Offshore Strategies

KT-511-903

Offshore Strategies

Professor Barry Spitz

Former adviser to the IRS and the US Congress. Adviser to international corporations, high-net worth individuals and governments. Barrister at law. Professor of International Tax Planning, Graduate School of Administration, Rice University, Houston, Texas; HEC School of Management, Paris.

Tolley
LexisNexis™

Members of the LexisNexis Group worldwide

United Kingdom	Butterworths Tolley, a Division of Reed Elsevier (UK) Ltd, Halsbury House, 35 Chancery Lane, LONDON, WC2A 1EL, and 4 Hill Street, EDINBURGH EH2 3JZ
Argentina	Abeledo Perrot, Jurisprudencia Argentina and Depalma, BUENOS AIRES
Australia	Butterworths, a Division of Reed International Books Australia Pty Ltd, CHATSWOOD, New South Wales
Austria	ARD Betriebsdienst and Verlag Orac, VIENNA
Canada	Butterworths Canada Ltd, MARKHAM, Ontario
Chile	Publitecsa and Conosur Ltda, SANTIAGO DE CHILE
Czech Republic	Orac sro, PRAGUE
France	Editions du Juris-Classeur SA, PARIS
Hong Kong	Butterworths Asia (Hong Kong), HONG KONG
Hungary	Hvg Orac, BUDAPEST
India	Butterworths India, NEW DELHI
Ireland	Butterworths (Ireland) Ltd, DUBLIN
Italy	Giuffré, MILAN
Malaysia	Malayan Law Journal Sdn Bhd, KUALA LUMPUR
New Zealand	Butterworths of New Zealand, WELLINGTON
Poland	Wydawnictwa Prawnicze PWN, WARSAW
Singapore	Butterworths Asia, SINGAPORE
South Africa	Butterworths Publishers (Pty) Ltd, DURBAN
Switzerland	Stämpfli Verlag AG, BERNE
USA	LexisNexis, DAYTON, Ohio

© Reed Elsevier (UK) Ltd 2001

All rights reserved. No part of this publication may be reproduced in any material form (including photocopying or storing it in any medium by electronic means and whether or not transiently or incidentally to some other use of this publication) without the written permission of the copyright owner except in accordance with the provisions of the Copyright, Designs and Patents Act 1988 or under the terms of a licence issued by the Copyright Licensing Agency Ltd, 90 Tottenham Court Road, London, England W1P 0LP. Applications for the copyright owner's written permission to reproduce any part of this publication should be addressed to the publisher.

Warning: The doing of an unauthorised act in relation to a copyright work may result in both a civil claim for damages and criminal prosecution.

Crown copyright material is reproduced with the permission of the Controller of HMSO and the Queen's Printer for Scotland. Any European material in this work which has been reproduced from EUR-lex, the official European Communities legislation website, is European Communities copyright.

A CIP Catalogue record for this book is available from the British Library.

ISBN 0406 948712
Typeset by M Rules, London
Printed and bound in Great Britain by The Cromwell Press, Trowbridge, Wiltshire

Visit Butterworths LexisNexis *direct* at www.butterworths.com

Preface

'When your strategy is deep and far-reaching, then what you gain by your calculations is much, so you can win before you even fight. When your strategic thinking is shallow and nearsighted, then what you gain by your calculations is little, so you lose before you do battle. Much strategy prevails over little strategy, so those with no strategy cannot but be defeated. Therefore it is said that victorious warriors win first and then go to war, while defeated warriors go to war first and then seek to win.'

The Art of War Sun Tzu

To succeed in war or in a lawsuit or in competitive sport, you must be aware of the strategy of the other side quite as much as of your own strategy. So, too, in the preparation of an international tax plan, it is essential to engage in deep and far-reaching calculations regarding, not merely strategic opportunities, but equally any material 'anti-avoidance' measures.

This work focuses on state-of-the-art methodology of structuring international operations and transactions in the light of current unilateral, bilateral and multinational anti-avoidance. For specific domestic anti-avoidance provisions, the reader is referred to the chapters in Part One of the *Spitz Tax Havens Encyclopaedia*, published by Butterworths, and now incorporated into Section D of Volume One of *Butterworths Offshore Service*, edited jointly by Giles Clarke and myself.

The aim of this new publication is to give practical hands-on guidance on strategic planning issues. The checklists of opportunities and caveats, contained in each chapter, are structured so as to assist the practitioner in safely achieving the optimal strategy. The format is as follows:

First, an introduction to the recent changes in the offshore scene (Chapter 1), the evolution of the International Offshore Financial Centres (Chapter 2) and the new developments in offshore operations and transactions (Chapter 3).

Then follow three chapters dealing with planning techniques, based on sections of my book titled *International Tax Planning* (Butterworths 1972), duly updated and re-edited, ie the preparation of the database (Chapter 4), double taxation (Chapter 5), and designing the offshore tax plan (Chapter 6).

These issues require a more detailed analysis of the three major topics which together account for the vast majority of international tax cases worldwide. The successful practitioner has no choice but to get these right: intra-group transfer pricing and offshore treasury management (Chapter 7), offshore planning strategies for individuals including offshore expatriates (Chapter 8) and offshore trusts and asset protection (Chapter 9).

Chapter 10 deals with the Internet as a research tool.

The two final chapters of the work deal with what every strategist has to know about the international measures against privileged tax regimes (Chapter 11), and 'all crimes' and 'money laundering' measures (Chapter 12).

The Appendices contain strategic checklists for offshore companies (Appendix 1) and offshore trusts (Appendix 2), in the most important of the international offshore financial centres.

Winning consists, above all, of not losing. The words written by Sun Tzu 2500 years ago, in his manual for military strategists, applies every bit as much to international tax planning strategists today.

Barry Kuper Spitz
1601 Elm Street, Suite 3000
Dallas, Texas 75201

Dedication

I dedicate this book to my beloved children Perri, Roy, Roger, Brad, Russell and Andrew.

Acknowledgements

My profound gratitude goes to colleagues and friends who so kindly contributed new material, in particular: Roger Bray, Charles Cain, Gerrit Disbergen, Richard Duke, Barry Engel, John Garland, Stephen Gray, Milton Grundy, Cym Lowell, Michael Maskall, Paul Roper, and Daniel Saksenberg; to the International Law and Tax Institute and the OECD for permission to copy excerpts from their publications; and to Chris Way-Jones, Jason Spriggs, and Theresa Lewarne for editorial support.

Roger Bray and Gerrit Disbergen

Roger Bray and Gerrit Disbergen are former corporate finance vice-presidents of Merrill Lynch. They currently advise international companies seeking to raise capital on world markets.

Charles A. Cain

Charles Cain, MA, ACIB is an Associate of the Chartered Institute of Bankers and a member of the Society of Trust and Estate Practitioners, the European – American Tax Institute, the International Fiscal Association, and the International Tax Planning Association. He is an affiliate of the American Bar Association and editor of the journal *Offshore Investment*. His company, Skyefid Ltd (www.skyefid.co.im), is located in the Isle of Man. He can be reached at charles.cain@skyefid.com

J. Richard Duke

J. Richard Duke, LLM, of the Duke Law Firm, PC, in Birmingham, Alabama, is a fellow and honorary legal scholar at the Centre for International Legal Studies, Salzburg, Austria, and Adjunct Professor, Cumberland School of Law. He is a member of the Asset Protection Planning Committee of the American bar, International Tax Planning Association, Society of Trust and Estate Practitioners, The Offshore Institute, and the Tax and International Law sections of the American, Alabama, and Florida Bars. He can be reached at (1205) 823–3900.

Barry S. Engel, together with John Garland

Barry Engel, Esq., is President Emeritus and a fellow of the Isle of Man – based Offshore Institute. He is a member of the Asset Protection Planning Committee of the American Bar Association Section of Real Property, Probate and Trust Law, and of the American Bar Association Section of International Law and Practice. He is also a fellow of the National Network of Estate Planning Attorneys and a member of the International, American, and Colorado Bar Associations. He is a principal in Colorado – based Engel, Reiman & Lockwood, PC bse@erl-law.com.

Milton Grundy and Stephen Gray

Milton Grundy, MA (CANTAB), FTII, is an English barrister and head of Gray's Inn Tax Chambers, London. He is President of the International Tax Planning Association (www.itpa.org) and the author of *Offshore Business Centres* (Sweet & Maxwell, 7th Edition, 1997) and (with John Briggs and Joseph Field) of *Asset Protection Trusts* (Keyhaven, 3rd Edition, 1997). He can be reached at grundy@itpa.org.

Acknowledgements

Stephen Gray, BA, JD, LLM – TAX. Of counsel to Shutts & Bowen in London, Stephen Gray is an American lawyer specialising in tax and immigration planning for wealthy individuals. Educated at Johns Hopkins University (BA), American University (JD), and Georgetown University (LLM – Tax), he previously served as a Trial Attorney/Assistant United States Attorney with the US Department of Justice (Tax Division).

Cym H. Lowell

Cym H Lowell, Esq., is a partner in the law firm of Gardere & Wynne, LLP, in Dallas and an adjunct professor of law at Southern Methodist University. He is the author of several books, including *US International Transfer Pricing and US International Taxation*. He can be reached at (214) 999–4239 or by email at Chlowell@aol.com.

Paul E. W. Roper

Paul Roper, BA, LLB, LLM, MIT, FILPA CFP, TEP, consulting editor of Trusts and Trustees, senior manager of the Stonehage Group, head of South African operations of ABSA Offshore.

Daniel L. Saksenberg

Daniel Saksenberg is an actuarial consultant for Southern Africa Actuarial Consultants. He is a statistical and financial policy advisor to several government agencies and senior tutor of the International Law & Tax Institute. He can be reached at danofinstitute@aol.com.

Contents

Contents

Chapter 5   Tax Treaties and the Question of Double Taxation

Chapter 6   Designing the Offshore Tax Plan

Chapter 7   Intra-group Transfer Pricing and Offshore Treasury Management Strategies

Chapter 8   Offshore Planning Strategies for Individuals

Contents

Table of Statutes

TABLE OF STATUTES BY JURISDICTION

Table of Cases

TABLE OF CASES BY JURISDICTION

Bahamas

Cook Islands

Jersey

United Kingdom

United States

1 A Time of Change

STRATEGIC ISSUES, OPPORTUNITIES AND CAVEATS

CARDINAL RULES GOVERNING OFFSHORE STRATEGIES
- The most important strategic issue: the need for due diligence.

- The greatest strategic opportunities: the result of due diligence.

- The essential *caveat*: neglect due diligence at your peril!

CHANGES IN THE MAJOR AREAS OF ACTIVITY
- Electronic commerce (e-commerce).

- Offshore trusts.

- Tax havens.

- High tax jurisdictions with preferential tax regimes.

- Transfer pricing.

- The Internet as a research tool.

ELECTRONIC COMMERCE (E-COMMERCE)
- E-commerce is reshaping the structures of commerce, and with this comes a major revolution in traditional methods of taxation.

- Revenue authorities are faced not only with the challenge of tax collection, but also with having to play a major role in realising the potential of what is already one of the greatest economic forces of the 21st century.

OFFSHORE TRUSTS AND SETTLOR CONTROL ISSUES
- Whether a court will attempt to compel distributions from a trust.

- Whether a creditor or spouse will succeed in an attempt to seize property from a trust.

- Whether upon a bankruptcy filing, assets will be included in the bankruptcy estate.

- Whether the settlor will be personally liable for the income taxes generated by the trust.

- Whether gift or estate taxes may be assessed at the time of funding, the time of a distribution, or the time of the settlor's death.

VALIDITY OF SETTLOR DRIVEN TRUSTS

- Where a settlor of a trust controls the trustee's decision-making powers or the trust assets, the courts may consider the trust a sham or the alter ego of the settlor.

- *Caveat:* The response of many offshore trust companies has been to refuse to follow requests from settlors or beneficiaries, thus attracting great displeasure on the part of the settlors.

THE ATTACK ON HARMFUL TAX COMPETITION AND TAX HAVENS

- The general concern of the OECD is with defence of the taxation base of Member countries.

- The main focus of the OECD's work is on financial and other service activities.

- *Caveat:* Specifically, the OECD is concerned to assure that Member countries are able to: (a) obtain information concerning Member country taxpayers' use of tax havens and preferential tax regimes and (b) design appropriate countermeasures to deal with such uses deemed abusive.

THE ATTACK ON TRANSFER PRICING

- The growth of multinational enterprises (MNEs) presents increasingly complex taxation issues for both tax administrations and the MNEs themselves since separate country rules for the taxation of MNEs cannot be viewed in isolation but must be addressed in a broad international context.

- *Caveat:* There is much concern among those advising multinational corporations that, without the OECD having stated so in as many words, the OECD attack on tax havens and preferential tax regimes is directed also at the transfer pricing structures of multinational corporations.

THE ATTACK ON MONEY LAUNDERING

- Tax dodging in other countries, as well as at home, has been criminalised under the 'All Crimes' legislation of most high tax jurisdictions as well as many offshore jurisdictions.

- Exchanges of information are being widened and enforcement procedures are being strengthened on a worldwide basis.

- *Caveat*. The criminal penalties are such that no one dare ignore the risks of participation in any of the offences listed in the 'All Crimes' legislation of other countries.

THE INTERNET AS A RESEARCH TOOL

- The Internet is one of the most powerful tools at the disposal of any person seeking information on matters of foreign taxation and offshore financial centres.

- *Caveat*. The reliability of the available information on the Internet is often questionable.

THE MAJOR CHANGES

1.1 There are several major trends in international taxation that will have significant impact on the nature of the environment in which offshore transactions are conducted, and that will have to be taken into account in evaluating existing, or in planning new, strategies. These are, above all, the following developments:

- The evolution of electronic commerce means that traditional geographic boundaries are of far less significance (see para 1.50 below).

- There is no longer any necessary geographic or territorial imperative for the performance of high technology research and development or related activities, so that multinationals are able to utilise the talents of engineers or other professionals located in under-developed regions of the world where highly-skilled and trained professionals can be found. This means that high technology activity requires no institutional physical presence in a given geographic location.

- These trends easily facilitate the location of an increasingly wide range of business functions or risks in jurisdictions that have advantageous tax regimes. This has, in turn, caused the OECD, the United Nations and the European Union to be concerned that these trends provide increasing incentive to utilise so-called tax haven countries or preferential tax regimes that provide harmful tax competition.

1.2 Inevitably, the principal changes in the world of taxation are in the biggest areas of activity. First, there are significant tax and legal changes affecting offshore trusts. It is estimated that some 20% of all the money in the world may be held in or through offshore trusts. Secondly, tax havens and high tax jurisdictions with favoured tax regimes are coming into the firing line. This includes the vast majority of countries in the world. And thirdly, transfer pricing is now under direct attack in all major countries. Approximately one-quarter of all international transactions measured in money take place between related companies, and a high percentage of major tax cases now involve pricing.

OFFSHORE TRUST ISSUES

1.3 The trust is the wonder product of English law; it is much older than the company and very much smarter. Above all, it has the unique feature of separating legal ownership and beneficial ownership. In this way the trust has become the tailor-made vehicle for protecting and administering the assets of the wealthy.

1.4 A Time of Change

1.4 Since its earliest origins in Mediaeval England, the trust has been used to get around inconvenient rules of law. Its forerunner, the so-called 'use', was a frequently employed device to overcome feudal dues.

1.5 Take the case of the knight dying and leaving his estate to his minor son. The lord of the manor would be entitled to use the heir's land for his own benefit until the youngster turned 21. The lord could even select a bride for the heir and, if the heir had different ideas about conjugal bliss and refused to marry her, the lord could exact a fine. On turning 21 the heir was obliged to pay over to the lord an additional sum amounting to a half-year's profits of the land before he could receive outright transfer.

1.6 Enter the *use*. On his deathbed a knight would convey the land to his friends to hold *to the use* of his son. In this way, his heir would not become the legal owner and the lord would be deprived of his feudal rights. This old-fashioned bit of tax avoidance worked so effectively that the only way in which King Henry VIII could lay his hands on the church lands was through the abolishment of the use by the Statute of Uses in 1535.

1.7 The trust proved to be irrepressible, and by the end of the 19th century the trust was well and truly in position to fulfil its prime vocation of income tax and estate duty avoidance. It has steadily maintained its place as the favoured tax game of the rich.

1.8 As a logical countermove, the trust became a target of British anti-avoidance measures. Because the moves to restrict the free operation of the tax avoidance games were domestic, however, the wealthy had an easy riposte. They duly set up their trusts offshore: in the Channel Islands, Bermuda, and the Caribbean islands, where the British Empire had carried the English law of trusts but not the British tax system. The United Kingdom then retaliated by enacting far-reaching legislation to prevent avoidance through the transfer of assets by UK residents to foreign trusts.

1.9 No sooner had the trust come to fulfil its major vocation of income tax and estate tax avoidance than it inevitably became a target of anti-avoidance measures, first in the UK, then in the US and then everywhere. But since the early moves to restrict the free operation of the trust were domestic, the wealthy simply moved their trusts offshore. Separately from tax issues, foreign situs trusts were found to be more protective as an asset protection device than domestic trusts, since they create practical barriers to litigation.

1.10 Indeed, so successful did the offshore trust become, that it is estimated that approximately one-fifth of all the money in the world may be held directly or indirectly through offshore trusts. And it is this that inevitably triggered major changes in tax and in law.

1.11 On the one hand, fiscal anti-avoidance measures have come to be aggressively directed at the offshore trust. In current US and UK tax law it may be far more onerous to have an offshore trust than an onshore trust. So much so, that many offshore trusts are simply being brought back home.

1.12 On the other hand, and in an unrelated development, the courts are questioning the legal validity of offshore trusts. A number of recent judgments in Jersey, Guernsey, the UK, the US and elsewhere have upheld attacks on offshore trusts by creditors, spouses and the Revenue, mainly on the grounds of settlor control. Courts have even put settlors in jail for contempt of court when they claim that they cannot control the trustees. Trust companies risk losing their licenses, paying fines and seeing their officers serve time. The late Professor Willoughby expressed the view that 90% of all offshore trusts may be invalid.

1.13   The issue of settlor control inevitably exercises a substantial impact on the offshore trust in several ways, including:

- whether a court will attempt to compel distributions from a trust;

- whether a creditor or spouse will succeed in an attempt to seize property from a trust;

- whether upon a bankruptcy filing, assets will be included in the bankruptcy estate;

- whether the settlor will be personally liable for the income taxes generated by the trust; and

- whether gift or estate taxes may be assessed at the time of funding, the time of a distribution, or the time of the settlor's death.

1.14   Simply, where a settlor of a trust controls the trustee's decision-making powers or the trust assets, the courts may consider the trust a sham or the alter ego of the settlor. The response of many offshore trust companies has been to refuse to follow requests from settlors or beneficiaries, thus attracting great displeasure on the part of the settlors. (See also Chapter 9.)

THE ATTACK ON HARMFUL TAX COMPETITION

1.15   The OECD issued its report titled 'Harmful Tax Competition: An Emerging Global Issue' in April 1998 (the 'Report'). The thrust of the Report is an outline of guidelines to be considered for dealing with the perceived problems of inappropriate tax competition (tax havens and preferential tax regimes) by Member countries. The general concern of the OECD is with defence of the taxation base of Member countries. Specifically, the OECD is concerned to assure that Member countries are able to: (a) obtain information concerning Member country taxpayers' use of tax havens and preferential tax regimes; and (b) design appropriate countermeasures to deal with such uses deemed abusive. The OECD has repeatedly indicated that effective tax rates (or no tax rates) are not, as such, the target of the Harmful Tax Competition initiative.

1.16   The Forum has identified a number of preferential regimes in member countries as potentially harmful.

1.17   The OECD has recommended that countries strengthen their domestic and bilateral measures against harmful tax practices. Member States are encouraged to refrain from adopting new measures that constitute harmful tax practices, to review existing measures, and to remove within five years any harmful features of preferential tax regimes.

1.18   At the national level, OECD countries are encouraged to adopt controlled foreign corporation (CFC) or equivalent legislation. Bilaterally, OECD countries are encouraged to intensify their exchange of information on tax havens and preferential tax regimes. A provision is being considered for the OECD's Model Tax Convention that would deny entities operating under harmful tax regimes access to certain or all of the Convention's benefits. Furthermore, the OECD report asks countries to consider terminating any treaties they might have with tax havens. The OECD has also established the Forum on Harmful Tax Practices in order to provide a framework for implementation of the 19 recommendations contained in the Report.

1.19   The main focus of the OECD's work is on financial and other service activities because these are the activities that are the most geographically mobile and therefore the most sensitive to tax differentials. Financial markets are constantly evolving, and innovative financial products are continually being created. Such instruments have the potential to be used to assist harmful tax competition, as well as being used for legitimate business purposes. The OECD has stated its intention to ensure that financial innovation is not used to assist harmful tax competition.

1.20   Another proposal that could have wide-reaching effects is that high tax countries impose withholding taxes on certain payments to residents of countries that engage in harmful tax competition. It is considered by the OECD that the imposition of withholding taxes at a substantial rate on certain payments to countries that engage in harmful tax competition, if associated with measures aimed at preventing the use of conduit arrangements, would act as a deterrent for countries to engage in harmful tax competition and for taxpayers to use entities located in those countries.

THE ATTACK ON THE TAX HAVENS

1.21   The OECD attack on the tax havens focuses on the following factors to determine whether a jurisdiction qualifies as such:

- The jurisdiction imposes no or only nominal taxes and offers itself, or is perceived to offer itself, as a place to be used by non-residents to escape tax in their country of residence.

- Practices of the jurisdiction prevent the effective exchange of relevant information with other governments on taxpayers benefiting from the low or no tax jurisdiction.

- A lack of transparency exists.

- There is an absence of a requirement that the activity be substantial, since this would suggest that a jurisdiction may be attempting to attract investment or transactions that are purely tax driven.

- There is no or only nominal taxation within the jurisdiction.

1.22   If combined with a situation in which the jurisdiction offers itself as a place where non-residents can escape tax in their country of residence, any of the above factors may be sufficient to identify a tax haven.

1.23   The OECD's concept of 'tax haven' thus refers to tax jurisdictions that offer themselves as a place that non-residents can use to escape tax obligations in their countries of residence. A number of factors identify these jurisdictions, in particular the virtual absence of taxes (combined with minimum business presence requirements) and a lack of legislative and administrative transparency. Bank secrecy and other features that prevent effective exchange of information are frequently also discernible.

1.24   A list of jurisdictions meeting the tax haven criteria of the 1998 Report were endorsed by the Council on 16 June 2000.

1.25   Perhaps the most effective attack by the high tax jurisdictions on the potential loss of revenue through tax haven activities, lies in the restriction of deductions for payments to tax haven entities. A number of countries have rules imposing restrictions on the deduction of payments made to tax haven countries or rules imposing a reversal of the onus of proof in case of such payments.

1.26   The offshore jurisdictions have treated the attack by the OECD and its Member States very seriously. A high percentage of jurisdictions identified as meeting the tax haven criteria have made a commitment to eliminate their harmful tax practices by the end of 2005, and others are expected to do so shortly.

THE ATTACK ON TRANSFER PRICING

1.27   The OECD countries are also encouraged to adhere to certain defined standards in providing tax rulings and to apply strictly the 1995 OECD Transfer Pricing Guidelines, which provide for internationally agreed-upon standards for establishing prices on intra-group transactions. This reflects the concern of Revenue departments worldwide that there was tremendous scope for the erosion of their tax bases if uncontrolled pricing of goods and services were allowed to continue.

1.28   The growth of multinational enterprises (MNEs) presents increasingly complex taxation issues for both tax administrations and the MNEs themselves since separate country rules for the taxation of MNEs cannot be viewed in isolation but must be addressed in a broad international context. These issues arise primarily from the practical difficulties, for both MNEs and tax administrations, of determining the income and expenses of a company or a permanent establishment that is part of an MNE group that should be taken into account within a jurisdiction, particularly where the MNE group's operations are highly integrated. In the case of MNEs, the need to comply with laws and administrative requirements that may differ from country to country creates additional problems. The differing requirements may lead to a greater burden on an MNE, and result in higher costs of compliance, than for a similar enterprise operating solely within a single tax jurisdiction.

1.29   In the period since the release of the Harmful Tax Competition Report, it appears that a critical motivating element of the efforts of the OECD is the perceived need to capture information to facilitate adjustments as may be necessary to assure arm's length dealing and compliance with particular domestic tax regimes, in particular via transfer pricing or controlled foreign corporation (CFC) legislation. There also appears to be an effort to utilise information obtained from potential harmful regimes in order to allow tax administrations to identify issues that may not be addressed by the OECD Transfer Pricing Guidelines or pertinent domestic tax regimes.

1.30   There is thus much concern among those advising multinational corporations that, without the OECD having stated so in as many words, the OECD attack on tax havens and preferential tax regimes, is directed also at the transfer pricing structures of multinational corporations. Since more than a quarter of all international transactions are estimated to take place within groups, this widening of the information base going beyond the scope of the existing transfer pricing guidelines, creates a new, and unwelcome, dimension.

1.31   An early step has been the creation of the Forum on Harmful Tax Competition (the 'Forum'), formed shortly after release of the Report, an important function of which is to identify those regimes that are viewed as being tax havens or preferential tax regimes. The next major step is the development of appropriate countermeasures as proposed in the Report. These include the co-ordination of:

- domestic legislation — including CFC regimes, foreign investment fund (additional 'clawback') rules, restriction on participation exemptions for foreign source income, information reporting, access to banking information by other countries' tax authorities, provision of rulings, and the application of the OECD Guidelines;

- tax treaties — including exchange of information, treaty benefit entitlement, compatibility of domestic anti-abuse rules, limitation of income exclusion provisions, termination of treaties with tax havens, co-ordinated or simultaneous tax examinations, and assistance in recovering tax claims of treaty partner countries;

- endorsement of the Guidelines;

- police 'links' between Member countries and tax haven dependencies to prevent harmful tax practices in the dependent tax havens;

- developing principles of good tax administration; and

- association of non-Member countries.

1.32   The release of the Report generated a vigorous debate between the OECD and the international business community concerning the actual intention of the OECD and the propriety of these intentions. Officials of some Member countries have been reported to have used rather strident language to suggest the need for dealing with harmful preferential tax regimes. There has been significant criticism from the business community as well as commentators with respect to the content of the Report and the manner in which it was released.

1.33   These criticisms include concern that the tone of the Report that may be appropriate for money-laundering or other criminal matters, is not appropriate for the routine international business arrangements made by multinationals in order to achieve a lower worldwide tax burden, and the primary purpose of which is to remain competitive with competitors that may have a lower international tax cost due to the regimes available in their home countries. From the standpoint of multinationals, the presence of tax competition between countries is a healthy phenomenon, which lowers overall tax burdens of multinationals and provides a means of equalising the tax burdens of companies based in high and low tax countries, all of which may be OECD Member countries. Furthermore, there are many reasons for locating business operations in countries offering tax incentives other than the incentives themselves, such as lower labour, geographic proximity to suppliers and markets, favourable government attitudes to inbound investment, and availability of developed internal infrastructure (telecommunications, natural resources, utilities — such as electricity, water, airport or harbour capacity).

1.34   In addition, the emergence of a global economy and resultant relaxation of trade and investment barriers (often led by the OECD itself) have led to a significant increase in the overall tax revenues of developed countries.

1.35   Finally, it has been noted that the tax base leakage issues that are at the heart of the Report, and which are legitimate concerns to tax administrations, would appear to be satisfactorily addressed by the OECD's Transfer Pricing Guidelines, Model Income Tax Convention, and domestic regimes of Member countries (such as controlled foreign corporation-type 'clawback' provisions, which typically require deemed repatriation of passive income earned in foreign subsidiaries — controlled foreign corporation-type regimes). The overall object of the Guidelines is, consistent with the mechanisms of the Model Income Tax Convention, to provide parameters for the allocation of income from international operations among multinational controlled taxpayers (and their respective countries) on the basis of function performed and risk assumed in each country. In this connection, the approach of the Report could be viewed to simply add another layer of international tax allocation principles on top of existing regimes.

1.36   Inevitably, the business community is showing considerable concern that the principal motivating elements of the Report may be to capture information and to allow tax administrations to identify issues that may not be addressed by the transfer pricing Guidelines or pertinent domestic tax regimes.

1.37   To the extent that this is an accurate assessment of the motivation behind the Report, it may be that the implication of the recommendations, and potential Guidelines to be forthcoming from the Forum activities, will be the evolution of a more uniform and complete system of information gathering from tax haven jurisdictions, followed by more uniform application of transfer pricing and domestic tax legislation principles, including domestic information reporting by multinationals. This may, in turn, not actually reflect an additional tax compliance burden being imposed upon multinationals. Indeed, such evolution may reflect little more than a recognition that documentation and penalty regimes, typically relating to transfer pricing, are spreading among Member countries and the need for co-ordination to assure that multinationals do not become subject to a crazy quilt of documentation-penalty regimes.

1.38 It seems likely that the increasing importance of electronic commerce as a medium of conducting international business provides encouragement for these information and tax administration co-ordination efforts of the Member countries.

1.39 While information and tax administration co-ordination efforts may be benign, there are other possibilities that would pose far more serious questions for both multinational taxpayers and tax administrations. It may be, for example, that the evolution of Forum activities and Guideline formulation would produce an environment in which Member countries would determine that harmful preferential tax regimes should be ignored for purposes of applying treaties between Member countries.

1.40 In the event that the process evolves in this direction, there are several potential implications, including the following:

- Such an evolution of Member country activity would have potentially ominous implications for all non-Member countries, not just those countries deemed to provide harmful preferential tax regimes. Such countries often seek to attract external investment with a favourable tax incentive structure.

- A country deemed to provide harmful preferential tax regimes would have an apparent incentive to enter information sharing agreements with Member countries.

- Multinationals would have even greater incentive to seek advance agreements with the tax authorities of the principal countries in which it conducts business, via advance pricing agreement or other mechanisms.

- A base may be laid for worldwide allocation of income, at least among Member countries.

1.41 It thus seems apparent that the OECD Member countries perceive that there is a clear logical relationship between transfer pricing documentation-penalty regimes (to provide tax authorities with information about worldwide related party functional and risk activities, and segmented financial information), domestic tax regimes (such as CFC clawback and domestic exit tax regimes — which provide bases for deeming the repatriation of income to the mother country), and the need to obtain complete information from countries deemed to provide harmful preferential tax regimes.

1.42 It may or may not be the case that these comments reflect the underlying motivations for the Report. Nonetheless, it does seem clear that the rather contentious debate that has been generated by the Report would benefit from a more complete statement of the underlying objectives of the Member countries by the OECD.

1.43 In the face of these developments, a critical concern of participants in the offshore industry could be the effect that the Harmful Tax Competition initiative of the OECD could have on the evolution of the industry.

1.44 Recommendations are currently being made that a co-ordinated approach be made by the participants in the offshore industry to work with the Forum in addressing the concerns of the OECD and its Member countries. It is seriously evident that a failure to do so would allow the debate to evolve with an important voice absent from the table. (See also Chapter 7.)

THE ATTACK ON MONEY LAUNDERING

1.45   Money laundering knows no frontiers. Money laundering is ubiquitous. Money laundering is an evolving activity. It follows that, in order to be effective, any action to combat money laundering must rely on effective cooperation between experts from a wide range of disciplines: legal and judicial, financial and regulatory, and law enforcement.

1.46   The main issues of concern include:

● the vulnerabilities of Internet banking;

● the increasing reach of alternative remittance systems;

● the role of company formation agents and their services; and

● international trade-related activities as a cover for money laundering.

1.47   The Financial Action Task Force (FATF) was established by the G7 Summit in Paris in 1989 in order to examine measures to combat money laundering. In 1990, the FATF issued Forty Recommendations for action against money laundering.

1.48   As the primary objective of its current mandate, the FATF is committed to promoting anti-money laundering initiatives in all continents and regions of the globe and to building a worldwide anti-money laundering network. Considerable progress has been made by FATF members in implementing anti-money laundering measures.

1.49   From the point of view of offshore tax planning, the main effects of these measures are threefold:

● Tax dodging in other countries has been criminalised under the 'All Crimes' legislation of most high tax jurisdictions as well as many offshore jurisdictions.

● Exchanges of information are being widened and enforcement procedures are being strengthened on a worldwide basis.

● The criminal penalties are such that no one dare ignore the risks of participation in any of the offences listed in the 'All Crimes' legislation of other countries.

THE INTERNET AS A RESEARCH TOOL

1.50   The Internet is the greatest advance in the communication of information since the telephone and the fax machine. Never before has so much information been so readily available to so many people. In every conceivable manner and by every conceivable method, the Internet has had a profound effect in all areas within its considerable and ever growing domain. While the reliability of the available information is often questionable, there is no doubt that with proper use the Internet is one of the most powerful tools at the disposal of any researcher (see Chapter 10).

2 Evolution of International Offshore Financial Centres (IOFCs)

STRATEGIC ISSUES, OPPORTUNITIES AND CAVEATS

TYPICAL OBJECTIVES OF IOFCS

- To provide for:

    - offshore companies;

    - offshore trusts;

    - offshore banking;

    - offshore insurance;

    - offshore shipping;

    - offshore funds;

    - co-ordination centres;

    - headquarters companies;

    - management and administrative offices.

- To create a new source of invisible earnings for the country.

- To increase the inflow of foreign currency and attract foreign qualifying companies.

- To generate employment.

- To create training and educational opportunities.

- To enhance the financial strength and status of the country.

- To foster the introduction and increased use of modern technology.

- To develop exports and associated activities.

- To develop tax and/or non-tax incentive programs.

OECD'S CONCEPT OF 'TAX HAVEN'

- The jurisdiction imposes no or only nominal taxes and offers itself, or is perceived to offer itself, as a place to be used by non-residents to escape tax in their country of residence.

- Practices of the jurisdiction prevent the effective exchange of relevant information with other governments on taxpayers benefiting from the low or no tax jurisdiction.

- A lack of transparency exists.

- There is an absence of a requirement that the activity be substantial, since this would suggest that a jurisdiction may be attempting to attract investment or transactions that are purely tax driven.

- There is no or only nominal taxation within the jurisdiction.

- The jurisdiction offers itself as a place where non-residents can escape tax in their country of residence.

- *Caveat:* The OECD is introducing measures to counter the distorting effects of tax havens on the economies of other countries.

CLASSES OF IOFCS OR TAX HAVENS

- Countries that have no income tax or that grant extensive tax exemptions.

- Countries that only tax locally arising income (territorial basis of taxation that exempts foreign income).

- Countries that combine features of either of the above with a treaty network.

- Low tax financial centres in countries offering special incentives and privileges, including international business company legislation.

- High tax countries offering special incentives for offshore companies and qualifying holding companies.

HIGH TAX JURISDICTIONS WITH IOFC FEATURES

- An extremely large percentage of otherwise high tax countries have special regions or regimes where offshore activities can be conducted.

- *Caveat:* Such favoured tax treatment is under attack from the OECD, the European Union and the United Nations.

WHAT IS 'OFFSHORE'?

2.1 The term *offshore* was used originally to refer to the tax havens off the shores of the United Kingdom and the United States, and by extension to any company or trust located in a tax haven or a country where tax can be kept low. It is being used more and more in connection with financial transactions.

2.2 The offshore scene is currently undergoing some important changes.

2.3   The main new development is the amount of money offshore (estimated at 60% of the world's money). It is considered that half the world's financial transactions measured in money take place offshore. There are now almost 60 offshore financial centres in the world, many within the jurisdiction of major economic powers with ostensibly high levels of taxation. Wealth, like any other commodity, tends to gravitate to where it will earn its greatest return (in economic terms, of course, after-tax return is the only really relevant statistic). As a result of this phenomenon, huge amounts of funds have been transferred to offshore locations over the last 30 years.

2.4   Another very significant feature is the vast increase in the number of persons participating in offshore activities. Never before have so many offshore companies and trusts been set up or have so many expatriates changed residence for purely fiscal reasons.

2.5   Then there is the increase in the number of countries offering tax haven or finance centre possibilities. In particular, the seeming high tax jurisdictions are actively seeking new 'offshore' business.

2.6   Another important recent development in the offshore area is to be found in the widened scope of offshore transactions and operations. The esoteric is becoming more and more commonplace, and there is an ongoing merging of onshore and offshore. This has led to a major counter-attack by the high tax jurisdictions, which have experienced a whittling away of their tax bases, not only by the offshore jurisdictions, but also through harmful tax competition by other high tax jurisdictions (see Chapter 11).

2.7   The term *international offshore financial centre*, or *IOFC*, is an alternative term for a 'tax haven'. The OECD has redefined the term in its Harmful Tax Competition Report and has established criteria that have permitted the creation of a list of jurisdictions classified as tax havens (see Chapter 11).

2.8   The classical tax havens generally have a common denominator of no or low taxes on income and capital, bank and commercial secrecy, no exchange controls (at least for offshore), an active banking sector, good communications, an appearance of political and economic stability, a favourable disposition toward foreign capital, and adequate professional advisors. The classical havens of this type are the Bahamas, Bermuda, and the Cayman Islands. More recently the Turks & Caicos Islands and the Cook Islands have started to make their presence felt.

2.9   Hong Kong's special position has been a result of the territorial tax system (no taxes on foreign source income) and an incomparable infrastructure.

2.10   Another group of little countries, such as Gibraltar, Guernsey, the Isle of Man, Jersey, Liechtenstein, and the Netherlands Antilles, has captured a large slice of the tax haven industry by offering reduced rates, special tax exemptions, incentives, and privileges, as well as excellent financial and professional infrastructures. The insecurities that threatened Panama caused a major move of offshore companies in favour of the British Virgin Islands, which is now developing into a major new financial centre with more new company incorporations than any other tax haven.

2.11   You can add to these groups half of the islands in the Caribbean and a good representation of tropical paradises from the South Pacific and the Indian Ocean, all with tax haven pretensions of one kind or another.

2.12   The number of tax havens and the variety of types of tax havens and offshore situations are multiplying all the time. This is a fascinating and proliferating species. Just the

2.13 Evolution of International Offshore Financial Centres

past few years have seen the arrival of active newcomers such as Mauritius, Samoa, Nevis, and Aruba.

2.13 There is so much offshore business around that it is not particularly surprising that the major countries do not want to waste it all on the palm-tree economies, and they are making a strong bid for their share of the action. Many of them offer very tempting packages.

2.14 There are probably nearly as many offshore possibilities as there are countries. High in the tax haven league you will find some very improbable candidates, like Belgium, the Netherlands, Singapore, and Switzerland. Their offshore products have unusual features, and they are usually styled financial centres rather than tax havens.

2.15 In the 1960s, financial institutions and banks were mostly interchangeable words for the same entity. The term *financial institution* began to pull away from the traditional legal entity of the bank as international finance projects and international tax planning strategies became more sophisticated. Yet the single most important factor in the development of offshore centres was the development of communications technology.

2.16 The ability to communicate with foreign subsidiaries quickly and effectively opened up the real possibility of firms maintaining funds offshore in relatively unsophisticated consumer market surroundings, such as on an island. Financial institutions on the (comparatively) unregulated islands were free to enter different types of business forbidden to banks in high tax jurisdictions. These types of business included provision of insurance, equity ownership in companies, organisation of new structures to protect corporate income from taxation, and the creation of new financial vehicles and methods tailored to the customers' needs.

2.17 Newly semi-independent jurisdictions, mainly former British colonies, in pursuit of potential financial centre fees and jobs, emerged as competitors for the business of financial institution incorporations. The islands used the new fee revenue to set up communications infrastructures and build financial districts. The islands' parliaments passed modern corporate legislation based on their common law traditions, and enacted laws insuring capitalist stability based on the English heritage. The Bahamas, the Cayman Islands, Bermuda, Turks and Caicos, the Isle of Man, Jersey, Guernsey, and the Cook Islands are good examples of this trend.

2.18 Offshore jurisdictions also include seemingly high tax jurisdictions that allow their tax treaties to be used for treaty conduit purposes (see Chapter 11).

WHAT DO THE OFFSHORE CENTRES OFFER?

2.19 The principal products stocked by the offshore supermarkets are companies and trusts. *Offshore companies* usually hold investments and may get involved in trading. *Offshore trusts* protect the ownership of assets and frequently of the companies themselves. The true beneficiaries are usually individuals residing in high tax countries.

2.20 *Offshore companies* and *trusts* hold every imaginable kind of asset: real estate, art collections, jewellery, stocks and bonds, insurance policies, contingent claims, in fact anything at all. And offshore is not only for the very wealthy and the multinationals. Depending on what you want and which haven you use, an offshore company and trust do not need to cost all that much. A few thousand dollars initial outlay can usually take care of both.

2.21 No one can count the number of *offshore companies*, and the number is expanding exponentially. They are put there for a very good reason: an offshore company can be used for any purpose for which a company in a high tax country can be used, and it mostly does not have to pay tax in the offshore jurisdiction. The bulk of offshore companies simply collect income consisting of dividends, loan interest or patent royalties and license fees. But many are also used for business purposes. Handled correctly, the offshore company plays a turntable role using tax-exempt income to make more tax-exempt income. Apart from tax, an offshore company can be used for other purposes such as privacy and freedom from exchange control, or protection of assets against future developments in the home country. Though companies in most offshore jurisdictions offer basic similarities, there are useful differences. For example, what information must be contained in the by-laws? Can the true promoters and beneficial owners be kept entirely out of the picture? What are the costs of incorporation? How much time is involved, and can it be accelerated? Are there limits on the powers of the company? Is there any limitation of liability? Can there be bearer shares, no par value shares, preference shares, redeemable shares, shares with special rights?

2.22 The wonder product is the *offshore trust*. The trust concept is over 600 years old, older than company law. The trust vehicle, from the tax planning perspective, may allow a taxpayer to break the connecting factor between the trust assets, the taxpayer, and the taxing jurisdiction. A huge and increasing volume of *international banking* takes place offshore. Indeed it is extremely easy for an individual or a company with acceptable references to open a bank account offshore, and even numbered accounts are possible. In most countries, one of the terms of the relationship between banker and customer is that the banker will keep the customer's affairs secret. In some tax havens this rule is now being widened and made a marketing feature. However, the whole world is moving toward greater openness, and severe pressure is currently being brought to bear on onshore and offshore jurisdictions to fight money laundering (see Chapter 12).

2.23 Other products on the shelves of the offshore supermarkets are finance subsidiaries, captive banks, captive insurance companies, shipping and trans-shipment companies, licensing companies, headquarters companies, limited liability companies, foundations, management services companies, manufacturing and export bases, and tax shelters.

2.24 A *captive bank* is a banking subsidiary set up in a tax haven or financial centre that operates principally for the benefit of the members of a multinational group and their customers and suppliers. Such captive banks may also operate as merchant banks and offer commercial banking as well as financing services.

2.25 Similarly, a *captive insurance company* is an insurance company that is fully owned (directly or indirectly) by a non-insurance commercial company and exclusively insures or reinsures the risks of the parent company and/or its affiliated companies. The function is thus one of self-insurance from the group point of view. Captives are now becoming more and more commonplace.

2.26 Owing to the innate mobility of the *shipping* industry, it has always been normal practice for ship owners and operators to have recourse to tax havens. Frequently, the ownership, operation, administration, and registration are situated in fiscally favourable (and often different) jurisdictions in order to keep global tax burdens at a low level. The list of flags of convenience countries gets longer every year.

2.27 Technology that can be the subject matter of licensing covers all forms of industrial enterprises. It embraces industrial property that may be protected by patents, trademarks, etc., as well as technology that cannot be patented. The Netherlands is the grand master of the international royalties game, owing to its wide networks of treaties and the special concessions at home. And an increasing number of cinema and television companies are joining the ranks of the technology companies in exploiting these opportunities.

2.28   *Headquarters offices* are offices situated abroad to exercise certain management, co-ordination, and control functions for the sole or principal benefit of an enterprise or group. Headquarters offices may benefit from a favourable tax regime even in an otherwise high tax jurisdiction like Belgium, France, or Germany. The competition between these countries is resulting in the *de facto* introduction of more and more favourable tax regimes through what may amount to a partial system of unpublished revenue rulings.

2.29   One of the main features of high tax systems with offshore potential is the *tax shelter*, which is really an investment with a flow-through of tax benefits. Artificial losses may be offset not only against income from the investment out of which they arise, but also against the taxpayer's other income, usually from his regular business or professional activity. Skilled players are able to sit tight onshore and simply let tax shelters transform their *onshore* earnings into *offshore* earnings.

CLASSES OF IOFCs

2.30   There are five basic classes of IOFCs, many of which are known as tax havens:

- countries that have no income tax or that grant extensive tax exemptions;

- countries that only tax locally arising income (territorial basis of taxation that exempts foreign income);

- countries that combine features of the two items above with a treaty network;

- low tax financial centres in countries offering special incentives and privileges, including international business company legislation; and

- high tax countries offering special incentives for offshore companies and qualifying holding companies.

2.31   Examples of IOFCs by category are set out below in a non-exhaustive list:

- Countries that have no income tax or that grant extensive tax exemptions: Andorra, Anguilla, the Bahamas, Bahrain, Bermuda, Brunei (individuals), Campione, the Cayman Islands, the Cook Islands, French Polynesia, Grenada, Kuwait, Maldives, Monaco, Nauru, Oman (individuals only), the Turks and Caicos Islands, United Arab Emirates, Uruguay and Vanuatu.

- Countries that impose no income tax on foreign source income: Costa Rica, Djibouti, Dominican Republic, Ecuador, France (special rules), Guatemala, Hong Kong, Ireland (non-resident company), Jordan, Kenya, Lebanon, Liberia, Macau, Panama, Swaziland, Uruguay and Venezuela.

- Countries that can be used as low tax areas but also have certain tax treaty benefits: Cyprus, the Netherlands, the Netherlands Antilles and Switzerland.

- Low tax financial centres and countries offering special incentives and privileges: Angola, Anguilla, Antigua, Barbados, the British Virgin Islands, Brunei, Cyprus, Gibraltar, Grenada, Guernsey, Hong Kong, Ireland, the Isle of Man, Jamaica, Jersey, Liechtenstein, Luxembourg, Macau, Madeira, Malta, the Marshall Islands, Mauritius, Montserrat, the Netherlands, Nevis, Philippines, Puerto Rico, Samoa, San Marino, Seychelles, Solomon Islands, Sri Lanka, St. Helena, St. Vincent and Switzerland.

Note: Certain countries above also offer tax treaty benefits.

- High tax countries offering special incentives and privileges. See paras 2.32–2.42.

HIGH TAX JURISDICTIONS WITH IOFC FEATURES

2.32   An extremely large percentage of otherwise high tax countries have special regions or regimes where offshore activities can be conducted. However, such favoured tax treatment is clearly on its way out.

2.33   *Ireland* is probably the high tax country with the widest range of offshore features, from manufacturing and exports to computer and financial services. The favourable tax regimes for financial services and manufacturing companies will not be renewed, and Irish Government proposals to address this dilemma have been accepted by the European Commission. The proposals entail introducing a single low rate of corporation tax of 12.5% for financial service companies.

2.34   The *United Kingdom* is the world's prime residential haven.

2.35   *Belgium* has the typical structure of a high tax jurisdiction. However, in its attempt to become one of the major financial centres of the European Union, the government introduced a system favouring the establishment in Belgium of headquarters companies and co-ordination centres where international corporations pay tax on a nominal basis only.

2.36   Similarly, *France, Germany*, the *Netherlands, Singapore*, and the *United Kingdom*, all high tax countries too, offer management company, administrative, headquarters company, and/or co-ordination centre facilities that can effectively be used as tax haven entities.

2.37   *Cyprus, Denmark*, the *Netherlands*, and *Switzerland* allow their tax treaties with other countries to be used in combination with special domestic tax concessions so as to produce an extremely low effective tax burden.

2.38   *Switzerland* gives favoured tax treatment to holding companies. For purposes of qualification, a holding company is defined as a Swiss corporation that owns at least 20% of the capital of another company or a participation valued at more than 2 million Swiss francs, to include capital gains. The ownership threshold for relief is limited to 20% of the capital in another company provided the participation has been held for more than one year.

2.39   *Spain* has introduced a special tax regime for a new type of holding company, the Entidad de Tenencia de Valores Extranjeros (ETVE), which follows the pattern of the Netherlands holding company participation privilege. The ETVE is an ordinary Spanish company whose primary purpose is the administration and management of participations in equity of non-resident companies. The principal benefits are as follows:

- total participation exemption for dividends and capital gains is realised on the disposal of shares in a non-resident company, provided the ETVE holds at least 5% of the share capital for at least one uninterrupted year before distribution;

- distribution of non-Spanish source dividends is exempt from any withholding tax;

- interest payments are fully deductible;

- no capital duty is payable on issue of share capital for entities established in certain provinces and on share-for-share contributions;

- overseas branch income is exempt; and

- advance rulings on transactions are available.

2.40 Following along these lines, *Denmark* is moving towards the abolition of withholding taxes on overseas dividends in a move that could create serious competition for existing European low-tax holding company regimes in the Netherlands, Luxembourg, Belgium, Switzerland, Spain and Austria. This would promote the participation exemption regime that enables Danish companies repatriating profits to receive dividends tax-free from foreign subsidiaries. The only requirements are that the Danish company must own at least 25% of the foreign company and that the foreign company must be active. This abolition of withholding taxes on overseas dividends could make Denmark the most direct route for investing from offshore to onshore.

2.41 *Singapore* has widened its existing range of offshore facilities to include the following:

● full tax exemption for fund managers managing a minimum S$5bn in offshore money (those managing less than S$5bn can qualify on a case-by-case basis);

● no tax on disposal gains from unit trusts with immediate effect;

● two-year suspension of the tax deduction limits for general provisions made by banks from year of assessment 1998;

● no tax on fee income from arranging debt securities in Singapore;

● 10% tax on bond interest and bond trading income with immediate effect;

● extension of the tax exemption for syndicated offshore credit and underwriting for five years to March 2003;

● five-year extension on the tax holiday for the Singapore International Monetary Exchange (SIMEX);

● up to a five-year extension on the tax concession for venture capital; and

● tax concession for offshore income from Internet transactions to 2004.

2.42 For further examples of high tax jurisdictions with IOFC features, see Chapter 3, Chapter 4 and Chapter 11, para 11.41.

ANATOMY OF A TYPICAL IOFC

Background

2.43 Many offshore financial centre operations and transactions traditionally take place in the entirely tax-exempt environments characteristic of tax havens such as the Cayman Islands or the Bahamas.

2.44 Offshore financial centre operations and transactions may also take place within a high tax system (technically onshore) but benefit from certain special features that enable them to function outside of the normal tax and exchange control restraints; these features are to be found typically in such onshore financial centres as London, Amsterdam, Zurich, or Singapore.

2.45 In many otherwise high tax jurisdictions, the creation of an offshore environment for certain forms of activity has proved valuable in attracting international capital and associated employment. Conversely, countries that have not done so may find their international competitiveness impaired. Developing countries with convenient geographical access to major markets can derive particular benefits from the development of an offshore sector.

Typical IOFC Structures

2.46   The typical IOFC may be structured to accommodate many, and sometimes all, of the following:

● to provide for

   — offshore companies

   — offshore trusts

   — offshore banking

   — offshore insurance

   — offshore shipping

   — offshore funds

   — co-ordination centres

   — headquarters companies

   — management and administrative offices;

● to create a new source of invisible earnings for the country;

● to increase the inflow of foreign currency and attract foreign qualifying companies;

● to generate employment;

● to create training and educational opportunities;

● to enhance the financial strength and status of the country;

● to foster the introduction and increased use of modern technology;

● to develop exports and associated activities; and

● to develop tax and/or non-tax incentive programs.

Benefits of an IOFC Program

Inflow of New Revenue — Tax and Non-tax

2.47   The potential revenue sources from a thriving IOFC include a wide range of income items, such as:

● incorporation and annual fees for companies;

● stamp duties on companies and trusts, registration of deeds, and certain transactions;

● increased use of facilities, such as transport communications, postal services, hotels, etc.;

● indirect benefits from transactions in the banking, insurance, and other financial sectors;

● indirect benefits from transactions in the legal, accounting, and other professional services sectors; and

● indirect benefits from the property and construction sectors.

Generation of Employment and Creation of Training Opportunities

2.48   At the time of granting permission to companies to set up in an IOFC, rules and procedures sometimes attach conditions of employment and training of local staff. This is common in the incentive programs of many high tax jurisdictions.

2.49 Evolution of International Offshore Financial Centres

2.49 Similarly, in order to qualify for favoured treatment, an applicant company may be obliged to create new training opportunities. For example, the Irish incentives have as an important objective that the new generation should be given financial skills and be trained in processing, programming, computer software development, telecommunications, and other related skills.

Enhancing the Financial Strength and Status of the Country

2.50 The offshore industry inevitably benefits the economy, and it may lead to an improvement in the status of the country as a financial and business centre. One need only make reference to a financial centre such as Luxembourg or Singapore for an example of the role that financial centre activities have played in the strengthening of the national economies.

Introduction and Increased Use of Modern Technology; Transfers of Technology

2.51 It may be made a condition for the grant of special tax and non-tax treatment that a qualifying company be obliged to affect certain technology transfers.

Costs and Related Considerations

2.52 Costs of setting up and maintaining financial centre structures are relatively low in relation to the benefits. Such costs may include the following:

Setting Up and Administration

2.53 A number of new laws and procedures would be required in order to create the necessary infrastructure for a financial centre.

2.54 A special agency or 'authority' is normally created for the entire offshore project. Efficient administration will maximise benefits to the economy by both reducing the cost of the offshore program and increasing its attractiveness. Multinational operators are particularly sensitive to streamlined, fast, and inexpensive procedures.

Infrastructure and Facilities

2.55 It is essential that there should be an adequate infrastructure with comprehensive facilities. It may be taken as an essential feature of an IOFC that there be state-of-the-art communications technology and facilities. The existence of professional firms of attorneys and accountants, as well as banks and other financial service companies, is vital. The opportunity will create the need, and, conversely, the need will create the opportunity. Existing hotel and related accommodations may have to expand. Additionally, it is of the greatest importance that adequate office accommodations should be available.

Promotion

2.56 Many IOFCs engage in a major promotion of their offshore facilities. In view of the large number of IOFCs and their broad similarities, certain IOFCs seek to develop innovative features and focus on these in addition to the favourable characteristics of the country itself.

OFFSHORE ENTITIES

2.57 Different legal systems contain a variety of companies, trusts, partnerships, and other legal entities.

2.58   The selection of the form to be given to the proposed entity is often made as a function of the whole body of rules (both tax and non-tax) governing formation, administration, and dissolution.

Companies

2.59   A company is an association of persons formed for the purpose of an undertaking or a business carried on in the name of the association.

2.60   The company laws of different offshore jurisdictions may show considerable variations of structure and detail.

2.61   The general requirements and conditions governing incorporation are important, and it is helpful to know what information must be contained in the memorandum and articles of association, by-laws, statutes, or other incorporation documents; whether a Table A system is employed; which persons are authorised to handle incorporation; and who usually do. (Table A is a model of by-laws (articles) that may be adopted by any company if it wishes and usually applies unless the company makes provision to the contrary. Table A is to be found in UK companies legislation and in other systems that are patterned thereon.)

2.62   Limits on the powers of the company may be important, particularly where borrowing rights are concerned, and it is sometimes useful to know in advance to what extent the powers of the company may be circumscribed in the incorporation documents or subsequently and whether there is an ultra vires doctrine. Limitation of liability should be checked.

2.63   Certain provisions governing the share capital of the company may have to be taken into account (i.e., the minimum issued and paid-up capital and the types or classes of shares that may be issued), in particular, whether bearer shares, no par value shares, preference shares, redeemable shares, shares with special (or no) voting rights, or classes of shares with different rights as to income or capital are permitted.

Example

Assume that an Anglo-American type of company has a share capital consisting of 100 A shares and 1,000 B shares. The A shares carry 10 votes for each B share. In all other respects the two classes of shares are equal.

As part of an international company reorganisation, it is proposed to establish a Swiss company, the share capital of which will be divided into two classes having the same rights as the existing A and B shares.

For the purpose of the proposed arrangement, it is considered that a branch of the existing company would not be appropriate and that a partnership would be an unsuitable type of entity.

The choice is thus between a joint stock company *Société anonyme* (SA) or *Aktiengesellshaft* (AG) and a limited liability company (*Société à responsabilité* (SARL) or *Gesellschaft mit beschränkter Haftung* (GmbH).

The joint stock company (*Code des Obligations* or *Obligationsrechts*, arts. 620 to 763) is the usual form of company used for business operations in Switzerland. It approaches most closely to the Anglo-American type of company. There are no nationality requirements for shareholders, but the majority of the directors must be both nationals of and resident in Switzerland. This requirement can, however, be overcome by the appointment of nominees.

The limited liability company (*Code des Obligations* or *Obligationsrechts*, arts. 772 to 827) is similar to the joint stock company in many respects. However, members participate in the capital with a fixed amount that does not correspond to a share in a company. There are no nationality or residence requirements for members or directors. However, a manager who is resident in, but not necessarily a national of, Switzerland must be appointed and registered as such. Though establishment and operating costs of a joint stock company are slightly higher than those of a limited liability company, the amount of money involved in the proposed arrangement is such that this difference in expenditure is considered to be irrelevant.

The crucial difference between the two types of companies from the point of view of the shareholders in the existing company is that there are no shares in the limited liability company and the transfer of participations would be much more difficult than in the case of the shares of a joint stock company.

For this reason, the type of entity chosen is the joint stock company. The next difficulty to be overcome is the differentiation between the A and B shares, since it is not possible to issue shares with increased voting rights, as in the case of an Anglo-American type of company (*Code des Obligations* or *Obligationsrechts*, arts. 692 and 693).

However, it is possible to create a class of shares enjoying increased rights as to dividend and liquidation distributions but with the same voting rights as other classes of shares (*Code des Obligations* or *Obligationsrechts*, arts. 656 and 693).

The solution to this problem is as follows: 100 A shares and 100 B shares are issued in the Swiss company. Each B share has a nominal value of 10 times that of each A share and entitles the holder to receive 10 units in respect of all distributions, whether in the form of dividends, liquidation dividends, or otherwise.

	A Shares	B Shares
Existing company		
Share capital	100:	1,000
Nominal value, in the ratio of	1:	10
Voting rights, in the ratio of	1:	1
Distribution rights, in the ratio of	1:	10
Swiss company		
Share capital	100:	100
Nominal value, in the ratio of	1:	10
Voting rights, in the ratio of	1:	1
Distribution rights, in the ratio of	1:	10

2.64 The rules applying to the organs and officers of the company are often material from the point of view of the nationality or residence of shareholders and directors, the requirement of and the place of the holding of meetings and the disclosure of names. The fees of local officers or nominees where these are required or desired should usually be ascertained in advance.

2.65 Requirements with regard to the maintenance of a local registered office and of statutory records, and the duty to file information returns, in particular financial statements, should be noted. Requirements with regard to auditors vary considerably. Sometimes the auditors (or *commissaires aux comptes*) constitute an organ of the company. In certain cases the ease with which a company can be wound up is valuable. Winding-up rules should generally be checked for possible problems. Government and professional/banking fees payable not merely on incorporation but annually and on winding up usually merit scrutiny. In some cases regard should be had to the rules governing increases or reductions of capital, reconstructions, invitations to the public to subscribe, and the public raising of loan capital.

2.66 Depending on the proposed operations, it may be important to examine whether the type of company contemplated may receive favoured treatment or be subject to any special requirements or restrictions.

2.67 It is sometimes advantageous to make use of a company incorporated elsewhere, and in such cases it is necessary to know whether there are any special requirements in order to carry on business or to have a branch or permanent establishment of such foreign company.

2.68 Special treatment is often accorded to holding companies. The definitional content of the term *holding* company may vary from one legal system to another.

2.69 In certain legal systems it implies the holding of a majority or the whole of the equity capital of one or more other companies. In other systems the criterion may be the holding of as little as 5% of the equity capital of the subsidiary, or simply the holding of shares in other companies. The shareholding qualification may result in the reduction of tax or other consequences either by virtue of the provisions of the domestic system or by virtue of a tax treaty. The term holding companies is sometimes employed more loosely to refer to companies that are used to control industrial or commercial companies; to act as investment funds; to finance the other companies in their group by supplying them with funds that they may obtain through the floating of bond issues; or to collect income in the form of dividends, loan interest or patent royalties, and licensing fees.

2.70 Often holding companies are intermediary companies in a group structure and hence are also subsidiaries of their parent companies. A financial holding company is generally established as a wholly owned subsidiary of a foreign parent company for the purpose of channelling financial transactions such as the issue of debentures or notes in the Eurocurrency market and the taking up of bank loans under the guarantee of the parent.

Segregated Portfolio Companies (Protected Cell Companies)

2.71 This concept applies primarily to offshore insurance companies, but also has a natural application in the mutual fund industry.

2.72 A segregated portfolio company may create segregated portfolios to segregate the company's assets and liabilities held in that portfolio from:

- company assets and liabilities held in other segregated portfolios; or

- assets and liabilities of different lines of business to protect the assets supporting these lines.

Partnerships

2.73 A partnership is an association of two or more persons (individuals or companies) normally formed for the purpose of making a profit. Such an association may be based on an oral or written agreement. A partnership can be a *general partnership* or a *limited partnership*, depending on the extent of each party's liability. A general partnership is characterised by the unlimited liability of the general partners for partnership debts. A limited partnership comprises at least one general partner who has unlimited liability for partnership debts, and one or more limited partners who are liable only to the extent of their capital contributions; limited partners, however, may not participate in the management of the business. The characterisation of a partnership is normally a function of the domestic law. At times, however, it may be that this question falls to be determined by a foreign legal system.

Example

In characterising business entities, US Treasury Regulations (Treasury Regulations issued pursuant to s 7701 of the Internal Revenue Code, Regulations 301.7701–1 to 301.7701–4) invoke the six corporate characteristics identified by the Supreme Court (*TA Morrisey, Trustee*, 36–1 USTC 9020, 296 US 344, 56 S Ct 289 (1953))

- associates;
- objective to carry on business and divide the profits;
- continuity of life;
- centralised management;
- free transferability of ownership interests; and
- limited liability.

Since the existence of the first two items are common to both the corporation and the partnership, in differentiating between these business forms only the remaining four corporate characteristics are considered, and a highly mechanical test is adopted:

'An unincorporated organization shall not be classified as an association (taxable under the Code as a corporation) unless such organization has more corporate characteristics than non-corporate characteristics.' (Regulations § 301.7701–2(a)(3).)

Thus, under existing law, if a business organisation has no more than two of the corporate characteristics of the third item through to the last item, it will be characterised as a partnership for US tax purposes.

2.74 In certain jurisdictions, a partnership may have a corporate form, and in such a case a checklist would resemble a checklist for a company. However, even if a partnership does not have a corporate form, requirements relating to formation and registration, the citizenship and/or residence of parties, limited liability, and restrictions on activities should be examined in the context of the general law governing partnerships.

2.75 It may be necessary to take into account whether or not a partnership constitutes a taxable person from the point of view of each of the legal systems involved.

2.76   The legal and tax position not merely of foreign partners but of the foreign partnership itself may require consideration.

2.77   In a 1998 case, the United Kingdom Court of Appeal clarified the question of the legal personality of a foreign partnership. The Court held that either the individual partners of a foreign partnership or the partnership itself could be sued in the English courts even if the partnership did not carry on business within the jurisdiction and was not a company. The reasoning given by the Court is that the partnership had a legal personality, enabling it to enter into contracts.

2.78   In this case (*Oxnard Financing SA v Rabn* [1998] 3 All ER 19, the plaintiffs' payment claim was for the balance of the share purchase price from a Swiss banking partnership in which the four defendants were partners. Under Swiss Law, a general partner is an entity distinct from individual partners; it could make contracts in its name, could sue or be sued in its name, and could own property. Individual partners were liable for the partnership's debts but could only be sued if a partner became bankrupt or if the partnership were dissolved.

2.79   It was held that it was permissible under English law to sue the Swiss banking partnership in England by naming as defendants the individual natural persons who were partners in it, who traded under that name, and who were sued in that capacity as partners. In the judgment of the Court, the claim was against the bank, while the individuals were being sued only in their capacity as partners in the foreign entity. It was the foreign general partnership that was being sued by joining the individual partners. Thus, they were being sued in the capacity of partners with respect to the contract made by the partnership. It followed that the foreign entity could be sued by reference to either the partners or the Swiss banking partnership.

Trusts

2.80   The word *trust* refers to the duty or aggregate accumulation of obligations that rest upon a person described as a trustee.

2.81   The responsibilities are in relation to property held by the trustee or under the trustee's control. The trustee is obliged to administer the trust property in the manner lawfully prescribed by the trust instrument (trust deed or settlement) or, in the absence of specific provision, in accordance with equitable principles or statute law. The administration will thus be in such a manner that the consequential benefits and advantages accrue not to the trustee but to the beneficiaries.

2.82   The Anglo-Saxon trust is merely a bundle of rights and obligations in equity and is thus not strictly speaking a legal entity. Though the law of trust varies from system to system, those patterned on the English law of trusts resemble one another closely, differences usually being of statutory origin. In the case of civil law systems in which the trust is to be found, it is invariably a creature of statute and may take the form of a legal entity.

2.83   Trust deeds and ancillary or related documents should always be drafted or checked by a local expert. It is obvious that a trust or settlement must be valid from the point of view of the domestic law; however, in certain cases it is important to consider its validity and characterisation from the point of view of any other legal system the courts or administrative tribunals of which may be called upon to construe it.

2.84   The rules governing the rights and duties of settlors, trustees, beneficiaries, and third parties; the legal effect of discretionary trusts; the possible role of protectors;

perpetuity periods; registration requirements; and the ability to transfer the situs of a trust from one jurisdiction to another are factors that should be taken into account.

2.85   The trust is often the key element of an arrangement seeking to sever or to prevent the formation of a connecting factor with a high tax jurisdiction. Certain legislation has been drafted with this objective, such as the Cayman Islands Trusts Law (Law No. 6 of 1967 as amended), from the tax point of view, and Gibraltar and Turks and Caicos Trust Laws, from the asset protection point of view.

2.86   Certain offshore jurisdictions that do not enjoy the Anglo–American trust traditions have introduced domestic equivalents by legislative procedures (e.g., Liechtenstein, Monaco, and Panama). (See Chapter 9.)

Sole Proprietorships

2.87   The sole proprietorship is not a common offshore vehicle. However, it may sometimes be convenient to operate in an individual capacity, and here the principal points to watch for usually relate to work permits and business licenses.

Other Legal Entities

2.88   A certain number of other legal entities that are *sui generis* to a given legal system may merit consideration as they have features that may be particularly appropriate for the purposes of a proposed arrangement.

2.89   Liechtenstein, for example, has the following entities (in addition to the company (that is, the joint stock company (*Aktiengesellschaft*), which corresponds to the Anglo-American type of company) and two types of trusts (that is, the trust organisation (*Treuunternehmen*), which is a separate legal entity managed by one or more trustees, and the private trust, which can be set up by private agreement between a settlor and a trustee)): the establishment, or *Anstalt*, and the foundation, or *Stiftung*.

2.90   The establishment, or *Anstalt*, is an extremely flexible form of legal association that is very suitable for international setups. Such an entity may be set up by one or more founders who need not have Liechtenstein nationality or residence.

2.91   The establishment is governed by the founder or by any one or more persons to whom the founder's rights have been assigned. The founder appoints the beneficiaries to whom the net profits are to be allotted. In the absence of such designation, the founder is the beneficiary.

2.92   The foundation, or *Stiftung*, of Luxembourg law is used primarily for the management and investment of family property or for charitable purposes, though it may also have a commercial object. The transfer of property to the foundation may be made irrevocably or with the right of revocation reserved. The foundation is managed by one or more managers appointed by the founder.

2.93   A new type of offshore entity is the private foundation recently introduced by Netherlands Antilles law. The *stichting*, or foundation, has been recognised for many years in the Netherlands and the Netherlands Antilles. It has always been used as a vehicle for charitable, social or non-profit-making purposes. Realising that there is a need for a vehicle such as the foundation for private purposes, the Netherlands Antilles legislators introduced the concept of a 'private foundation'.

2.94   The private foundation is a foundation that is established as such in accordance with its articles. The determining factor is the purpose clause. The private foundation may have any purpose that is legal under the laws of the Netherlands Antilles that is not against public order to pursue. The private foundation can make any distribution that is appropriate under its purpose clause. The purpose clause may not, however, include the running of a business or enterprise, but this prohibition does not extend to the active management of the funds of the foundation. The foundation is allowed to hold shares in a company which, in turn, runs a business. The private foundation is a suitable vehicle to separate the legal and economic ownership of assets. Unlike a company, a foundation does not have shares that entitle the shareholders to the underlying assets in the company or to its income.

2.95   The beneficiaries of a foundation are appointed by the board, subject to the prior approval and direction of the founder, if the articles so provide. A beneficiary of a foundation is entitled to distributions of income and/or capital from the foundation only after his or her appointment as such by the board, in accordance with the articles of the foundation. Until such an appointment is made, a contingent or future beneficiary does not have any claim against the assets or the income of the foundation.

2.96   The most important difference between a private foundation and a common law trust is that the foundation is a legal entity, while the trust is not. On formation, the founder transfers full ownership of the assets to the foundation as a separate legal entity. The affairs of the foundation are then managed by its board. There are no specific residency rules for private foundations. There are no statutory accounting or audit requirements other than those stipulated in the articles of the foundation.

NON-TAX FEATURES OF IOFCS

2.97   Non-tax factors that may have to be taken into account obviously vary from case to case. The following indications are thus only of a general nature.

Legal and Administrative Systems

2.98   The legal and administrative systems of a given country may be relevant from the point of view of practice and procedure.

Political and Economic Stability

2.99   The political and economic stability of the countries involved in a proposed arrangement and likely future developments should always be considered. This is an essential precaution where it is proposed to invest capital in a foreign country or where any funds or other assets are exposed to the risk of nationalisation, expropriation, or outright confiscation. Cuba left the kind of memories that threatened for a moment to destroy the offshore financial centre operations of Panama under Manuel Noriega.

Professional, Commercial, and Banking Facilities

2.100   The availability of good lawyers, accountants, and secretarial and other staff, and of commercial and banking facilities, may be of considerable importance in deciding whether to locate a subsidiary, branch, or trust in a particular country.

2.101 Evolution of International Offshore Financial Centres

Business Climate

2.101 Note should also be taken of the business climate in any country included in an international arrangement, since considerably different standards may be encountered with respect to business ethics.

Incentives

2.102 See Chapter 4, paras 4.164–4.165.

Position of Foreigners

2.103 It is advisable to know in advance whether foreign individuals and entities are subject to legal or factual disabilities as compared with residents and, if so, whether there is any simple method of overcoming them (e.g., by the use of nominees).

Communications

2.104 In addition to the essential requirement of good telecommunications, another factor that may be of some importance is the availability of good air and sea links and of good postal and telecommunications services. Transportation facilities are particularly relevant in the case of manufacturing subsidiaries.

Markets

2.105 It may be material in certain cases also to take into account the natural markets of a given country as well as any agreements giving it preferential treatment. Such agreements may be bilateral or multilateral and may be institutional (i.e., creating international customs or economic unions or communities).

Labour

2.106 The availability of skilled and unskilled labour and rates of pay may be important with regard to operations in a given country.

Accountancy Laws, Procedure, and Customs

2.107 Accountancy laws, procedure, and customs may also have to be taken into consideration for the purposes of an international setup. Problems may arise in connection with consolidated accounts and with the computation of depreciation allowances, which may have a direct effect on the tax position.

Languages

2.108 Difficulties may be encountered in handling and presenting material in foreign languages. It is important to establish contact with lawyers, accountants, and banks operating in foreign countries with whom it is possible to communicate in a language understood by the parties.

Exchange Control

2.109 Offshore money normally seeks to keep clear of exchange controls and restrictions.

2.110   In IOFCs that have exchange restrictions, special provisions normally govern non-resident or external accounts (i.e., the accounts of account holders not regarded as resident or carrying on business in that country) and the facilities and limitations attached to such accounts.

2.111   However, offshore operations do very often start onshore where they may be subject to domestic exchange controls and restrictions.

2.112   The exchange control system of a country is a body of statutory and administrative regulations and rules the principal objects of which are to control that country's liquid resources abroad and the international movement of currency owned by its residents. The main heads of classification employed by the International Monetary Fund in its Annual Report on Exchange Restrictions are the administration of control; the prescription of currency; non-resident accounts; imports and import payments; payments for invisibles; exports and export proceeds; proceeds from invisibles; capital; and gold.

2.113   Exchange control is an essential factor to be taken into account in the creation of an international tax plan, since restrictions on convertibility and transferability of funds may have the effect of making a contract unenforceable or of rendering any international transaction, operation, or relationship unworkable.

2.114   The problems attendant upon the appreciation of this factor are considerable, as it is necessary to take into account not only existing restrictions but also likely future developments. This kind of prediction is often difficult in the case of short-term developments and is nearly always impossible in the case of long-term developments. It is therefore advisable to seek undertakings from the appropriate authorities *prior* to investing in a foreign country, with a view to insuring the right to transfer and convert current profits and (on the realisation of the investment) the capital proceeds.

2.115   In certain cases, import and export restrictions may affect a project, and it may thus also be advisable to obtain undertakings from the appropriate authorities with respect to future rights to import and export.

Currency and Exchange Rates

2.116   The currency and exchange rates may act as deterrents to using certain countries as IOFCs (for example, South Africa, which would otherwise be an excellent tax treaty conduit country).

2.117   An exchange rate is the price at which one currency can be exchanged for another, expressed in units of such currencies. Like all other prices, exchange rates tend to vary from time to time, however slightly.

2.118   Far more extensive and sudden rate variations result from the devaluation and revaluation of currencies. In periods of monetary instability, the greatest possible care must be exercised in determining the currencies to be employed with respect to the various elements of a proposed international structure. Changes in international monetary markets may result in substantial losses to the one party and corresponding gains to the other.

2.119   In the case of contracts for imports, exports, licenses, and many other international business agreements, possible changes in exchange rates require careful consideration for the selection of a currency for stipulating prices. Fluctuations in the exchange rates are of particular importance in the case of loans.

2.120 This is well illustrated in the choice of currencies for Eurobond issues. In the early days of this market, most Eurobonds were expressed in US dollars, as this was considered to be the most stable currency. However, as other currencies strengthened, it became more common to find issues in DMs, Swiss francs, and Dutch guilders.

2.121 The use of forward markets may constitute a useful hedge against adverse currency changes. To protect the value of future receipts in a foreign currency, a company may sell forward the foreign currency, though only effecting delivery of such foreign currency at the time provided for in the contract. Prices vary according to the currencies involved but are normally related to current interest rates.

2.122 The forward market may also be used as a protection against the devaluation of the currency of a country where a foreign subsidiary is located. In such a case, a parent company may sell forward in the amount required for the operations of the subsidiary. Sometimes it is necessary for a borrower or an importer to use forward markets as a protection against the devaluation of a particular currency.

STRATEGIC CHECKLISTS

GENERAL AND CORPORATE ACTIVITIES CARRIED ON IN IOFCS

- Holding companies.

- Finance companies and partnerships.

- International headquarters and administration.

- International shipping and air transport vehicles.

- Insurance, life insurance, and reinsurance companies.

- International pension funds.

- Trust corporations and related activities.

- Banking, finance, and treasury management.

- Brokerage and arbitrage activities.

- Venture capital funds and offshore funds.

- Counter trade activities.

- Joint ventures.

- Funds for leveraged buyouts.

- Location for ownership of intangible rights and licensing companies.

- Assembly and manufacturing.

- Professional services.

- International and wholesale trading with third parties.

- Joint ventures and partnerships in construction, mining, onshore and offshore drilling, and exploration activities.

- Leisure industry activities.

- Hotels and resorts.

- Property and investment and international real estate ownership.

- Time-share and holiday homes.

SERVICES FOR INDIVIDUALS CARRIED ON IN IOFCS

- Offshore trusts and trust management.

- Employment trusts and employee share ownership plans.

- Offshore employment companies.

- Investment holding companies and private group holding companies.

- Property and portfolio investments.

- Insulation vehicles for estate and capital taxes.

- Exchange control vehicles and planning.

- Investment services and asset administration.

- Offshore ownership of intellectual property rights.

- Offshore roll-up funds and investment trusts.

- Life insurance free of withholding taxes.

- Offshore banking activities and brokerage advice.

- Venture capital planning.

- Retirement location.

- Vacation resorts and time-sharing.

- Location for producing works of artistic and cultural merit.

- Pension planning.

- Location for tax residence and tax shelter.

- Tax deferment and secondary sheltering opportunities.

KEY SELECTION FACTORS OF AN IOFC LOCATION

- Political and economic stability.

- Guarantees against future taxation.

- Guarantees against expropriation or nationalisation.

- Freedom from exchange controls.

- Good professional and banking facilities.

- Favourable long-term government policies.

- Favourable attitude to offshore activities.

- Confidentiality.

- Strength of banking and commercial secrecy.

- Freedom from banking controls and availability of local capital.

- Location of offshore banking activities.

- Effective legal, accounting, and administrative systems.

- Favourable company law requirements.

- Ability to use IOFC for central distribution activity.

- Availability of duty-free zones.

- Minimum import duty scales.

- Good communications and transportation facilities.

- Ability to conduct substantial business activities.

- No withholding taxes.

- Liberality of corporation legislation.

- Low or no direct or indirect taxes on all or certain types of income and capital.

- No inheritance taxes.

- Flexibility to move out of tax haven location.

- Minimum governmental controls.

- Minimal currency risks.

- Opportunity to obtain local tax rulings.

- Acceptable level of fees and legal costs.

- Availability of tax treaties.

- Availability of investment concessions.

- Freedom to import necessary raw materials and obtain work permits.

- Security of property rights.

- Minimal filing requirements (tax and corporate).

- Ability to take advantage of redomiciliation provisions.

- Bearer shares availability.

- Availability of share warrants to bearer or no par value shares.

- Legislation permitting exempt companies and trusts.

- Acceptance of trust legislation.

- Ability to use nominee shareholders.

- Good local directors.

- Availability of qualified local staff.

OECD'S TAX HAVENS LIST

Andorra	The British Virgin Islands
Anguilla	The Cook Islands
Antigua and Barbuda	Dominica
Aruba	Gibraltar
The Bahamas	Grenada
Bahrain	Guernsey/Sark/Alderney
Barbados	Isle of Man
Belize	Jersey

Liberia	Samoa
Liechtenstein	Seychelles
The Maldives	St. Lucia
The Marshall Islands	St. Christopher & Nevis
Monaco	St. Vincent and the Grenadines
Montserrat	Tonga
Nauru	The Turks & Caicos Islands
Netherlands Antilles	The US Virgin Islands
Niue	Vanuatu
Panama	

COUNTRIES THAT HAVE NO INCOME TAX OR THAT GRANT EXTENSIVE TAX EXEMPTIONS

Andorra	Grenada
Anguilla	Kuwait
The Bahamas	Maldives
Bahrain	Monaco
Bermuda	Nauru
Brunei (individuals)	Oman (individuals only)
Campione	The Turks and Caicos Islands
The Cayman Islands	United Arab Emirates
The Cook Islands	Uruguay
French Polynesia	Vanuatu

COUNTRIES THAT IMPOSE NO INCOME TAX ON FOREIGN SOURCE INCOME

Costa Rica	Ecuador
Djibouti	France (special rules)
Dominican Republic	Guatemala

Hong Kong	Macau
Ireland (non-resident company)	Panama
Jordan	Swaziland
Kenya	Uruguay
Lebanon	Venezuela
Liberia	

COUNTRIES THAT CAN BE USED AS LOW TAX AREAS BUT ALSO HAVE CERTAIN TAX TREATY BENEFITS

Cyprus	The Netherlands Antilles
The Netherlands	Switzerland

LOW TAX FINANCIAL CENTRES AND COUNTRIES OFFERING SPECIAL INCENTIVES AND PRIVILEGES

Angola	Liechtenstein
Anguilla	Luxembourg
Antigua	Macau
Barbados	Madeira
The British Virgin Islands	Malta
Brunei	The Marshall Islands
Cyprus	Mauritius
Gibraltar	Montserrat
Grenada	The Netherlands
Guernsey	Nevis
Hong Kong	Philippines
Ireland	Puerto Rico
The Isle of Man	Samoa
Jamaica	San Marino
Jersey	Seychelles

Solomon Islands   St. Vincent

Sri Lanka   Switzerland

St. Helena

Note: Certain of the above countries also offer tax treaty benefits.

OECD MEMBER COUNTRIES WITH HARMFUL PREFERENTIAL TAX REGIMES

- *INSURANCE*

Australia	Offshore Banking Units
Belgium	Co-ordination Centres
Finland	Åland Captive Insurance Regime
Italy	Trieste Financial Services and Insurance Centre
Ireland	International Financial Services Centre
Portugal	Madeira International Business Centre
Luxembourg	Provisions for Fluctuations in Re-Insurance Companies
Sweden	Foreign Non-life Insurance Companies

- *FINANCING AND LEASING*

Belgium	Co-ordination Centres
Hungary	Venture Capital Companies
Hungary	Preferential Regime for Companies Operating Abroad
Iceland	International Trading Companies
Ireland	International Financial Services Centre
Ireland	Shannon Airport Zone
Italy	Trieste Financial Services and Insurance Centre
Luxembourg	Finance Branch
The Netherlands	Risk Reserves for International Group Financing

The Netherlands Intra-group Finance Activities

The Netherlands Finance Branch

Spain   Basque Country and Navarra Co-ordination Centres

Switzerland   Administrative Companies

- ## *FUND MANAGERS*

Greece   Mutual Funds/Portfolio Investment Companies
                (Taxation of Fund Managers)

Ireland   International Financial Services Centre (Taxation of
                Fund Managers)

Luxembourg   Management companies (Taxation of management
                companies that manage only one mutual fund (1929
                holdings))

Portugal   Madeira International Business Centre (Taxation of
                Fund Managers)

- ## *BANKING*

Australia   Offshore Banking Units

Canada   International Banking Centres

Ireland   International Financial Services Centre

Italy   Trieste Financial Services and Insurance Centre

Korea   Offshore Activities of Foreign Exchange Banks

Portugal   External Branches in the Madeira International
                Business Centre

Turkey   Istanbul Offshore Banking Regime

- ## *HEADQUARTERS REGIMES*

Belgium   Co-ordination Centres

France   Headquarters Centres

Germany   Monitoring and Co-ordinating Offices

Greece   Offices of Foreign Companies

The Netherlands Cost-plus Ruling

Portugal Madeira International Business Centre

Spain Basque Country and Navarra Co-ordination Centres

Switzerland Administrative Companies

Switzerland Service Companies

- *DISTRIBUTION CENTRE REGIMES*

Belgium Distribution Centres

France Logistics Centres

The Netherlands Cost-plus/Resale Minus Ruling

Turkey Turkish Free Zones

- *SERVICE CENTRE REGIMES*

Belgium Service Centres

The Netherlands Cost-plus Ruling

- *SHIPPING*

Canada International Shipping

Germany International Shipping

Greece Shipping Offices

Greece Shipping Regime (Law 27/75)

Italy International Shipping

The Netherlands International Shipping

Norway International Shipping

Portugal International Shipping Register of Madeira

- *MISCELLANEOUS ACTIVITIES*

Belgium Ruling on Informal Capital

Belgium Ruling on Foreign Sales Corporation Activities

Canada   Non-resident Owned Investment Corporations

The Netherlands Ruling on Informal Capital

The Netherlands Ruling on Foreign Sales Corporation Activities

United States   Foreign Sales Corporations

3 New Developments in E-commerce and Other Offshore Operations and Transactions

STRATEGIC ISSUES, OPPORTUNITIES AND CAVEATS

E-COMMERCE

- Estimates are that, in 30 years time, consumer activity on-line could represent 30% of total consumer activity, and probably a very much higher percentage as measured in value.

- The framework for the taxation of e-commerce addresses four areas: (a) tax treaties, (b) consumption taxes, (c) tax administration, and (d) taxpayer service.

- *Caveat*: The taxation principles that guide governments in relation to conventional commerce tend to guide them also in relation to e-commerce.

KEY E-COMMERCE ISSUES ADDRESSED BY THE REVENUE

- Whether a web site or a server can constitute a permanent establishment giving rise to tax jurisdiction in a country. (Note: There is broad consensus that a web site cannot, in itself, constitute a permanent establishment.)

- How payments for digitised products should be characterised under tax treaties.

- For a consumption tax, defining (a) the place of consumption, (b) services, and (c) intangible property.

- Adopting conventional identification and internationally compatible information requirements.

- The role of Internet banking in money laundering.

OFFSHORE BANKING

- A considerable volume of international banking takes place offshore. Many of the world's major banks have banking and trust company operations in one or more IOFCs.

- Most IOFC jurisdictions strictly control banking and trust company activities.

- 'Know your customer' rules are becoming the norm.

- *Caveat:* Banking secrecy is progressively becoming more historical than real.

OFFSHORE FINANCIAL AND BUSINESS OPERATIONS

- Nearly every kind of operation or transaction that takes place onshore can also take place offshore.

- *Caveat:* The regulation of offshore operations and transactions is becoming progressively stricter.

OFFSHORE SHIPPING AND AIRCRAFT OPERATIONS

- Ownership, operation, administration, and registration may be situated in fiscally favourable (and even different) jurisdictions.

- Flags of convenience are still the norm.

- Ownership of aircraft via a group company in an IOFC can be hired out to a related operating company on an arm's length basis in order to make a profit on operations in an IOFC.

- *Caveat:* Most flag of convenience countries comply with international non-tax norms, such as safety at sea and manning requirements.

OFFSHORE PROVISION OF INTERNATIONAL SERVICES

- Offshore employment companies can be utilised to give effect to a separate contract of employment for offshore employment duties to minimise home country tax.

- Professional partnerships can employ staff in low tax jurisdictions for international consulting projects.

- Offshore services offered by banks and trust companies normally include a fairly wide range of trusteeship, management, and related services.

- *Caveat:* Watch out for variations in fees and quality of service. Check on everything.

HEADQUARTERS, ADMINISTRATIVE OFFICES, MANAGEMENT COMPANIES

- A number of otherwise high tax jurisdictions grant special tax treatment to attract the administrative offices of multinationals.

- Tax is normally levied at standard rates on a tax base calculated on a cost-plus basis.

- *Caveat:* The company is not normally permitted to engage in trade or certain other activities that are not of an administrative or management nature.

CO-ORDINATION CENTRES

- Co-ordination centres are typically subject to tax on a notional base, with the tax base normally determined as a percentage of certain operating costs borne by the co-ordination centre. However, personnel costs and financing costs may be excluded from the calculation of the notional tax base.

- The co-ordination centre must form part of an international group of affiliated companies with a very substantial aggregate capital and annual turnover. Banks, insurance companies, and certain other financial institutions may be excluded from establishing a co-ordination centre.

- *Caveat:* The activities that may be carried out in a co-ordination centre are normally restricted to activities that are specifically authorised.

CAPTIVE INSURANCE COMPANIES

- A captive insurance company may be set up by a non-insurance commercial company to insure or reinsure the risks of the parent company and/or its affiliated companies.

- A foreign captive insurance company may be used to insure against certain risks that the normal insurance market will not accept or to obtain broader types of insurance, to reduce the price cycle, to obtain an acceptable rating, to obtaining cover in difficult cases, and to obtain adequate service.

- Tax advantages may be obtained through the deductibility of premiums.

- Money savings can be achieved through the use of reinsurance as opposed to direct insurance.

- Captive insurance companies located in IOFC jurisdictions are often not subject to the same controls as insurance companies located in the country of the parent company and can invest surplus accumulations relatively freely, including investments for the direct or indirect benefit of the parent company or other affiliated companies.

- *Caveat:* There is a limit to the extent to which risks can be shifted and diluted.

INTERNATIONAL INVESTMENT TRUSTS

- Collective investment has become a huge, highly technical, and fast-developing sector.

- Recent developments encourage collective investment-based provision for retirement benefits.

OFFSHORE FUNDS

- An offshore fund may take the form of an investment company, unit trust, mutual fund, or other entity incorporated and resident in an IOFC, and may be open-ended or closed.

- Since the bulk of investors in offshore funds are residents or citizens of high tax countries, many of which severely restrict the local marketing activities of funds.

- Offshore funds can be used to raise low cost finance; to invest in zero coupon bonds, as well as growth stocks and securities on behalf of foreign investors; to raise venture capital finance; to raise funds for use in leveraged and management buyouts; to act as offshore multi-currency roll-up funds; and to invest in gilt-edged stocks.

- Other activities can include equity funds, bond funds, and funds specialising in particular sectors.

- Umbrella offshore funds can offer investors the possibility of investing in different portfolios.

- An offshore fund may enter into a professional services agreement with an independent broker, advisor, or merchant bank located in another international financial centre for the provision of investment advice at a fee based on market rates.

- *Caveat:* Though offshore funds generally enjoy greater investment flexibility than do funds located in high tax countries, there is a growing tendency to require greater disclosure and, generally, to tighten the regulations governing offshore funds.

OFFSHORE IPOS

- Cross-border initial public offerings ('IPOs' or listings) on offshore and foreign exchanges create the opportunity to access hitherto untapped financial markets.

- Listing on alternative exchanges provides access to a widespread international investor base.

- *Caveat:* Any IPO, irrespective of where it is finally executed, is a complex and long-term exercise that requires due diligence and careful consideration.

3.1 New Developments in Offshore Operations

SCOPE OF OFFSHORE OPERATIONS AND TRANSACTIONS

3.1 Many of the operations and transactions that can be performed onshore can potentially also be performed offshore. Every day, new technology reduces the number of business, commercial, financial, and professional activities that are entrapped onshore.

3.2 The most important development of all is the impact of electronic commerce.

ELECTRONIC COMMERCE

The Importance of Electronic Commerce (E-commerce)

3.3 E-commerce is reshaping the structures of commerce, and with this comes a major revolution in traditional methods of taxation. Revenue authorities are faced not only with the challenge of tax collection, but also with having to play a major role in realising the potential of what is already one of the greatest economic forces of the 21st century.

3.4 Jean-Baptiste Colbert, treasurer to King Louis XIV of France, advised that: 'The art of taxation consists in so plucking the goose to obtain the largest amounts of feathers, with the least possible amount of hissing.' In the world of electronic commerce, the tax collector's problem lies not in obtaining the most feathers but in getting hold of any at all. In fact, the real problem is getting hold of the goose; geese have gone virtual.

3.5 The Internet simply eliminates borders between countries and furthermore makes businesses virtually invisible.

3.6 At the consumer end, electronic commerce makes the tracing of transactions and thus the taxing of goods and services sold and distributed via the Internet almost impossible. As a result, state and national governments' tax bases are, or are at risk of, being eroded.

3.7 One problem with tracing 'intangible goods' sold via the Internet, such as an electronic newspaper or a software program, is that the marginal cost of providing an extra unit is close to zero. Since no additional inputs are required, tax authorities can no longer crosscheck a firm's units of input with its claimed units of o' put.

3.8 The development of electronic cash as opposed to credit card systems will probably further facilitate both electronic commerce and tax evasion since payment no longer leaves a paper trail but is rather anonymous and untraceable. Today tax inspectors can check reported income and spending against bank and credit card statements. At present, 90%, by volume, of all financial transactions with respect to consumption take place using cash, checks, and credit cards. These systems usually involve intermediaries such as banks, credit card companies, or other financial institutions that leave an audit trail of payment. In the world of the Internet, such an audit trail may not exist.

3.9 The Internet may also reduce the role of these intermediaries — important to tax authorities as they report financial transactions. Such intermediaries allow tax inspectors to compare interest income declared by the individual with that paid out by banks. The Internet removes, to some extent, this middleman and thus the source for crosschecking. Furthermore, it will be increasingly easy for the average citizen to access offshore financial centres in cyberspace. These virtual tax havens are likely to further paralyse the tax collector.

3.10 Though Internet commerce is in its earliest stages, rapid growth is anticipated. As cryptology programs are developed that protect all forms of transmitted digital data, electronic commerce will certainly expand. Consumers will become confident that their payment information is protected, and businesses will be able to insure payment for the use of their products and services. The number of companies and individuals offering products and services on the Internet will also increase with the development of legal principle and enforcement systems worldwide in the areas of trademark infringement and domain names, copyright infringement, the application of traditional intellectual property principles to cyberspace, and problems relating to jurisdiction. Some estimates are that, in 30 years time, consumer activity on-line could represent 30% of total consumer activity, and probably a very much higher percentage as measured in value.

The OECD's role in creating a favourable tax climate for E-Commerce

3.11   The OECD has once more bitten the tax bullet, and is dealing with the tax effects of the communications revolution that is dismantling national borders and changing the face of domestic and cross-border commerce. The OECD Committee on Fiscal Affairs is actively working on the taxation issues related to e-commerce, and has invited substantial involvement from the business community and countries outside the OECD. The Committee has developed Taxation Framework Conditions setting forth the governing principles, and has specified a detailed work program that is intended to lead to a fiscal climate where e-commerce can flourish.

3.12   The Taxation Framework Conditions, adopted by the OECD Committee on Fiscal Affairs in June 1998, were welcomed by Ministers at a Ministerial-level Conference on e-commerce held in Ottawa in October 1998. The key conclusion:

> The taxation principles that guide governments in relation to conventional commerce should also guide them in relation to e-commerce.

3.13   The Committee has stated that, at this stage of development of the technological and commercial environment, existing taxation principles can implement these principles.

3.14   The framework for taxation of e-commerce addresses four areas:

- tax treaties;
- consumption taxes;
- tax administration; and
- taxpayer service.

3.15   In the tax treaty area, the framework provides that the present international norms are capable of being applied to e-commerce, but that some clarifications should be given as to how these norms, and that in particular the Model Tax Convention applies. In the consumption tax area, the framework provides that taxation should occur in the jurisdiction where consumption taxes place, and that the supply of digitised products should not be treated as a supply of goods. In the tax administration area, the information reporting requirements and tax collection procedures being developed must be neutral and fair, so that the level and standard are comparable to what is required for traditional commerce (although different means may be necessary to achieve those requirements). And a number of options have been identified for using the new technologies to improve taxpayer service.

3.16   Representatives of OECD governments have agreed on a number of important conclusions and recommendations that pave the way for greater certainty among businesses and consumers in relation to the taxation of e-commerce. These cover three main areas:

3.17   New Developments in Offshore Operations

- *international direct taxation*, with particular regard to the interpretation of existing permanent establishment rules that are fundamental for deciding where profits on the conduct of e-commerce can be taxed;

- *consumption taxes*, with particular regard to identifying pragmatic ways of achieving the desired result of effective taxation in the place of consumption; and

- *tax administration*, with particular regard to the administrative challenges and opportunities facing tax administrations, and on the sort of responses that governments need to consider.

3.17   There is broad consensus on clarification of the Commentary on the OECD Model Tax Convention ('Model') in respect of the application of the current definition of *permanent establishment*. In short, the clarification of the Committee states:

- that a web site cannot, in itself, constitute a permanent establishment;

- that a web site hosting arrangement typically does not result in a permanent establishment for the enterprise that carries on business through that web site;

- that an Internet service provider normally will not constitute a dependent agent of another enterprise so as to constitute a permanent establishment for that enterprise and that while a place where computer equipment, such as a server, is located may in certain circumstances constitute a permanent establishment, this requires that the functions performed at that place be significant as well as an essential or core part of the business activity of the enterprise.

The OECD Fiscal Committee's Work Program for 2001–2003

3.18   The principal features of the OECD Fiscal Committee's work program for 2001–2003 include:

- *On direct taxes*: work (a) on issues associated with the attribution of profits to a server permanent establishment; (b) on the refinement of the 'place of effective management' concept in determining residence for taxation purposes; and (c) further evaluation of the adequacy of the current treaty rules in the context of e-commerce, taking into account possible alternatives and the possible clarification or modification of the existing rules.

- *On consumption taxes*: work (a) on the feasibility of technology-based collection mechanisms, (b) on simplification opportunities, and (c) on means of promoting more effective international administrative co-operation.

- *On tax administration issues*: work (a) to strengthen the compliance tools available to tax administrations, (b) to share 'best practice' and (c) to promote further taxpayer service initiatives.

3.19   The release of discussion papers by the OECD Fiscal Committee is an important part of the process, and much further work still remains to be done in several fields.

Consumption Tax Issues

3.20   The Committee's Report on Consumption Taxes notes that it is necessary to define the principle of taxation in the place of consumption more clearly and to identify the collection mechanisms that can best support the practical operation of that principle.

3.21   The Report proposes Guidelines to define the place of taxation for cross-border services and intangible property by reference to the business establishment of the recipient business in the case of B2B (business-to-business) transactions, and by reference to the recipient's usual jurisdiction of residence for B2C (business-to-consumer) transactions.

3.22   On collection mechanisms, the Report identifies a self-assessment mechanism for B2B transactions as the most viable option. For B2C transactions, the report points toward the potential in the medium term for technology-facilitated options, while accepting that, in the interim, simplified registration-based mechanisms may be required.

Tax Administration Issues

3.23   The Committee's Report on the Tax Administration Aspects of E-commerce addresses such issues as how tax administrations can ensure effective tax collection in an electronic environment, and the steps that they may need to take to strengthen their co-operation internationally. It also identifies a range of initiatives that tax administrations across the world are already taking to improve the quality of service that they provide to taxpayers.

Report by the Technical Advisory Group on Treaty Characterisation of E-Commerce Payments

3.24   The OECD Model Tax Convention, first published in 1963 and regularly updated since then, is the basic reference manual used by both OECD and non-OECD countries for the negotiation, application and interpretation of bilateral tax treaties co-ordinating their direct tax systems.

3.25   The Technical Advisory Group (TAG) on Treaty Characterisation was set up in 1999 by the OECD's Committee on Fiscal Affairs with the mandate 'to examine the characterisation of various types of e-commerce payments under tax conventions with a view to providing the necessary clarifications'. Members of the TAG included tax officials from OECD and non-OECD countries as well as representatives from the business community.

3.26   The TAG released on 1 February 2001, its final Report on how various types of payments for e-commerce transactions should be characterised for purposes of applying tax treaties.

3.27   The Report, which was unanimously approved by TAG members, deals with the interpretation of tax treaties for the purpose of determining which provisions apply to various types of e-commerce payments, thereby ultimately determining which country may tax these payments and under what conditions. It includes analysis, conclusions and recommendations concerning which treaty provisions apply in particular cases, as well as the TAG's views on how such recommendations would apply in 28 typical categories of e-commerce transactions.

3.28   Some of the TAG's principal conclusions and recommendations are:

- in the case of transactions that permit the customer to electronically download digital products for that customer's own use or enjoyment (for instance, where a customer orders software or music from an Internet web site and that digital product is downloaded from that site), the payment should be characterised as business profits rather than as a royalty;

- whilst e-commerce transactions resulting in know-how payments which constitute royalties are relatively rare, the report provides a number of criteria and examples to help distinguish the provision of services from the provision of know-how;

- payments for time-limited use of digital products or for transactions such as data warehousing cannot be considered as payments for the use of, or the right to use, an industrial, commercial or scientific equipment so as to constitute royalties under some conventions;

- where the consideration for the payment covers various elements but one element is predominant and the others are only of an ancillary and unimportant character, it would be more practical to apply the treatment applicable to the principal part to the whole consideration.

3.29   The recommendations of the Report, and in particular the suggestions for changes to the Commentary of the OECD Model Tax Convention that it includes, will be examined by the Committee on Fiscal Affairs with a view to quickly making the appropriate changes to the OECD Model Tax Convention.

The Embedded Software issue

3.30   The issue of the characterisation of e-commerce transactions is one of the most intriguing international taxation debates at the present time. The range of potential issues is rather wide, depending on the nature of the transactions in question.

3.31   Specifically, the issue is whether software that is required in order for a hardware system to be operational should be treated as a unit or separated for taxation purposes (including updates of the software). In essence, this is another manifestation of the characterisation issues relating to the treatment of software and e-commerce transactions. Not surprisingly, specific multinational enterprises (MNEs) in specific situations may prefer one characterisation as opposed to another.

3.32   In order to develop guidelines for determination of such characterisation issues, the OECD has established Technical Advisory Groups ('TAGs') to focus on each of the critical e-commerce issues, including characterisation of the transactions. The TAG on 'characterisation' has released a draft paper addressing some 26 common transactions and how it is proposed such matters be characterised as involving sale, royalty or service transactions (including majority and minority views on certain issues).

3.33   Among the most important issues addressed by the TAG concerns the treatment of so-called embedded software — for example, computer equipment with software 'embedded' in the hardware. Such transactions could be characterised as involving a sales transaction, which would normally be treated as business profits under OECD Model Income Tax treaties, the licensing of intangibles (with attendant potential withholding in the payor country), or services.

3.34   The embedded software issue was addressed in the TAG's Illustration 6 ('Single-use software and other digital product'), in the following manner: the customer receives the right to use software or other digital products one time. The product may be either downloaded or used remotely (e.g. use of software stored on a remote server). The customer does not receive the right to make copies of the digital product other than as required to use the digital product for its intended use. Some members view this type of transaction as contracts for services. Other members disagree and yet others consider that it would then be important to distinguish between cases where the product is downloaded onto the customer's hard disk or other non-temporary media from those where it is not (e.g. where it is used remotely or copied into RAM only) as only the former would give rise to royalty characterisation.

OFFSHORE BANKING OPERATIONS

Offshore Banking

3.35   A considerable volume of international banking takes place offshore, and many of the world's major banks have banking and trust company operations in one or more IOFCs.

3.36   Most IOFC jurisdictions have enacted legislative provisions and set up administrative authorities whose function is to control banking and trust company activities.

3.37   Banking services offered in the tax havens are of different types: The commercial banks offer full commercial and retail facilities to both residents and non-residents of the jurisdictions where they are located. These banks usually provide an extremely wide range of services through their network of branches, their ability to move funds swiftly, and their expertise in handling international transactions.

3.38   Representative offices in IOFC jurisdictions offer a more limited range of services than do the commercial banks; however, they do normally handle currency transactions, deposits, and the issue of letters of credit. Representative offices of banks located elsewhere are usually licensed as non-resident banks.

3.39   Non-resident banks are licensed to serve only those clients who reside outside the tax haven jurisdiction or to transact business of a non-local character. The precise terminology and the limitations may vary according to the jurisdiction in question.

3.40   Switzerland is the unquestioned leader of the world's offshore private banking industry. London, Switzerland's nearest competitor, manages less than half as much as the combined totals of Zurich, Geneva, and Lugano, Switzerland's three main private banking centres. Switzerland's share of the world private banking market is estimated to be in the range of 30–40%, and the funds deposited with Swiss banks have been estimated to exceed 2.5 billion Swiss francs. Approximately two-thirds of this amount belongs to private clients, the majority of whom reside outside Switzerland.

3.41   Private banking, unlike global investment banking, is one area where Swiss banks have always been market leaders. Now, predictably, private banking activities have become a focus not only of Swiss banks themselves but also of many foreign banks carrying on activities in Switzerland. Private banks are concentrating more on investment advice and portfolio management, and less on trading and investment banking, due to the low risks and high returns that can be generated. Private bankers are entrepreneurs in a privately-owned sector, who carry out their business using their own assets, assuming unlimited liability with their entire commercial and private fortunes, and exercising independent powers of decision. The core activity of private bankers traditionally has been and still is asset management for private clients. Private banking is not only performed by private bankers. Many former private bankers have converted their partnerships into private or publicly-traded corporations in order to have limited liability and to be able to benefit from financing opportunities on the capital markets. In the past few years, the activities of many private banks have been extended to the management of assets for national and international institutional investors. This new class of client is very attractive for the banks because of the accumulated savings and potential market they represent. Institutional clients are, in general, very demanding in respect to the performance of their portfolios, and they benchmark performance on a regular basis. Due to the high volume of business they represent, institutional investors are putting substantial pressure on private banks' fee structures and forcing them to enhance their technical expertise. Private banks are also becoming active on the stock exchanges and many of them are also involved in under-writing and placement. In addition to catering to institutional investors, private banks are now establishing investment funds. The investment fund business has attracted new clients to private banks who either wish to invest in very specialised funds or whose assets are not substantial enough to justify the structuring of individualised portfolios.

Captive Banks

3.42   The term *captive bank* is sometimes used to refer to a banking subsidiary set up in an IOFC tax haven or financial centre that operates principally for the benefit of the members of a multinational group and their customers and suppliers. Such captive banks may also operate as merchant banks and offer commercial banking as well as financing services.

Banking Secrecy

3.43   In most countries, one of the terms of the relationship between banker and customer is that the banker will keep the customer's affairs secret. Staff members are normally required to sign a declaration of secrecy concerning the business of the banks. If numbered accounts are used, their purpose is to limit the number of persons who know the identity of the client.

3.44   In certain countries, specific legislation makes breaches of bank secrecy subject to criminal law sanctions. However, in all legal systems (including Switzerland), there are specific cases in which the duty of secrecy of a banker is discharged. Furthermore, the current attacks being waged worldwide against money laundering have resulted in significant restrictions and controls on bank secrecy. The level of secrecy in the Swiss banking industry is now not much different than most developed countries. In fact, it is arguable that Swiss 'know-your-customer' rules are much stricter than elsewhere. The Swiss banks have become more responsive to foreign requests to block questionable funds in Swiss banks. Furthermore, the negative publicity that has resulted from the past Swiss tradition of banking secrecy is now turning from an asset into a liability. The exchange of information clause contained in most tax treaties may enable the tax administration of one treaty country to obtain information concerning bank accounts that its residents have in the other country.

3.45   In a major new development, the worldwide attack on money laundering is creating very considerable pressure towards more open access to banking information.

Back-to-Back Loans

3.46   Back-to-back loans are matching deposit arrangements. They may be used to solve a financing or exchange control problem. However, in the case of certain IOFCs, the function of back-to-back loans is to reduce the taxable base subject to withholding taxes on interest payments, by interposing an intermediary subsidiary company between the source of the income and the recipient. For example, an intermediary company located in the Netherlands or the Netherlands Antilles may be interposed to take advantage of a favourable tax treaty. In such cases, the authorities usually require a certain spread or 'turn' on the rates to create a small profit that is subject to tax locally.

3.47   This type of transaction involves the prospective lender placing funds or securities on deposit with a bank operating in the lender's own country or elsewhere, while an associate of that bank (or the same bank) operating locally or in that other country lends an equivalent amount to an associate of the lender in another country. It is an arrangement for the avoidance of withholding tax on interest paid to a foreign country and of exchange controls on the remittance of funds outside the borrower's country.

3.48 The advantage of using an IOFC as a location for the initial deposit is that the interest received on the bank deposit will be paid free of tax. In the country of the back-to-back loan, the loan interest should be designed to be an allowable tax deduction. This structure may be utilised in financing structures for the purchase of property in high tax jurisdictions. It is also used to route money from IOFC jurisdictions to high tax countries, without the use of conduit vehicles using tax treaty structures.

Eurocurrencies and Eurobonds

3.49 Eurocurrencies are currencies other than the domestic currency of the country in which the bank taking the deposit or lending the funds is located. Originally, the US dollar was deposited and lent by West European banks, hence the term Eurodollars, which may be defined as an entry denominated in US dollars on the books of a non-US bank. All major currencies are now dealt in Eurocurrencies, so the prefix *Euro* is now a misnomer because the term applies outside Europe. The market is not subject to exchange controls or like restrictions, although investors and borrowers may be subject to them in their own countries.

3.50 Eurobonds are long-term loans issued in terms of US dollars or other currencies or in terms of composite units of account. They may take the forms of loans, debentures, or convertible debentures.

3.51 When the Eurobond market started in 1963, the borrowers were mainly governments, nationalised industries, and public utilities. These were soon joined by large companies, particularly as a result of the restrictions imposed during the 1960s on US enterprises with regard to their investments abroad. The market has since enjoyed considerable growth.

3.52 Eurobonds are usually issued in countries where interest payments are not subject to withholding tax. Major issues are normally handled by international underwriting syndicates, including major world banking and financial institutions.

OFFSHORE FINANCIAL AND BUSINESS OPERATIONS

Multi-Currency Management Centre

3.53 The objectives of a multi-currency management centre (MMC) can be combined with those of an international financing company.

3.54 In addition, the centre must be capable of transferring funds freely without exchange control restrictions.

3.55 The MMC would be remunerated on an arm's-length basis and would charge a fee for its services to recover its costs plus a reasonable mark-up.

Brokerage and Securities Operations

3.56 It is possible to use a tax haven or an IOFC for these activities since it is quite feasible, with electronic mail and information systems, for the whole operation to be carried on at the IOFC location.

Dealing in Commodities or Financial Futures

3.57 The above comments relating to brokerage and securities operations apply equally to commodity dealing and financial futures. As long as there is no need to take physical delivery of the commodities traded, the geographic location of the business is unimportant, provided that the tax haven or IOFC chosen is fully equipped with the most up-to-date methods of communicating with the outside world, as well as a suitable commercial and financial environment.

Debt Factoring

3.58   This is another example of a genuine trading operation that can be wholly carried on in a tax haven or an IOFC. The debt factoring company purchases the debts of group trading companies at an arm's-length valuation. The tax liabilities of the group trading companies will be reduced by the difference between the face value of the debts and the amount actually received. The debt factoring company collects the debts, and any profits it makes may be free of tax.

Leasing Company and Plant Rentals Company

3.59   A company could be established in an IOFC to purchase business assets and lease them to the user. The user may obtain a tax deduction for the lease rent, which would be tax-free in the hands of the lessor or taxable at a low rate.

Trading Operations

3.60   There is much scope for conducting trading operations through a tax haven or an IOFC. The type of business or trade selected should be suitable for being carried on in that jurisdiction.

3.61   Some offshore companies specialise in activities such as advertising, marketing, architecture, electronics, audio and video services, computerised information, printing and publishing, engineering, and consultancy services, as well as administration, invoicing, and re-invoicing services.

3.62   Many IOFCs offer incentives for warehousing as well as duty-free zones.

3.63   Sales, distribution, and agency companies trading internationally often have flexibility as to where the dealing profit or agency commission can be taken, and it may be advantageous to establish an offshore sales or distribution company. The key to effective planning in this area is to insure the offshore vehicle is trading *with* and not *within* high tax countries. To this end, it is very important to avoid creating an onshore permanent establishment of the offshore vehicle. It is also necessary to show substance (i.e., real commercial activity at arm's-length prices) and to write sales contracts from within the offshore location.

Intangibles

3.64   Intangibles are intellectual property rights that may be owned by a vehicle (company or trust) located in a tax haven or suitable IOFC. It is important to determine the structure correctly at the outset and to insure that the rights that are to be licensed arise in the tax haven or IOFC, or are at least acquired at market price by the tax haven or IOFC vehicle before they have any real value. This is to insure that only minimal tax problems are encountered in transferring the rights from the country where the property (which is the subject matter of the rights) has been developed.

3.65   The licensees in high tax countries, then pay tax-deductible arm's-length royalties, fees, etc. Similar structures may apply for other intangibles including franchising.

Joint Ventures and Partnerships

3.66 Joint ventures and partnerships, including professional service partnerships, are sometimes formed and operated in an IOFC.

International Construction Company

3.67 A construction company located in an IOFC could recruit a team of engineers and other specialists and hire its personnel to work on construction projects in high tax jurisdictions. Profits, and in many cases the employees' salaries, may be tax-free, or only subject to a low rate of tax.

Mail Order Trading Centre

3.68 Mail order is a good example of the type of business that may be carried on genuinely and legitimately in an IOFC since the business does not always need to take delivery of the goods that it buys and sells. Business newsletters can also be written, edited, and mailed from these locations.

Purchase and Sale of Special Items and Bulk Purchase Companies

3.69 Where opportunities arise to purchase a single item for resale at a substantial profit, an IOFC company could be used to take the profit (e.g. purchase of liquidation goods, etc.). A similar structure could be used for a bulk purchase of goods for subsequent on-sale in smaller lots. Substantial discounts may be obtained by purchasing in bulk from third parties for onward sale to group companies or third parties.

Assembly and Testing Operations

3.70 An IOFC can be used to carry out such operations for a group. Payment for its services or goods on an arm's-length basis should be tax deductible to the companies in a high tax jurisdiction using the products and tax-free or taxed at low rates in the tax haven.

Research and Development

3.71 An IOFC may be a suitable location for carrying on a particular type of research or development work.

OFFSHORE SHIPPING AND AIRCRAFT OPERATIONS

3.72 Owing to the innate mobility of the shipping industry, it is common for ship owners and operators to have recourse to tax havens. Frequently, the ownership, operation, administration, and registration are situated in fiscally favourable (and often different) jurisdictions to keep global tax burdens at a low level.

3.73 International shipping companies are often incorporated for commercial reasons under flags of convenience in countries that either are IOFCs or offer special tax treatment. It is common to have only one ship owned by each company for insulation purposes.

3.74 Shipping companies have used IOFCs to shelter income from chartering and other activities. Container leasing is also sometimes operated from IOFCs.

3.75 Even a landlocked IOFC can have a maritime flag.

3.76 New Developments in Offshore Operations

3.76 The flag of a ship is the flag of the country of its registration. The term *flag of convenience* refers to the flag of a country that is chosen for ship registration in order to achieve fiscal benefits (no income tax being levied by such countries on international shipping operations) and other non-tax advantages relating to lower labour costs and manning scales, officer and crew requirements, trade union practices, etc. In the past there used to be considerable differences with regard to international safety standards; however, satisfactory standards are now generally being applied by most convenience flag countries.

3.77 Ownership of the ship is frequently vested in a company incorporated in the country of the flag.

3.78 In addition to Liberia and Panama, the following countries offer flag of convenience facilities: the Cayman Islands, Costa Rica, Cyprus, Gibraltar, Haiti, Honduras, Hong Kong, Malta, Morocco, the Netherlands Antilles, Singapore, and Vanuatu.

3.79 Some private groups own their aircraft via an IOFC vehicle. The aircraft is then hired out to operating companies on an arm's-length basis in order to make a profit on operations in an IOFC.

OFFSHORE PROVISION OF INTERNATIONAL SERVICES

3.80 A large number of banks located in IOFCs offer trust services. In addition, there are trust companies specifically offering trust services.

3.81 Services offered by banks and trust companies normally include a fairly wide range of trusteeship, management, and related services. The trusteeship services involve not merely acting as trustee of settlements but many other services such as acting as trustee for debenture holders or as custodian trustee for pension funds, acting as the executor or administrator of estates, including acting as the attorney for foreign executors, etc. Management services are not limited to investment and holding companies and, in appropriate cases, are extended to the activities of trading companies. The management services usually include attending to statutory requirements and the maintenance of financial records. Often, nominee shareholders, directors, and other officers are furnished. Investment management services are normally provided; in certain cases, the management of specific assets is undertaken. Services may also extend to such activities as the preparation of share issues and participation in the registration and transfer work.

3.82 Fee scales tend to vary from country to country and from institution to institution. However, there is often a fixed schedule of acceptance fees, annual fees, and withdrawal fees for acting as trustee, executor, or administrator or for providing the headquarters and nominee shareholders, directors, etc., of a company. In addition, there may be special fees for unduly onerous or prolonged administration; dealing with a business; administering real property, mortgages, or foreign assets; litigation; the preparation of investment valuations or tax returns and claims; etc.

3.83 IOFC locations are often utilised to employ international staff. Offshore employment companies are also utilised to give effect to a separate contract of employment for offshore employment duties to minimise home country tax, and professional partnerships often employ staff in low tax jurisdictions for international consultancy projects.

3.84 A management advisory services company may be used, for example, in the hotel industry, where a hotel is situated in a high tax jurisdiction. The service company located in an IOFC could provide co-ordination and advisory services to the hotel located in a high tax jurisdiction, for which a tax-deductible fee would be paid. The service company should have substance, personnel, and premises if it is sought to deduct such service fees for tax purposes in the high tax jurisdiction (See also paras 3.85–3.90).

HEADQUARTERS, ADMINISTRATIVE OFFICES, MANAGEMENT COMPANIES

3.85   Headquarters offices may be defined as offices that belong to an enterprise or an international group of enterprises that are situated abroad and that exercise certain management, co-ordination, and control functions for the sole or principal benefit of the enterprise or group. Headquarters offices may benefit from a favourable tax regime even in an otherwise high tax jurisdiction. Such an office may take any legal form; in particular, it may be a subsidiary company or a branch of a foreign company.

3.86   An administrative office is frequently located in a country other than that of the headquarters office, the parent company, or a country of operation. The role of such an administrative office may be to co-ordinate international or regional activities, to provide particular services (such as management analysis, financial, or other related services), or to perform a given function (such as marketing). A number of otherwise high tax jurisdictions grant special tax treatment to attract the administrative offices of multinationals.

3.87   Belgium, France, Germany, Malaysia, Monaco, Singapore, the United Kingdom, and many other countries are in active competition to attract these kinds of centres and offices. In many of these countries, there are government departments actively soliciting multinationals to base operations in their countries. The benefits, in terms of prestige, white-collar employment, and general economic development, are universally considered sufficiently attractive for a variety of specific incentives to be introduced. It is particularly valuable that large, reputable companies with bona fide multinational activities should be associated with an IOFC to offset the impact in terms of image and credibility of the inevitable abuses of offshore structures by certain less-scrupulous operators.

3.88   The two key features of headquarters, administrative offices, and management companies are as follows:

- *Tax at standard rates is levied on a tax base calculated on a cost-plus basis.* For example, if the office spends $100,000 and if the cost-plus basis negotiated with the tax administration is 5%, then the deemed tax base will be $5,000.

- *The company must not be engaged in trade or certain other activities that are not of an administrative or management nature.*

3.89   The example of a UK management company illustrates this point, since a management company is on a deemed tax basis not otherwise within the charge to corporation tax unless it trades in the United Kingdom. The question whether a company is exercising a trade within the United Kingdom is a question of fact. Most important is the place where the contracts for the sale of the goods or the rendering of the services in question are made. If the contracts are made in the United Kingdom, a trade is being carried on within that country, but if the contracts are made abroad, it may be possible to show that no trade is being carried on within the United Kingdom. However, the contract test may not be decisive in all circumstances. There can be cases in which, although the contract with the customer is made abroad, nevertheless the negotiations for the sale and even the complete carrying out of the contract may take place in the United Kingdom in such circumstances as to show that the trade was exercised in the United Kingdom. As a practical matter, such a company should not send its invoices out of the United Kingdom; payments by customers should not be received in the United Kingdom; and, similarly, payments should not be effected from the United Kingdom.

3.90 New Developments in Offshore Operations

3.90 Many of the features of headquarters and administrative offices and management companies are replicated in co-ordination centres. (See also paras 3.91–3.119.)

CO-ORDINATION CENTRES

3.91 Co-ordination centres were originally developed in Belgium and are now found in other jurisdictions such as the Netherlands and Luxembourg.

3.92 Operating through a co-ordination centre allows multinational groups to carry out a large variety of financial and management services on a virtually tax-free basis.

Requirements for Recognition as a Co-ordination Centre

3.93 To qualify for co-ordination centre status, a number of conditions must usually be satisfied.

International Group

3.94 The co-ordination centre must form part of an international group of affiliated companies with a very substantial aggregate capital and annual turnover. A group is normally defined to include all companies in which the common shareholdings, direct or indirect, represent a certain minimum percentage of capital.

Exclusion of Financial Institutions

3.95 Banks, insurance companies, and certain other financial institutions may be excluded from establishing a co-ordination centre.

Qualifying Activities

3.96 The activities that may be carried out in a co-ordination centre are normally restricted to activities that are specifically authorised.

Employment Requirements

3.97 It is normally a condition for co-ordination centre status that the co-ordination centre have a specified number of full-time employees.

3.98 There is normally no condition as to the citizenship or rank of the employees. Generally, personnel transferred from an affiliated company may be counted toward fulfilment of the employee requirement.

Tax Concessions for Co-ordination Centres

Corporation income taxes

3.99 Co-ordination centres are typically subject to tax on a notional base only. The tax base is determined as a percentage of certain operating costs borne by the co-ordination centre. However, personnel costs and financing costs may be excluded from the calculation of the notional tax base.

3.100 The percentage to be applied to the remaining costs depends upon the mark-up applied by the co-ordination centre itself in charging affiliated companies for its services. This leaves the discretion to the centre itself, within certain parameters, to determine the formula for the notional tax system. Corporation tax will be calculated according to the normal rate on the tax base computed in this manner.

3.101 The arm's-length character of internal group payments forming part of the taxable base should be determined by comparing them to similar operations carried out between unrelated parties. Provided that the terms offered by the co-ordination centre to group members are no less favourable than those applied between independent parties, there would be no problem.

Exemption from Withholding Taxes

3.102 Co-ordination centres are normally not subject to withholding taxes.

3.103 In application of this principle, all payments of dividends, interest, and royalties by a co-ordination centre are excluded from application of the normal withholding tax.

3.104 It is also recognised that co-ordination centres may receive investment income. For this reason, payments of interest on deposits made by co-ordination centres with banks and other financial institutions may be exempt from withholding tax.

Concessions for Expatriate Employees of Co-ordination Centres

3.105 Foreign executives and researchers are normally exempted from the requirement to obtain a work permit.

3.106 Foreign executives, researchers, and other specialists who meet the requirements for non-resident status are normally entitled to substantial concessions for personal income taxes. These concessions consist principally in the exclusion from personal income tax of a variety of expatriate allowances representing the special cost of living allowances, housing allowances, tuition, and home leave grants, as well as tax equalisation payments.

Procedure for Co-ordination Centre Recognition

3.107 Co-ordination centre concessions are not normally automatic but are granted only on the basis of a written request followed by a favourable decision by the relevant department.

3.108 The request for recognition should contain a detailed description of all the activities of co-ordination and centralisation that are intended for the centre. Applicants are usually also encouraged to include activities that are not planned for the initial stages of operations but might be added later on.

3.109 Once the department is satisfied that all conditions are met, formal recognition will be granted for the co-ordination centre during a fixed period.

Broad Range of Uses for Co-ordination Centres

3.110 The principal attraction of the co-ordination centre system is that it allows, besides support services to group members, a broad range of sophisticated intra-group financing to be carried out in a virtually tax-free environment. These latter operations include leasing, re-invoicing, and factoring as well as more traditional group lending activities.

3.111 Multinationals have found a great variety of uses for co-ordination centres. The system permits each multinational to construct a 'tailor-made' co-ordination centre as a function of its present and future needs, provided that services are performed solely for the benefit of group members.

3.112   As a general rule, a co-ordination centre may centralise specific activities for affiliated companies, charge affiliates for such services, and even recover a profit margin on a 'cost-plus' formula. However, the centre may not perform services for other companies that are not members of the group.

3.113   The activities that can be carried out by co-ordination centres generally fall into two principal categories:

● support services rendered directly to other members of the group; and

● financial services provided indirectly through inter-company transactions.

Support Services Rendered Directly to Group Members

3.114   The first category comprises a variety of support services provided directly to other group members. Such centralised services make unnecessary the duplication of the same activities in a variety of different locations. This increases efficiency and can result in important cost savings.

3.115   Services in this category are normally charged directly by the co-ordination centre to the affiliated companies that receive them. Generally, such charges are based on the costs incurred by the centre in carrying out the services, often with a small profit margin calculated according to a cost-plus formula.

Financial Services provided Indirectly through Inter-company Transactions

3.116   The second major category of activities carried out in co-ordination centres consists of inter-company transactions with the objective to centralise financial management and the hedging of foreign exchange risks.

3.117   A common feature of these activities is that they are not rendered directly by the co-ordination centre and invoiced as management services to the affiliated companies of the group. Instead these services are carried out in the form of inter-company transactions, such as leasing and factoring. The co-ordination centre covers its costs with revenues from the transactions themselves. Such revenues take a variety of forms (interest, lease payments, etc.) depending on the nature of the particular transactions.

3.118   This category of activities enables multinational companies to carry out a variety of centralised financing operations in a favourable tax climate and to take advantage of the country's network of tax treaties.

3.119   The advantages of a group using a co-ordination centre are, above all:

● to provide centralised support services to other members of the group, thus taking advantage of 'economies of scale';

● to meet the various financing needs of group members by taking advantage of the absence of withholding taxes, of double taxation treaties, and of a virtually tax-free environment; and

● to provide foreign-exchange risk hedging to group members and indeed to reduce the risk itself, with no exchange control restrictions, by aggregating a variety of sources of fluctuations.

OFFSHORE LICENSING

3.120   Technology that can be the subject matter of licensing covers all forms of industrial enterprise. It embraces industrial property that may be protected by patents, trademarks, etc., as well as technology that cannot be patented.

3.121   Industrial enterprises frequently exploit their technology by transferring it to licensing companies in tax havens so that royalties and other sums may be received by the licensing company from related companies or third parties, thus reducing the total tax burden.

3.122   The anti-avoidance provisions of certain developed countries have limited the use of tax havens for this purpose.

3.123   When it comes to international licensing, a suitable country for sublicensing arrangements would require the following elements:

- a usable tax treaty or network of treaties;

- the reduction in withholding taxes that are normally levied abroad on royalties paid to a licensing company, pursuant to the tax treaty or treaties negotiated by that country;

- the concessions given to group or other licensing companies by the tax administration in that country on the spread of taxable income receivable; and

- the absence of any withholding tax on the onward payment of royalties to any non-resident.

3.124   The Netherlands is the world leader in offering favoured treatment to licensing companies. The benefits of using a Netherlands licensing company lie, above all, in the reduced rates of withholding in treaty countries. The withholding rates for royalty payments under many of the treaties concluded with the Netherlands are either zero or very low. There is no withholding tax in the Netherlands on payments of royalties.

3.125   A choice that would normally have to be made would be between:

- obtaining a ruling that is issued in appropriate cases by the Netherlands Tax Administration, or

- simply using a third party bona fide resident company or individual in the Netherlands for this purpose.

3.126   In the usual structure, a related Netherlands licensing company would sublicense the rights.

3.127   The Netherlands Tax Administration usually gives a ruling fixing the taxable base of a licensing company that is a related party to the principal licensor. The administration normally requires, as the taxable base, a minimum spread between royalties received and royalties paid.

OFFSHORE INSURANCE

Offshore Captive Insurance Companies

3.128   The term *captive insurance company* is used to refer to an insurance company that is owned (directly or indirectly) by a non-insurance commercial company and exclusively insures or reinsures the risks of the parent company and/or its affiliated companies. The function is thus one of self-insurance from the group point of view. The underlying reasons for the formation of foreign captive insurance companies are usually of an insurance and business nature quite apart from any fiscal benefits that may accrue.

3.129   Foreign captive insurance companies are located in a certain number of tax havens, in particular, in Bermuda, and to a lesser extent in the Bahamas, the Cayman Islands, Guernsey, Hong Kong, the Isle of Man, Jersey, Panama, and Vanuatu. A major reason for using one of these jurisdictions is to obtain freedom from the onerous requirements and restrictions of insurance legislation in the principal countries where the group operates.

3.130   A foreign captive insurance company may be used to insure against certain risks that the normal insurance market will not accept or to obtain broader types of insurance that the commercial insurance companies do not have the flexibility to provide.

3.131   Money savings can be achieved through the use of reinsurance as opposed to direct insurance. Also, as distinct from direct insurance where premiums are paid in advance, payments by a captive insurance company to a reinsurance company are generally made at the close of a predetermined period.

3.132   Furthermore, captive insurance companies located in IOFC jurisdictions are often not subject to the same controls as insurance companies located in the country of the parent company and can invest surplus accumulations relatively freely, including investments for the direct or indirect benefit of the parent company or other affiliated companies.

3.133   An offshore captive insurance company is thus a limited-purpose, wholly owned insurance subsidiary, which has as its primary function the insuring of some of the exposures and risks of its parent and the parent's affiliates. A protected cell company or segregated portfolio company may also be used.

3.134   A captive thus usually takes the form of a wholly owned foreign subsidiary incorporated in a jurisdiction that levies little or no foreign tax on premiums or investment income from the insurance of the worldwide risks of the captive's parent and related domestic or foreign subsidiaries. Thus tax advantages may be obtained through the deductibility of premiums.

3.135   Apart from any fiscal benefits that may accrue, the objectives of setting up a foreign captive insurance company are of an insurance and business nature, such as meeting insurance needs, providing a funding mechanism, reducing the price cycle, obtaining an acceptable rating, obtaining cover in certain particularly difficult cases, and obtaining adequate service.

Tax Considerations

3.136   Tax legislation in most jurisdictions makes a sharp distinction between insurance premiums (which are tax deductible) and risk-related provisions (which are not). From a business point of view, there is no material difference (although provisions can provide the equivalent of insurance only for large companies with highly diversified risks). Yet the rule makes a company's risk-management strategy entirely dependent on the vagaries of an insurance market that is unable to provide adequate cover for a whole series of significant risks.

3.137 Captive insurance is a powerful tool to solve, at least partly, this problem. The tax benefit is obvious: paying premiums to an offshore subsidiary in effect makes provisions tax deductible. However, this in itself makes no contribution to improved insurance cover (leading some jurisdictions to disallow premiums paid to captive subsidiaries that do not spread and transfer risk). The decision to set up an offshore captive insurance company, while ostensibly a tax planning tool, should in fact be primarily driven by insurance considerations.

3.138 Most high tax countries seek to limit the tax advantages, but even on an arm's-length basis these can be significant. Generally, a company can deduct insurance premiums as expenses to reduce its taxable income if the premiums are ordinary and necessary to the conduct of its business.

3.139 One major attack the courts have aimed at companies attempting to convert non-deductible self-insurance reserves into deductible self-funding arrangements with bona fide insurance companies is that the premium payments made to the insurer are not, in fact, premium payments for insurance, but payments into a self-insurance reserve merely held by the insurer as agent of the insured and thus not deductible.

3.140 Before an insurance payment can be classified as a premium, two essential factors must be present: *risk shifting* and *risk distribution*. To shift the risk, the insured must transfer it to another who has the financial capacity to make good the losses. Distribution of the risk is a device by which the insurer combines large numbers of unrelated risks and thus reduces the risk through the law of probability.

The Reinsurance Market

3.141 The reinsurance market usually enables the buyer to obtain a more attractive discount or credit for his self-retention than would be possible from the direct insurance market. The main reason for the differential between these two parts of the insurance industry is that the direct insurer has very considerable expenses, most of which are funded by the premium he receives from the low-level loss area. On the other hand, the re-insurer has minimum expenses, since the services it provides are not as comprehensive as those that the direct insurer has to provide to its customers, and particularly to its private customers, who need much greater attention and service than the major industrial buyer.

3.142 Companies considering the establishment of captive insurance companies recognise that one of the major advantages is access to the reinsurance market.

The Management Decision

3.143 There is a limit to the extent to which risks can be shifted and diluted. Ultimately, there is one reinsurance market with a finite number of operators and a finite amount of capital. As shown by the Lloyd's debacle of the early 1990s, that market can collapse if its cover is incorrectly priced or if it is dealing with risks that do not obey the law of large numbers. Captives may be more efficient than outside insurance, but they cannot escape the market altogether.

Implementation

3.144 Implementation of an offshore captive insurance strategy requires a clear decision concerning:

3.145   New Developments in Offshore Operations

- the most suitable location of the captive, taking into account the most important factors, such as convenience, government attitude, and taxation;

- whether the multinational company should manage the captive itself or use outside services;

- the tax implications of the decision in relation to both the captive location that is being considered and the attitude of the country's domestic revenue authorities;

- whether the fronting companies will require parental guarantees or letters of credit;

- whether there are any international problems in the form of insurance legislative difficulties, exchange control, or political problems that need to be taken into account;

- the political considerations to be taken into account both domestically and elsewhere in the world;

- in relation to the risks that the captive will be retaining and its overall exposure, the needs for capitalisation and the attitudes of the company to solvency margin (i.e., the ratio between total assets (weighted for differential liquidity where appropriate) and total insured risk (net of reinsurance where appropriate)); and

- whether there are any exchange control restrictions that need to be taken into account in relation to capitalising the captive both from the company's domicile and to the location that is being chosen.

Choice of Location of the Captive (Domestic or Offshore)

3.145   In principle there is no reason why a captive insurance company cannot be established in any country where insurance legislation permits insurance companies to operate. From a practical point of view, domestic captives, located in the country of origin of the parent, are usually subject to additional legislation, high capitalisation, high taxation, and the onerous data requirements of the authorities. There may, however, be cases in which, for political reasons, it is necessary to form the captive domestically, particularly if the parent company is government owned or the government has a substantial shareholding.

3.146   One of the benefits of the domestic captive is that it is convenient from an operational point of view and can be managed within the operations of the parent corporation. A possible disadvantage, however, is that in some parts of the world the domestic captive may not be able to select the risks that would be most beneficial, since there may be some pressure from the authorities for it to participate in other classes. This is a particular problem in countries where there is a method of sharing substandard risks for compulsory insurances through the whole insurance community. The captive in this environment might be involved automatically in underwriting outside business of an undesirable underwriting nature.

3.147   Most captives are located offshore in an environment that is reasonably free of legislative restraints and has a low taxation position. This offers clear benefits in relation to the build-up of reserves, reduction of management time, and the cost and speed of establishment. In many of these offshore locations it would be possible to form a captive within 30 days and to render information to the authorities on a very limited basis and in total confidence. However, even in IOFCs insurance legislation is a factor that needs to be taken into account when deciding on the best location so far as the parent company is concerned.

OFFSHORE FUNDS AND INTERNATIONAL INVESTMENT TRUSTS

Offshore Funds

3.148 An offshore fund is generally an investment company, unit trust (a trust in which the investing public are the beneficiaries), mutual fund, or other entity usually incorporated and resident in an IOFC. The fund may be open-ended or closed.

3.149 The majority of offshore funds are open-ended investment companies; however, funds may take any of the forms permitted by the legal system or systems concerned. The more popular locations for offshore funds are Bermuda, the Cayman Islands, Guernsey, Hong Kong, the Isle of Man, Jersey, and Luxembourg.

3.150 Offshore funds generally enjoy greater investment flexibility than do funds located in high tax countries. However, there is a growing tendency to require greater disclosure and, generally, to tighten the regulations governing offshore funds.

3.151 The bulk of investors in offshore funds are residents or citizens of high tax countries, many of which severely restrict the local marketing activities of funds.

3.152 The fund will be designed to be free of income tax in its chosen location, and it may be able to make bank deposits and other investments without suffering withholding taxes in the source country. The fund will also be designed to be exempt from tax on any capital gains arising from the sale of investments.

3.153 Funds located in suitable IOFCs have been used to raise low cost finance (e.g., by way of preference shares in bearer form); to invest in zero coupon bonds, as well as growth stocks and securities on behalf of foreign investors; to raise venture capital finance; to raise funds for use in leveraged and management buyouts; to act as offshore multi-currency roll-up funds; and to invest in gilt-edged stocks. Other activities include equity funds, bond funds, and funds specialising in particular sectors.

3.154 Umbrella offshore funds have been introduced to offer investors the possibility of investing in different portfolios. These may offer a variety of investment strategies incorporated in a single investment vehicle.

3.155 An offshore fund located in a suitable IOFC will generally be 'managed' by a management company owned by the fund's promoters. Such a management company may also be located in the same IOFC as the offshore fund or possibly in another favourable IOFC location.

3.156 Alternatively, or in addition, the fund may enter into a professional services agreement with an independent broker, advisor, or merchant bank located in another international financial centre for the provision of investment advice at a fee based on market rates.

International Investment Trusts

3.157 Since mutual funds and unit trusts are to be found in high tax jurisdictions and since investors too are to be found onshore as well as offshore, the laws governing the onshore taxation and regulation of onshore investment trusts will, of necessity, seek to accommodate the requirements of the onshore investor.

3.158   New Developments in Offshore Operations

3.158   Minimising the tax burden on the international transactions of an onshore investment fund (as distinct from genuine inflows from, and outflows to, investors) will typically be a key objective.

3.159   Collective investment is a huge, highly technical, and fast-developing sector. It is a useful indicator of the way in which business issues, including tax, should be seen within a wider economic and even political context. Recent developments have been driven primarily by two objectives:

- to stimulate saving and investment in order to promote economic growth and job creation; and

- to reduce the demographic pressure on unfunded entitlement schemes by encouraging collective investment-based provision for retirement benefits.

3.160   Favourable treatment for schemes such as pension funds is explained by their perceived ability to contribute simultaneously to both these objectives. Conversely, their failure to do so would certainly trigger significant changes in the rules.

3.161   The use of specific incentives for tax-planning purposes is inseparable from anti-avoidance issues. Any scheme promoting investment funds could also, prima facie, provide an opportunity for money laundering, even without any genuine saving element. Many of the complications in the regulations of high tax jurisdictions derive specifically from attempts to prevent such 'non-saving' use.

OFFSHORE IPO STRATEGIES

The New Global Opportunities

3.162   The surge in cross-border initial public offerings ('IPOs' or listings) on offshore and foreign exchanges creates the opportunity to access hitherto untapped financial markets. Notwithstanding the spectacular performance of US markets during the past decade, Americans are coming more and more to participate in the wider exploitation of other potential international stock exchanges. There are many exciting opportunities in addition to the NYSE or NASDAQ.

3.163   The benefits of globalisation are evident in the many financial markets that exist, not merely offshore, but within first world and especially European markets. From a perspective of young and fast growing companies, attractive opportunities exist within the United Kingdom, for example the Alternative Investment Market (AIM) and the London Stock Exchange, and in Germany where the Neuer Markt is receiving attention. Also EASDAQ (European Association of Securities Dealers Automated Quotation), the only pan-European stock market, is now a very successful exchange attracting top-drawer companies and sophisticated investors. Listing on alternative exchanges provides access to a widespread international investor base.

3.164   More and more foreign and offshore stock exchanges are attracting interest due to the large amounts of capital that are being invested in companies on these exchanges and the tremendous growth in equity values resulting from the availability of such large pools of capital. Canadian, Italian, and French stock exchanges are becoming the high growth markets of tomorrow.

3.165   The FTSE's Offshore Investment Companies and Funds sector now contains over 90 foreign companies originating from a wide range of locations, including Bermuda, the British Virgin Islands, Canada, the Cayman Islands, Guernsey, Ireland, Luxembourg,

Mauritius, the Netherlands, Singapore, and South Africa. As a general rule, open-ended funds tend to list on offshore exchanges where the IPO requirements are less onerous than on the major exchanges. The Dublin stock exchange has gone out of its way to attract funds, as have exchanges in Bermuda, the Cayman Islands, the Channel Islands and Luxembourg.

3.166 A sophisticated market will be receptive to a large variety of instruments that can be traded on various markets, such as traditional equities, depositary receipts, tracking stocks, warrants and other derivative instruments.

3.167 The competition in terms of number of companies listed on first world stock exchanges is tough and therefore, if the IPO candidate can generate more awareness and attention by offering different trading instruments, this may act in its favour. The market's understanding and experience of such instruments may thus be crucial.

3.168 Large amounts of capital destined for public, private equity, and venture capital investments are present in world markets, and investors are eagerly moving into young and fast growing companies. The emphasis, as in the United States, is primarily focusing on technology issues, but other fast growing and promising enterprises have also been very successful. There is a strong new trend for Europeans to invest more and more in equities, and European-based investment is a driver of these markets. Another equally important factor is that Europeans are embracing all forms of technology, which is driving the demand for technology products and services, thereby fuelling the rapid growth of technology companies many of which are listed on the offshore and foreign exchanges. Any IPO, irrespective of where it is finally executed, is a complex and long-term exercise that requires due diligence and careful consideration.

Launching a Company on a Foreign Exchange

3.169 Initial public offerings (IPOs) on foreign exchanges have many similarities to IPOs in the United States. However, there are some unique aspects to consider. The following checklist will highlight the essential pieces of any offshore IPO.

Selecting the Exchange

3.170 If the listing candidate qualifies according to these guidelines, consider the alternative markets available and discuss them with reputable investment bankers and other experienced advisors. This process is onerous, but differs less than may be expected from country to country.

3.171 The IPO itself is only the start of a very long and demanding process of performing to investors' expectations and in the public eye. This is true regardless of which offshore or foreign stock exchange is chosen, as standards and criteria must be adhered to in all credible markets.

Timing

3.172 Obtaining a listing is subject to similar vicissitudes in most offshore and foreign markets. The completion time is dependent on variable factors including:

- The availability of recently audited financial information.

- A formalised group structure, bearing in mind that many existing structures must be changed prior to a planned listing.

3.173 New Developments in Offshore Operations

- Compliance with statutory requirements.

- The availability of information on the group, its operations, and history, as well as on its directors and senior management.

- The speed and efficiency of the professional firms and financial institutions handling the listing.

3.173 The above information is required for any form of admission document, prospectus, or other disclosure document required by the selected offshore stock exchange.

Costs

3.174 Although the costs of floatation may not appear to be material in the larger scheme of things, one should be aware of the continuing costs associated with being quoted on an international stock exchange.
Included in the costs are:

- Publishing expenses (annual reports, circulars, printed announcements, etc.).

- Annual stock exchange listing fees.

- Compliance with the various rules and requirements of the particular stock exchange.

- The need to consult with expensive experts and advisors on an ongoing basis regarding such compliance.

- Fees of corporate advisors when contemplating and executing acquisitions, disposals, etc.

3.175 Such costs can be demanding, and the IPO candidate should ensure that the long-term benefits of being listed outweigh the costs. This is a vital factor that requires skilful consideration, especially when an attractive international alternative outside the United States has been identified for the proposed IPO.

3.176 Although media coverage and exposure may work as easily against as for the company, any coverage will expose the company to potential capital investors.

Secondary or Dual Floatations

3.177 Many companies float the same entity on more that one stock exchange. There are many variations on the theme.

3.178 The major reason to have a secondary or dual floatation is to attract capital from the other regions in which the company operates so as to enlarge its international investor base. Another reason could be to raise its profile and to seek credibility in a new market that it wishes to penetrate.

Continuing Obligations

3.179 Adherence to the selected exchange's rules and requirements is essential, especially in the execution of transactions, the application of good corporate governance, and the regular and timely reporting of financial results.

3.180 The duties of the directors and management of the now publicly quoted company require careful monitoring in order to meet the continuing obligations of the relevant stock exchange and to ensure that there are no late — and costly — surprises.

STRATEGIC CHECKLISTS

OFFSHORE BANKING OPERATIONS

- Taking deposits.

- Non-bank lending and syndicated loans, including related off-balance-sheet transactions.

- Buying and selling foreign currencies, both spot and forward.

- Interest rate and currency swaps.

- Future rate agreements.

- Inter-bank deposits.

- Fund management.

- Trading bonds and other financial instruments.

- Credit sales.

- Factoring.

- Hire purchase of goods and equipment.

- Leasing.

- Credit card operations.

- Offshore Financial and Business Operations.

- Multi-currency management centre.

- Brokerage and securities operations.

- Dealing in commodities or financial futures.

- Debt factoring.

- Leasing company and plant rentals company.

- Trading operations.

- Intangibles.

- Joint ventures and partnerships.

- International construction company.

- Mail order trading centre.

- Purchase and sale of special items and bulk purchase companies.

- Assembly and testing operations.

- Research and development.

MULTI-CURRENCY MANAGEMENT CENTRE OBJECTIVES

- To exercise strict control over international payments in order to plan and effectively control the liquidity of an international group (the centre should be able to channel funds to those companies that need them most or where borrowing costs are highest).

- To pool exchange risks in one location.

- To execute foreign exchange transactions at the lowest costs.

- To reduce foreign exchange risks through:

  — matching income and outgoing payments in the same currency;

  — leading and lagging of payments;

  — hedging operations (e.g., forward contracts, borrowing, depositing in domestic and/or foreign markets)

- To decrease overall borrowing costs.

- To house medium and long-term inter-company and other loans.

- To provide inter-company loans.

FLAG OF CONVENIENCE COUNTRIES

In addition to Liberia and Panama:

- The Cayman Islands
- Costa Rica
- Cyprus
- Gibraltar
- Haiti
- Honduras

- Hong Kong
- Malta
- Morocco
- The Netherlands Antilles
- Singapore
- Vanuatu

TYPICAL CLASSES OF FEES CHARGED BY OFFSHORE TRUST COMPANIES

- Acceptance fees.

- Annual fees.

- Withdrawal fees.

- Fees for the provision of headquarters.

- Fees for the provision of nominee shareholders, directors, etc.

- Special fees for unduly onerous or prolonged administration.

- Fees for dealing with a business, administering real property, mortgages, or foreign assets.

- Fees for litigation.

- Fees for the preparation of investment valuations.

- Fees for the preparation of tax returns.

Note: Fee scales tend to vary from country to country and from institution to institution.

HIGH TAX JURISDICTIONS OFFERING FAVOURED TAX TREATMENT TO HEADQUARTERS, ADMINISTRATIVE OFFICES, MANAGEMENT COMPANIES

- Belgium
- France
- Germany
- Malaysia
- Singapore
- The United Kingdom

REQUIREMENTS FOR RECOGNITION AS A CO-ORDINATION CENTRE

- International group with minimum percentages of common shareholdings.

- Exclusion of banks, insurance companies, and certain other financial institutions.

- Qualifying activities restricted.

- Minimum employee requirements.

SUPPORT SERVICES RENDERED BY CO-ORDINATION CENTRES DIRECT TO GROUP MEMBERS

- Advertising and sales promotion.

- Collection and dissemination of information.

- Insurance and reinsurance.

- Scientific research.

- Accounting, administrative, and electronic data processing activities.

- Preparatory and auxiliary activities.

FINANCIAL SERVICES PROVIDED BY CO-ORDINATION CENTRES INDIRECTLY THROUGH INTRA-COMPANY TRANSACTIONS

- Re-invoicing.

- Factoring.

- Leasing.

- Financing.

PREFERRED LOCATIONS OF FOREIGN CAPTIVE INSURANCE COMPANIES

- The Bahamas
- The Isle of Man
- Bermuda
- Jersey
- The Cayman Islands
- Panama
- Guernsey
- Vanuatu
- Hong Kong

SCREENING CONSIDERATIONS FOR THE SETTING UP OF A CAPTIVE INSURANCE COMPANY

- The savings in insurance premiums, and their impact on cash flow, taking account of investment income on the savings.

- Future developments in the insurance market, to the extent that they can be anticipated.

- The impact the captive will have on loss control in the company.

- Whether the captive will improve the insurance cover available to the company.

- Whether the captive will improve the company's overall risk financing strategy.

- Problems of local implementation throughout the world.

- Opportunities to optimise the funding mechanism.

- The tax position.

- The implementation of an overall risk retention program.

PREFERRED LOCATIONS OF OFFSHORE FUNDS

• Bermuda	• The Isle of Man
• The Cayman Islands	• Jersey
• Guernsey	• Luxembourg
• Hong Kong	

PRE-QUALIFICATIONS FOR A NEW IPO (LISTING)

- A top quality management and executive team with appropriate back-ups and succession plans.

- A focused and niche market in which the company operates or will operate.

- Unique skills, products, and intellectual capabilities that give the company a competitive advantage.

- A strategic investor or industry leader as a major shareholder to add credibility to the candidate.

- A strong balance sheet, with an emphasis on cash availability.

- Strong potential revenue and profit streams; investors are now placing more emphasis on the generation of profits than in the past.

- An existing presence in the market the company serves, preferably including general brand awareness, product knowledge, and operational experience in these markets.

- A suitable investment community in the market where the listing is planned.

- The market's understanding of, previous experience with, and appetite for other companies with similar activities and risk profiles.

STRATEGIC ISSUES, OPPORTUNITIES AND CAVEATS

SCOPE OF OFFSHORE STRATEGIES

- Tax planning is the process of taking into consideration all relevant tax factors, in the light of the material non-tax factors, for the purpose of determining

  — whether (and if so),

  — when,

  — how, and

  — with whom

  to enter into and conduct transactions, operations, and relationships, with the object of keeping the tax burden falling on taxable events and persons as low as possible while attaining the desired business, personal, and other objectives.

- Offshore tax planning is tax planning in which factors involving more than one country are included in the original database and an offshore element is introduced as an extension of domestic tax planning.

- In this context, the term *offshore* applies to countries or transactions:

  — where there are no relevant taxes;

  — where taxes are levied only on internal taxable events, but not at all, or at low rates, on profits from foreign sources; or

  — where special tax privileges are granted to certain types of taxable persons or events (such special tax privileges may be accorded by the domestic internal tax system or may derive from a combination of domestic and treaty provisions).

DATABASE REQUIRED FOR THE DESIGN OF AN OFFSHORE TAX PLAN

- The facts

- Tax factors

- Non-tax factors

THE FACTS

- The particular situation of a taxpayer and the business and other objectives vary from case to case.

- It is obviously not possible to draw up a correct offshore tax plan without a comprehensive and accurate briefing on the facts.

- *Caveat:* Bad briefing results partly from the lack of awareness that it is possible to take into account all possible solutions to a problem and avoid pitfalls only with access to the full and accurate database containing all the material facts.

TAX FACTORS

- In analysing the tax factors of an international tax plan, it is necessary to examine:

  — the domestic internal tax systems of the countries involved in the project; and

  — the manner in which the general rules embodied in such systems are affected by the introduction of the offshore factor.

- *Caveat:* Given the wide differences in the types of offshore jurisdictions, it should not be assumed that offshore taxes may be ignored. On the contrary, there are a number of classes of direct and indirect taxes and duties that may be encountered offshore.

NON-TAX FACTORS

- Non-tax factors may also have to be taken into consideration for the purposes of a proposed offshore tax plan.

- These can be every bit as important as the tax factors.

- *Caveat:* The tax tail must never be allowed to wag the business dog.

BREAKING THE CONNECTING FACTOR

- Liability to tax is dependent upon the existence of a connecting factor between a taxing jurisdiction on the one hand and a taxpayer or taxable event on the other.

- The most effective offshore tax plans derive from the ability to sever the nexus or connecting factor with a taxing country in favour of an offshore country or to rearrange the connecting factors in such a way that a lower overall tax burden is suffered.

THE RELATIONSHIP OF THE TAXPAYER TO OTHER PERSONS

- The relationship of the parties may determine whether an item is included in the taxable base. It may also affect the rate of tax.

- The key issue is frequently the controlled foreign company (or corporation) issue, where domestic shareholders may be taxed on the income of a foreign company.

- *Caveat:* In most tax systems and tax treaties, special provisions govern parent and subsidiary or otherwise associated companies, as variously defined. There are considerable differences encountered in the definitional content of the term *holding company*.

TAX INCENTIVES IN OFFSHORE STRATEGIES

- Nearly all countries grant tax incentives of some kind as part of their general or regional economic development programs.

- Tax incentives are tax concessions that are granted to attract local or foreign investment capital to particular activities or areas.

- Tax incentives may convert otherwise high tax countries into limited purpose tax havens.

- *Caveat:* Tax incentives in high tax countries are in the firing line of the international measures to combat harmful tax competition.

ANTI-AVOIDANCE

- As a general principle, there is no obligation, either morally or legally, to suffer a heavier tax burden than is necessarily attendant upon a given taxable event.

- *Caveat:* Even though a taxpayer may stay within the letter of the law, there is usually a limit to the tax minimisation steps that he may take. Most tax systems contain some general or specific anti-avoidance provisions. The substance *versus* form rule enables the revenue to disregard appearances and to rewrite transactions so as to reflect the true situation.

- Sometimes loopholes in anti-avoidance provisions offer comparatively simple solutions to tax problems.

- *Caveat:* These loopholes are frequently plugged as soon as the tax authorities become aware of their potential for abuse, and most anti-avoidance provisions become progressively more comprehensive as taxpayers grow more ingenious.

- Offshore counters to anti-avoidance provisions are structures whereby the taxpayer's affairs are arranged in such a way that, as far as possible, they do not fall within the taxing net.

- *Caveat:* This general principle is, however, being narrowed considerably by the international measures to combat harmful tax practices.

EXCHANGES OF INFORMATION

- The principal formal exchange of information mechanism is the tax treaty. Most tax treaties contain an article providing for the exchange of information between the competent authorities.

- *Caveat:* Frequently, too, provision is made for the contracting states to render to each other administrative and legal assistance in connection with the assessment and collection of taxes.

- *Caveat:* Though no statistics are available, it may be assumed that informal exchanges of information between the administrations are on the increase.

FOREIGN CURRENCY GAINS AND LOSSES IN OFFSHORE TRANSACTIONS

- Frequently, offshore transactions are conducted in whole or in part in foreign currency.

- The translation of foreign currency into the domestic currency may follow various methods (e.g., the profit and loss method, the net worth method, or the transaction method).

- In the case of an intermittent user of foreign currency, the transaction method deals with each foreign transaction separately and computes the domestic income at the appropriate exchange rate for that transaction.

- *Caveat:* The tax laws of different countries must be applied against the background of foreign exchange markets.

TAX PLANNING IN GENERAL

4.1 It is both lawful and sensible to arrange business and personal affairs in such a way as to attract the lowest possible incidence of tax. The widening scope of tax laws, the complexity of their provisions, and high tax rates make it more necessary than ever for business enterprises and individuals alike to plan their taxable events with considerable care.

4.2 For a commercial or industrial enterprise, an unnecessarily increased tax burden represents a business waste that not only reduces its distributable profits but may well make it uncompetitive.

4.3 In the case of an individual, the net return from personal endeavour and the investment of capital is in most countries so severely reduced by the Revenue that the failure to take advantage of potential tax minimisation benefits may have a considerable effect on his spending power and accumulated wealth. The omission to anticipate death duties and inheritance taxes will frequently cut an unnecessarily deep wedge into his estate.

4.4   Preparation of the Database

4.4   Offshore tax planning is tax planning in which factors involving more than one country are included in the original database and an offshore element is introduced as an extension of domestic tax planning.

4.5   The different ways in which two or more systems may be linked offer considerable scope for tax minimisation or deferral, particularly where at least one of the countries is offshore, since offshore does, by its very nature, generally refer to a better tax deal in a foreign country.

4.6   On the other hand, where a project crosses frontiers, there are far more tax and non-tax factors to be taken into account than in a purely domestic case. It follows that offshore tax planning may often be exceedingly complex.

THE OFFSHORE DATABASE

4.7   With the expansion of international trade and private foreign investment, it has become increasingly necessary to have access to a database containing general information regarding tax and business laws and practices in foreign countries. This need is catered to by a number of publications and online services, which are of varying degrees of accuracy, completeness, and speed of updating (see also Chapter 10).

4.8   However, most of the available information is far from comprehensive, and it therefore follows that one is dependent to a greater or lesser extent on second-hand information.

4.9   The difficulty of obtaining adequate information is aggravated in the case of countries where administrative rulings (and even judicial decisions) are not published fully and quickly, where the ultimate tax bill is subject to negotiation (especially where such negotiation is open to graft), and generally where there is a contrast between the printed word and actual practice.

4.10   One is thus frequently obliged to obtain advice from experts in foreign countries involved in a proposed arrangement. Depending on the available documentation, it may be desirable to seek such advice at the outset, during the course of the research, or only at a much later stage for the purpose of controlling whether a possible benefit or pitfall may not have been overlooked.

4.11   The database required for the design of an offshore tax plan consists of:

- the facts;
- tax factors; and
- non-tax factors.

The Facts

4.12   The particular situation of a taxpayer and the business and other objectives vary from case to case. It is obviously not possible to draw up a correct offshore tax plan without a comprehensive and accurate briefing on the facts.

4.13   Bad briefing results partly from the lack of awareness that it is possible to take into account all possible solutions to a problem and avoid pitfalls only with access to the full and accurate database containing all the material facts.

Tax Factors

4.14 In analysing the tax factors of an offshore tax plan, it is necessary to examine:

- the domestic internal tax systems of the countries involved in the project; and

- the manner in which the general rules embodied in such systems are affected by the introduction of the offshore factor.

4.15 Given the wide differences in the types of offshore jurisdictions, it should not be assumed that offshore taxes may be ignored. On the contrary, there are a number of classes of direct and indirect taxes and duties that may be encountered offshore.

Non-tax Factors

4.16 Non-tax factors may also have to be taken into consideration for the purposes of a proposed offshore tax plan. These can be every bit as important as the tax factors since the tax tail must never be allowed to wag the business dog.

DEFINITIONAL CONTENT OF TERMS

4.17 When dealing with foreign countries, it may be important to understand the precise nature of a foreign tax or duty. Similar terms frequently have quite different connotations in other systems. The particular taxes and duties that are imposed and the extent to which they overlap may vary considerably from one system to another.

4.18 Problems may arise in determining the definitional content of terms, either within the context of the legal system or in relation to another onshore or offshore system or a tax treaty. The meaning of terms that are constantly employed in treaties and domestic laws (such as *income tax, total income, residence, domicile, immovable property*, and *permanent establishment*) may vary considerably according to the context.

4.19 The presence of different languages may lie at the root of the difficulty. The literal translation of terms may prove treacherous. Treaties are frequently concluded in more than one language. In such cases, it is specifically provided whether such texts are equally authentic or whether one text is to prevail in case of doubt.

4.20 A major part of tax planning involves the use of tax treaties. Treaties normally define certain terms that are employed. Recent treaties show a tendency toward the unification of these definitions. An important number of such treaties have been modelled on the draft conventions of the Fiscal Committee of the Organisation for Economic Co-operation and Development (OECD) for the Avoidance of Double Taxation on Income and Capital, and on Estates and Inheritances.

4.21 In the absence of a definition, reference is made to the domestic law of the countries concerned. A standard clause contained in many treaties runs along the following lines:

'As regards the application of the Convention by a Contracting State any term not otherwise defined shall, unless the context otherwise required, have the meaning which it has under the laws of that Contracting State relating to the taxes which are the subject of the Convention.'

4.22 Sometimes interpretative rulings are issued for the purpose of determining whether a foreign tax falls within the scope of a treaty or legislative provision. It may also occur that the tax authorities of the countries concerned enter into an agreement to settle such questions.

Example

The US Internal Revenue Code, s 901, allows a credit against US tax for foreign income, war profits, and excess profits taxes. For a tax paid to a foreign country to qualify as an income tax, it must be shown that the tax imposed by the foreign country is a tax on income within the US concept thereof, or is a tax in lieu of an income tax within the meaning of s 903. S 903 provides that the phrase 'income, war profits, and excess profits taxes' includes 'a tax paid in lieu of a tax on income, war profits, or excess profits otherwise generally imposed by any foreign country'.

The question arose as to whether the Italian tax bonds (*imposta sulle obbligazioni*) qualified as an 'income tax' for the purposes of the foreign tax credit provisions of s 901.

The tax on bonds and like securities issued in Italy is payable by the issuers who are entitled to recover it from the bondholders. The tax is imposed at a rate based on the taxable value of the bonds. The value of the bonds is determined on the basis of the latest stock exchange settlement price prior to the closing of the taxpayer's balance sheet, or in the case of unlisted bonds or bonds that are listed but have no settlement price, the nominal value. In defining taxable value, it is provided that the tax is payable on the aggregate value of the bonds as shown in the issuer's balance sheet, reduced by one-half for the bonds issued in the second half of the fiscal year.

The IRS issued a ruling holding that the Italian tax on bonds bears no relation to the income or profits of the issuer or to the interest payable with respect to the bonds. It is therefore not an 'income tax' within the meaning of s 901, nor a tax paid in lieu of an income tax within the meaning of s 903. It is therefore not a creditable tax under s 901.

4.23 Even where a term is defined for the purposes of the tax treaty, a dispute with the tax authorities may nevertheless arise on the question as to whether the particular facts fall within the definition.

4.24 A number of reported cases deal with the question of the existence of a *permanent establishment*. This term is frequently used in tax treaties as a basis for the apportionment of taxable income (particularly with regard to industrial and commercial profits). The term is usually defined for the purposes of such treaties owing to variations in its precise definitional content.

Example

The Italian branch office of a French corporation was involved in buying wine in Italy for the French corporation. The goods acquired by the branch office were regularly invoiced to the head office in France.

The question arose as to whether the branch office was a 'permanent establishment' for the purposes of the France–Italy Tax Treaty (Treaty of 29 October 1958, as amended) and therefore subject to Italian tax. Article 3(4)(1) of the treaty states that offices shall be deemed to be permanent establishments and that their profits are subject to tax in the State in which the office is located.

The tax commission in Milan decided that, as the branch office charged its head office the same prices as it had paid for the goods, it was not engaged in commercial activities but merely provided the head office with merchandise. The branch office was not, therefore, a permanent establishment and was not subject to Italian tax.

4.25   However, it may happen that a particular treaty does not define a term that it employs. In such a case, the courts or the revenue authorities may be called upon to furnish the definition. Frequently, reference is made to the provisions of the OECD Model Conventions.

Example

The taxpayer was a French citizen resident in France who had contracted with an unrelated US corporation to be his representative in connection with concert appearances in the United States. The corporation was under a contractual duty to promote the taxpayer's career in the United States and had exclusive power to execute contracts for his services; the corporation received a percentage of the taxpayer's earnings for performing these functions. Inquiries concerning the taxpayer's concert tour in the United States could be made only to the corporation's offices.

Article 14(2) of the France–United States Tax Treaty provides that income derived by a resident of one of the treaty countries in respect of independent activities performed in the other country is not taxable in that other country if:

- the recipient of the income is present there for a period not exceeding 183 days; and

- the recipient does not maintain a fixed base in the other country for a period not exceeding 183 days.

Fixed base is not defined by the convention, and the meaning of the term is derived from Article 14 of the OECD Model Convention. Article 14 equates 'fixed base' with 'permanent establishment', which means a centre of industrial or commercial activities of a fixed or permanent character. Under Article 4(5) of the France–United States Tax Treaty, a resident of one of the treaty countries is not deemed to have a permanent establishment in the other country merely because he carries on business there through an independent agent acting in the ordinary course of business.

The taxpayer's concert tour in the year in issue required him to spend a total of 36 days in the United States. He was thus not liable for tax in the United States as neither of the necessary conditions was fulfilled.

THE CONNECTING FACTOR

4.26   The most effective offshore tax plans derive from the ability to sever the nexus or connecting factor with a taxing country in favour of an offshore country or to rearrange the connecting factors in such a way that a lower overall tax burden is suffered. Liability to tax is dependent upon the existence of a connecting factor between a taxing jurisdiction on the one hand and a taxpayer or taxable event on the other.

4.27   In the case of an individual taxpayer, the principal connecting factors are residence, ordinary residence, domicile, and citizenship (nationality). In the case of a company, they are management and control, beneficial ownership, place of incorporation, and location of the registered office. In the case of a trust, they are the place of creation, the applicable law, the place of administration or trusteeship, and the residence, domicile, or citizenship of the beneficiaries or trustees.

4.28   Other important connecting factors may be the centre of economic interests, the presence of a permanent establishment, and effectively connected income.

4.29   The principal connecting factor with regard to a taxable event is the real or deemed source. For example, in the case of profits deriving from the sale of goods, the source might be the place of the execution of the contract, the place where a trader or manufacturer employs his capital or where activities are exercised, while in the case of a real property tax or a capital gains tax on the sale of real property, geographic source or situs would normally constitute the connecting factor.

4.30   Many parameters relating to the taxpayer, the source, or the nature of the taxable event may affect (a) the liability to tax, (b) the computation of the tax burden, and (c) whether the connecting factor has indeed been severed with the taxing country in favour of an offshore country.

4.31   The definitional content and criteria affecting the existence or otherwise of a connecting factor and its characterisation must be determined from within any given legal system or treaty.

Residence, Domicile, and Citizenship

4.32   Issues of personal residence, domicile and citizenship are dealt with in Chapter 8.

Tax Treaty Definition of the Residence Companies

4.33   Article 4.1 of the OECD Model Convention deals with the question of residence as follows:

> 'For the purposes of this Convention, the term "resident of a Contracting State" means any person who, under the law of that State, is liable to tax therein by reason of his domicile, residence, place of management or any other criterion of a similar nature. But this term does not include any person who is liable to tax in that State in respect only of income from sources in that State or capital situated therein.'

4.34   The OECD Commentary on paragraph 1 of Article 4 deals with the definition of the expression 'resident of a Contracting State' for the purposes of the Convention. The definition refers to the concept of residence adopted in the domestic laws. As criteria for the taxation as a resident, the definition mentions: domicile, residence, place of management or any other criterion of a similar nature. As far as individuals are concerned, the definition aims at covering the various forms of personal attachment to a State which, in the domestic taxation laws, form the basis of a comprehensive taxation (full liability to tax). It also covers cases where a person is deemed, according to the taxation laws of a State, to be a resident of that State and on account thereof is fully liable to tax therein (e.g. diplomats or other persons in government services). In accordance with the provisions of the second sentence of paragraph 1, however, a person is not to be considered a 'resident of a Contracting State' in the sense of the Convention if, although not domiciled in that State, he is considered to be a resident according to the domestic laws but is subject only to a taxation limited to the income from sources in that State or to capital situated in that State. That situation exists in some States in relation to individuals, e.g. in the case of foreign diplomatic and consular staff serving in their territory.

4.35 *Note*: The definition of a resident of a Contracting State excludes foreign held companies which are exempt from tax on their foreign income by virtue of provisions designed to attract conduit companies, but this exclusion should be interpreted restrictively.

Residence of Companies

4.36 The 'resident' issue can arise in the multinational group context in designing offshore legal entity structures. For example, in evaluating holding company structures for international operations, the typical choice has been between utilisation of treaty countries and non-treaty countries. It is also interesting to determine whether it is possible to devise a structure that has the benefits of treaty country status (availability of tax treaty protection) as well as the benefits of low effective tax costs of non-treaty, tax advantageous jurisdictions.

4.37 The 1996 US Model provides that the treaty will apply only to residents of one or both Contracting States. The definition of 'resident' is contained in 1996 US Model Article 4, which provides with respect to companies, in pertinent part, that a person is a resident of a State if it is liable to tax therein due to place of management, place of incorporation, or any other criterion of a similar nature. The term does not include a person 'who is liable to tax in that State in respect only of income from sources in that State, in respect only from sources in that State, or in respect of profits attributable to a permanent establishment in that State' (1996 US Model Article 4(1)). In the case of an entity that is transparent under the laws of either State, an item of income, profit, or gain is treated as derived by a resident of a State to the extent the item is treated as such in the case of a resident of the State (1996 US Model Article 4(1)(c)) If a company is treated as resident in both States, it will then be treated as a resident of the State of creation (incorporation or organisation) (1996 US Model Article 4(3)).

4.38 Even if a resident, a company must also satisfy the limitation of benefits article before it is eligible for treaty benefits (1996 US Model Article 22(1)).

Case study

An interesting point came up for consideration by the IRS in cases where it was ruled that the term 'liable to tax' in Article 4.1 of the US Model Treaty does not require actual taxation.

In Revenue Ruling 2000–59 (Rev. Rul. 2000–59, 2000–52 IRB 1), the Service addressed the situation of two companies and a trust:

Situation 1. Entity A is a business organisation in Country X, which has an income tax treaty in effect with the United States that is identical to the 1996 US Model. Under the laws of Country X, Entity A is an investment company taxable on income from all sources at the entity level by reason of being incorporated in Country X. Similar to other domestic corporations, distributions from a Country X investment company are generally treated as dividends and do not retain the character or source of the underlying income. However, net capital gains and, in some cases, tax-exempt interest, retain their character when they are distributed to the investment company's interest holders. Further, a Country X investment company may *deduct distributions* of current income to its interest holders in computing taxable income.

Entity A distributes its net income and capital gains on a current basis to its interest holders so that it will not actually bear tax. Country X imposes a withholding tax on Entity A's dividend distributions to its foreign interest holders regardless of the source of Entity A's underlying income. If Entity A did not distribute such amounts, Entity A would be taxed by Country X on such amounts. Entity A receives dividend income from the United States.

Country X has not announced by public notice that investment companies such as Entity A are not residents of Country X, and there is no competent authority agreement providing that such entities are not residents of Country X. Further, the US competent authority has not issued a public notice indicating that treaty benefits to such entities are being denied because, and to the extent that, Country X will not grant treaty benefits to similar US entities.

Situation 2.   Entity B is an investment company organised in Country Y, which has an income tax treaty in effect with the United States that is identical to the 1996 US Model. Under the laws of Country Y, corporations organised in Country Y are generally taxable on income from all sources at the entity level by reason of being incorporated in Country Y. A specific provision in Country Y law, however, exempts the income of investment companies such as Entity B from taxation. Under Country Y law, the character and source of distributions from Entity B to all its interest holders are determined based on the distributions themselves rather than on the character and source of Entity B's underlying income. Further, Country Y imposes a withholding tax on distributions to its foreign interest holders regardless of the source of the underlying income. Entity B receives dividend income from the United States.

The last paragraph of Situation 1 is the same in Country Y.

Situation 3.   Entity C is a trust established and administered in Country Z, which has an income tax treaty with the United States identical to the 1981 US Model Income. The trust exclusively provides pension benefits. Entity C's trustee is a resident of Country Z. Under the laws of Country Z, because Entity C's trustee is a resident of Country Z, Entity C is treated as a resident trust taxable at the entity level. However, because Entity C is established and operated exclusively to provide pension benefits, a provision of Country Z law exempts Entity C from Country Z income tax. Entity C receives dividend income from the United States.

The last paragraph of Situation 1 is the same in Country Z.

4.39   The Service noted that the term 'liable to tax' in Article 4.1 of both the 1996 US Model and 1981 US Model does not require actual taxation. Thus, the fact that a person is only nominally taxable does not preclude that person from meeting the applicable 'liable to tax' standard of these residence articles. For purposes of these residence articles, whether a person will be liable to tax in, and thus a resident of a jurisdiction depends on the facts and circumstances. However, in the context of a bilateral income tax treaty, a person will not be considered a resident of a Contracting State if:

- the treaty partner has announced by public notice that such persons are not residents of that state;

- there is a competent authority agreement or separate specific treaty provision providing that such persons are not residents of that State; or

- the treaty partner would not treat similar US persons as residents of the United States, and the Service has issued a public notice indicating that treaty benefits to such entities are consequently being denied. Conversely, a person may be treated as a resident of a Contracting State if there is a competent authority agreement or separate specific treaty provision providing that such persons are residents of that State.

4.40 Applying these criteria, the Service ruled that in Situation 1, Entity A is 'liable to tax' even though it is only nominally taxable in Country X because:

- it may be taxed by Country X on its worldwide income;

- but for the deduction regime, Country X would have imposed a tax on Entity A as it would any corporation incorporated in Country X;

- the character and source of certain distributions by Entity A are determined independent of the character and source of Entity A's income, and Country X imposes a withholding tax on such distributions by Entity A to its foreign interest holders regardless of the source of Entity A's underlying income;

- Country X has not announced by public notice that persons such as Entity A are not residents of Country X; there is no competent authority agreement providing that such persons are not residents of Country X; and

- the US competent authority has not issued a public notice indicating that treaty benefits to such persons are being denied because Country X will not grant treaty benefits to similar US persons.

4.41 Accordingly, the Service ruled that Entity A is liable to tax in Country X by reason of its place of incorporation within the meaning of Article 4(1) of the US–Country X Treaty, and thus is a resident of Country X for purposes of the US Country X Treaty. In order to obtain treaty benefits, however, Entity A must still meet all other applicable requirements for such benefits, including the applicable limitation on benefits provision and, if Entity A is viewed as fiscally transparent under the laws of either the United States or Country X, those provisions of Treas. Reg. § 1.894–1(d).

4.42 A similar conclusion was reached with respect to Situation 2 where Entity 2 was only nominally liable to tax in Country Y, and in Situation 3 where Entity C was only nominally taxable in Country Z due to the exemption from tax for Country Z entities that provide pension benefits.

4.43 The explanation 'liable to tax' in the context of the 'resident' article of the US Model Treaty is interesting, confirming the application of treaties in the context of foreign entities organised in countries that provide significant tax base limitation benefits.

The Legal Status of the Taxpayer

4.44 In most tax systems, the legal personality of the taxpayer has a direct effect on liability to tax.

4.45 Individuals, companies, trusts, partnerships, and other types of legal entities may be subject to different tax burdens or may benefit from different deductions or credits. Frequently, too, they suffer tax at different rates.

4.46   Other notions may also be relevant, such as 'controlled foreign company', 'foreign personal holding company', 'close company', 'private company', 'dealer', 'trader', 'profit-making institution', 'importer', 'married person', 'head of the household', etc.

4.47   Sometimes legal status is determined by rulings of the tax administration.

Example

Under Article 11(3)(c) of the Belgium–Switzerland Tax Treaty (Treaty of 28 April 1978) interest paid on any loan guaranteed by a Swiss bank (which is not embodied in a bearer instrument) is exempt from tax in the country of source. Article 11(3) of the Spain–Switzerland Tax Treaty (Treaty of 26 April 1966) provides that interest arising in Spain and paid to a Swiss bank over five years or more may not be taxed in Spain.

The question arose as to which kinds of financial institutions should be regarded as 'Swiss banks' for the purposes of these treaties. It has been agreed among Switzerland, Spain, and Belgium that a 'Swiss bank' is either (a) a normal bank or savings institution, or (b) a financial institution or private enterprise that has the characteristics of a bank and that solicits deposits from the general public; therefore it fulfils all the conditions imposed by the Federal Law on Banks and Savings Institutions and submits to the Federal Bank Commission's control.

If a Swiss financial institution has been wrongly granted exemption under the treaties, because it does not come within the requirements of a 'Swiss bank', the Swiss tax administration has the right to inform the foreign tax administration, collect the relevant tax, and remit it to the appropriate country.

The Source of the Income or Gain

4.48   Source is normally the most significant connecting factor in determining the tax liability of the income or gain.

4.49   The typical offshore tax plan locates the source of the taxable event well and truly offshore. This is because geographic source is frequently the sole or the principal connecting factor between a taxing jurisdiction and a taxable event.

Example

A French reinsurance broking company had its registered office (*siège*) and its regular offices (*bureaux*) in France. It carried on business in France and abroad, but foreign operations were exclusively carried out by correspondence or through sub-brokers established abroad.

The *Conseil d'Etat* held that in such a case the income derived through foreign contracts is in fact derived through activities carried on in France and must therefore be considered as domestic source income. The company was thus liable to corporate income tax with respect to contracts concluded abroad.

Example

A non-resident alien sold and conveyed motion picture rights in a literary work to a US corporation. The contract for the deal was negotiated in New York, executed in Hungary, and paid for in New York.

Gross income from sources within the United States includes payments of royalties derived from intangible property such as patents, copyrights, secret processes and formulas, goodwill, trademarks, trade brands, and franchises.

It was held that the payment was gross income from US sources and subject to tax, in spite of the fact that the contract gave worldwide rights.

4.50 More than one country may consider income or a gain as deriving from a source within its jurisdiction. Furthermore, there may be a conflict between this and another connecting factor. These situations may result in cases of double taxation. Sometimes provision is made with regard to the tax position in cases where sources are partly in and partly out of the country concerned.

The Nature of the Transaction or Operation

4.51 The nature of the transaction or operation may determine whether it is subject to tax at all and, if so, whether expenditure incurred in connection with it is deductible from the taxable base.

4.52 In many tax systems, the crucial distinction is between income and capital. These notions are often not defined in the tax legislation, and their precise meanings must be obtained from judicial and administrative decisions and rulings.

Example

The taxpayer was a New Zealand company that entered into an agreement with a US company under which the latter agreed to supply it for a period of 15 years with technical knowledge, plans and facilities, new developments, etc. The consideration was in the form of royalty payments.

After the agreement had been running for five years, the taxpayer negotiated the cancellation of the agreement in consideration of a lump-sum payment.

This payment was effected in order to achieve an economy in working expenses and left the capital structure of the taxpayer unaffected.

The taxpayer treated this expenditure as being on revenue account and deducted this sum from its assessable income.

The New Zealand commissioner of Inland Revenue disallowed the deduction claimed.

On appeal, the New Zealand Supreme Court held that the royalties represented expenditure incurred by the taxpayer in operating its manufacturing process to best advantage.

4.53 Preparation of the Database

> Since the expenditure was on revenue account, it was deductible from the taxpayer's assessable income.

4.53 Income arising from mergers or similar types of operations may receive favoured tax treatment or may suffer from various kinds of economic double taxation. The tax position may also vary according to whether the operation crosses frontiers or is purely domestic.

The Relationship of the Taxpayer to Other Persons

4.54 The relationship of the parties may determine whether an item is included in the taxable base. It may also affect the rate of tax.

4.55 The key issue is frequently the controlled foreign company (or corporation) issue, where domestic shareholders may be taxed on the income of a foreign company. (See *Butterworths Offshore Service*, Spitz and Clarke, Vol I, Pt D.)

4.56 In most tax systems and tax treaties, special provisions govern parent and subsidiary or otherwise associated companies, as variously defined. There are considerable differences encountered in the definitional content of the term *holding company*.

4.57 Sometimes special tax benefits favour certain relationships, for example, in the cases where subvention payments are allowed or where the losses of an associated company may be deducted.

4.58 In certain countries, provision is made for the profits and losses of a group of companies to be consolidated and taxed as if the various companies were one company. The existence of the consolidated subsidiary or subsidiaries is to a large extent ignored for corporation tax purposes.

4.59 Fiscal unity can be advantageous as it can help in avoiding the payment of tax in one group company where the other group company suffers loss. Without fiscal unity a group cannot easily transfer losses from one company to another, nor can assets easily be transferred at book value if the real value is higher.

4.60 In other cases, the fact that companies are related may attract the operation of anti-avoidance provisions, particularly where transactions are not at arm's length.

4.61 The amount of a share participation may also have a material effect on the determination of the tax burden, for example, in the case of a Netherlands holding company or a Swiss substantial participation holding company.

4.62 The amount of a share participation is also relevant for the purposes of a number of tax treaties. Dividends may benefit from a reduction in the withholding tax where a company of one Contracting State controls more than a certain percentage of the voting power of a company of the other Contracting State. In certain cases, a qualifying percentage may entitle the shareholder to an indirect credit in respect of taxes paid by the company in the other country.

4.63 For example, many of the tax treaties contain a provision to the effect that the country of which the company paying the dividends is resident may tax such dividends in most cases at a maximum rate, such maximum rate being reduced to 5% or 10% if the recipient company that is resident in the other country controls a certain minimum percentage of the voting power of the company paying the dividends. In certain of these treaties, there is also an indirect credit available to a company controlling 10% of the voting power of the distributing company for the tax payable in the other country by the distributing company in respect of the profits out of which the dividend is paid.

4.64   In the case of individuals, kinship may also be material. Often gifts between spouses, and the income deriving therefrom, are not subject to tax. On the other hand, income deriving from gifts to children may be treated as income in the hands of the donor parent. This is to prevent the avoidance of tax through the splitting of income among members of the family.

4.65   In many cases, estate, inheritance, and gift tax laws reduce the rate of tax or the taxable base in the case of heirs, legatees, and donees that are close relatives.

TAX INCENTIVES IN OFFSHORE TAX PLANNING

4.66   Tax incentives may convert otherwise high tax countries into limited purpose tax havens (see Chapter 11). Tax incentives are tax concessions that are granted to attract local or foreign investment capital to particular activities or areas. Nearly all countries grant tax incentives of some kind as part of their general or regional economic development programs.

4.67   At the international level, the sphere of application of a tax incentive may be extended by way of a tax sparing clause in a tax treaty between a capital importing country and a capital exporting country. Tax sparing clauses allow residents of the capital exporting country a credit against their domestic tax for profits or gains derived in the developing country in respect of which all or specified taxes are subject to exemption or reduction in the latter country.

4.68   As the legal and tax systems of different countries and the economic exigencies that lie behind the tax incentives vary inter se, so too do the form and the scope of the incentives. The benefits that may be derived from tax incentives must be judged against their total background.

4.69   Since *offshore* does by definition imply that there is a tax (or other) deal available elsewhere that is better than if one stayed within the confines of the normal tax or regulatory system, tax incentives do by their very nature introduce an offshore factor into the planning equation.

4.70   The attacks by the OECD and the European Union on what are becoming known as 'harmful preferential tax regimes' are likely to curtail the proliferation and operation of tax incentives. Such preferential tax regimes are to be found in the fields of insurance, financing and leasing, fund management, banking, headquarters, distribution centres, service centres, shipping, and other miscellaneous activities.

Categories of Tax Incentives

4.71   Most tax incentive measures fall into one or more of the following categories:

- tax exemption (tax holiday);
- deduction from the taxable base;
- reduction in the rate of tax;
- tax deferral.

4.72 Preparation of the Database

Tax Exemption

4.72 The tax exemption, or tax holiday, is the most valuable form of tax incentive. However, it may be subject to important conditions. Furthermore, in the absence of official undertakings or guarantees against future taxes for a specified period, an exemption may fail to attract long-term investment capital.

Deduction from the Taxable Base

4.73 A deduction from the taxable base is the most frequently encountered form of tax incentive. It is granted with respect to expenditure and losses that would not normally be deductible under the general principles of the tax system.

4.74 Common examples of such deductions are allowances granted in cases of expenditure on industrial buildings and structures, machinery and plant, hotels, foreign market development, industrial and intellectual rights, scientific research, and training of staff.

4.75 Many of these allowances are depreciation allowances. They may be in the form of:

- an *initial allowance*, which is a type of accelerated depreciation whereby a larger than normal deduction is obtained upon the acquisition or construction of certain assets;

- an *investment allowance*, which is an exceptional additional deduction that does not reduce the full cost of the asset, which may thus still be written off in full; or

- *annual allowances,* which are deducted annually until the deductible value of the asset is exhausted.

4.76 In some cases, the incentive is the right to carry forward certain expenditure, losses, and unabsorbed depreciation for more years than would normally be permitted under the general principles of the tax system.

Reduction in the Rate of Tax

4.77 A large number of systems impose tax on certain types of entities or particular activities at a lower rate than is normally applicable.

4.78 Sometimes the reduction in the tax rate takes the form of a refund of a percentage of the tax paid in respect of the particular item of income.

Tax Deferral

4.79 A tax deferral may operate either to postpone the inclusion of the income or gain in the taxable base or to postpone the date upon which the tax itself becomes due or payable.

4.80 For example, in the case of a merger or similar operation, the gain may not be subject to tax until a later year.

Scope of Tax Incentives

4.81 Tax incentives may be of general or regional application. At the international level, the sphere of application of a tax incentive may be extended by way of a tax sparing clause in a tax treaty between a capital importing country and a capital exporting country.

4.82 Tax incentives frequently favour specific activities such as farming, prospecting for minerals and mining, shipping, and air transport.

4.83 Many countries provide either an exemption or some type of special tax treatment with regard to certain categories of interest income, such as, in particular, national or local government-sponsored bonds. Non-residents will most often benefit little, if at all, from such concessions, since they will generally be subject to tax on the interest in question in the country of residence. The few tax treaties that do contain tax sparing clauses usually limit their operation to concessions applying within the framework of a development program.

4.84 A concession may apply in respect of national taxes or only in respect of taxes imposed at a lower level in the constitutional hierarchy (e.g., provincial taxes, cantonal taxes, etc.). In countries where there are scheduler taxes, the incentive may well relate to only certain types of tax.

4.85 Sometimes concessions are granted in favour of indirect taxes only, such as reductions of the rate of, or exemptions from, turnover taxes or import and export duties.

4.86 Often a tax concession is available without regard being had to the person benefiting. In other cases, however, the concession may be available only to residents or to non-residents, or only to individuals or to companies (or to certain special types of companies).

4.87 Tax incentives may be limited in time. This is usually so in the case of tax holidays, and particularly where government guarantees are granted.

4.88 In certain cases, there is a ceiling on the amount of a tax benefit. Sometimes the ceiling affects only the tax year in question with the right to carry over any excess into subsequent tax years. In other cases, the ceiling is absolute, and any amount in excess of such ceiling will be included in the taxable base.

4.89 The grant of favoured tax treatment may be subject to conditions that are able to be fulfilled only by a limited clientele. An example is the Belgian Law on Co-ordination Centres.

4.90 Non-tax incentives are frequently included in incentive packages. These may include subsidised factory sites, training of local staff, transportation facilities, soft loans, and other benefits.

Special Incentives and Grants

Financial and Banking Facilities

4.91 In addition to the credit facilities of private banks, government-sponsored finance houses operating on a commercial basis may make capital available to industry by way of medium- and long-term loans, direct share investment, and hire-purchase and equipment leasing finance. They may also act as underwriters for public issues of shares. Special arrangements may be made for the provision of finance for undercapitalised concerns.

4.92 Such finance houses may also initiate and facilitate mergers by providing financial advice, undertaking share valuations, advising on terms for mergers, and assisting in the carrying through of negotiations and formalities. In cases where finance is required in connection with a merger operation, they may provide facilities.

4.93 Preparation of the Database

4.93 Commercial banks often establish subsidiary organisations to provide an extended range of financial services and to facilitate increased investment in the industrial and commercial sectors.

Reductions in Corporation Tax

4.94 Companies providing certain financial services may also benefit from reduced rates. A special license may be required. The activities that may qualify may include the following:

- foreign currency transactions normally provided by banks;

- international financial activities including global money management, insurance, and related activities and dealings in foreign currencies, options, and similar financial assets;

- services or facilities for processing, control, accounting, communication, clearing, settlement, or information storage in relation to financial activities;

- the development and supply of computer software for use in the provision of the services or facilities referred to above or for reprocessing and analysing information on financial activities;

- dealing in commodity futures or commodity options on behalf of unconnected persons who are not themselves involved in commodity trading;

- trading operations similar or ancillary to any of the above and that contribute to the use of the area as an international financial services centre;

- life assurance business with policyholders and annuitants abroad; and

- the management of the investments of unit trusts.

4.95 Reductions in corporation tax are frequently granted to manufacturing companies from the sale of manufactured goods. The term *manufacturing* may be extended to include commodities or materials belonging to another person that are subjected to a process of manufacturing.

4.96 A reduction in corporation tax may also be extended to certain trading operations of a qualified company carried on within specified zones.

4.97 The classes of trading operations may be extended to the repair or maintenance of aircraft and to trading operations that contribute to the use or development of an airport.

Cash Grants and Other Incentives for Industrial Development

4.98 Development authorities may provide non-refundable cash grants toward the cost of the fixed assets of new industries that are considered to have good prospects of success and permanence in free trade conditions and are likely to contribute to the growth of the economy. For the purposes of cash grants, 'fixed assets' may include the factory site, site development, factory buildings, and new machinery, plant, and equipment. Higher grants are usually available in the designated areas (i.e., certain underdeveloped areas).

4.99 Specially arranged packages of incentives, embracing industrial grants, interest subsidies, loan guarantees, and training grants, may be provided for approved subjects. Industrial and commercial facilities and important financial incentives may also be made available in the airport or other customs-free zones.

4.100   Incentive programs may permit the carrying on of trade, business, or manufacture under license within the airport or other zones and may grant exemptions from payment of tax on profits from certain business operations.

4.101   Such programs may also assist the establishment of new projects through the payment of cash grants, the amount of any such grant usually being subject to negotiation.

Machinery and Plant

4.102   An initial allowance may be granted in respect of capital expenditure incurred on the provision of new machinery or plant.

4.103   An annual allowance is usually available in respect of reasonable wear and tear of machinery and plant.

4.104   A form of free depreciation may also be available in the case of new machinery or plant acquired for use in a development area. The system of free depreciation allows the writing off of machinery or plant to be accelerated according to the specifications of the taxpayer.

4.105   A balancing allowance or charge may be made where machinery or plant ceases to belong to the trader or permanently ceases to be used for the purposes of his trade.

Industrial Buildings and Structures

4.106   Initial allowances of capital expenditure incurred on the construction of an industrial building or structure are usually granted.

4.107   An annual allowance may also be available in respect of capital expenditure incurred on the construction of industrial buildings or structures.

4.108   If an industrial building or structure is purchased prior to the exhaustion of the annual allowance, an adjustment may be made with regard to the allowance that may be claimed by the new owner.

4.109   A balancing allowance or charge may be made where an industrial building or structure is sold, destroyed, or ceases to be used and the residue of the expenditure on construction that has not been allowed for tax purposes exceeds or falls short of the amount of sale, insurance, salvage, or compensation moneys received.

Training of Local Staff

4.110   A trader proposing to manufacture goods for sale, or in the case of certain other qualifying activities, may claim an allowance for the full amount of certain expenditure incurred, before the commencement of trading, on recruitment and training of personnel.

Regional Development Grants

4.111   Regional development grants on buildings and equipment may be granted in the form of cash grants to encourage investment in industry in development areas. Training grants may also be granted on the cost of internal and external training programs for work in new industries.

4.112 Preparation of the Database

Export Sales Relief

4.112 Companies that export manufactured goods frequently benefit from a reduction in corporation tax.

4.113 The definition of *manufacture* may be extended to include a wide range of items, such as the following:

- goods processed by a company and then returned to the foreign owner;

- design and planning services carried out on behalf of non-resident persons in connection with a variety of projects such as chemical, civil, electrical, or mechanical engineering works, carried on abroad; and

- shipping profits, gold transactions, and financial futures transactions.

Export Credit Guarantees

4.114 There may be provision for exporters to insure with an official insurance corporation the credit they give their overseas customers. The basic export credit insurance policy provides cover against the main risks of non-payment, whether this arises from insolvency, default, or political causes.

Pioneer Industries

4.115 Pioneer industries may be entitled to complete freedom from income tax on the basis of the product investment levels, skills, and advanced technology, and dividends paid out of the exempt income may also be free of tax.

4.116 Pioneer status may be extended to companies providing engineering, technical, and computer-based industrial design services.

4.117 Post-pioneer companies may also be taxed at a concessionary rate.

Investment Allowances

4.118 Investment allowances may be granted as an alternative to the pioneer and export incentive holidays.

Expansion of Established Enterprises

4.119 Existing businesses may be entitled to a tax holiday if the enterprise incurs, or intends to incur, capital expenditure on productive equipment, and dividends paid out of the exempt income may also be free of tax.

Free Zones and Free Ports

4.120 Free zones are designated areas that receive special treatment through their exclusion from the area to which the country's normal customs rules apply. A free port is one at which imports may be landed without paying customs duties. The system of free zones or free ports favours export processing, transhipment, and the entrepôt trade since there is no need to pay and then reclaim customs duties.

4.121 Warehousing and servicing companies may receive favoured treatment in respect of these services generally or in respect of certain designated products only.

4.122 Though free zones are often part of a tax incentive package in what would otherwise be a high tax jurisdiction, they may also be found in tax havens, such as Freeport in the Bahamas.

Venture Capital Incentives

4.123 An investor investing in an approved venture company that is developing or using a new technology that is of economic or technical benefit may be allowed to deduct up to the full amount of the investment, or any loss arising from the sale of shares or from the liquidation of the approved venture company.

Research and Development

4.124 The entire amount of capital expenditure incurred on scientific research may, subject to certain conditions, be written off.

4.125 Research and development activities may benefit from incentives in the form of accelerated depreciation, investment allowances, etc.

4.126 A product development assistance scheme may also be set up to make grants to manufacturing companies developing certain new products.

Patents

4.127 Income from registered patents could receive favoured treatment and may be tax-free.

4.128 If a trader incurs capital expenditure for the purpose of acquiring certain patent rights, he may be allowed an annual allowance amortised or spread over a period of years or over the remaining life of the patent.

4.129 A balancing allowance or charge may be made where patent rights terminate or are sold for less or for more, as the case may be, than the residue of the expenditure that has not yet been allowed.

Urban Renewal Incentives

4.130 Urban renewal incentives may be granted for buildings that would not otherwise qualify once the premises are in use for the purposes of a trade. Similarly, a lessee of an industrial building who is engaged in a trade or profession may be entitled to claim a special additional deduction in respect of the amount of rent actually paid.

Joint Ventures

4.131 Favoured treatment may be accorded to companies engaged in certain joint ventures where they carry on such activities through the medium of tax-efficient partnerships or limited partnerships.

Film Production

4.132 Favoured treatment, normally including at least a tax deduction, may be accorded to companies in respect of investments in film production companies.

4.133 Preparation of the Database

Capital Assistance Scheme

4.133 Capital insurance schemes may provide funding for projects that are considered to be of benefit to the economy.

Operational Headquarters

4.134 Operational headquarters providing management, technical, or other supporting services to subsidiaries and/or associated companies in other countries may benefit from favoured tax treatment.

Tax Shelters

4.135 A *tax shelter* or *tax sheltered investment* may be defined as an investment with a flow-through of tax benefits, generally having some or all of the following characteristics: deferral of taxes, conversion of ordinary deductions for future capital gains, and leverage.

4.136 The flow-through of tax benefits is a material factor, whether the entity is organised as a limited partnership, joint venture, trust, or company and whether it is offered to investors as a private or public program.

4.137 The term is applied generally to a variety of devices that allow taxpayers to deduct certain artificial losses (i.e., losses that are not really economic losses but represent losses that are available as deductions under the current tax laws). These artificial losses may be offset not only against income from the investment out of which they arise, but also against the taxpayer's other income, usually from his regular business or professional activity.

Tax Sparing

4.138 The sphere of application of a tax incentive may be extended by way of a tax sparing clause in a tax treaty between a capital importing country and a capital exporting country.

4.139 Such clauses allow residents of the capital exporting country a credit against their domestic tax for profits or gains derived in the developing country in respect of which all or specified taxes are subject to exemption or reduction in the latter country.

4.140 The failure of a capital exporting country to provide for tax sparing or some similar arrangement leads to a distortion of competition at the international level, since investors who are taxed on foreign income in their country of residence are at a disadvantage as compared with investors who are resident in countries giving full or partial exemptions for foreign source income, and also as compared with investors resident in the developing country itself.

4.141 A tax sparing arrangement is thus a concession offered by a capital exporting or investing country to ensure that an incentive offered by a developing country is effective. Without it, the incentive offered by the developing country may be nullified because it merely results in more tax being payable in the investing country.

Example

Assume that the taxpayer is a company resident in a developed country that is operating a branch in a developing country that has granted it a five-year tax holiday on all income and withholding taxes. A comprehensive tax sparing provision is in the tax treaty between the two countries. In year three of the holiday, the taxpayer earns $1 million in the developing country. It pays no foreign tax because of the tax holiday.

Assume further that such companies are taxable on foreign earnings, subject to a tax credit. Thus the taxpayer would normally be subject to full tax in its country of residence on the $1 million of earnings. Moreover, it would normally not be able to credit any foreign tax because it paid none.

The tax sparing article provides that the company may take a tax credit against taxes in its country of residence (subject to normal limitations) in the amount of the taxes it would have paid to the developing country if there had been no tax holiday.

Caveat

4.142 It will be seen from the above that many otherwise high tax countries offer significant *offshore* features through the creation of tax and non-tax incentives.

4.143 Investment incentive programs, together with, or in the absence of, tax incentives, may well prove decisive in the choice of location of a project. Such programs are particularly attractive where substantial grants, interest-free or low-interest loans, factory sites, etc., are available in addition to tax incentives.

4.144 There are two areas where care should be exercised:

• the international measures to contain preferential tax regimes and tax havens (see Chapter 11); and

• the question as to whether the incentive is really beneficial.

4.145 *Caveat emptor* — let the buyer beware!

ANTI-AVOIDANCE

4.146 As a general principle, there is no obligation, either morally or legally, to suffer a heavier tax burden than is necessarily attendant upon a given taxable event. This general principle is, however, being narrowed considerably by the international measures to combat harmful tax practices.

4.147 Even though a taxpayer may stay within the letter of the law, there is usually a limit to the tax minimisation steps that he may take. Most tax systems contain some general or specific anti-avoidance provisions. The substance *versus* form rule enables the revenue to disregard appearances and to rewrite transactions so as to reflect the true situation.

4.148 Sometimes loopholes in anti-avoidance provisions offer comparatively simple solutions to tax problems. These loopholes are frequently plugged as soon as the tax authorities become aware of their potential for abuse, and most anti-avoidance provisions become progressively more comprehensive as taxpayers grow more ingenious.

4.149 Offshore counters to anti-avoidance provisions are structures whereby the taxpayer's affairs are arranged in such a way that, as far as possible, they do not fall within the taxing net.

4.150 Preparation of the Database

4.150 Though most offshore tax plans are conceived by taxpayers, it may also happen that the game is played by governments themselves.

4.151 An example of this is the legislative repartee between the United Kingdom and the Cayman Islands.

Example

The UK Income Tax Act 1952, s 412 (as it then was) was designed to prevent the practice of transferring stocks and shares and other assets by UK residents to foreign companies and trusts in such a way that the UK transferor would be able to enjoy the income yielded by the assets while only being subject to UK tax on the amount of income remitted to that country. One of the requirements of this anti-avoidance provision was that an individual should have 'rights' to the income in question.

It was clearly with s 412 and analogous provisions in other countries in sight that the Cayman Islands Trust Law 1967 laid down that:

'where any right or remedy in respect of a Caymanian exempted trust would vest in one or more of the beneficiaries under any such trust, the right or remedy in question would instead vest in and be exercisable by the Registrar of Trusts; and

no beneficiary would enjoy in relation to the trust fund or its income any right or remedy at law or in equity.'

Offshore tax planners were immediately enthusiastic and assiduous in exploiting the divesting techniques offered by such exempted trusts.

To counter the Caymanian counter–anti-avoidance measures, the UK Finance Act 1969, s 33, amended s 412 in such a way that it was no longer a requirement that an individual should have 'rights' to enjoy the income in question, and the Caymanian divesting provision thus lost much of its relevance for offshore planning arrangements of UK residents.

4.152 Many systems contain anti-avoidance provisions that hit at dividend stripping and bondwashing arrangements.

4.153 Dividend stripping is a device whereby a favourably placed person from the tax point of view purchases shares prior to a declaration of a large dividend and thereafter resells the shares to the original purchaser at a lower price.

4.154 Bondwashing is a device similar to dividend stripping whereby a high-rate taxpayer owning securities in respect of which interest is due shortly thereafter agrees to sell such securities to a low-rate or exempt taxpayer with the right to repurchase the securities after the accrual of the interest.

4.155 In the case of a gift by a corporation or trust, the anti-avoidance provision may be directed at the individual at whose instance the gift is made.

4.156   A tax court often penetrates the memorandum and articles of association or the by-laws of a company and looks to the real situation. This is particularly so for the purposes of determining the residence of a corporation.

Example

Three wholly owned subsidiaries of a UK company were companies regis-tered in Kenya. The meetings of the directors of these subsidiaries, in whom the powers of management were vested by the subsidiary companies' arti-cles of association, could not validly be held in the United Kingdom.

Initially, the management of the Kenyan subsidiaries was carried on in Kenya. Subsequently, the control and management of the Kenyan subsidiaries was taken over by the parent company, and de facto control of the Kenyan sub-sidiaries was exercised by the directors of the parent company in London (though this was contrary to the articles of association of the Kenyan sub-sidiaries). The local directors of the Kenyan subsidiaries stood aside and did not exercise their powers of management.

A UK subsidiary of the parent company sought to deduct, in a computation of its profits for income tax purposes (under the law as it then was), payments made to the Kenyan subsidiaries as being subvention payments to associ-ated companies. A company could not be an 'associated company' unless it was resident in the United Kingdom.

The House of Lords held that the place where the central management and control of a company was situated in fact determined the place of residence of the company, even though their being situated there was irregular and con-trary to the constitution of the company.

Accordingly, the Kenyan subsidiaries were considered to be resident in the United Kingdom, and the subvention payments were deductible in computing the profits of the UK subsidiary.

4.157   Where a corporation is merely a conduit or a dummy that does not carry on sub-stantial activity, courts frequently refuse to treat it as having legal personality for tax purposes.

Example

A Swedish prize-fighter, Ingemar Johannson, incorporated a Swiss corpora-tion of which he was the sole employee and source of revenue. He entered into an agreement with this corporation, under which he was entitled to receive 70% of the company's gross income plus a pension fund.

He thereafter fought in the United States for the heavyweight boxing cham-pionship of the world and was assessed by the US tax authorities on the income earned in the United States from his boxing and certain related activities.

He claimed tax exemption under the Switzerland–United States Tax Treaty on the grounds that he was a Swiss resident.

The US Tax Court, however, held that the taxpayer was not a resident of Switzerland for the purposes of the treaty and that the Swiss corporation had no legitimate business purpose but was a device used by the taxpayer as a controlled depository and conduit by which he attempted to divert temporarily his personal income, earned in the United States, so as to escape US tax. The taxpayer was held liable for the taxes assessed against him.

4.158   In most tax systems, there are transfer pricing provisions giving the tax authorities the power to reallocate profits and losses where the parties are related and/or the transactions in question are not at arm's length or for a legitimate business purpose.

Example

Corporation A and Corporation B had at least one common shareholder. A granted interest-free loans to B and also bought goods from B at an inflated price.

Under the French General Tax Code, taxpayers are allowed to deduct expenses only when incurred with a view of furthering their own business interests.

The French tax administration reallocated the profits of both corporations, on the grounds that, despite the fact that they had a common shareholder, they were in fact two distinct legal entities and therefore the expenses incurred by A in making the loans and purchasing the goods were not in furtherance of their own business interests. Therefore A's income was increased by the amount of the charges incurred to grant the advantages to B.

Example

The taxpayer, a Belgian corporation, allowed overdrafts on current accounts to two subsidiaries in Panama. No interest was payable on the overdrafts. The tax authorities considered that the non-payment of interest amounted to 'advantages granted to related enterprises' and added a fictitious interest charge to the profits of the Belgian corporation for the purpose of computing tax.

The court agreed with the view of the tax authorities and held that the subsidiaries, which were separate legal entities, had benefited from interest-free loans and that the advantages so obtained were to be added to the profits of the Belgian corporation. Because of the distinct legal personalities of the taxpayer and its subsidiaries, no double taxation relief could be sought for the alleged double taxation of the fictitious interest added to the profits and dividends actually received.

4.159   In many tax systems, the main anti-avoidance provisions relating to arm's-length transactions refer specifically to international situations. Tax havens are often used for the purpose of transfer pricing or re-invoicing.

4.160   In the first place, a manufacturing company located in a high tax jurisdiction could effect sales to a related company in a tax haven jurisdiction at cost or at prices involving a very small profit margin; the tax haven company could then in turn sell the goods to one or more related marketing companies in high tax jurisdictions at high prices, which would produce a low profit in the hands of the latter company or companies. A variation of this technique would involve selling to unrelated marketing companies at arm's-length prices, the primary object of the exercise still being achieved since the manufacturing company would have avoided taxation on the real profits that would otherwise have accrued to it.

4.161   Secondly, raw materials or goods or components manufactured at a very low cost abroad could be purchased by a tax haven company and then sold to a related company in a high tax jurisdiction at high prices, which would give the latter company a substantially lower profit than if purchases had been effected directly.

4.162   Often transfer pricing takes place by companies merely passing invoices without the subject matter of the sale actually being transferred to or by the intermediary company.

4.163   Most developed tax systems have anti-avoidance provisions aimed directly at counteracting the tax-saving effects of transfer pricing (see Chapter 7).

ENFORCEMENT OF FOREIGN REVENUE JUDGMENTS

4.164   As a traditional rule, the courts of most countries did not entertain a claim by a foreign government for its taxes or recognise or enforce a foreign revenue law judgment. This rule did not necessarily mean that courts would countenance transactions that are knowingly designed to violate the revenue laws (such as fraudulent tax evasion schemes) of a foreign and friendly State. For example, in *Re Emery's Investment Trusts, Emery v Emery* [1959] Ch 410, [1959] 1 All ER 577, an English court refused to recognise a transaction carried out in contravention of a US revenue law. (While the meaning of the term *revenue law* may vary from one legal system to another, it generally includes income taxes, capital gains taxes, capital taxes, succession and estate duties, customs duties, stamp duties, and profit levies.)

Example

A company that was registered in the United Kingdom but carried on business in India sold its undertaking to the Indian government for a sum of money that was immediately remitted to the United Kingdom. After the company had gone into voluntary liquidation, the Indian commissioner of income tax claimed payment of a large sum of income tax in respect of the capital gain derived from the sale of business.

The House of Lords followed the generally accepted rule that no action lies in the United Kingdom for the enforcement of a foreign revenue law. It made no difference that the country in question was a Commonwealth country.

4.165   A narrowing of the traditional rule of non-enforcement of foreign revenue judgments is currently accompanying the international regulation of offshore activities.

EXCHANGE OF INFORMATION

Treaty Provisions for Formal Exchanges of Information

4.166   The principal formal exchange of information mechanism is the tax treaty. Most tax treaties contain an article providing for the exchange of information between the competent authorities. Frequently, too, provision is made for the Contracting States to render to each other administrative and legal assistance in connection with the assessment and collection of taxes.

Example

Under the Austrian Federal Fiscal Code, the Austrian tax authorities are entitled to request that information that is relevant for the imposition of taxes be disclosed. Every person is obliged to pass on such information, even if his own tax liability is not affected thereby.

The Law on Fiscal Penalties provides that no such information should be disclosed by the authorities unless the disclosure:

● supports the enforcement of tax proceedings;

● is required in the public interest or by law; and

● does not violate any legitimate interest of the taxpayer.

The Austria–France Tax Treaty authorises the full exchange of all information between the two countries relevant to the proper collection of taxes, unless such information, because of its nature, cannot be obtained under the laws of the country; would disclose a manufacturing process, industrial, commercial, or professional secret; or would endanger law and order.

The French tax authorities sought information regarding an Austrian corporation from the Austrian tax authorities. The corporation refused to give the information to the Austrian authorities on the grounds that disclosing it to the French authorities would constitute a violation of its rights under the Law on Fiscal Penalties.

The Austrian Administrative Court ruled that the corporation had to provide the information and that the Austrian authorities could furnish it to the French authorities without violating the corporation's rights. The court held that, as the Law on Fiscal Penalties prohibits only the unauthorised disclosure of information, and since the Austria–France Tax Treaty authorised the Austrian authorities to disclose the information to the French authorities, such disclosure would not constitute a violation of the Law on Fiscal Penalties.

It follows that the much-vaunted Austrian banking secrecy regulations would take second place to an exchange of information provision in a tax treaty.

4.167   Although the exact wording of the exchange of information article may differ from treaty to treaty, the article will typically be based on Article 26 of the 1963 OECD Model Convention as amended in 1992 and 1997.

4.168   In general terms, Article 26 comprises three elements:

● the information that can be exchanged;

● the secrecy of such information; and

● the steps a treaty country must take to comply with its obligations.

4.169   It is likely that information relating to offshore operations and transactions may be the subject of exchanges of information between high tax jurisdictions.

The Information that can be Exchanged

4.170   The first principle is that the only information that can be exchanged is that which is necessary to secure the correct application of the treaty, and the domestic laws of the treaty countries concerning taxes covered by the treaty.

4.171   This means, for example, that a request for information concerning sales tax need not be complied with as it is not covered by the treaty. Conversely, in the context of granting an exemption from withholding tax pursuant to the royalty article, a request by one country to the other treaty country as to whether the recipient of the royalty is in fact a resident of that country and the beneficial owner of the royalties is within the scope of the provisions. Furthermore, in the context of applying domestic transfer pricing provisions, a request by one treaty country to the other concerning the price a company in the other country paid for goods bought from a company in the requesting country would be within the scope of information that can be exchanged.

Secrecy of Information

4.172   The second principle is that any information that is exchanged must be kept secret, taking into account a country's domestic laws on this point. Therefore information communicated under the provisions of a treaty must be treated as secret in the receiving country in the same manner as information obtained under the domestic laws of that country. Similarly and logically, sanctions for the violation of such secrecy are to be governed by the administrative and penal laws of that country. If the information appears to be of value to the receiving country for purposes outside the scope of the treaty, the country may not use the information for such other purposes. Rather, it must resort to means specially designed for those purposes (e.g., in the case of a non-fiscal crime, to a treaty concerning judicial assistance).

Compliance Steps

4.173   Subject to the above qualifications, however, the competent authority of State A is obliged to collect the information that State B requires 'in the same way as if its [State A's] own taxation was involved'. As pointed out in *United States v AL Burbank & Co* 525 F 2d 9, the avowed intent of a tax treaty is to prevent fiscal evasion. It follows 'that if [State A] is investigating the tax liability of [a taxpayer] who is potentially delinquent to it, the [State B] may utilise the same investigative techniques that it would employ if that [taxpayer] were under investigation [in State B] for a domestic tax liability. To do otherwise would be to negate the very purpose of the Treaty'.

4.174   Another principle is that a country is not bound to go beyond its own internal laws and administrative practice in putting information at the disposal of the other treaty country. Subject to this rule, the OECD commentary illustrates the different ways in which information is likely to be exchanged (i.e., when there is a specific request by a tax authority for information or, if none, then either automatically or spontaneously). Insofar as the latter is concerned, no doubt many advisors among the readers will have come across the situation in which they have been negotiating with their own tax authorities and, as part of the 'give and take', the tax authorities have innocuously referred to the possibility of spontaneously exchanging information with their counterparts in other relevant countries.

Informal Exchanges of Information

4.175   Though no statistics are available, it may be assumed that informal exchanges of information between the administrations are on the increase.

4.176 Preparation of the Database

4.176   Also the leverage of the major powers on the small tax haven jurisdictions may be considerable. In the case of any confrontation between the United States and a Caribbean haven, the United States would be able to destroy the latter's offshore economy overnight by a refusal to process dollar transfers.

4.177   The recent UK case of *R v Allcock* (unreported) has shed much light on informal exchange of information and has caused much concern among certain taxpayers.

Mutual Assistance Directive of the European Union (77/799)

4.178   The directive provides that information may be exchanged to enable a correct assessment of taxes on income and capital. In comparison, Article 26 refers to the correct application of a treaty and the domestic laws of a treaty country concerning taxes covered by a treaty. The scope of the directive would appear in certain instances to be wider.

Extended Scope of Exchanges of Information

4.179   See Chapters 11 and 12.

CHOICE OF LAW

4.180   Choice of law is a conflict of laws (private international law) issue, and the rules are part of the domestic law of each country. Choice of law problems frequently arise with respect to entities that are known to, or do not enjoy legal personality in, a foreign system. The determination of the applicable law for the purpose of characterising such entities varies from one legal system to another. For example, an unusual type of entity, such as the Liechtenstein *Anstalt*, might be treated as a company in one country and as a trust in another country.

Example

A Netherlands partnership carried out the demolition of one of the pavilions at the Brussels World Fair.

The Belgian tax authorities thereafter sought to assess one of the partners individually for the full amount of income tax due on the total income derived from the partnership in Belgium.

Under Belgian law, a partnership is a legal entity, and its distributed profits are subject to tax as if they were dividends distributed by a company.

Under Netherlands law, on the other hand, a partnership is not a legal entity, and the members are taxed individually on their share of the partnership profits.

The Brussels Court of Appeal held that the Netherlands partnership could not be considered a legal entity for the purposes of Belgian taxation and, consequently, that each of the partners should have been assessed individually for his respective share of the profits.

The effect of this decision is that, under Belgian law, the tax status of foreign entities is to be determined according to the law of the country of their establishment.

4.181 The precise meaning of terms may vary from one context to another, and it may be necessary for a court to decide which law is applicable for the purpose of characterising one or more of the elements of the taxable event.

Example

The taxpayer, a UK company, had a minority shareholding in an Italian corporation that issued a substantial amount of shares at a premium. From these issues, a certain sum was entered in the Italian corporation's share premium reserve, and a distribution was thereafter effected out of this reserve.

Under Italian law, 5% of the net annual profits of a corporation must be placed in a legal reserve until such reserve reaches 20% of the share capital. Sums received in consideration for the issue of shares at a premium cannot be distributed until the legal reserve reaches 20% of the share capital, the excess being normally transferred to the share premium reserve, which may then be distributed by resolution at a general meeting.

The receipt by the taxpayer of its corresponding share of the dividend, the source of which was the share premium reserve, was assessed to UK tax as an 'income receipt' (i.e., as a dividend).

Under Italian law, such a distribution is a return of capital, and thus no Italian withholding tax was due on the distribution.

The issue between the UK company and the Board of Inland Revenue was whether the distribution was a return of capital (Italian law) or an income distribution (English law). It was thus necessary for the court to decide which was the applicable law for the purpose of characterisation.

The High Court of Justice (Chancery Division) held that Italian law decided the characterisation issue, and the amount distributed from the Italian corporation's share premium reserve was a return of capital.

FOREIGN CURRENCY GAINS AND LOSSES IN OFFSHORE TRANSACTIONS

4.182 Frequently, offshore transactions are conducted in whole or in part in foreign currency. Problems therefore arise involving changes in exchange rates. Are the gains and losses attributable to changes in rates to be treated as capital or as income? At what date are such gains or losses to be taken into account for tax purposes? What exchange rates should be used for translating foreign branch profits into the domestic currency?

4.183 The tax laws of different countries must therefore be applied against the background of foreign exchange markets.

4.184 The translation of foreign currency into the domestic currency may follow various methods (e.g., the profit and loss method, the net worth method, or the transaction method).

4.185 In the case of an intermittent user of foreign currency, the transaction method deals with each foreign transaction separately and computes the domestic income at the appropriate exchange rate for that transaction.

Example

The taxpayer, a US corporation, and its wholly-owned foreign subsidiary entered into business transactions with each other. The transactions were recorded on the taxpayer's books as accounts payable or accounts receivable, depending on the nature of the transactions. In assessing its taxable income, the taxpayer adjusted the accounts to give effect to fluctuations in the foreign exchange prevailing at the end of the taxable year; for the year in question, this adjustment resulted in an overall loss. The question was whether a foreign exchange loss is allowable under s 164 of the Internal Revenue Code.

Section 165(a) provides that any loss sustained during the taxable year should be allowed as a deduction if it is not compensated for by insurance or other method. Section 1.165–1(b) of the Income Tax Regulations provides, however, that, if a loss is to be allowed as a deduction under s 165, it must be the result of closed and completed transactions, fixed by identifiable events.

In the present case, it was held that, as the accounts payable to and receivable from the subsidiary remained on the taxpayer's books for subsequent payment and collection, the loss suffered by the taxpayer was not the result of completed transactions. The taxpayer was not, therefore, entitled to a deduction under s 165.

PROCEDURAL AND RELATED MATTERS

4.186   Matters of procedure are regulated by the law and practice of the taxing State.

4.187   Local law governs all matters relating to the collection of taxes (in particular, the form and time of presentation of tax returns).

4.188   Provision is often made for the withholding of tax at source and the prepayment of provisional payment of tax. Such withholding may have an effect on offshore tax planning.

4.189   The duty to make payment may in certain cases fall not on the taxpayer himself but on the company paying him dividends, the debtor paying him interest, the employer paying his salary, the trustee or the administrator handling a trust, or an estate of which he is beneficiary.

4.190   Objection to assessments and administrative and judicial appeals also follow the procedure laid down in the country concerned.

STRATEGIC CHECKLISTS

TYPES OF TAXES ENCOUNTERED IN FOREIGN COUNTRIES

- Individual and corporate income taxes.

- Capital gains taxes.

- Special taxes on dividends, interest, and royalties.

- Withholding taxes on salaries, dividends, interest, royalties, etc.

- Capital taxes (e.g., property, patrimony, net worth taxes, etc.) imposed on individuals and companies.

- Payroll taxes.

- Company duties.

- Business taxes.

- Business license and other trade taxes.

- Stamp duties.

- Transfer duties.

- Registration duties.

- Customs duties and other import and export duties.

- Sales and use taxes.

- Turnover taxes on value added.

- Capital transfer taxes.

- Estate and inheritance taxes.

- Gift taxes.

TAX CONNECTING FACTORS (NEXUS)

- Residence.

- Ordinary residence.

- Domicile.

- Citizenship (nationality).

- Management and control.

- Beneficial ownership.

- Place of incorporation.

- Location of the registered office.

- Place of management and control.

- Place of creation of a trust, the applicable law, residence of the trustees or beneficiaries.

- Centre of economic interests.

- Permanent establishment.

- Effectively connected income.

- Real or deemed source.

COMMON DOMAINS FOR TAX AND NON-TAX INCENTIVES

- Exports.

- Export-related services.

- Technical services including construction, distribution, design, and engineering services.

- Consultancy, management, supervisory, or advisory services relating to any technical matter or to any trade or business.

- Fabrication of machinery and equipment and procurement of materials, components, and equipment.

- Data processing, programming, computer software development, telecommunications, and other computer services.

- Professional services including accounting, legal, medical, and architectural services.

- Educational and training services.

- Technopark.

- Freeport.

- Warehousing and servicing incentives.

- Operational headquarters.

- Management companies.

- Administrative offices.

- The exporting of manufactured goods by a special trading house where the goods are sold by wholesale.

- Repair and maintenance of aircraft and aircraft engines or components.

- Film production.

- Meat processing.

- Remanufacture and repair of computer equipment of subassemblies.

- Defined processes or series of defined processes applied to material acquired in bulk.

- The alteration of articles without changing their character.

- Refurbishment of articles.

- Financial and banking facilities.

- Reductions in corporation tax.

- Foreign currency transactions normally provided by banks.

- International financial activities including global money management, insurance, and related activities and dealings in foreign currencies, options, and similar financial assets.

- Services or facilities for processing, control, accounting, communication, clearing, settlement, or information storage in relation to financial activities.

- The development and supply of computer software for use in the provision of the services or facilities referred to above or for reprocessing and analysing information on financial activities.

- Dealing in commodity futures or commodity options on behalf of unconnected persons who are not themselves involved in commodity trading.

- Trading operations similar or ancillary to any of the above and that contribute to the use of the area as an international financial services centre.

- Life assurance business with policyholders and annuitants abroad and management of the investments of unit trusts.

- Cash grants and other incentives for industrial development.

- Machinery and plant.

- Training of local staff.

- Regional development grants.

- Export sales relief.

- Design and planning services carried out on behalf of non-resident persons in connection with a variety of projects such as chemical, civil, electrical, or mechanical engineering works, carried on abroad.

- Shipping.

- Gold transactions.

- Financial futures transactions.

- Export credit guarantees.

- Pioneer industries.

- Investment allowances.

- Expansion of Established Enterprises.

- Free zones and free ports.

- Venture capital incentives.

- Research and development.

- Patents.

- Urban renewal incentives.

- Joint ventures.

- Film production.

- Capital assistance scheme.

- Operational headquarters.

- Tax shelters.

INCENTIVE DUE DILIGENCE

- Are the reasons that influenced the government to introduce the concessions (usually the underdevelopment of the area) likely to constitute a disadvantage with regard to the proposed investment?

- If the absence of good communications was the principal reason why the region became backward in the first place, has there been an improvement in the situation, or, if not, would this constitute a disadvantage if the incentive were to be used for the purposes of the project under consideration?

- Is there any likelihood of nationalisation or other political or economic risk attendant upon investment in the incentive area?

- Are there any exchange controls, and, if so, are there any guarantees with regard to the repatriation of profits and investment capital under the incentive scheme?

- Are there any special difficulties affecting foreign controlled enterprises?

- Are there any strings attached to the grant of the concession that may subsequently prove to be a disadvantage?

EXCHANGES OF INFORMATION

- Treaty provisions for formal exchanges of information.

- Lack of secrecy of information.

- Compliance steps.

- Informal exchanges of information.

- Mutual assistance.

- Extended scope of exchanges of information.

- Anti-tax avoidance co-operation.

- Anti-tax evasion co-operation.

- Anti-money laundering co-operation.

STRATEGIC ISSUES, OPPORTUNITIES AND CAVEATS

INTERNATIONAL DOUBLE TAXATION

- International double (or multiple) taxation occurs when the tax authorities of two or more countries concurrently impose taxes having the same bases and incidence, in such a way that a person incurs a heavier tax burden than if he were subject to one tax jurisdiction only.

- Tax treaties, which are intended to avoid such incidence of double taxation, may inadvertently create opportunities where global tax burdens may be reduced in a manner unintended by the treaty partners.

ECONOMIC DOUBLE TAXATION

- Economic double taxation can cause the same profits to be subject to tax at more than one level.

- *Caveat:* The most important example is the case in which corporate profits are first taxed in the hands of a company and then, upon distribution, are once again taxed in the hands of shareholders.

TAX TREATY CONDUIT HAVENS

- Offshore jurisdictions also include countries that allow foreign corporations to borrow their tax treaties.

- *Caveat:* Many countries will simply disregard the treaty when the ultimate beneficiary is not a bona fide resident of a treaty country.

REDUCTION IN WITHHOLDING RATES

- Treaties normally also reduce the amount of tax a country is allowed to withhold on income being repatriated to another treaty partner country.

- *Caveat:* For this type of structure to prove efficient, the costs of the structure plus the aggregate tax burden suffered in the third country by the conduit company should not exceed the high tax country's tax burden.

BUSINESS PROFITS AND THE PERMANENT ESTABLISHMENT RULE

- Tax treaties lay down which country will be entitled to tax business profits that an enterprise of one country makes in the other country.

- In most cases, this is by reference to whether there is a permanent establishment in such other State.

- In situations in which companies wish to take advantage of the certainty and better provisions of double tax treaties, the possibility of structuring business transactions with or in a high tax country through a third country with which it has a tax treaty should be investigated in the diagnostic.

- It may be possible for an offshore company located in a country that does not have tax treaties to take advantage of the vast network of tax treaties of other countries (such as Switzerland and the Netherlands) provided that the structure attracts very little corporate tax in the home country. The company could take advantage of all the treaty advantages since it would be a bona fide Swiss or Netherlands company, notwithstanding the fact that there is little Swiss or Netherlands tax to be paid and the operations would take place in the IOFC.

- The advantage of using a company incorporated in a country with tax treaties, such as a Swiss or a Netherlands company, is the possibility offered by the treaties to reduce worldwide taxes on business profits, while structuring the operations so as to attract very little tax in the country of incorporation. This is as a function of the provisions of tax treaties that make it possible to avoid tax on business profits in a foreign treaty country even where the Swiss or the Netherlands company has profits in the other country. The critical point is to avoid the creation of an office or a branch (permanent establishment) in the country concerned.

- *Caveat*: Always read carefully the definition of 'permanent establishment' as it may vary from treaty to treaty.

TREATY SHOPPING

- 'Treaty shopping' is the attempt by third parties to benefit artificially from tax treaties intended to benefit the bona fide residents of the two treaty countries.

- Both the OECD Model Income Tax Convention on Income and Capital (Article 10) and the US Treasury Model Income Tax Treaty (Article 16) contain provisions limiting the use of treaty shopping.

- *Caveat*: Additionally, a provision is being considered for the OECD's Model Tax Convention to deny entities operating under harmful tax regimes access to certain or all of the Convention's benefits.

MEASURES TO COMBAT HARMFUL TAX PRACTICES

- Countries that allow their treaties to be used for treaty shopping are directly in the firing line of the OECD attack on harmful tax practices.

- *Caveat*: Always refer to the international measures to combat harmful tax practices.

5.1 Tax Treaties and the Question of Double Taxation

TAX TREATY CONDUIT HAVENS

5.1 Offshore jurisdictions also include countries that allow foreign corporations to borrow their tax treaties.

5.2 Tax treaties are primarily contracts between countries regarding the countries' respective rights to tax the income or capital attributable to corporations or individuals when that income or capital may attract tax in both countries if there were no tax treaty.

Tax Treaties and Withholding Rates

5.3 Treaties normally also reduce the amount of tax a country is allowed to withhold on income being repatriated to another treaty partner country. For example, a subsidiary transferring a $1,000,000 dividend to its parent in a foreign country may have to withhold say 30%, or $300,000, of tax from the dividend. That tax is paid over to the revenue. If the country of the parent has a tax treaty with the subsidiary's country, then the withholding may be only 5%, or $50,000 (an up-front saving of $250,000). Where the withholding tax is not a final payment, the difference may eventually cancel out, but when one takes account of the time value of money, it may still be a material factor.

5.4 If the parent's country does not have a treaty with the subsidiary's country, then the parent may establish an intermediary company in a country that does have tax treaties with both the subsidiary's country and that of the parent. The withholding tax burden using the intermediary structure may be reduced to $100,000, not as good as $50,000 but better than $300,000. If the intermediary company costs $10,000 yearly, then the parent realises a $190,000 savings.

5.5 In the above example, the intermediary jurisdiction gains the extra 5% of tax plus the $10,000 cost of the company. The intermediary jurisdiction that allows a foreign corporation to borrow its treaties, as per the above example, is thus also an offshore jurisdiction.

Offshore Trading Companies and Tax Treaties

5.6 In situations in which offshore companies wish to take advantage of the certainty and better provisions of double tax treaties, the possibility of structuring trade with a high tax country through a third country with which it has a tax treaty should be investigated in the diagnostic. For this type of structure to prove efficient, the costs of the structure plus the aggregate tax burden suffered in the third country by the conduit company should not exceed the high tax country's tax burden.

5.7 The objective of an offshore trading company is to trade within the offshore jurisdiction so that the diverted profits only occur in the offshore jurisdiction. Alternatively, one may want profits to be taxed in a foreign jurisdiction if the effective tax rate there is lower than that at home. Also, if there are accumulated losses abroad with the time limit of carry forward provisions, it may be possible to place the trading profits in that country to absorb the losses.

5.8 An alternative to establishing a conduit company in a country that has both a tax treaty with the high tax country and a nominal rate of tax lower than the high tax country's rate may be to choose a conduit country where, although the nominal rate of tax is in excess of the high tax country, the effective rate of tax can be reduced by extraction and diversion techniques to below that of the high tax country.

5.9 For this technique to be efficient, the rates of withholding tax on the diverted and extracted tax profits will need to be low. For example, both the Netherlands and Switzerland offer this possibility because of their domestic tax provisions concerning the exemption of foreign branch income.

5.10 When a company considers having commercial presence in a foreign country, but wants to avoid unnecessary foreign tax exposure, it may be allowed to set up either a non-taxable representative office that does not undertake activities that constitute a permanent establishment or a headquarters office. On the other hand, it may establish a service subsidiary and take care that its tax base is kept as low as possible by paying the subsidiary or headquarters office on a cost-plus basis. The cost represents the expenses of maintaining the subsidiary, while the plus represents a percentage of the costs. That percentage will be the taxable base.

5.11 To avoid foreign tax on 'trading' operations, you should first analyse exactly those tax laws of the foreign country that subject trading transactions to tax. It is a general principle of most countries' tax laws that a tax treaty cannot impose a liability where none existed before. If one is not trading in a country according to its domestic law, then a tax treaty provision cannot impose tax.

5.12 Domestic tax laws imposing tax on trading transactions (source-based connecting factor) can vary significantly in detail. In general, they approximate to the definition of a permanent establishment found in the OECD Model Tax Treaty and bilateral tax treaties. In many cases, domestic tax laws imposing tax are wider than the permanent establishment provisions in tax treaties. In this situation, it is very advantageous to be able to rely on permanent establishment provisions in a tax treaty to limit the local source rule.

5.13 The local government will aim to increase a country's tax base, especially concerning international income. If a country finds that foreign companies make many sales to its residents, it may decide to base local taxability on the place where the sales are performed. Similarly, where services are frequently rendered locally or production is carried out locally, the location of those rendering the services, or the place where production is carried out, may determine whether a trade is being conducted within the country.

5.14 Even with clear domestic legislation concerning source rules, it is difficult to analyse precisely when a company is trading 'within', as opposed to trading 'with', another country. Much has to do with the revenue's attitude on a given day. Some civil law jurisdictions do not adhere to previous court decisions. Countries that do have adherence to previous decisions allow the revenue to overrule those decisions with newer notices. Whether a trade is being conducted in a particular country will be a question of fact, thus at the revenue's discretion. Therefore, it is usually better to rely on the terms of double tax treaties, which are often tighter than domestic law.

Treaty Shopping

5.15 Treaty shopping is the use of a tax treaty by a person resident in a country that is not a party to the treaty.

5.16 Both the OECD Model Income Tax Convention on Income and Capital (Article 10) and the US Treasury Model Income Tax Treaty (Article 16) contain provisions limiting the use of treaty shopping.

5.17 Tax Treaties and the Question of Double Taxation

5.17 Additionally, a provision is being considered for the OECD's Model Tax Convention to deny entities operating under harmful tax regimes access to certain or all of the Convention's benefits (see Chapter 11).

DOMESTIC DOUBLE TAXATION

5.18 Domestic double taxation occurs where one tax jurisdiction imposes tax twice in respect of the same taxable event and person.

5.19 In most countries, there are equitable provisions to prevent or alleviate such cases. For example, many taxing statutes define *gross income* as 'the total amount received by or accruing to . . . a taxpayer'. If income were to accrue in one year and suffer tax, but payment were only to be effected in the following year, the taxpayer would not in most cases be subjected to tax twice on the same amount.

5.20 The term *domestic double taxation* does not normally refer to cases where jurisdictions that are at different levels in a country's constitutional structure (e.g., federal, provincial, and municipal authorities) enjoy concurrent or overlapping taxing powers. Nor does it refer to cases in which an item is subject to two different types of taxes (e.g., income tax and value-added tax (VAT)).

5.21 Where the divisions of federal States enjoy parallel taxing powers, incidents of double taxation may well occur that are technically closer to international than domestic double taxation.

INTERNATIONAL DOUBLE TAXATION

Definition

5.22 International double (or multiple) taxation occurs when the tax authorities of two or more countries concurrently impose taxes having the same bases and incidence, in such a way that a person incurs a heavier tax burden than if he were subject to one tax jurisdiction only.

5.23 *Note:* The term *double taxation* is normally used as referring only to cases of international double or multiple taxation.

Causes of Double Taxation

5.24 The cause of double taxation lies in the fact that the various possible connecting factors between taxing jurisdictions on the one hand and taxpayers on the other are not mutually exclusive.

5.25 These connecting factors may relate to a quality of the taxpayer (e.g., citizenship, residence, domicile, place of incorporation, etc.), of the income (real or deemed source usually constituting the relevant link), or of the property (usually situs, but sometimes source, being material).

5.26 One of the most common cases of overlapping tax jurisdictions is the combination of residence taxation and source taxation. This would occur, for example, where a taxpayer who is resident in a country that taxes on worldwide income derives income from a foreign country that imposes tax on the basis of source. If there were no tax treaty between the two countries nor any unilateral measures in either country to protect him from having to pay tax twice in respect of the same income, he would be subject to a double tax burden, which could conceivably even exceed the total amount of the income in question.

5.27 However, it may also occur that more than one jurisdiction regards an individual or a company as resident for tax purposes.

5.28 For example, it would be possible for a taxpayer to be considered resident in Ireland by the Irish tax authorities on the grounds of his renting an apartment in Dublin that he visits from time to time and considered resident in Belgium by the Belgium tax authorities on the grounds of his centre of economic activities being located there, even though he was ordinarily resident in some third country for all practical purposes.

5.29 He could thus be taxed as a resident in all three countries. If he were also a citizen of a country that taxed on the basis of citizenship (e.g., the United States), he could also be subject to tax in that country, even though he never set foot there from one year to another and did not derive any income from sources in that country or own any property situated there.

5.30 Similarly, a company may be considered resident in Sweden by the Swedish tax authorities on the grounds of its being incorporated there and considered resident in the United Kingdom by the UK tax authorities on the grounds of its central management and control being located in the United Kingdom.

5.31 Just as criteria of residence are not mutually exclusive, so too with criteria of source. Even in the case of countries where the notion of 'source' receives substantially similar treatment and judicial decisions of the one country are persuasive authority in the other (e.g., Singapore and South Africa), the respective tax authorities and even the appeal courts may well come to different conclusions in a given case.

5.32 For example, this situation could easily arise with regard to the source of income deriving from a contract concluded in one country but providing for performance in the other (or partially in one and partially in the other).

Relief Provisions

5.33 Many tax systems provide a measure of unilateral tax relief in cases of double taxation. These provisions present considerable differences in form as well as scope.

5.34 Furthermore, a number of countries have entered into bilateral double taxation treaties. Treaty provisions regulating bilateral tax situations often differ in material respects from the unilateral provisions normally applied by the contracting parties. Unfortunately, however, treaty networks are very far from being comprehensive, and the existing treaties show a considerable lack of harmony with regard to their provisions.

5.35 Unilateral and treaty provisions normally provide for one of the following types of relief:

- *tax exemption*, whereby all or part of the taxpayer's foreign source income or foreign situs property is excluded from the taxable base (it is frequently a condition that such income or property should have been subjected to tax in the foreign country);

- *tax credit*, whereby foreign tax, paid or payable, is credited against the taxpayer's domestic tax bill;

- *tax reduction*, whereby foreign tax, paid or payable, is deductible from the domestic taxable base; and

- *reduction in the rate of tax*, whereby foreign income or assets are taxed domestically at a lower rate.

5.36 Different national systems and tax treaties offer a wide variety of formulas for the computation of the amount of relief available.

5.37 For a foreign tax to be eligible for a tax credit or other relief treatment, it is normally required that it should be of the same generic type as the tax normally imposed by the domestic country (e.g., the United States).

5.38 Similarly, reciprocity may be required for tax relief to be granted.

Example

Under the German Net Worth Tax Law, individuals with a domicile or customary place of abode in Germany and legal entities with their place of management in Germany are subject to German net worth tax on their worldwide property. German net worth tax liability does not, however, apply to certain fixed assets situated in a foreign State with which Germany has not concluded a double taxation treaty.

The Ministry of Finance of Bavaria issued a ruling stating that this relief would be granted but only on the basis of reciprocity. The relief does not apply where the foreign country does not impose a net worth tax, as no double taxation occurs. Therefore immovable property and fixed assets belonging to a permanent establishment in those countries, owned by taxpayers who are German residents, would normally be subject to net worth tax in Germany.

The ruling has been approved by the Federal Ministry of Finance.

5.39 In certain cases, there are territorial extensions of a tax treaty, for example, UK or Netherlands tax treaties that have been extended to its colonies and former colonies.

5.40 The presence of a tax sparing clause in a tax treaty may also be relevant. A tax sparing clause allows residents of a capital exporting country a credit against domestic tax for profits or gains in a developing country in respect of which foreign taxes benefit from an exemption or reduction.

5.41 Care should be taken to note whether a tax treaty is applicable to the taxes of the divisions of federal States as well as to the federal taxes.

Example

The deceased died resident in Texas. Among the assets of his estate were mortgages on real estate located in Canada.

These mortgages were omitted from the State inheritance tax return by the attorney for the estate on the grounds that Texas did not have jurisdiction, under Texas inheritance tax law, over mortgage on real property situated in Canada.

The argument of the attorney for the estate was based on the situs rules contained in the United States–Canada Estate Tax Treaty (Treaty of 17 February 1961), Article II, and his case was that the treaty precluded the State of Texas from including in the estate the indebtedness and mortgage securing the payment thereof.

However, Article I provides that the tax referred to in the treaty with regard to the United States is the 'federal estate tax'.

In the opinion of the Attorney General, the legal ownership of intangibles by a person in Texas gives such intangibles a business situs in Texas and makes them 'property without the jurisdiction of this State'.

It therefore followed that the value of an indebtedness secured by mortgages against real estate located in Canada and held by a resident deceased of Texas was to be included in the estate when computing the amount of inheritance taxes due.

5.42 Special unilateral provisions may govern the application of the provisions of a tax treaty in the domestic law, e.g. the Swiss measures for the prevention of the improper use of tax treaties.

Tax Treaties

5.43 Tax treaties (or double taxation agreements — DTAs) are international agreements or conventions concluded with the object of eliminating double taxation by the Contracting States. International double taxation may be loosely defined as the imposition of comparable taxes in two (or more) States on the same taxpayer in respect of the same subject matter and for identical or overlapping periods. The most harmful effects of double taxation are on the exchange of goods and services and on the movement of capital and persons.

5.44 Tax treaties frequently contain provisions reducing the rates of withholding taxes. It is the existence of these provisions in a wide network of treaties that enables countries such as Switzerland (notwithstanding its measures against the abuse of tax treaties) and the Netherlands to be used as conduits.

5.45 Normally tax treaties are not concluded between high tax jurisdictions and tax havens. In line with this approach, certain tax treaties specifically exclude from their scope entities that benefit from specially favoured tax treatment (e.g., the exclusion of Luxembourg holding companies from the provisions of tax treaties concluded with Luxembourg).

5.46 When relying on a tax treaty, care should always be taken to insure that it is applicable. It is important to check whether there are any amending treaties or protocols and whether there are any interpretative rulings or official statements concerning the scope of the treaty.

Withholding Taxes

5.47 Withholding taxes are taxes that are part of a country's income tax system and that the payer of a dividend, royalty, interest payment, etc., must withhold from each such payment and must pay over to his own tax authorities. In the case of non-residents, a withholding tax may be a final tax or it may only constitute the advance payment of tax.

5.48   Tax Treaties and the Question of Double Taxation

5.48   The rates of withholding taxes are frequently reduced by tax treaties. Indeed, certain jurisdictions qualify as tax havens by virtue of the exemptions or the reductions in the rates of withholding taxes to which their residents become entitled in accordance with the provisions of one or more (sometimes a network of) tax treaties. The use of such tax treaties may thus permit the creation of a conduit whereby profits are transferred from one country to another via a third country, thus suffering the smallest possible total tax burden.

5.49   The cost of withholding taxes may not be immediately apparent. However, it may be costly to ignore the time value of money. Receiving a dollar tomorrow is not the same as receiving a dollar today. The dollar received today will enable you to pay back debt (thereby avoiding interest charges) or to make an investment (thereby producing a stream of income). The difference in value between a dollar tomorrow and a dollar today is precisely the return earned by today's dollar between now and tomorrow.

5.50   In technical terms, this is known as the 'discount rate'. It is a key element in planning that has to be determined by each decision maker on the basis of an assumption about what an extra dollar today would earn in the future. The lowest reasonable discount rate is the current interest rate on risk-free securities such as treasury bonds. Most businesses, however, can expect to earn more than this (otherwise they would quite rapidly go out of business), and their discount rate should take account of the average return on their available investment opportunities. Typical rates of return for large corporations are in the region of 6% to 10% per annum. Small businesses may have much higher rates, especially when they have investment opportunities they regard as attractive for which they are unable to borrow money or raise equity.

5.51   Using a discount rate of x%, the value of a future dollar declines exponentially at a rate of x% per year. A few simple calculations show how dramatic the effect of discounting can be on deferred income. After ten years, a sum of money has lost 44% of its value at 6% p.a., 54% at 8%, 61% at 10%, and 75% at 15%.

5.52   Tax effects are typically over shorter periods, but they can still be significant. Overlapping connecting factors can lead to economically disadvantageous multiple taxation. Taxing authorities are subject to conflicting pressures: they have a vested interest in maintaining and stimulating taxable income, but they are also playing a 'tax game' with other taxing authorities, the rules of which they do not control.

5.53   It follows that, while most tax systems contain unilateral mechanisms mitigating double taxation, these are generally both inadequate and uncoordinated — they may even aggravate the problem they purport to solve. Bilateral (or multilateral) treaties can be viewed as imposing stricter and more effective rules on the tax game that countries play.

OECD Model Convention

5.54   In July 1958, the Council of the Organisation for European Economic Cooperation (OEEC) instructed its Fiscal Committee to submit a draft convention for the avoidance of double taxation with respect to taxes on income and capital, together with concrete proposals for the implementation of such a convention. In September 1961, the Organisation for Economic Cooperation and Development (OECD) was established to succeed the OEEC, and the mandate of the Fiscal Committee was confirmed.

5.55   On 6 July 1963, the Fiscal Committee submitted a draft convention in a report to the council. In April 1972, and at subsequent sessions, the Committee on Fiscal Affairs (the former Fiscal Committee) adopted revised texts of various articles. The revised wording has been incorporated in the text of that 1963 draft convention.

5.56   In 1977, an updated model convention was published in a report to the Council of the OECD by the Committee on Fiscal Affairs. The 1977 model convention incorporated, with further amendments, the revisions mentioned above.

5.57   In 1992, a similar updating process culminated in the release of the present OECD Model Convention.

5.58   The members of the OECD are Australia, Austria, Belgium, Canada, Denmark, Finland, France, Germany, Greece, Iceland, Ireland, Italy, Japan, Luxembourg, the Netherlands, New Zealand, Norway, Portugal, Spain, Sweden, Switzerland, Turkey, the United Kingdom, and the United States.

5.59   The draft conventions have exercised a considerable influence on most tax treaties, including treaties between countries that are not members of the OECD, as well as on the US Treasury Model.

US Treasury Model Income Tax Treaty

5.60   The US Treasury uses its own model income tax treaty as a starting point in its negotiation of tax treaties with other countries.

5.61   On 20 September 1996, the US Treasury Department released a revised Model Income Tax Convention ('the 1996 Model') to serve as its basic negotiating document. The 1996 Model draws on the previous 1981 Model, which was withdrawn on 17 July 1992, as well as on the current OECD Model Tax Convention on Income and Capital, existing US tax treaties, recent negotiating experience, current US tax laws and policies, and the comments of interested parties.

5.62   The 1996 Model is designed to provide a basic explanation of US treaty policy and to facilitate negotiations by identifying differences between income tax policies in the two countries. But it does not represent an ideal US income tax treaty. Particular income tax treaties may depart from the 1996 Model on account of a variety of factors related to the tax laws and policies of the other country, their interaction with the treaty and US tax law, treaty precedents, and the relative economic positions of the treaty parties.

ECONOMIC DOUBLE TAXATION

Definition

5.63   The term *economic double taxation* is used to indicate, by analogy, the case in which the same profits are subject to tax at more than one level.

5.64   The most important example is the case in which corporate profits are first taxed in the hands of a company and then, upon distribution, are once again taxed in the hands of shareholders.

5.65   Economic double taxation is not strictly speaking a case of double taxation since the taxpayers are different legal personae and the quality of the income changes upon distribution. However, the practical effect is often similar to that of double taxation *stricto sensu*.

Relief Provisions

5.66   In many countries, inter-corporate distributions are not taxed or they receive favourable treatment in the hands of a recipient company.

5.67 Tax Treaties and the Question of Double Taxation

5.67 For example, the imputation system is a system under which at least part of the tax paid by a company on its profits is credited against the tax liability of shareholders in receipt of distributions paid by the company out of those profits. Imputation reduces or eliminates the double taxation of distributed profits that arises under the classical system of taxation. Under an imputation system, all taxable corporate profits, whether or not distributed, are subject to corporate income tax at statutory rates. When the corporate profits are distributed, an individual or corporate shareholder is entitled to a full or partial credit for the underlying corporation tax that can be attributed to the dividends.

5.68 The problem usually arises in cases in which the shareholder is an individual. At the one end of the spectrum are the countries that make no provision at all for the avoidance or mitigation of this form of double taxation.

5.69 At the other end are those countries that aim to eliminate entirely the double taxation burden. In between are the systems offering different types of relief, the most common being:

● systems in which the distributed and undistributed profits are taxed at different rates;

● systems in which the shareholder pays tax on his dividend income at a lower rate than he would normally pay on the slice of income in question; and

● systems in which all corporate profits are taxed at substantially the same rate but a refund is granted at the shareholder level.

5.70 The problem of economic double taxation is most acute in the case of distributions from a company in one country to shareholders in another country where the relief measures do not dovetail in a satisfactory manner.

5.71 This would, for example, be the case of a company that is resident and makes profits in a country that taxes companies at a uniform rate in respect of both distributed and undistributed profits (even though it granted a tax credit to resident shareholders in respect of tax suffered at the corporate level) but the shareholders are resident in a country that taxes distributed corporate profits at a reduced rate and does not in consequence grant any tax credit at the shareholder level. If there were no unilateral or treaty provision for relief, the profits of a company would be taxed in full in its hands, and its distributions would be taxed once more in full in the hands of the shareholders. Certain treaty provisions deal specifically with this problem, for example, the extension of the French *avoir fiscal* to certain foreign shareholders.

THE PERMANENT ESTABLISHMENT CONCEPT

Taxation of Business Profits

Basis for Taxation

5.72 The treaties lay down which State will be entitled to tax business profits that an enterprise of one State makes in the other State. In most cases, this is by reference to whether there is a permanent establishment in such other State.

5.73 The relevant provision relating to business profits is contained in Article 7(1) of the OECD Model Convention, which states:

'The profits of an enterprise of a Contracting State shall be taxable only in that State unless the enterprise carries on business in the other Contracting State through a permanent establishment situated therein. If the enterprise carries on business as aforesaid, the profits of the enterprise may be taxed in the other State but only so much of them as is attributable to that permanent establishment.'

5.74   The rest of Article 7 explains how the profits of a permanent establishment are determined.

5.75   The main use of the concept of a permanent establishment is thus to determine the right of a contracting state to tax the profits of an enterprise of the other Contracting State.

5.76   It follows that the key to preventing exposure to tax on business profits arising in foreign treaty countries lies in avoiding the creation of a permanent establishment in such countries.

5.77   In effect, provided that a Swiss or a Netherlands company is not considered to have a permanent establishment in a treaty country, it will not be liable to tax on its business profits there. It could carry on business transactions and operations freely without tax implications.

Definition of a Permanent Establishment

5.78   The definition of *permanent establishment* may be found in Article 5 of the OECD Model Convention.

5.79   The term *permanent establishment* means a fixed place of business in which the business of the enterprise is wholly or partly conducted. Permanent establishment includes especially:

- a place of management;

- a branch;

- a factory;

- a workshop;

- a mine, quarry, or other place of extraction of natural resources; and

- a building site or construction or assembly project that exists for more than 12 months.

5.80   Under the OECD Model Tax Treaty, a permanent establishment will generally be deemed to exist if a 'fixed place of business' is maintained in a country.

5.81   An alternative feature of the OECD Model Tax Treaty is the negative definition of permanent establishment.

5.82   The term *permanent establishment* does not include the following:

- the use of facilities solely for the purpose of storage, display, or delivery of goods or merchandise belonging to the enterprise;

- the maintenance of a stock of goods or merchandise belonging to the enterprise solely for the purpose of storage, display, or delivery;

- the maintenance of a stock of goods or merchandise belonging to the enterprise solely for the purpose of processing by another enterprise; or

- the maintenance of a fixed place of business solely for the purpose of purchasing goods or merchandise, or for collecting information, for the enterprise.

5.83 The OECD Model Tax Treaty further provides that the term *permanent establishment* shall not be deemed to include 'the maintenance of a fixed place of business solely for the purpose of advertising, for the supply and collection of information, for scientific research or for similar activities which have a preparatory or auxiliary character'. The official OECD commentary on the model treaty explains that these words extend the exemption by stating that all activities that fall within the spirit of the provisions above should be exempted, thus avoiding an exhaustive list of exceptions. These negative provisions may be useful in enlarging the scope of activities that companies will be permitted to carry out without incurring local tax liability.

5.84 To avoid mingling income from a business activity that of itself would not constitute a permanent establishment with income from other business activities that fall within the permanent establishment definition, it may be useful to form a subsidiary. The subsidiary could undertake the activities that would constitute a permanent establishment. The non-taxable activities pursuant to the permanent establishment article could then be conducted by the non-resident parent and these activities would be insulated from the subsidiary's taxable activities.

The Case of an Independent Agent

5.85 Under all treaties, where an enterprise carries on business dealings through a broker, general commission agent, or any other agent of an independent status in a treaty country, it cannot be taxed by such country in respect of those dealings if the agent is acting in the ordinary course of his business.

5.86 A person will not constitute a permanent establishment of the enterprise on whose behalf he acts provided that:

- he is independent of the enterprise both legally and economically; and

- he acts in the ordinary course of his business when acting on behalf of the enterprise.

5.87 Whether a person is independent of the enterprise represented depends on the extent of the obligations that such person has vis-à-vis the enterprise. Where the person's commercial activities for the enterprise are subject to detailed instructions or to comprehensive control by it, such person cannot be regarded as independent of the enterprise. Another important criterion will be whether the entrepreneurial risk has to be borne by the person or by the enterprise the person represents. A subsidiary is not to be considered dependent on its parent company solely because of the parent's ownership of the share capital. Persons cannot be said to act in the ordinary course of their own business if, in place of the enterprise, such persons perform activities that, economically, belong to the enterprise rather than to that of their own business operations.

5.88 It is generally accepted that the existence of a subsidiary company does not, of itself, constitute that subsidiary company a permanent establishment of its parent company. This follows from the principle that, for the purpose of taxation, such a subsidiary company constitutes an independent legal entity. Even the fact that the trade or business carried on by the subsidiary company is managed by the parent company does not constitute the subsidiary company a permanent establishment of the parent company.

5.89 However, a subsidiary company will constitute a permanent establishment for its parent company under the same conditions stipulated above, as are valid for any other unrelated company (i.e., if it cannot be regarded as an independent agent and if it has and habitually exercises an authority to conclude contracts in the name of the company).

5.90 The same rules would apply to activities that one subsidiary carries on for any other subsidiary of the same company.

The Case of a Dependent Agent

5.91 Persons whose activities may create a permanent establishment for the enterprise are so-called dependent agents (i.e., persons, whether employees or not, who are not independent agents). Persons having the authority to conclude contracts can lead to permanent establishment for the enterprise maintaining them. In such a case, the person has sufficient authority to bind the enterprise's participation in the business activity in the country in question. The use of the term *permanent establishment* in this context presupposes, of course, that the person makes use of this authority repeatedly and not merely in isolated cases.

5.92 The authority to conclude contracts must cover contracts relating to operations that constitute the business proper of the enterprise. Moreover, the authority has to be habitually exercised in the other country; whether or not this is the case should be determined on the basis of the commercial realities of the situation. A person who is authorised to negotiate all elements and details of a contract in a way binding on the enterprise can be said to exercise this authority in the other country, even if the contract is signed by another person in the country in which the enterprise is situated.

5.93 It should be borne in mind, however, that a dependent agent simply provides an alternative test of whether an enterprise has a permanent establishment in a State. If it can be shown that the enterprise has a permanent establishment within the meaning of another provision of the permanent establishment article of the relevant tax treaty, it will not be necessary to show that the person in charge is a dependent agent pursuant to the treaty.

5.94 It follows that either an independent or a dependent agent of the operating company could carry on international operations without attracting tax in the countries of operation, provided that care is taken not to create a permanent establishment in such countries.

Tax Treaty Protection

5.95 It would be possible for an offshore company located in a country that does not have tax treaties to take advantage of the vast network of tax treaties of other countries (such as Switzerland and the Netherlands) in the following way: a Swiss or Netherlands company is set up with the profit centre in a foreign permanent establishment. This would attract very little corporate tax in either Switzerland or the Netherlands. The company could take advantage of all the treaty advantages since it would be a bona fide Swiss or Netherlands company, notwithstanding the fact that there is little Swiss or Netherlands tax to be paid and the operations would take place in the IOFC.

5.96 The advantage of using a company incorporated in a country with tax treaties, such as a Swiss or a Netherlands company, is the possibility offered by the treaties to reduce worldwide taxes on business profits. This is as a function of the provisions of tax treaties that make it possible to avoid tax on business profits in a foreign treaty country even where the Swiss or the Netherlands company has profits in the other country. The critical point is to avoid the creation of an office or a branch (permanent establishment) in the country concerned.

5.97 Tax Treaties and the Question of Double Taxation

5.97 *Caveat*, however, the international measures to combat harmful tax practices (see Chapter 11).

Switzerland as an Illustration of the Planning Process

5.98 Switzerland is normally a high tax jurisdiction like any other. However, there are certain provisions that can make a Swiss company a suitable vehicle for the proposed structure.

5.99 Swiss taxes are frequently settled by negotiation with the tax administration before setting up. The effective tax may be substantially less than the amounts provided in Federal Direct Taxes Law or in the various cantonal tax codes.

5.100 At the federal level, corporation income tax is imposed on annual worldwide income, after deduction of business expenses.

5.101 However, an important exception should be noted: this is a proportional reduction of tax due on business income earned through a permanent establishment outside Switzerland (e.g. an offshore company). The income is included in the company's taxable income; a reduction of the resulting tax is then granted in the proportion that the qualifying foreign net income bears to the company's total net income.

Domiciliary Company

5.102 Important tax savings can also be achieved by operating through a domiciliary company. The distinguishing feature of the domiciliary company is that it conducts no business activities in Switzerland. There is no limitation as to its business activities worldwide, but it will generally have little more than a registered office (a nameplate) in Switzerland.

5.103 A domiciliary company is granted no federal tax relief. Its income will primarily be from foreign sources. Most cantons give extremely favourable cantonal tax treatment to domiciliary companies. It should be noted that the exact tax status of each domiciliary company is normally a matter of negotiation with the cantonal authorities.

Permanent Establishment Exemption

5.104 A valuable planning possibility lies in the rule contained in paragraph 1 of Article 55 of the Direct Taxes Law (IDN). According to this rule, all income from foreign sources is included in Swiss taxable income with the exception of income attributable to a foreign permanent establishment and income from foreign immovable property. The tax rate, however, is determined on the basis of total income.

5.105 The following points should be noted:

- The Swiss tax authorities may require the company to prove the existence of a foreign permanent establishment, which in the absence of an applicable treaty is defined in domestic law as being a 'fixed place of business where a qualitatively or quantitatively essential part (partie notable) of the business of the enterprise is carried on' (Article 6 IDN).

- The income attributable to the foreign permanent establishment is included with the other income of the company (if any) for the purposes of calculating the rate of tax applicable, but a reduction of the resulting tax is then granted in the proportion that the qualified foreign income bears to the net income.

- The Swiss tax authorities have issued comprehensive guidelines for the purpose of determining the amount of income that may be allocated to the foreign permanent establishment, but they are generally willing to accept the book profit or loss of the permanent establishment as a basis of the computation.

- At first sight it might seem that a Swiss company whose entire income was attributable to its overseas establishment would avoid payment of any federal or cantonal direct income taxes on its profits, but this will not necessarily be the case because of a rule that allows the tax authorities to attribute a percentage of net profits (between 10% and 30%) to the Swiss head office on the basis that the Swiss head office exercises some managerial function that contributes to the profit-generating activity of the overseas branch. The amount so attributed is known as the 'preciput' and is taxable in Switzerland at the rate determined under the above rules.

- Most cantonal tax codes follow the principles of federal taxation outlined above, but the question may be an academic one if the Swiss company is incorporated in a canton that grants a full exemption for cantonal tax purposes for all overseas income (the domiciliary company exemption).

5.106 It follows that if the Swiss company were to attach all or some of its business profits to a foreign permanent establishment (say in an offshore jurisdiction), this could lead to substantial savings at the federal level.

Effective Swiss Tax Burden

5.107 It follows that there would be little corporate tax in either country provided that the income is earned by qualifying a foreign branch.

5.108 However, there are withholding taxes in Switzerland. For this reason, it would be advisable to reduce the taxable base in Switzerland by making deductible payments to other group companies. Such deductions should be in respect of items and in amounts acceptable to the revenue in the country concerned. This could leave a relatively small tax base.

Caveat

5.109 Given the proposed international measures to curb harmful preferential tax regimes, it is questionable for how long this type of tax structure will be practical (see Chapter 11).

STRATEGIC CHECKLISTS

POSITIVE DEFINITION OF 'PERMANENT ESTABLISHMENT'

The term *permanent establishment* means a fixed place of business in which the business of the enterprise is wholly or partly conducted. Permanent establishment includes especially:

- a place of management;

- a branch;

- a factory;

- a workshop;

- a mine, quarry, or other place of extraction of natural resources; and

- a building site or construction or assembly project that exists for more than twelve months.

NEGATIVE DEFINITION OF 'PERMANENT ESTABLISHMENT'

The term *permanent establishment* does not include the following:

- the use of facilities solely for the purpose of storage, display, or delivery of goods or merchandise belonging to the enterprise;

- the maintenance of a stock of goods or merchandise belonging to the enterprise solely for the purpose of storage, display, or delivery;

- the maintenance of a stock of goods or merchandise belonging to the enterprise solely for the purpose of processing by another enterprise; or

- the maintenance of a fixed place of business solely for the purpose of purchasing goods or merchandise, or for collecting information, for the enterprise.

THE INDEPENDENT AGENT AS A PERMANENT ESTABLISHMENT

A person will not constitute a permanent establishment of the enterprise on whose behalf he acts provided that:

- he is a broker, general commission agent, or any other agent of an independent status in a treaty country;

- he is independent of the enterprise both legally and economically; and

- he acts in the ordinary course of his business when acting on behalf of the foreign enterprise.

THE DEPENDENT AGENT AS A PERMANENT ESTABLISHMENT

Persons whose activities may create a permanent establishment for the enterprise are:

- persons, whether employees or not, who are not independent agents;

- persons having the authority to conclude contracts for the enterprise maintaining them, making use of this authority repeatedly and not merely in isolated cases;

- persons fulfilling orders from a stock of goods.

STRATEGIC ISSUES, OPPORTUNITIES AND CAVEATS

ANALYSIS OF THE EXISTING DATABASE

- Start with an analysis of the different items of tax involved in the project.

- Compute as accurately as possible the likely total tax burden, in the light of the likely gross return of the project and the non-tax expenditure involved.

- *Caveat.* Where there is relatively little money in issue, care should be taken not to incur expenditure in connection with the preparation and implementation of an offshore tax plan that is out of proportion to the possible savings.

STRUCTURAL STRATEGIES

- The structural design of an international arrangement may involve one or more of the following:

  - the selection of the form of an international transaction, operation, or relationship;

  - the selection of a foreign investment country or new country of residence;

  - the introduction of one or more additional offshore jurisdictions, and joint ventures.

- Where all countries are determined in advance, the planning process may not go beyond the stage of selecting the most favourable form of a transaction, operation, or relationship from the tax point of view.

- Dividends, interest, royalty receipts, and capital gains frequently receive quite different tax treatment at the domestic level and at the treaty level.

- *Caveat.* Do not let the tax tail wag the business dog.

SELECTION OF A FOREIGN INVESTMENT COUNTRY OR NEW COUNTRY OF RESIDENCE

- Where there is a choice between two or more possible opportunities in different countries, examine comparative tax burdens in the light of the business considerations.

- In deciding between offers to take up shares in companies in different countries, the following considerations should, *inter alia*, be taken into account:

  - the rate of tax imposed on corporate profits in the investment countries under examination;

  - whether dividend distributions are subject to withholding taxes, and if so, at what rates; and

  - whether any tax credits or deductions are available in the country of residence of the shareholder in respect of taxes paid in the investment countries under examination.

- *Caveat*: In the case of sales and manufacture, take into account sales taxes and turnover tax on value added (VAT).

INTRODUCTION OF ADDITIONAL OFFSHORE JURISDICTIONS

- Examine the tax savings that may be achieved by the careful selection of the form of an international transaction, operation, or relationship.

- Then examine the possible benefits and pitfalls through the introduction of one or more IOFCs.

JOINT VENTURES

- Begin with a close analysis of:

  - what each of the parties is required to contribute to the venture;

  - how the profits (if any) are to be divided between them;

  - how losses are to be borne;

  - how the venture can be unscrambled.

- *Caveat*: Joint ventures go wrong far more often than is expected by the parties when they are first put together.

MOVING PROFITS FROM AN OFFSHORE ENTERPRISE

- Management charges, technical assistance fees, or royalties.

- Payment for supplies or raw materials bought from, or product supplied to, other members of the group.

- Interest payments.

- Business profits.

EVALUATING THE OFFSHORE TAX PLAN

Compute all variables as accurately as possible for each of the following hypotheses:

- if the plan is not adopted;

- if the plan is adopted and succeeds; and

- if the plan is adopted and fails.

SEEK LOCAL ADVICE

- It is impossible for an outsider to be aware of all the pitfalls that lie in foreign legal, tax, and exchange control systems or of the special difficulties that may be encountered in operating in a foreign country.

- *Caveat.* Entities that are valid in one system of law may not be recognised by the courts of other countries.

SUBSTANCE *VERSUS* FORM

- The rule that the substance of a transaction, rather than its mere form, controls tax liability is one of very wide application.

- This rule can affect the amount of taxable income arising from practically any type of transaction.

- *Caveat.* This rule is also applied frequently to settle questions of who is taxable on certain taxable events.

APPLICABILITY OF TAX TREATIES

- When relying on a tax treaty, care should always be taken to insure that it is in force and that it applies to the parties.

- *Caveat.* It is always important to check whether there are any amending treaties or protocols and whether there are any interpretative rulings or official statements concerning the scope of the treaty.

SUBSTANTIAL RISKS OR DISADVANTAGES

- Where there are substantial risks or disadvantages attendant upon the proposed tax plan and these cannot be easily avoided by the modification of the plan, it may be necessary to abandon the project altogether or to adopt the next most satisfactory of the alternative possible solutions considered.

- *Caveat.* Any such alternative solution must in turn be examined for weaknesses and pitfalls.

6.1 Designing the Offshore Tax Plan

UPDATING THE TAX PLAN

- Even after a plan has been adopted and the project has been embarked upon, always watch for any changes in the law or practice of any of the countries involved, which may have an effect on any of the elements of the arrangement.

- *Caveat:* Also watch for any changes in the facts as time goes on.

ANALYSIS OF THE EXISTING DATABASE

6.1   The first stage in the tax planning process is to analyse the different items of tax involved in the project and to compute as accurately as possible the likely total tax burden.

6.2   It is only by considering each of the tax elements both separately and as a whole that it is possible to formulate an efficient tax plan.

6.3   It may also be necessary to take into account the likely gross return of the project and the non-tax expenditure involved.

6.4   *Caveat:* Where there is relatively little money in issue, care should be taken not to incur expenditure in connection with the preparation and implementation of an offshore tax plan that is out of proportion to the possible savings.

DESIGN OF ONE OR MORE POSSIBLE TAX PLANS

6.5   The design of an international arrangement may involve one or more of the following:

- the selection of the form of an international transaction, operation, or relationship;

- the selection of a foreign investment country or new country of residence;

- the introduction of one or more additional offshore jurisdictions, and joint ventures.

Selection of the Form of an International Transaction, Operation or Relationship

6.6   In most international tax situations, at least two of the countries are determined in advance. In such cases, the planning process may not go beyond the stage of selecting the most favourable form of a transaction, operation, or relationship from the tax point of view.

6.7   Dividends, interest, royalty receipts, and capital gains frequently receive quite different tax treatment at the domestic level and at the treaty level. It would thus be necessary to take such differences into account in deciding, for example, whether an investment should take the form of a dividend-producing share participation or an interest-producing loan. In the case of industrial and intellectual property, it might be necessary to decide whether the rights should be sold or be exploited by way of royalty arrangement.

Example

The taxpayer was a UK company that manufactured electric power tools and had evolved various secret production methods and drawings. It was faced with difficulties in connection with its established export trade to India, owing to the Indian government's policy of encouraging local factories.

The taxpayer decided to set up a new company in India to manufacture its tools and to provide the new Indian company with the necessary know-how and goodwill, the consideration therefore being in the form of shares in the Indian company.

A comprehensive arrangement was thus entered into between the two companies in accordance with which the taxpayer was to provide the Indian company for a fixed number of years with all present and future drawings, designs, schedules, and technical knowledge and data necessary for the establishment of a factory for the production of certain portable electric tools, and to assign to the Indian company all the Indian patents and the benefit of all future inventions relating to the selected tools. The taxpayer undertook further not to provide the above facilities to any other party in India nor to compete with the Indian company in India.

The United Kingdom had not yet introduced the tax on long-term capital gains, and it would obviously make a substantial difference to the taxpayer if such consideration were treated as being on capital and not on revenue account. Though the United Kingdom no longer exempts capital gains from tax, this distinction is still crucial in a number of jurisdictions that were inspired by the earlier UK legislation and that continue only to tax gains that are revenue gains or that tax capital gains at a substantially lower rate.

If the transaction represented a method of trading by which the taxpayer acquired the shares as part of the gains of its trade, this income gain would have been taxable. If, however, the transaction represented the receipt of shares in return for the transfer to the Indian company of capital assets, the consideration would not have been subject to tax.

On appeal from the decision of the special commissioners, the court held that the effect of the arrangement was that the taxpayer transferred to the Indian company two capital assets comprising:

- a fund of confidential material in relation to its manufacture of tools; and

- its pre-existing goodwill with exclusive rights precluding it from competing with the Indian company in India.

The consideration received by it was therefore on capital account and not on revenue account, and was therefore not subject to tax.

6.8 In certain countries, dividends arising from substantial share participations (as variously determined) receive favoured tax treatment in the hands of corporate shareholders, for example, the Netherlands substantial participation (*deelneming*) exemption, where, subject to certain conditions, a 5% or greater shareholding can produce a 0% corporate tax base. This can prove an important consideration in fixing the amount of a proposed shareholding.

6.9 Designing the Offshore Tax Plan

6.9 The tax consequences of operating through a subsidiary, through a branch office, or through an independent agent are frequently quite different. These differences may be crucial in determining the manner in which a proposed operation is to be conducted.

6.10 In many countries, the notion of 'permanent establishment' is employed for the purpose of determining the tax liability of non-resident taxpayers carrying on business within such countries. In addition, this notion is frequently used in tax treaties as a basis for the apportionment of taxable income (particularly in the case of industrial and commercial profits).

6.11 This feature in tax treaties can be particularly valuable where there is no tax at home since it can be used to turn a high tax jurisdiction into a virtual tax haven for the purposes of a particular transaction or operation.

Example

An Australian company that carried on theatrical enterprises in Australia and abroad planned to promote a number of touring shows in New Zealand.

Under the former Australia–New Zealand Tax Treaty, Article III(1), an Australian enterprise was not subject to tax in respect of its New Zealand source industrial or commercial profits, unless these are derived through a permanent establishment in New Zealand, in which case they may be subject to New Zealand tax.

Article II(1) defines 'industrial or commercial profits' as including 'the profits of an industrial or commercial enterprise but does not include . . . income arising from, or in relation to, contracts or obligations to provide the services of public entertainers, such as stage, motion picture, television or radio artistes, musicians, and athletes'.

Article II(1)(m) defines a 'permanent establishment' as 'a branch agency or other place of business', including a 'management'. It is further provided in Article III(1)(m)(ix) that 'where an enterprise of one of the Contracting States . . . has an agent in that other State other than an agent who has, and habitually exercises, a general authority to negotiate and conclude contracts on behalf of that enterprise . . . that enterprise shall not, merely by reason thereof, be deemed to have a permanent establishment in that other Contracting State'.

The Australian company did not wish to pay New Zealand tax on the commercial profits that would accrue to it as a result of its New Zealand promotions. It therefore aimed to carry on its theatrical enterprises in such a way that it would not be considered to be engaged in trade or business in New Zealand through a permanent establishment in that country.

With regard to the definition of the term *permanent establishment* in the treaty, the Australian company organised its operations in New Zealand in the following way:

- its executives and artistes were brought from overseas on tour;
- the Australian company did not open an office in New Zealand;

- the duties of the touring manager who accompanied each show did not go beyond the performance of the small tasks arising out of the day-to-day production of a show on tour;

- in respect of any major decision, the touring manager was required to refer to his principals in Australia who were alone empowered to make such decisions; and

- the only New Zealand staff engaged was casual staff in the nature of ushers, stage staff, etc.

There was thus no branch, agency, other place of business, management, or agent who had, and habitually exercised, a general authority to negotiate and conclude contracts on behalf of the Australian company in New Zealand. It was therefore held that the Australian company was not engaged in trade or business in New Zealand through a permanent establishment, and consequently it was not subject to New Zealand tax in respect of the commercial profits derived by it from its theatrical productions.

Example

The taxpayer was a Canadian company that entered into a number of transactions in the United States. For the purposes of its negotiation, it used certain US resident individuals in a representative capacity.

The taxpayer did not wish to have a permanent establishment in the United States since it is provided under the former United States–Canada Tax Treaty, Article I, that:

'An enterprise of one of the Contracting States is not subject to taxation by the other Contracting State in respect of its industrial and commercial profits except in respect of such profits allocable in accordance with the Articles of this Convention to its permanent establishment in the latter State.'

The Protocol to the treaty, paragraph 3, defines the term *permanent establishment* as including branches, fixed places of business, etc., and goes on to state:

'When an enterprise of one of the Contracting States carries on business in the other Contracting State through an employee or agent established there, who has general authority to contract for his employer or principal, or has a stock of merchandise from which he regularly fills orders which he receives, such enterprise shall be deemed to have a permanent establishment in the latter State.

The fact that an enterprise of one of the Contracting States has business dealings in the other Contracting State through a commission agent, broker or other independent agent or maintains therein an office used solely for the purchase of merchandise shall not be held to mean that such enterprise has a permanent establishment in the latter State.'

Therefore to insure that it did not have such a permanent establishment, the taxpayer arranged its affairs in such a way that it did not have, in the United States:

6.12 Designing the Offshore Tax Plan

- a real office;
- officers, directors, or employees;
- a bank account or books of account;
- a telephone listing;
- its name on any door or office; or
- an employee or agent with general authority to contract for it.

The taxpayer was thus not subject to US tax on its industrial and commercial profits.

6.12 The method to be employed in analysing and comparing the relative tax burdens and other expenditure attendant upon the project

- if no tax minimisation plan is adopted; and
- if a tax minimisation plan is adopted, and it (a) succeeds or (b) fails,

is considered below.

Selection of a Foreign Investment Country or New Country of Residence

6.13 Offshore tax planning may be occasioned by a choice between two or more possible investments in different countries. In examining their relative merits, it is important to regard not only business considerations but also comparative tax burdens.

6.14 For example, in deciding between offers to take up shares in companies in different countries, the following considerations should, *inter alia*, be taken into account:

- the rate of tax imposed on corporate profits in the investment countries under examination;
- whether dividend distributions are subject to withholding taxes, and if so, at what rates; and
- whether any tax credits or deductions are available in the country of residence of the shareholder in respect of taxes paid in the investment countries under examination.

6.15 In the case of the setting up of a manufacturing subsidiary, the tax and non-tax factors to be compared will be somewhat more complex. It may also be necessary to take into account the turnover tax on value added.

6.16 Value added tax (VAT) is a general tax on consumption expenditure incurred in respect of:

- deliveries of goods;
- the rendering of services; and
- imports.

6.17 In the case of deliveries and services, the total tax is collected in fractional payments from the various persons involved, on the basis of the value added by them. In the case of imports, the tax is imposed on the value of the goods imported.

6.18   There is usually an exemption on exported goods and services or a refund of any VAT already paid on the exported goods or services.

6.19   The business effect of VAT is that export enterprises enjoy a distinct pricing advantage in both their own countries and foreign countries vis-à-vis enterprises located in countries that employ direct, rather than this form of indirect, taxation.

6.20   The following example illustrates this effect in a somewhat oversimplified way, deliberately ignoring the complex business considerations governing the fixing of prices.

Example

Assume that company A is located in country A, which has introduced VAT, while company B is located in country B, which has not introduced VAT and relies instead on direct taxation. Assume further that a product manufactured by each such company costs 70 units to manufacture. VAT imposed by country A on this project is at the rate of 10%.

Taking into account the domestic tax structure, company B sets the domestic retail price of its product at 110.

The domestic retail selling price of company A's product is similarly 110, i.e., a basic price of 100 plus the 10% VAT.

When company B exports its product to country A, the addition of the 10% VAT will produce a retail selling price of 121, i.e., 11 units more expensive than company A's product.

In country B, on the other hand, the position will be the reverse. Country A will take off the 10% VAT on exportation and the product will therefore be priced in country B at 100, while the product of company B will be priced there at 110, again allowing company A's product to be marketed at a lower price in country B than company B's product.

6.21   Individuals frequently emigrate for business, pleasure, and health reasons.

6.22   International and particularly offshore planning may thus be required by a proposed change in residence, domicile, or nationality.

6.23   In such cases, it is necessary to take into account the tax (including especially estate and inheritance taxes) and the exchange control implications of the change.

6.24   Switzerland is considered to be one of the most desirable countries by many emigrants. As a general policy, Switzerland rigidly controls the influx of new residents and admits only a limited number of applicants who (apart from the employees of international organisations and certain companies) are usually individuals who have retired for reasons of age or sickness. Those who are fortunate enough to obtain residence permits in Switzerland may, under certain conditions, benefit from favoured tax treatment at federal level. Similar tax treatment is also available in certain cantons to resident aliens not carrying on trade or business in the canton in question.

6.25   Frequently the preferred country of residence imposes a high rate of income tax, net worth tax, and estate duty on the worldwide income and property of residents.

6.26   In such cases, the emigrant may find it advisable to resort to an offshore set-up that could result in the divestment of certain assets prior to establishing residence in the new country.

6.27   Of considerable importance is the question of whether the connecting links with a former country of residence have been effectively severed from the tax point of view.

Example

The taxpayer was a Belgian citizen who had lived abroad for a long period of time. He had, however, maintained a home and a bank account in Belgium and had acquired some real property there.

The question at issue was whether the taxpayer maintained a *domicile* (the connotation of the French word *domicile* is closer to the English notion of dwelling place or home rather than to the English concept of domicile) or seat of fortune in Belgium and therefore was to be considered a Belgian resident taxpayer.

The Belgian Tax Code does not define *domicile*, but the courts take two factors into account, physical presence in Belgium and the intention to establish the main residence in Belgium on a permanent basis. A seat of fortune is considered to be the place where the fortune was administered, and not the place where the properties of the individual were situated.

The Supreme Court held that the taxpayer was not a Belgian resident. In reaching this decision, the Court took into account the fact that the taxpayer did not and had no intention of returning to his former home, which was occupied by his wife and children from whom he lived separately. It also noted that the real property was held to provide his child with income and that the Belgian bank account was used only to hold funds during his visits to Belgium.

Example

The taxpayer was resident in Germany and also had the centre of his vital interests there. He was a partner in a German limited partnership. He stayed in Austria for eight to ten days per month for the management of a permanent establishment there owned by the partnership, and he had a customary place of abode there. The taxpayer sought to deduct losses incurred by the Austrian permanent establishment from his personal tax liability in Austria.

The Austrian Administrative Court (*Verwaltungsgerichtshof*) ruled that a taxpayer can have only one customary place of abode and that since his residence and the centre of his vital interests were in Germany, that was where he was resident for tax purposes.

6.28   Tax liability in a previous country of residence or citizenship may cling for many years after a change (e.g., in the United States, Germany, or Denmark). This is especially to be weighted for in the use of a move to an offshore country.

Introduction of Additional Offshore Jurisdictions

6.29 In many cases, considerable tax savings may be effected not only by the careful selection of the form of an international transaction, operation, or relationship, but by the introduction of one or more IOFCs in addition to those countries that are already included in the database.

6.30 International tax planning may be merely a simple extension of national tax planning through the introduction of a foreign element, such as the creation of a trust or holding company in a tax haven or other country where low tax rates prevail.

Example

A US resident was the owner of certain oil and gas leases in the United States.

With a view to minimising the tax burden arising therefrom, he set up a Swiss company and transferred to it the major part of his interest in the leases in exchange for a 100% share participation in the Swiss company.

Under the Switzerland–United States Tax Treaty (Treaty of 24 May 1951), Article III(1)(a), a Swiss enterprise is not subject to tax in the United States in respect of its industrial and commercial profits unless it is engaged in trade or business in the United States through a permanent establishment situated therein.

Care was taken to insure that the Swiss company carried on substantial business activity and was managed as a going concern so that it would be recognised as a separate taxable entity under US tax law.

To this effect, it did all the necessary things to act like a viable company. It purchased and held title to working interests in oil and gas leaseholds; assumed and paid its proportionate share of the obligations under the operating agreement covering such leaseholds; executed division order for the disposition of production income; signed contracts to the management of its producing properties; collected income and deposited it in a bank account; paid expenses incurred in connection with its activities; and invested excess funds in securities.

The US Tax Court held that the Swiss company was a separate entity for US tax purposes and that its undistributed income was not subject to tax in the taxpayer's hands.

6.31 If there is already at least one foreign element in a project, the inclusion of an additional tax jurisdiction for the purposes of a tax minimisation arrangement may be both obvious and simple to achieve.

Example

An Italian engineering company was engaged to undertake certain works in Switzerland, principally in the canton of Valais.

6.32 Designing the Offshore Tax Plan

The Swiss Federal Constitution, Article 46(2), prohibits the double imposition of tax on income and net worth by the cantons. In the absence of further legislative provisions, the rule has been consistently applied by the Swiss courts to the effect that if an enterprise that is established in one canton derives income from sources in another canton through a permanent establishment located in the latter canton, such income is subject to tax only in the canton where the permanent establishment is situated.

The Swiss cantons constitute different tax jurisdictions and in this respect resemble different countries.

On an examination of the tax rates applying in the various Swiss cantons, it was observed that the canton of Zug would produce the lowest tax burden on the proposed operation, and for this reason it was decided to set up a permanent establishment in Zug with the function of directing the project.

A major tax saving could have been effected if the inter-cantonal rule had applied to a foreign company in the position of the taxpayer.

However, the federal court held that this rule does not apply where foreign countries are involved. Nevertheless, the allocation between cantons, with respect to both income and net worth taxation, did result in the reduction of the total Swiss tax burden.

6.32 In more complicated cases in which it is decided that it is appropriate to investigate the potential advantages of introducing one or more additional countries into the existing international database, a preliminary examination should be made of combinations of bilateral tax situations, with special regard to the following:

• any particularly favourable provisions contained in the tax treaties concluded with other countries by each of the countries already involved (it is frequently here that the key to the most favourable set-up is to be found); and

• the potential benefits of using a tax haven or some other country offering tax incentives or other special tax or non-tax benefits.

6.33 Thereafter, a number of different possible schemes should be improvised, using various combinations of countries, transactions, operations, and relationships. There is scope for considerable imagination and ingenuity. It will usually be found that at least a few different arrangements would be suitable for the purposes of a tax minimisation plan.

6.34 The number of possible parameters may in certain cases be extremely large. Each additional IOFC that it is proposed to include in the tax plan should be examined in the light of the existing database and all new tax and non-tax factors that are material to such inclusion.

6.35 In designing the most appropriate arrangement, it is above all important to consider the following:

• whether ownership of the various rights, securities, etc., should be vested in one or more companies, individuals, trusts, or a combination of these;

• what should be the relationship *inter se* of the various individuals and entities; and

• insofar as this is not already predetermined, where each such entity should be located, since the characteristics of IOFCs may differ considerably.

Preventing Local Taxable Presence

6.36   A common planning paradigm for international transactions in establishing a legal entity and transfer pricing arrangement for a foreign service provider structure, may be the desire to avoid having a taxable presence in the foreign country to the greatest extent possible. A common situation is set out in the following example.

Example

A United States corporation is a manufacturer of electrical generation equipment. The corporation's equipment has been selected for installation in a new project to be developed where the domestic entity will need to provide technical support for a significant project in a foreign country ('the local country'). In order to complete its contractual responsibilities, the US corporation will build and ship the electrical generation equipment for a conventional facility from its manufacturing facilities in the United States. In addition, the US corporation will need to provide on the ground in the local country the services of a large number of technical experts to supervise various aspects of the installation process.

The US corporation desires to minimise its taxable presence in the local country and to earn as much of the income as possible in the United States, its home country. Specifically, the US corporation seeks to avoid: (a) having a permanent establishment in the local country; (b) being subject to income taxation in the local country; (c) being subject to any withholding taxes on remittances of income from the local country; and (d) any ambiguity with respect to these issues.

The international tax executives of the US corporation have checked their sources of information about the local country and find that there is no reliable information concerning the current law and practice of the tax authority of the local country with respect to these issues.

6.37   The situation in the above example is a typical outbound technical service arrangement. In order to provide the tax executive with the information that is required to structure the transaction, it would be appropriate to obtain general guidance with respect to a checklist, commentary, and legal agreements for establishing a foreign service provider arrangement. In order to achieve the objectives of the US corporation in the above example, it may be appropriate to form a local subsidiary corporation, which would, in turn, enter an appropriate agreement to be a service provider to the US corporation for the purpose of installing the equipment in the project. This could be in the form of a technical services agreement. The enumerated objectives of the US corporation could be established in the adaptation of such an agreement to the situation at hand.

6.38   Complexity may be expected to arise in two areas. One is the foreign. There may be local income tax, withholding, VAT, and other issues. Often these issues are not addressed in a practical sense in any data source in English, certainly as more than general background. In such a situation, it would be appropriate for the US corporation to prepare a brief summary of how it seeks to handle the allocation of income (transfer pricing) from the project and permanent establishment exposures, and then design a structure to accomplish this result.

6.39   It will then be appropriate to find a local advisor (which can often be located through industry sources or trusted external advisors) and pose the list of appropriate questions of local law. It is then typically possible to meet with the local tax authorities to obtain appropriate rulings to eliminate any risk.

6.40   This approach should provide a means for the US corporation to achieve the objectives that are desired by its tax executives.

Joint Ventures

6.41   When examining the setting up of joint ventures from scratch, it is useful to begin with a close analysis of what each of the parties is required to contribute to the venture, how the profits (if any) are to be divided between them, and how losses are to be borne. It is also helpful to consider how the venture can be unscrambled. Joint ventures go wrong far more often than is expected by the parties when they are first put together.

6.42   There are four broad ways by which profits from a venture can be moved offshore. These may be subject to difficult business considerations, which could in turn have an effect on tax considerations, in the case of joint ventures, and particularly so in the case of joint ventures where there are minority holdings.

● *Management charges, technical assistance fees, or royalties.* These will, subject to transfer pricing constraints, be allowed as a deduction against taxable profits in the country of source. They will be taxed in the country of destination, which may or may not be the parent company. Double tax agreements may be relevant.

● *Payment for supplies or raw materials bought from, or product supplied to, other members of the group.* This affords some scope for the transfer of taxable profits but is severely limited by transfer pricing rules. Related to this is the possibility of factoring where one company in the group purchases the receivables of another company at a substantial discount and proceeds to collect the full amount of the receivables itself.

● *Interest.* This may be interest on loans within the group. It may be arm's-length interest. The group has a choice between borrowing and claiming a deduction at parent level (injecting funds into the subsidiaries' paid-up capital) or operating and claiming the deduction at subsidiary level. This may be constrained by 'thin capitalisation' or, in the case of the United States, 'interest stripping' rules. Double tax agreements will often be relevant.

● *Profits.* Profits may be taxed in the country of source and then distributed as dividends either to the parent or to an intermediate company. There will then normally be a credit for the underlying tax paid. Again, double tax agreements will be relevant.

6.43   In the cases of the first three items above, a management charge (for instance) will typically be at the expense of all the shareholders. This can create intractable problems unless the intention to make such payments is built into the terms of the original agreements and compensated for by adjustments in the percentage shareholdings, the prices paid for the shares, or by payments made to the other parties via different routes. This problem should always be considered.

6.44   In the case of the last item 'Profits' above, it is important to make sure either that all parties have the same strategy as to the proportion of profits distributed or retained or that more complex provisions are made in the statutes of the company to permit the different parties to each pursue its optimum tax strategy. There is sometimes scope for using 'dividend access shares', and problems can sometimes (but not always) be solved by interposing a local, 100%-owned 'dividend trap' subsidiary between the parent and the minority shareholding. One problem is how to obtain any relief for any losses. Most countries have provisions by which losses suffered in one group company can be offset against profits in another, but these are subject to two restrictions:

- a common degree of ownership is required; and

- loss relief may not apply across frontiers. Typically, a parent company can offset the losses of a foreign branch, but this does not extend to foreign subsidiaries and does not work in reverse.

6.45   The greatest and most cost-effective value can be obtained by setting up onshore and offshore structures from the beginning. In those cases, it is better for all of the parties to be involved at an early stage of negotiation of any joint venture, once agreement in principle has been reached. The best starting point is a draft letter of intent. It is then possible to indicate what further information is likely to be needed.

6.46   All onshore and offshore factors can thus be taken into account in designing a tax plan that will accommodate the interests of all parties.

EVALUATING THE OFFSHORE TAX PLAN

Method

6.47   Tax planning is only a part of business planning as a whole. It is therefore necessary to take into account, in addition to the tax burden, any differences in gross profits and non-tax expenditure that may result from the introduction of a tax plan.

6.48   These variables must be computed as accurately as possible for each of the following hypotheses:

- if the plan is not adopted;

- if the plan is adopted and succeeds; and

- if the plan is adopted and fails.

6.49   The purpose of a tax plan is in many cases the postponement of tax as well as or instead of any reduction in the aggregate tax burden. Where, therefore, tax would be chargeable at a different time as a result of the implementation of a tax plan, it is necessary to discount the tax burden back to the basic year (usually either the current tax year or the year of commencement of the project) for each year that is considered relevant for the purposes of comparison.

6.50   As in the case of the tax burden, the time at which income is received or expenditure incurred may make a considerable difference in calculating real savings or additional costs. It may thus also be necessary to discount each term that would be affected by the implementation of a tax plan back to the basic year.

6.51   Of course, it is not always necessary to discount each of these terms separately.

6.52   Where all the terms would change as a result of introducing a tax plan, the figure to be discounted is *gross profits less tax and non-tax expenditure*.

6.53   Where only tax and non-tax expenditure would change, the figure to be discounted is *the total of such expenditure*.

6.54 Designing the Offshore Tax Plan

6.54 Where only gross profits and the tax burden would change, the figure to be discounted is *gross profits less the tax burden.*

6.55 Where only the tax burden would change, *only this figure need be discounted.*

6.56 In this way, constant terms are ignored.

6.57 By calculating and comparing in this way the relative gross profits and tax and non-tax expenditure applying to the different hypotheses, it is possible to determine to what extent the implementation of a given tax plan will place the taxpayer in a better position if it succeeds, or in a worse position if it fails.

6.58 The taxpayer will not necessarily choose the most favourable solution on the basis of the above formula, since non-quantifiable factors (such as difficulties of changing over, exchange control restrictions, etc.) may persuade him to choose the more expensive solution as calculated in this way.

Comparing Alternative Tax Plans

6.59 The method described above is equally appropriate for the purpose of determining the most favourable form of a proposed transaction, operation, or relationship; deciding whether it is appropriate to include an additional country in the existing database, and if so, which; and comparing with one another the advantages of two or more possible plans.

Estimating the Chances of a Tax Plan Succeeding

6.60 While the win or lose odds of a tax plan can to a certain extent be calculated, the chances of a plan succeeding can only be estimated.

6.61 One often hears estimates being given in percentages. Such figures cannot be taken too literally. 'A 50–50 chance of success' really means little more than that it is considered to have an even chance of succeeding; 'a 90% chance of success', that there is a strong likelihood of succeeding.

6.62 Such percentage estimates may, however, assist counsel in explaining to his client the interrelationship between the estimated chances of success, on the one hand, and the win or lose odds (i.e., the calculated potential savings if the tax plan were to succeed or the additional costs if it were to fail) on the other.

6.63 A taxpayer might be tempted to take a chance on a plan, even if the odds of success were very small, provided that the estimated savings would be considerable if he succeeded, while the additional cost would be minimal if he lost. Say, for example, his only additional expenditure would be the cost of taking the matter on appeal, whereas taxwise he would be placed in the same position as if he had never adopted the plan at all or were merely liable for interest on the difference in tax for the relevant period.

6.64 Conversely, he would be most reluctant to adopt a tax plan where he stood to lose a substantial amount if it failed (e.g., as a result of penalties) in relation to his potential gain if it succeeded, unless the chances of success were overwhelmingly in his favour.

6.65 It may thus be helpful to be able to express the risk as a percentage chance of succeeding, the other term of the equation being the potential benefit resulting from success against the potential loss resulting from failure.

6.66   Considerable care must be taken in preparing a technical analysis in cases where the tax authorities have the power to allocate deemed income or losses.

Example

The taxpayer was a Belgian company. Its statutory director owned 96% of the shares. The director was also president of a Liechtenstein company, with which the Belgian company made an agreement not to conclude any transaction on its own account but to place all its organisation and personnel at the disposal of the Liechtenstein company. The latter company would reimburse all costs and expenses but would not provide any remuneration for the service.

Under Belgian law, if a business enterprise established in Belgium has, directly or indirectly, an interdependent relationship with an enterprise established abroad, all abnormal benefits granted to a foreign enterprise as a result of that relationship will be added to the Belgian enterprise's profits.

The Belgian tax administration added a deemed 5% brokerage fee to the taxable profits of the taxpayer. This was contested. However, the Brussels Court of Appeal upheld the assessment. In the first place, it was decided that there was a link of dependency between the two companies. Furthermore, the court considered it abnormal that a business company created with a view to making profits should have acted free of charge as a cashier for a foreign sister company, thus forgoing the usual minimum broker's fee.

DEBUGGING THE TAX PLAN

Local Advice

6.67   It is impossible for an outsider to be aware of all the pitfalls that lie in foreign legal, tax, and exchange control systems or of the special difficulties that may be encountered in operating in a foreign country.

6.68   The following example illustrates the danger that an individual who never sets foot in a particular country may, through his investing there, be taxed by such country as a resident.

Example

A resident of Monaco acquired immovable property in Belgium and share participations in several companies that were registered and established in Belgium, of which he became a director.

Under Belgian law, residents are subject to tax on their worldwide income, while non-residents are subject to tax only on their Belgian source income. An individual is considered to be a Belgian resident if his domicile or the centre of his economic interests is in Belgium.

Though he was a Monegasque resident and had no home whatsoever in Belgium, and despite the fact that he had substantial other business interests outside of Belgium, the taxpayer was deemed to have the centre of his economic interests in Belgium and hence to be a Belgian resident for tax purposes.

He was thus taxed in Belgium on his worldwide income, not merely on his Belgian source income. He was consequently subject to a tax burden considerably higher than if he had made the same investments in a country where, in identical circumstances, he would have been taxed as a non-resident.

6.69   When a decision has been taken as to what seems to be the most favourable arrangement on the basis of

- the objectives;

- the total tax burden, in relation to gross profits and non-tax expenditure, as discounted back to the basic year; and

- all other relevant considerations,

it is usually advisable to submit the proposed plan, for debugging, to a local expert in each of the foreign countries involved.

6.70   Where appropriate, foreign counsel should be asked to approach the necessary tax, exchange control, and other authorities to obtain rulings and, if possible, official commitments on matters that are essential to carrying out successfully a proposed arrangement.

Substance *versus* Form

6.71   The rule that the substance of a transaction, rather than its mere form, controls tax liability is one of very wide application. It can affect the amount of taxable income arising from practically any type of transaction. It is also applied frequently to settle questions of who is taxable on certain income.

6.72   The US Supreme Court (*Griffiths v Helvering* 308 US 355 (1939) and *Corliss v Bowers* 281 US 376) has stated:

'We cannot too often reiterate that taxation is not so much concerned with the refinements of title as it is with actual command over the property taxed — the actual benefit for which the tax is paid. And it makes no difference that such 'command' may be exercised through specific retention of legal title or the creation of a new equitable but controlled interest, or the maintenance of effective benefit through the interposition of a subservient agency.'

6.73   Though many of the decisions that involve the principle of substance *versus* form arise because the tax authorities have detected a tax avoidance motive, it must be stressed that such a motive will not normally establish liability if the transaction does not do so without it.

6.74   One of the circumstances that may cause the test of substance *versus* form to be applied is that the transaction involved was not an arm's-length transaction.

6.75   Application of the rule of substance *versus* form is often called for when several separate steps are taken to reach the final result.

6.76   In a number of varied types of cases, the courts have applied the 'business purpose' test. In most cases where the test is applied, the parties involved do not have adverse economic interests. They have consequently been held in many cases not to be dealing at arm's length.

6.77   Artificial avoidance schemes are particularly vulnerable to attack.

Example

The taxpayer had made a substantial capital gain and 'purchased' a scheme to avoid paying tax. The effect of the scheme was, by a series of transactions, to create a deductible capital loss equivalent to the gain. A 'real' loss was not suffered by the taxpayer because another effect of the scheme was to give rise to a tax-exempted capital gain to compensate for the loss. The taxpayer's only purpose in resorting to the scheme was to avoid tax. He relied on the fact that the form of transaction had often been held by the English courts to be more important than its overall effect, so that any loss or gain produced by the transaction would be upheld.

It has always been a principle of English law that the taxpayer is entitled to arrange his affairs so as to minimise his liability to tax, and, provided any steps taken were legal, the courts do not look behind a genuine document to seek the underlying substance of the transaction.

However, the House of Lords put a limit on this principle. The court looked at the scheme as a whole, instead of step-by-step as in previous cases, and said that the tax losses created were artificial losses and therefore were not deductible.

Example

The taxpayer was a Netherlands corporation, X. It had no offices in the Netherlands. In 1976, X held a 100% interest in four Swiss companies, none of which had offices or were staffed in Switzerland. The group also consisted of a holding company in the Netherlands Antilles, X Curaçao, which fully controlled X and which was, in turn, fully controlled by another corporation in Panama, X Panama. This corporation was owned by an individual resident in Germany, Mr N. X purchased the Swiss companies from X Curaçao by means of a loan from X Curaçao. X Curaçao had originally bought the four companies from X Panama, and X Panama had financed the necessary loan. All loan contracts provided that the debts would be repaid only out of dividend income. The Swiss companies withheld the 35% 'anticipatory tax' on the distributions of dividends to X. X then applied, in accordance with the Netherlands–Switzerland Tax Treaty (Treaty of 22 June 1966), for a full refund of the tax withheld on its dividends.

The issue in question was whether X was entitled to a full refund because it was resident in the Netherlands or only to a partial refund of 20%.

Under Swiss law, income from dividends, *inter alia*, is subject to a 35% withholding tax. Non-resident individuals and non-resident corporations having no permanent establishment in Switzerland are not entitled to receive a refund of withholding tax. Any refund of withholding tax must be claimed via the tax authorities of the country in which the claimant taxpayer is resident. The Netherlands–Switzerland Tax Treaty provides that the refund is available provided that insuring receipt of the total refund is not the main reason for the relationship between the two companies.

The Swiss Federal Tax Administration denied X the full refund of withholding tax on the grounds that the relationship between X and the four Swiss companies had been established primarily to receive the full refund and not for any sound business reasons.

X appealed against this ruling. The Federal Tax Administration held that, on the facts of this case, the issue raised was whether the transfer of control of the Swiss companies from X Panama to X Curaçao and then to X was primarily effected to avoid the 'anticipatory tax'. As an individual resident in Germany, Mr N was not entitled to receive a full refund of the withholding tax, only to a refund equal to 20% of the dividends, and the administration noted that through the scheme of transferring shares to X against a debt claim equal to the purchase price, Mr N was trying to have the reserves distributed to him without having to pay the withholding tax. The original decision of the Federal Tax Administration was thus upheld: X was not entitled to receive a full refund of the withholding tax paid in Switzerland, only to a refund equal to 20% of the dividends.

Applicability of Tax Treaties

6.78 When relying on a tax treaty, care should always be taken to insure that it is applicable. It is important to check whether there are any amending treaties or protocols and whether there are any interpretative rulings or official statements concerning the scope of the treaty.

Example

The taxpayer was a bank incorporated under Swiss law but with its central management and control in the United Kingdom. The Swiss branch of the bank had granted a loan to a bank in the United States and was in receipt of interest from sources in the United States.

The taxpayer fell within the provisions of the Switzerland–United States Tax Treaty (Treaty of 24 May 1951) Article II(f), which defines a Swiss corporation as a corporation created or organised under Swiss law. Under Article VII of the treaty, interest derived from sources in the United States by a Swiss corporation is subject to a tax of 5%, which is deducted at source.

On the other hand, the taxpayer also qualified as a resident of the United Kingdom under the former United Kingdom–United States Tax Treaty, which provides that a corporation is resident in the United Kingdom if its business is managed and controlled there. Interest from the United States to a UK resident is exempt from withholding tax (except where more than 50% of the debtor corporation is owned by the recipient corporation, which is not the present case).

A revenue ruling was issued that permits the taxpayer bank to choose the application of either the Swiss Treaty or the UK Treaty with the United States.

Example

There is an affiliation privilege in the internal tax legislation of Luxembourg. This insured the relief from double taxation in respect of dividends paid between affiliated enterprises. The Belgium–Luxembourg Tax Treaty (Treaty of 17 September 1970) provides for a reduction to 15% of the Belgian withholding tax on dividends. If a Luxembourg company directly holds at least 25% of the shares of the distributing Belgian company or if the direct holding was acquired for at least 250 million B Frs, the Belgian withholding tax is reduced to 10%. This means that Luxembourg companies entitled to an affiliation privilege can reduce or be exempt from Belgian withholding tax by using the provisions in the Belgium–Luxembourg Tax Treaty.

The Belgian Minister of Finance stated that no special measures need be enacted by Belgium to stop this practice, as the Luxembourg legislation was inspired by the *non bis in idem* principle, which is incorporated to a different degree in most countries, including Belgium.

Validity of Entities

6.79   Entities that are valid in one system of law may not be regarded as valid in the courts of other countries.

6.80   The following example illustrates a problem that arose in connection with the status of an *Anstalt*.

Example

Under Belgian civil law, the legal status of companies incorporated abroad is governed by their national law. They can therefore act in Belgium within the limits prescribed by that law but not in violation of the fundamental rules of Belgian law.

One of those fundamental rules is that all companies are based on a contract concluded between two or more partners. Therefore, 'one-man companies' are not recognised by the Belgian courts, although they are not actually void under the Belgian law.

This means that such an entity (an *Anstalt*) does not have a separate legal personality, and thus the sole founder is personally liable for any debts incurred by the entity.

Substantial Risks or Disadvantages

6.81   Where there are substantial risks or disadvantages attendant upon the proposed set-up and these cannot be easily avoided by the modification of the plan, it may be necessary to abandon the project altogether or to adopt the next most satisfactory of the alternative possible solutions considered.

6.82   Any such alternative solution must in turn be examined for weaknesses and pitfalls.

UPDATING THE TAX PLAN

6.83   Even after a plan has been adopted and the project has been embarked upon, it remains necessary to take into account any changes in the law or practice of any of the countries involved, which may have an effect on any of the elements of the arrangement.

6.84   This is comparatively easy with respect to one's own country. However, the financial press and various tax and business services usually provide only limited information with regard to changes in foreign countries.

6.85   It is therefore sound policy when briefing a foreign expert in connection with a proposed arrangement not only to ask specifically for information with regard to any impending or likely future changes in the existing law or practice of the country in question, but also to request him to report on any subsequent changes that may affect the arrangement.

6.86   Updating is the necessary corollary to the modifications that are concomitant with a dynamic society. By paying attention to future developments as well as to the present situation, it may be possible to lessen the harmful effects of some changes and to take full advantage of the potential benefits of others.

STRATEGIC CHECKLISTS

THE FORMULA FOR COMPUTING THE WIN OR LOSE ODDS

- Let A =   the estimated gross profits of the project if a tax plan is not adopted;

- Let B =   the estimated gross profits of the project if the tax plan is adopted;

- Let C =   the estimated tax burden if the tax plan is not adopted;

- Let D =   the estimated tax burden if the tax plan is adopted and succeeds;

- Let E =   the estimated tax burden if the tax plan is adopted and fails;

- Let F =   the estimated cost (other than tax) of setting up and running the project if the tax plan is not adopted; and

- Let G =   the estimated cost (other than tax) of setting up and running the project if the tax plan is adopted.

Certain items (e.g., future earnings, future taxable base, and tax rates) used for the purposes of calculating these terms can only be estimated. Since, however, the same figures are used to compare alternative arrangements, they nevertheless constitute a sound basis for comparison.

It is essential to be aware of any assumptions made in the database used for computing the various items and also of any non-quantifiable elements that have been left out of account.

Where identical items appear, respectively, in terms A and B; C, D, and E; or F and G, they may be ignored, as it is only comparative and not absolute figures that are required.

Where terms A and B, or F and G, are identical, they may be left out of account altogether.

Where additional expenditure is incurred as a result of introducing a tax plan, it is necessary to take into account any tax deduction that may be available in respect of such expenditure, otherwise a distortion may creep in regarding the comparison of the various alternatives.

In calculating term E, particular note should be taken of any applicable tax penalties.

APPLYING THE FORMULA IN EVALUATING AN OFFSHORE TAX PLAN

Obviously no tax plan should be adopted unless the tax saving, if the plan were to succeed, is substantially greater than the sum of any reduction in gross profits and any increase in expenditure resulting from its implementation.

That is, if $(A - F)$ is greater than $(B - G)$, the plan should not be adopted unless the difference is smaller than $(C - D)$.

Where the estimated tax burden if the plan is adopted and fails is materially greater than the estimated tax burden if the plan were not adopted at all (i.e., where E is materially greater than C), the decision as to whether or not to adopt a tax plan depends on the likelihood of the plan succeeding, and

- in the case where there is no material difference between gross profits less non-tax expenditure whether or not the plan is adopted, then: on a comparison between the total discounted tax burden if the plan is not adopted, and the total discounted tax burden if

  — the plan is adopted and succeeds; and

  — the plan is adopted and fails;

  that is, if there is no material difference between $(A - F)$ and $(B - G)$, then: on a comparison between $(C - D)$ and $(E - C)$

  or

- in the case where there is a material difference between the gross profits less non-tax expenditure according to whether or not the plan is adopted, then: on a comparison between the total discounted gross profits less the total discounted tax and non-tax expenditure if the plan is not adopted, and the total discounted profits less the total discounted tax and non-tax expenditure if

— the plan is adopted and succeeds; and

— the plan is adopted and fails.

That is, if there is a material difference between $(A - F)$ and $(B - G)$, then:

on a comparison between

$$[B - (D + G)] - [A - (C + F)]$$

and

$$[A - (C + F)] - [B - (E + G)]$$

By calculating and comparing in this way the relative gross profits and tax and non-tax expenditure applying to the different hypotheses, it is possible to determine to what extent the implementation of a given tax plan will place the taxpayer in a better position if it succeeds, or in a worse position if it fails.

7 Intra-group Transfer Pricing and Offshore Treasury Management Strategies

> ## STRATEGIC ISSUES, OPPORTUNITIES AND CAVEATS
>
> ### MULTINATIONAL ENTERPRISE (MNE) PRICING STRATEGIES
>
> - Transfer pricing issues account for more major tax cases worldwide than all other tax issues put together.
>
> - Get the MNE's pricing right from the start, since this can contribute substantially to its taking a stronger market position.
>
> - *Caveat:* Failure to get pricing right seriously increases the risk of double taxation.
>
> ### INTRA-GROUP SERVICES
>
> - MNE groups require a wide range of services for their members, in particular administrative, technical, financial, and commercial services.
>
> - Deductible payments by a corporation in a high-tax jurisdiction to a related offshore entity may result in a reduction in the group's overall tax burden.
>
> - Examples of intra-group services are:
>
>   — Administrative services such as planning, co-ordination, budgetary control, financial advice;
>
>   — accounting, auditing, legal services, factoring, and computer services;
>
>   — financial services, such as supervision of cash flows and solvency, capital increases, loan contracts, management of interest and exchange rate risks, and refinancing;
>
>   — assistance in the fields of production, buying, distribution, and marketing;
>
>   — services in staff matters such as recruitment and training;
>
>   — research and development or administration and protection of intangible property for all or part of the MNE group;
>
>   — overseas purchases and sales;
>
>   — multicurrency management;

— interest received/interest paid;

— debt factoring;

— advertising;

— transport/distribution/handling;

— travel;

— communications;

— captive insurance/reinsurance;

— royalties;

— computer charges;

— professional services;

— training;

— staff recruitment;

— printing and stationery.

OFFSHORE TREASURY MANAGEMENT

- The skilful treasury management of a multinational company can produce significant tax savings through arm's length deductions being paid by members of the group to an administrative office, headquarters company, or co-ordination centre.

- Deductions (particularly commissions) relate to gross income, thus making for a much higher percentage saving on net income. In some cases, a significant percentage of a group's net earnings may be paid out in the form of deductions.

- Where deductions are made to a related party in a lower tax or tax-free country, significant tax savings may be achieved.

- Care should always be taken to insure that any structure involving a preferential tax regime does not fall within the scope of any measures directed at the curtailing of such operations.

- *Caveat:* Payments between related parties must be arm's length. This could be on a cost-plus or any other basis, provided the arm's length quality of the payments can be substantiated.

DETERMINING ARM'S LENGTH CHARGES

- Before even considering the arm's length issue, it is always necessary to determine whether a bona fide intra-group service has, in fact, been rendered.

- If an intra-group service has been rendered, it is necessary, as for other types of intra-group transfers, to determine whether the amount of the charge, if any, is in accordance with the arm's length principle.

- *Caveat:* For tax purposes, such transactions should not be treated differently from comparable transactions between independent enterprises.

- Where a group member performs specific economic functions and takes all, or possibly none, of the risks that uncontrolled parties customarily undertake while performing the same activity, the group member should be entitled to the same prices or returns that are earned in uncontrolled transactions.

- Where the intra-company transaction involves the use of money by another controlled entity and the lender assumes the risks of an uncontrolled lender, then the lender should be entitled to the arm's length charge (i.e., interest) for the use of its money.

- *Caveat:* Although the lender also may be viewed as providing a service, the compensation of the lender in the case of the independent enterprise transactions is typically an interest charge for the funds loaned.

MAJOR NEW TECHNOLOGICAL TRENDS

- The evolution of electronic commerce means that traditional geographic boundaries are of far less significance.

- High technology activity requires no institutional physical presence in a given geographic location.

- These trends easily facilitate the location of an increasingly wide range of business functions or risks in jurisdictions that have advantageous tax regimes.

OECD APPROACH TO HARMFUL TAX COMPETITION

- The Harmful Tax Competition Report reflects the OECD's concern about tax havens and preferential tax regimes that proide harmful tax competition to Member countries of the OECD.

- *Caveat:* It appears that a critical motivating element of the efforts of the OECD is the perceived need to capture information to facilitate adjustments as may be necessary to assure arm's length dealing.

7.1 Intra-group Transfer Pricing

- *Caveat:* There also appears to be an effort to utilise information obtained from potential harmful regimes in order to allow tax administrations to identify issues that may not be addressed by the OECD Transfer Pricing Guidelines or pertinent domestic tax regimes.

- *Caveat:* There is thus much concern among those advising multinational corporations that, without the OECD having stated so in as many words, the OECD attack on tax havens and preferential tax regimes, is directed also at the transfer pricing structures of multinational corporations.

OECD PROPOSED COUNTER-MEASURES

- Domestic legislation — including CFC regimes, foreign investment fund (additional 'clawback') rules, restriction on participation exemptions for foreign source income, information reporting, access to banking information by other countries' tax authorities, provision of rulings, and the application of the OECD Guidelines.

- Tax treaties — including exchange of information, treaty benefit entitlement, compatibility of domestic anti-abuse rules, limitation of income exclusion provisions, termination of treaties with tax havens, co-ordinated or simultaneous tax examinations, and assistance in recovering tax claims of treaty partner countries.

- Endorsement of the OECD Transfer Pricing Guidelines.

- Police 'links' between Member countries and tax haven dependencies to prevent harmful tax practices in the dependent tax havens.

- Developing principles of good tax administration.

- Association of non-Member countries.

SCOPE OF THE TRANSFER PRICING ISSUE

7.1 When the Organisation for Economic Co-operation and Development (OECD) published its first major work on the topic of transfer pricing in 1979, it made reference to what had become the pivotal point around which all transfer pricing discussion revolves, namely the arm's length principle. This work reflected the concern of Revenue departments worldwide that there was tremendous scope for the erosion of their tax bases if uncontrolled pricing of goods and services were allowed to continue.

7.2 The growth of multinational enterprises (MNEs) presents increasingly complex taxation issues for both tax administrations and the MNEs themselves since separate country rules for the taxation of MNEs cannot be viewed in isolation but must be addressed in a broad international context. These issues arise primarily from the practical difficulties, for both MNEs and tax administrations, of determining the income and expenses of a company or a permanent establishment that is part of an MNE group that should be taken into account within a jurisdiction, particularly where the MNE group's operations are highly integrated. In the case of MNEs, the need to comply with laws and administrative requirements that may differ from country to country creates additional problems. The differing requirements may lead to a greater burden on an MNE, and result in higher costs of compliance, than for a similar enterprise operating solely within a single tax jurisdiction.

7.3   Currently, transfer pricing issues account for more major tax cases worldwide than all other tax issues put together.

7.4   If a MNE gets its transfer pricing right from the start, this can contribute substantially to its taking a stronger market position. There is a clear connection between double taxation and transfer pricing, since failing to get pricing right, seriously increases the risk of double taxation. With over 60% of the world's trade taking place within MNEs, it is inevitable that transfer pricing has become the key international tax issue.

7.5   In the context of the worldwide trend for tax authorities to create tough, hard-hitting transfer pricing rules and regulations, MNEs are aiming to achieve a global approach to designing and documenting their transfer pricing policies. They find that an integrated approach can save money. It may also provide an opportunity for spotting tax-planning opportunities. But at the very least, there is increased recognition of the need for consistent documentation to ward off the various tax administrations.

7.6   A recent survey conducted by Ernst & Young shows that the level of transfer pricing audit activity has increased overall. A very high number of audits occur in the field of intra-group services, and particularly so in those countries where tax administrations have augmented their rules and resources, with a high number of adjustments resulting in double taxation. Running tandem with the increasing appearance of, or intention to enact, new legislation, there is to be found a hardening attitude on tax-driven transfer pricing, bigger policing resources, and increased cross-border sharing of information. MNEs are obliged to deal with a relatively coherent and well-equipped establishment that is now examining their transfer pricing.

7.7   In addition to its strategy to improve the administration and enforcement of transfer pricing rules, the IRS has placed increased emphasis on industry-wide exchanges of information with treaty partners. Successful industry-wide exchanges of information in the transfer pricing area have involved the pharmaceutical, oil, grain, data processing, heavy construction and electronics industries. Simultaneous examinations are also undertaken pursuant to working arrangements between the IRS and the treaty partner tax authorities.

7.8   The 1999 Ernst & Young Survey on Transfer Pricing (available at http://www.eyi.com) shows that:

- 78% of US MNEs regard transfer pricing as an important current international tax issue, and 71% believe it will be the biggest issue they will face over the next two years.

- Only 26% of US MNEs consider transfer pricing issues at the strategic planning level. However, 78% of respondents believe the integration of tax and transfer pricing in business decisions could minimise their organisation's overall tax burden.

- Despite the rigorous comparability requirements necessary to use transaction-based methods in the United States, US MNEs continue to rely on them more than on profit-based methods.

- While 68% of US respondents believe an integrated approach to transfer pricing documentation is a priority, only 27% report using a globally integrated approach.

7.9 Intra-group Transfer Pricing

- 59% of US respondents examined in any country were examined in the United States. Canada (46%), the United Kingdom (35%) and Germany (34%) were also very active in examining US-based MNEs.

- 14% of the US parents report negotiating an Advance Pricing Agreement (APA) in the past, and 49% indicate they would consider one in the future.

STRATEGIES FOR INTRA-GROUP SERVICES

Payments to a Related Party in a Low-tax Jurisdiction

7.9 The International Transfer Pricing Guidelines have been adopted by all Organisation for Economic Co-operation and Development (OECD) countries and represent a consensus of policies and procedures. With more than 25% of the world's trade taking place within multinational enterprise (MNE) groups, there will inevitably be a number of transactions occurring between related parties. Hence, transfer-pricing rules must be applied to a substantial number of transactions.

7.10 The perception exists that transactions involving related offshore entities are often motivated by tax, rather than strictly commercial reasons. The OECD International Transfer Pricing Guidelines emphasise that taxpayers should be aware that the IRS and other countries' revenue services may pay closer attention to a transaction involving an entity resident in a country with lower tax rates than in the home country.

Intra-Group Services

7.11 Deductible payments by a corporation in a high-tax jurisdiction to an offshore entity will result in a reduction in the corporation's overall tax burden. Assuming that payments are made to a related party in a lower-tax or tax-free country, significant tax savings may be achieved. Multinational enterprise groups require a wide range of services for its members, in particular administrative, technical, financial, and commercial services. The cost of providing these services may be borne initially by the parent, a specially designated group member (i.e. a group service centre), or another group member.

7.12 A member of an MNE group in need of a service may acquire it directly or indirectly from independent enterprises, or from one or more associated enterprises in the same MNE group (i.e. intra-group), or it may perform the service for itself. The commercial character of transactions should therefore be studied in all proposed arrangements. Credibility may be dependent on the arrangements being substantive.

DETERMINING WHETHER SERVICES HAVE BEEN RENDERED

7.13 There are two issues in the analysis of transfer pricing for intra-group services:

- whether intra-group services have, in fact, been provided; and

- what the intra-group charge for such services for tax purposes should be in accordance with the arm's length principle.

7.14 Under the arm's length principle, the question of whether an intra-group service has been rendered when one group member performs an activity for one or more other group members should depend on whether the activity provides a respective group member with economic or commercial value that might enhance its commercial position. This can be determined by considering whether an independent enterprise in comparable circumstances would have been willing to pay for the activity or perform it for itself in-house. If the independent enterprise would not have been willing to pay for or perform the activity itself, the activity ordinarily should not be considered as an intra-group service under the arm's length principle.

7.15   In general, activities performed by one group member that merely duplicate a service that another group member is performing for itself — or that are being performed for the other group member by a third party intra-group — do not qualify as 'services rendered'. A duplicative service, however, may be found to constitute an intra-group service if it is rendered only on a temporary basis (e.g., where an MNE group is reorganising to centralise its management functions); or undertaken to reduce the risk of a wrong business decision (e.g., getting a second legal opinion on a subject).

Services that Provide Incidental Benefit

7.16   In certain circumstances, an intra-group service performed by one group member (e.g., a shareholder or co-ordinating centre) may relate only to some group members, but, incidentally, provide benefits to other members.

7.17   Other activities that may relate to the group as a whole are activities centralised in the parent company or a group service centre (e.g. a regional headquarters company), that are made available to the entire group. The activities that are centralised depend on the kind of business and on the group's organisational structure, but they may generally include the following:

● administrative services such as planning, co-ordination, budgetary control, financial advice;

● accounting, auditing, legal services, factoring, and computer services;

● financial services, such as supervision of cash flows and solvency, capital increases, loan contracts, management of interest and exchange rate risks, and refinancing;

● assistance in the fields of production, buying, distribution, and marketing;

● services in staff matters such as recruitment and training; and

● research and development or administration and protection of intangible property for all or part of the MNE group.

7.18   These types of activities are ordinarily considered intra-group services, because they are activities that independent enterprises would be willing to pay for or perform for themselves.

7.19   In considering whether a charge for providing services would be made between independent enterprises, it is also relevant to consider the form that an arm's length consideration would take had the transaction occurred between independent enterprises. For example, with respect to financial services (such as loans, foreign exchange, and hedging), remuneration would generally be built into the spread and it would not be appropriate to expect a further service fee to be charged.

Determining Arm's Length Charges

7.20   If an intra-group service has been rendered, it is necessary, as for other types of intra-group transfers, to determine whether the amount of the charge, if any, is in accordance with the arm's length principle. This means that the charge for these services should reflect a charge that would have been made and accepted between independent enterprises in comparable circumstances.

7.21 Intra-group Transfer Pricing

7.21 In other words, for tax purposes, such transactions should not be treated differently from comparable transactions between independent enterprises simply because the enterprises involved happened to be associated.

7.22 Where a group member performs specific economic functions and takes all, or possibly none, of the risks that uncontrolled parties customarily undertake while performing the same activity, the group member should be entitled to the same prices or returns that are earned in uncontrolled transactions. This practice is the essence of the separate-entity view of pricing. For example, when the intra-company transaction involves the use of money by another controlled entity and the lender assumes the risks of an uncontrolled lender, then the lender should be entitled to the arm's length charge (i.e., interest) for the use of its money. Because money is a fungible commodity, the arm's length charge is readily determinable.

7.23 Although the lender also may be viewed as providing a service, the compensation of the lender in the case of the independent enterprise transactions is typically an interest charge for the funds loaned.

MULTINATIONAL TRANSFER PRICING ISSUES

Major New International Taxation Trends

7.24 There are several major trends in international taxation that will have significant impact on the nature of the environment in which offshore transactions are conducted, and that will have to be taken into account in evaluating existing, or in planning new, strategies:

- The evolution of electronic commerce means that traditional geographic boundaries are of far less significance.

- There is no longer any necessary geographic or territorial imperative for the performance of high technology research and development or related activities, so that multinationals are able to utilise the talents of engineers or other professionals located in under-developed regions of the world where highly skilled and trained professionals can be found. This means that high technology activity requires no institutional physical presence in a given geographic location.

- These trends easily facilitate the location of an increasingly wide range of business functions or risks in jurisdictions that have advantageous tax regimes. This has, in turn, caused the OECD to be concerned that these trends provide increasing incentive to utilise so-called tax haven countries or preferential tax regimes that provide harmful tax competition to Member countries of the OECD.

The OECD Attack on Harmful Tax Competition

7.25 In the period since the release of the Harmful Tax Competition Report it appears that a critical motivating element of the efforts of the OECD is the perceived need to capture information to facilitate adjustments as may be necessary to assure arm's length dealing and compliance with particular domestic tax regimes, in particular via transfer pricing or controlled foreign corporation (CFC) legislation. There also appears to be an effort to utilise information obtained from potential harmful regimes in order to allow tax administrations to identify issues that may not be addressed by the OECD Transfer Pricing Guidelines or pertinent domestic tax regimes.

7.26 There is thus much concern among those advising multinational corporations that, without the OECD having stated so in as many words, the OECD attack on tax havens and preferential tax regimes, is directed also at the transfer pricing structures of multinational corporations. Since more than a quarter of all international transactions are estimated to take place within groups, this widening of the information base going beyond the scope of the existing transfer pricing guidelines, creates a new, and unwelcome, dimension.

7.27 The OECD issued its report titled 'Harmful Tax Competition: An Emerging Global Issue' in April 1998 (the 'Report'). The thrust of the Report is an outline of guidelines to be considered for dealing with the perceived problems of inappropriate tax competition (tax havens and preferential tax regimes) by Member countries. The general concern of the OECD is with defence of the taxation base of Member countries. Specifically, the OECD is concerned to assure that Member countries are able to: (a) obtain information concerning Member country taxpayers' use of tax havens and preferential tax regimes; and (b) design appropriate countermeasures to deal with such uses deemed abusive. The OECD has repeatedly indicated that effective tax rates (or no tax rates) are not, as such, the target of the Harmful Tax Competition initiative.

7.28 An early step has been the creation of the Forum on Harmful Tax Competition (the 'Forum'), formed shortly after release of the Report, an important function of which is to identify those regimes that are viewed as being tax havens or preferential tax regimes. It is anticipated that this list will be released in the coming months. The next major step is the development of appropriate countermeasures as proposed in the Report.

7.29 These include the co-ordination of:

● domestic legislation — including CFC regimes, foreign investment fund (additional 'clawback') rules, restriction on participation exemptions for foreign source income, information reporting, access to banking information by other countries' tax authorities, provision of rulings, and the application of the OECD Guidelines;

● tax treaties — including exchange of information, treaty benefit entitlement, compatibility of domestic anti-abuse rules, limitation of income exclusion provisions, termination of treaties with tax havens, co-ordinated or simultaneous tax examinations, and assistance in recovering tax claims of treaty partner countries;

● endorsement of the Guidelines;

● police 'links' between Member countries and tax haven dependencies to prevent harmful tax practices in the dependent tax havens;

● developing principles of good tax administration; and

● association of non-Member countries.

Criticisms by the International Business Community

7.30 The release of the Report has generated a vigorous debate between the OECD and the international business community concerning the actual intention of the OECD and the propriety of these intentions. Officials of some Member countries have been reported to have used rather strident language to suggest the need for dealing with harmful preferential tax regimes. There has been significant criticism from the business community as well as commentators with respect to the content of the Report and the manner in which it was released.

7.31 These criticisms include concern that the tone of the Report that may be appropriate for money-laundering or other criminal matters, is not appropriate for the routine international business arrangements made by multinationals in order to achieve a worldwide lower tax cost, and the primary purpose of which is to remain competitive with

7.32 Intra-group Transfer Pricing

competitors that may have a lower international tax cost due to the regimes available in their home countries. From the standpoint of multinationals, the presence of tax competition between countries is a healthy phenomenon, which lowers overall tax burdens of multinationals and provides a means of equalising the tax burdens of companies based in high and low tax countries, all of which may be OECD Member countries. Furthermore, there are many reasons for locating business operations in countries offering tax incentives other than the incentives themselves, such as lower labour, geographic proximity to suppliers and markets, favourable government attitudes to inbound investment, and availability of developed internal infrastructure (telecommunications, natural resources, utilities — such as electricity, water, airport or harbour capacity).

7.32   In addition, the emergence of a global economy and resultant relaxation of trade and investment barriers (often led by the OECD itself) have led to a significant increase in the overall tax revenues of developed countries.

7.33   Finally, it has been noted that the tax base leakage issues that are at the heart of the Report, and which are legitimate concerns to tax administrations, would appear to be satisfactorily addressed by the OECD's Transfer Pricing Guidelines, Model Income Tax Convention, and domestic regimes of Member countries (such as controlled foreign corporation-type 'clawback' provisions, which typically require deemed repatriation of passive income earned in foreign subsidiaries — controlled foreign corporation-type regimes). The overall object of the Guidelines is, consistent with the mechanisms of the Model Income Tax Convention, to provide parameters for the allocation of income from international operations among multinational controlled taxpayers (and their respective countries) on the basis of function performed and risk assumed in each country. In this connection, the approach of the Report could be viewed to simply add another layer of international tax allocation principles on top of existing regimes.

Suspected Motivation Behind the Report

7.34   Inevitably, the business community is showing considerable concern that the principal motivating elements of the Report may be to capture information and to allow tax administrations to identify issues that may not be addressed by the transfer pricing Guidelines or pertinent domestic tax regimes.

7.35   To the extent that this is an accurate assessment of the motivation behind the Report, it may be that the implication of the recommendations, and potential Guidelines to be forthcoming from the Forum activities, will be the evolution of a more uniform and complete system of information gathering from tax haven jurisdictions, followed by more uniform application of transfer pricing and domestic tax legislation principles, including domestic information reporting by multinationals. This may, in turn, not actually reflect an additional tax compliance burden being imposed upon multinationals. Indeed, such evolution may reflect little more than a recognition that documentation and penalty regimes, typically relating to transfer pricing, are spreading among Member countries and the need for co-ordination to assure that multinationals do not become subject to a crazy-quilt of documentation-penalty regimes.

7.36   It seems likely that the increasing importance of electronic commerce as a medium of conducting international business provides encouragement for these information and tax administration co-ordination efforts of the Member countries.

Implications for the Business Community

7.37   While information and tax administration co-ordination efforts may be benign, there are other possibilities that would pose far more serious questions for both multinational taxpayers and tax administrations. It may be, for example, that the evolution of Forum activities and Guideline formulation would produce an environment in which Member countries would determine that harmful preferential tax regimes should be ignored for purposes of applying treaties between Member countries.

7.38   In the event that the process evolves in this direction, there are several potential implications, including the following:

- Such an evolution of Member country activity would have potentially ominous implications for all non-Member countries, not just those countries deemed to provide harmful preferential tax regimes. Such countries often seek to attract external investment with a favourable tax incentive structure.

- A country deemed to provide harmful preferential tax regimes would have an apparent incentive to enter information sharing agreements with Member countries.

- Multinationals would have even greater incentive to seek advance agreements with the tax authorities of the principal countries in which it conducts business, via advance pricing agreement or other mechanisms.

- A base may be laid for worldwide allocation of income, at least among Member countries.

7.39   In conclusion, it seems apparent that the OECD Member countries perceive that there is a clear logical relationship between transfer pricing documentation-penalty regimes (to provide tax authorities with information about worldwide related party functional and risk activities, and segmented financial information), domestic tax regimes (such as CFC clawback and domestic exit tax regimes — which provide bases for deeming the repatriation of income to the mother country), and the need to obtain complete information from countries deemed to provide harmful preferential tax regimes.

7.40   It may or may not be the case that these comments reflect the underlying motivations for the Report. Nonetheless, it does seem clear that the rather contentious debate that has been generated by the Report would benefit from a more complete statement of the underlying objectives of the Member countries by the OECD.

7.41   In the face of these developments, a critical concern of participants in the offshore industry could be the effect that the Harmful Tax Competition initiative of the OECD could have on the evolution of the industry.

7.42   Recommendations are currently being made that a co-ordinated approach be made by the participants in the offshore industry to work with the Forum in addressing the concerns of the OECD and its Member countries. It is seriously evident that a failure to do so would allow the debate to evolve with an important voice absent from the table.

OFFSHORE TREASURY MANAGEMENT

7.43   The skilful treasury management of a multinational company can produce significant tax savings through arm's length deductions being paid by members of the group to an administrative office, headquarters company, or co-ordination centre.

7.44   Intra-group Transfer Pricing

7.44   Deductions (particularly commissions) relate to gross income, thus making for a much higher percentage saving on net income. In some cases, a significant percentage of a group's net earnings may be paid out in the form of deductions.

7.45   On the assumption that the deductions are made to a related party in a lower tax or tax-free country, significant tax savings may be achieved.

7.46   Payments between related parties must be arm's length. This could be on a cost-plus or any other basis, provided the arm's length quality of the payments can be substantiated.

7.47   Care should always be taken to insure that any structure involving a preferential tax regime does not fall within the scope of any measures directed at the curtailing of such operations (see Chapter 11).

7.48   The following are examples of tax-efficient structures that a multinational group might employ to accumulate income, and manage the income on the income, in an international offshore financial centre (IOFC):

- overseas purchases and sales;
- multicurrency management;
- interest received/interest paid;
- debt factoring;
- advertising;
- transport/distribution/handling;
- travel;
- communications;
- captive insurance/reinsurance;
- royalties;
- computer charges;
- professional services;
- training;
- staff recruitment;
- printing and stationery.

See Strategic Checklists below.

STRATEGIC CHECKLISTS

OVERSEAS PURCHASES AND SALES

Assume the following structure: a centralised overseas purchase and sales office is set up in an IOFC to handle buying and selling of certain products for the group.

The overseas purchase and sales office is paid commissions by group members, on an arm's length basis, for performing such functions.

TAX BENEFIT

The payment of commissions, on an arm's-length basis, would constitute an allowable deduction in the hands of the various group members.

Since less tax or no tax would be paid in the country where the overseas purchase and sales office is based, this differential would constitute an easily calculable tax saving.

DOS AND DON'TS

All payments between related parties should be at arm's length. It would in principle be easier for the revenue, as well as for the group, to obtain information on comparable uncontrolled percentages payable as commissions in cases of payments to third parties than in most other cases of international pricing. Charging more than the arm's-length price would be risky, while charging less could be wasteful.

Transactions must be *bona fide*.

Care should be taken to insure that the profits of the overseas purchase and sales office do not fall within the tax nets of the countries of operation.

MULTICURRENCY MANAGEMENT

Assume the following structure: a multicurrency management centre (MMC) is set up in an IOFC for the benefit of the group.

Specific objectives of the MMC will include some or all of the following:

● to exercise strict control over international payments in order to plan and effectively control the liquidity of an international group;

● to pool exchange risks in one location;

● to execute foreign exchange transactions at the lowest costs;

● to reduce foreign exchange risks through

— matching income and outgoing payments in the same currency,

— leading and lagging of payments, and

— hedging operations (e.g., forward contracts, borrowing, depositing in domestic and/or European markets);

- to decrease overall borrowing costs;

- to house medium- and long-term inter-company and other loans; and

- to provide inter-company loans.

The MMC can also be used as an international financing company.

The MMC would be remunerated on an arm's-length basis and would charge a fee for its services to recover its costs plus a reasonable mark-up.

Note: This could amount, at the very least, to 0.4% of all amounts owed or owing at any time in any foreign currency.

BUSINESS BENEFITS

See above assumptions.

TAX BENEFIT

Arm's-length fees payable by the various group members to the MMC would be deductible in their hands. At the very least, this would be 0.4% of any foreign currency owed or owing. These fees would be unconnected with any profits.

DOS AND DON'TS

All payments between related parties should be at arm's length.

Transactions must be *bona fide*.

Care should be taken to insure that the profits of the MMC do not fall within the tax nets of the countries of operation.

INTEREST RECEIVED/INTEREST PAID

Assume the following structure: an offshore finance company is used for certain lending and borrowing transactions of the group. The finance company participates in commissions and spreads.

BUSINESS BENEFITS

The profits do not get altogether wasted on the banks.

It is possible to control the transactions.

TAX BENEFIT

All of the above profits can be taken tax-free.

DOS AND DON'TS

All payments between related parties should be at arm's length.

Transactions must be bona fide.

Care should be taken to insure that the profits of the finance company do not fall within the tax nets of the countries of operation.

DEBT FACTORING

Assume the following structure: an offshore debt factoring company purchases the debts of the various group members at arm's-length prices in relation to those prices charged by unrelated debt factoring companies.

TAX BENEFITS

The tax liabilities of the group members would be reduced by the difference between the face value of the debts and the amount actually received by them.

Any profits of the debt factoring company from the successful collection of the debts would be made free of tax.

DOs and DON'Ts

All payments between related parties should be at arm's length.

Transactions must be bona fide.

Care should be taken to insure that the profits of the debt factoring company do not fall within the tax nets of the countries of operation.

ADVERTISING

Assume the following structure: a related offshore advertising agency handles advertising for all group members (the principals). The advertising agency receives a 15% commission from the media (newspapers, journals, TV, radio stations) for the placing of these advertisements.

Note: The average commission paid by the media internationally is 15%; the advertising agency uses sub-agents in the countries where the advertisements are placed; and the advertising agency splits the commission with the subagents 50–50.

BUSINESS BENEFIT

Saving of 15%, or such percentage that has not already been granted to the subagents (assumed for these purposes to be 7.5%).

TAX BENEFIT

Tax rate multiplied by 7.5% (assumed saving), say tax rate of 40% = 3%.

DOS AND DON'TS

Normally, the domestic tax authorities will not question this transaction since:

- the payment by the principal consists of a standard payment of the normal advertising fee; and

- the commission is paid by a third party (the media) to the advertising agency (i.e., the principals are not included).

It follows that there should not be any transfer pricing issues involved even though the advertising agency and the principals are related parties.

Care should be taken to insure that the profits of the advertising agency do not fall within the tax nets of the countries of operation.

TRANSPORT/DISTRIBUTION/HANDLING

Assume the following structure: a related overseas transportation and distribution office is set up in an IOFC.

This transportation and distribution office is responsible for transportation, distribution, freight, railage, shipping, handling, etc., required by the group members, and dealing with agents.

The transportation and distribution office is paid arm's-length commissions in line with those payable to any third party for the performance of these services.

TAX BENEFIT

The payment of the transportation, etc., charges, on an arm's length basis, would constitute allowable deductions in the hands of the paying company.

Since less tax or no tax would be paid in the country where the transportation and distribution office is based, this differential would constitute an easily calculable tax saving.

DOS AND DON'TS

All payments between related parties should be at arm's length. It would in principle be easier for the revenue, as well as for the group, to obtain information on comparable uncontrolled percentages payable as commissions in cases of payments to third parties than in most other cases of international pricing. Charging more than the arm's-length price would be risky, while charging less could be wasteful.

Transactions must be bona fide.

Care should be taken to insure that the profits of the transportation and distribution office do not fall within the tax nets of the countries of operation.

TRAVEL

Assume the following structure: an offshore travel agency is set up to handle all travel arrangements. The travel agency receives the usual agency commissions from the airlines, hotels, etc. (for example, in the case of most airlines, this is 9%).

Where the travel agency uses sub-agents, there would normally be a commission split, as in the case of advertising agencies. See above.

BUSINESS BENEFIT

Saving of full or partial commissions that would otherwise be wasted.

TAX BENEFIT

Tax rate multiplied by 5% (assumed saving), say tax rate at 40% = 2%.

DOS AND DON'TS

Normally, the domestic tax authorities will allow this deduction since the deduction consists of a standard payment of the normal travel commission paid by third parties.

The commission must be paid by third parties to the travel agency and not by the principals.

It follows that there should not be any transfer pricing issues involved, even though the travel agency is a related party to the principals.

Care should be taken to insure that the profits of the travel agency do not fall within the tax nets of the countries of operation.

COMMUNICATIONS

Assume the following structure: a centralised overseas communications office is set up in an IOFC to handle communications for group members. The communications office is paid an arm's length fee for performing such functions.

TAX BENEFIT

The payment of communications charges, on an arm's-length basis, would constitute an allowable deduction in the hands of the various group members.

Since less tax or no tax would be paid in the country where the communications office is based, this differential would constitute an easily calculable tax saving.

DOS AND DON'TS

All payments between related parties should be at arm's length.

Transactions must be bona fide.

Care should be taken to insure that the profits of the communications office do not fall within the tax nets of the countries of operation.

CAPTIVE INSURANCE/REINSURANCE

Assume the following structure: an offshore captive insurance company is set up to handle all insurance costs for the group.

The captive insurance company accepts for itself a lower slice on certain risks (technically known as 'deductibles').

The captive insurance company reinsures all the rest through a reinsurance company.

BUSINESS BENEFITS

It is possible to use a captive insurance company to obtain cover that the normal insurance market does not easily provide for, or does so only at very great expense.

It is possible to pay for reinsurance at the end of the stated term, whereas normal insurance premiums are paid at the beginning of the stated term.

If the members of the group are more careful than the average in the industry, it would be possible to achieve economies on insurance premiums that would not be possible in the normal course.

It is possible to obtain freedom from the onerous requirements and restrictions of insurance legislation in the principal countries where the group operates.

TAX BENEFIT

It may be possible to charge premiums representing greater deductions than are reflected in the actual insurance and reinsurance costs of the captive insurance company, with the deductibility of such 'inflated' premiums being accepted by the revenue as being in line with industry standards.

DOS AND DON'TS

There must be both *distribution* of risk and *spreading* of risk to insure that deductions for the payment of premiums will be allowed.

All payments between related parties should be at arm's length.

Transactions must be bona fide.

Care should be taken to insure that the profits of the captive insurance company do not fall within the tax nets of the countries of operation.

ROYALTIES

Assume the following structure: certain technology would be owned by an offshore licensing company.

The licensing company would use a sublicensing company in the Netherlands.

TAX BENEFIT

In tax treaties between the Netherlands and many other countries, withholding taxes on royalties are normally reduced to 0%.

Netherlands taxes on a flow-through of royalties can also be extremely low.

There is no withholding tax on payments of royalties by a Netherlands company.

DOS AND DON'TS

Payments of royalties are normally deductible subject to the following:

- All payments between related parties should be at arm's length. It would in principle be relatively easy for the revenue, as well as for the group, to obtain information on comparable uncontrolled royalty percentages.

- Transactions must be bona fide.

The United States–Netherlands Treaty cannot be used to benefit persons in third countries.

Care should be taken to insure that the profits of the licensing company do not fall within the tax nets of the countries of operation.

The source of the right must be situated in the correct profit centre (see also above).

COMPUTER CHARGES

Assume the following structure: a related computer services office located in an IOFC performs certain computer functions that can be performed abroad, taking into account the practicalities of the performance.

The computer services office is paid an arm's-length fee for performing such functions.

The reasonable amount payable for such services, if paid to a third party, would be greater than the real cost to the group.

TAX BENEFIT

The payment of the computer charges, on an arm's-length basis, would constitute an allowable deduction in the hands of the various group members.

Since less tax or no tax would be paid in the country where the computer services office is based, this differential would constitute an easily calculable tax saving.

DOS AND DON'TS

The tax saving on an assumed tax rate of 40% would have to produce a significantly greater benefit than the additional costs attached to having these computer-related services performed abroad — otherwise it would not be worth the cost and the inconvenience.

All payments between related parties should be at arm's length.

Transactions must be bona fide.

Care should be taken to insure that the profits of the offshore computer services office do not fall within the tax nets of the countries of operation.

PROFESSIONAL SERVICES

Assume the following structure: certain accounting, legal, engineering, etc., services are performed by one or more services companies overseas.

The billing for these services is in line with billing by comparable third parties.

TAX BENEFIT

Payments by the various group members would be deductible.

Profits in the hands of the services companies would not be subject to tax.

DOS AND DON'TS

All payments between related parties should be at arm's length.

Transactions must be bona fide.

Care should be taken to insure that the profits of the services companies do not fall within the tax nets of the countries of operation.

TRAINING

Assume the following structure: a specialised training company is set up overseas in an IOFC for the purpose of providing training to employees of the various group members.

Certain aspects of the training provided by this company would be effected abroad and other aspects would be on a distance-learning basis.

The reasonable amount that would be payable to a third party for similar services would be greater than the real cost to the group.

TAX BENEFIT

The training costs would be deductible in the hands of the various group members whose employees receive training from the training company.

The profits of the training company would suffer little or no tax in the other countries.

DOS AND DON'TS

All payments between related parties should be at arm's length.

Transactions must be bona fide.

Care should be taken to insure that the profits of the training company do not fall within the tax nets of the countries of operation.

STAFF RECRUITMENT

Assume the following structure:an offshore recruitment company is entrusted with recruitment of certain classes of employees for the various group members.

The billing for these services is in line with billing by comparable third parties.

Where the recruitment company uses sub-agents, there would normally be a commission split, as in the case of advertising agencies.

BUSINESS BENEFIT

Saving of full or partial commissions that would otherwise be wasted.

TAX BENEFIT

Tax differential multiplied by saving.

DOS AND DON'TS

Normally, the domestic tax authorities will allow this deduction since the deduction consists of a standard payment of commissions normally paid by principals to third party employment agencies.

All payments between related parties should be at arm's length.

Transactions must be bona fide.

Care should be taken to insure that the profits of the recruitment company do not fall within the tax nets of the countries of operation.

PRINTING AND STATIONERY

Assume the following structure: a printing and stationery company located in an IOFC handles any appropriate printing, stationery, and related requirements of the group members.

There is a justifiable profit margin.

BUSINESS BENEFIT

Potential cash earnings.

TAX BENEFIT

Payments by the various members would be deductible.

Profits in the hands of the printing and stationery company would not be subject to tax.

DOS AND DON'TS

The figures must take into account all material costs, including transport, to insure that the operation makes business sense.

All payments between related parties should be at arm's length.

Transactions must be bona fide.

Care should be taken to insure that the profits of the printing and stationery company do not fall within the tax nets of the countries of operation.

STRATEGIC ISSUES, OPPORTUNITIES AND CAVEATS

OFFSHORE TACTICS

- The combination of tax and non-tax factors applying to individuals focuses essentially on residence, domicile, and citizenship.

- *Caveat:* Offshore solutions to individual tax planning problems can be achieved only if the offshore component succeeds in breaking or modifying connecting factors between the individual and the relevant high tax jurisdictions.

RESIDENCE

- Residence is where one lives as well as where one has the right to live.

- Residence is the one single factor that can change dramatically the tax bill of an individual or a company, possibly running the full range from zero tax to the top marginal rate.

- The reason for this is that residence is the principal connecting factor in most tax systems. Residence normally decides, for most double taxation purposes, which will be the primary taxing country enjoying the right to tax general or specific taxable events.

- Many big earners use an offshore company to employ them. The company makes the profits and pays them a salary spread over a number of years.

- *Caveat:* Where there is a double taxation treaty between two countries, there will usually be 'tie-breaker' rules under which a dually resident individual's residence status is resolved.

DOMICILE

- Unlike residence, domicile has ramifications beyond the sphere of taxation.

- Domicile determines which system of law is to govern one's personal position in situations such as succession, marriage and divorce, legitimacy, and questions of legal capacity.

- *Caveat:* An individual may also be deemed to be domiciled in a particular country for tax purposes even though he is not domiciled there in general law.

THE UNITED KINGDOM AS THE WORLD'S PRIME RESIDENTIAL TAX HAVEN

- The UK tax regime is currently particularly favourable to individuals who are resident in the United Kingdom but not domiciled there.

- Where it is established that an individual is a UK-resident non-domiciliary, income tax is chargeable on all income arising in the United Kingdom and on any income arising outside the United Kingdom that is remitted to the United Kingdom.

- *Caveat*: The UK Revenue does, however, deem remittances to the United Kingdom to be income first, capital gains second, and capital last, unless proved otherwise. In order to differentiate between these, an individual should set up, outside the United Kingdom, three separate accounts before arrival in the United Kingdom:

  — A 'clean' capital account with all the available cash before arrival in the United Kingdom. Such moneys can be remitted to the United Kingdom from this account without any UK tax consequences.

  — An income account to receive all non-UK source income, both from non-UK employment and from non-UK investments. Moneys from this account should never be remitted to the United Kingdom, as they would be immediately liable to UK tax.

  — A capital account for the proceeds of sale of any non-UK assets concluded while the individual is resident in the United Kingdom. As with the income account, any remittance from this third account will be immediately liable to UK tax.

CITIZENSHIP

- Many offshore persons need more than just residence. Citizenship too can be critical.

- *Caveat*: The United States taxes on the basis of citizenship, and shedding US citizenship may be a painful procedure.

REMUNERATION OF OFFSHORE EMPLOYEES

- In structuring proposed arrangements, it is important to focus on the provision of internationally competitive rewards.

- *Caveat*: In order not to lose expatriate executives, pay specific attention to:

  — salaries;

  — similar cash entitlements;

  — bonuses;

— share participation;

— retirement benefits;

— a reward and benefit framework.

GROSS-UP PRINCIPLE

Assume an employee currently earning X pre-tax and paying tax at rate $t1$. Assume the employee is relocated, and as a consequence is taxable at the (higher) rate $t2$. He (reasonably) insists that his after-tax income be maintained. The employer therefore pays him an allowance of ($t2$ minus $t1$)X. But this allowance is taxable, which requires a further equalisation allowance of $t2(t2-t1)X$, and so on.

The problem has a simple algebraic solution. If A is the taxable tax equalisation allowance, then:

$$(1 - t_2)(X + A) = (1 - t_1)X$$

from which it follows:

$$A = \frac{t_2 - t_1\ X}{1 - t_2}$$

One needs only to assume that $t1$ = 30% and $t2$ = 60% (say), for A to be equal to 75% of X. If A could be paid tax-free, however, it would be only 30% of X, i.e. less than half the otherwise required tax-equalisation allowance.

THE INTERNATIONAL PERSON

8.1 Inevitably, offshore tax planning extends to the world of the 'international person' every bit as much as it does to the corporation. Indeed, much offshore business involves the affairs of entrepreneurs who have effective control over their activities.

8.2 While many similar tax considerations come into operation, the combination of tax and non-tax factors applying to individuals focuses essentially on residence, domicile, and citizenship. Offshore solutions to individual tax planning problems can be achieved only if the offshore component succeeds in breaking or modifying connecting factors between the individual and the relevant high tax jurisdictions.

Residence

8.3 One's residence is where one lives. But more important from some points of view is where one has the right to live.

8.4 As a general rule one can live in a country where one is a citizen. But one can normally also live in many other countries as well — sometimes casually, sometimes by virtue of a residence permit or merely a visa.

8.5 Offshore Planning Strategies for Individuals

8.5 In most countries resident individuals are subject to income and other taxes on worldwide income and assets, wherever situated. In some countries, like the United States, Denmark, and Germany, tax can follow an emigrant for a number of years after he or she leaves the territory.

8.6 Despite its importance, the meaning of *residence* is not comprehensively defined in most countries for either legal or tax purposes. Criteria for determining residence are generally based on practical considerations and derived largely from court cases, although many countries use as a test the number of days of presence in the country in some stipulated period. In the case of the United States, days in the current year as well as days in the previous two years are taken into account for determining residence for tax purposes.

8.7 If there is a double taxation treaty between two countries, there will usually be 'tiebreaker' rules under which a dually resident individual's residence status is resolved.

Emigration

8.8 Emigration to a tax haven or to a country offering special retirement incentives may serve to break totally or in part the link between a taxpayer and the high tax jurisdiction from which he or she is emigrating. Normally, it is the change in the place of residence that is material; however, in other cases a change in domicile or even citizenship (in the case of the United States) may be necessary. Anti-avoidance provisions or exchange controls may delay or render extremely difficult the coming into effect of the fiscal advantages of emigration.

8.9 In addition to countries where no relevant taxes are levied or where taxation is levied at very low rates, certain countries offer favourable tax treatment to all or certain categories of immigrants in respect of their foreign source income. Special exchange control treatment may also be granted to qualifying immigrants.

8.10 The obvious way of giving up one's residence is to emigrate. However, while the right of any person to leave any country is generally recognised, the right to *immigrate* — to choose a new country of residence — is not. Immigration is therefore the main practical issue in emigration.

8.11 All European Union (EU) citizens can choose any of the member countries, but those countries can and do tax.

8.12 Monaco, which is not an EU country, is fairly liberal with new residents of adequate means, although the procedure can be slow. Jersey and Guernsey are very difficult to get into, while the Isle of Man is more welcoming. Switzerland is theoretically difficult, although the right budget can usually do the trick.

8.13 Then there are specials like Austria, Costa Rica, Israel, Malta, the Philippines, and Sri Lanka that are keen to attract retirees with a bit of loose cash to invest and seek to tempt them with tax exemptions.

8.14 Many expatriates, of course, want to work in their new homes, and this requires the correct visa and/or work authorisation. An expatriate leaving home usually has a long checklist:

- buying or renting property in a new country;
- overseas removal;

- pre-retirement savings and investment;

- the pension position;

- social security benefits;

- private medical treatment and health care;

- exchange control;

- and of course, tax.

8.15   If the expatriate returns home — and many do — the checklist is shorter. Mainly it is tax and, particularly, estate tax. Becoming a full-scale non-resident creates a very special opportunity. In matters of estate planning and probate, remember the two folk adages: 'Have a little trust' and 'Where there's a will, there's a way'.

Artists and Athletes

8.16   Bjorn Borg and Anthony Burgess weren't the first, and Boris Becker and Ringo Starr aren't the last. Monaco is full of musical, literary, and sporting stars — many of them earning big bucks. And so are the other residential havens. The influx seems to be gathering momentum.

8.17   Some stars may decide to emigrate, but many don't. They just stay right where they are and treat their own countries as tax havens, often by turning their income into a capital appreciation in their own companies. This technique can work so well that companies have even been floated on the stock exchange on the basis of book earnings generated from the performances of the stars. Tom Jones and the Beatles were masters of this game.

8.18   Many big earners use an offshore company to employ them. The company makes the profits and pays them a salary spread over a number of years. Of course, this ploy doesn't always work. Take what happened to Ingemar Johannson, the Swedish prize-fighter. He had incorporated a Swiss company of which he was the sole employee and source of revenue; he was entitled to receive 70% of the company's gross income plus a pension fund. He then fought in the United States for the heavyweight boxing championship of the world and was hit for taxes on his prize winnings by the IRS. He claimed tax exemption under the Switzerland–United States Tax Treaty on the grounds that he and the company were really Swiss residents. That was one time the 'Hammer of Thor' well and truly got hammered. The IRS rejected his argument and so did the US tax court.

8.19   For every loser, however, there are many winners. There are people living for more than 10 months of the year in high tax countries where they are legally designated as non-residents for tax purposes; others who are deemed residents in havens of convenience and who barely spend more than a couple of days there from time to time. Sometimes one spouse is a resident and the other is not; though technically separated, they manage to live together happily ever after.

What About Taxes Abroad?

8.20   The offshore person has usually left old tax (and sometimes other) problems behind. But what about tax in the country of adoption? Is the expatriate off the tax hook in France, Italy, Spain, or Greece? No, indeed. The taxes in most of the countries on the Mediterranean shore are quite high indeed, and their systems contain a full barrage of income taxes, inheritance taxes, gift taxes, and wealth taxes.

8.21 Offshore Planning Strategies for Individuals

8.21 In the past, expatriates benefited from Mediterranean neglect. The local tax administration simply didn't bother with them. But that has changed. Not only is the expatriate an easy target of the computer and a welcome source of additional tax revenue, but European Union pressures are leading to a tightening of tax systems generally.

8.22 Having no tax address at all can sometimes work, but it could be more difficult to prove a clean break with the previous country of residence, particularly if the would-be expatriate still visits there.

Domicile

8.23 Domicile may have considerable practical significance for foreigners coming from abroad to visit or live in Anglo-American countries — also for those who leave those countries to make a new home in another country. Unlike residence, domicile has ramifications beyond the sphere of taxation. It determines which system of law is to govern one's personal position in situations such as succession, marriage and divorce, legitimacy, and questions of legal capacity.

8.24 It is a fundamental principle of Anglo-American legal systems that every individual must at all times have a domicile. Domicile of origin is a domicile automatically acquired by all individuals at birth and is determined solely on the basis of parentage, without reference to the place of birth. So an individual need never have set foot in the country of his domicile of origin.

8.25 An individual's domicile of origin continues indefinitely to be his domicile unless and until he acquires a new domicile. Children usually follow their parents' domicile. Otherwise, for a domicile of choice to be effective, two essential requirements must be met. First, the individual must take up residence in the country concerned; and secondly there must be an intention to remain indefinitely, or without time limit, in the adopted country. Married women can usually establish an independent domicile.

8.26 In determining domicile, the courts look at material factors such as the residence in the country concerned of members of the individual's family, cultural connections such as the ability to speak the local language, making a will and appointing locally resident executors, financial or business interests, and involvement in social activities such as membership in clubs, societies, and churches. Even expressing a desire to be buried in a particular country after death may be relevant, especially if a burial plot is actually acquired.

8.27 An individual may also be deemed to be domiciled in a particular country for tax purposes even though he is not domiciled there in general law.

The United Kingdom as the World's Prime Residential Tax Haven

8.28 The United Kingdom is the favourite residential tax haven of the world's rich and famous expatriates.

Basis for UK Tax Liability of Foreign Domiciliaries

8.29 Liability to UK tax on both income and capital is dependent on the two concepts of residence and domicile.

8.30 The UK tax regime is currently particularly favourable to individuals who are resident in the United Kingdom but are not UK domiciled. To benefit from such a position, it is necessary for non-UK domiciled individuals to insure that they retain some connection with, or desire to return to, their domicile of origin.

Residence. An individual is deemed to be resident in the United Kingdom if he is physically in the United Kingdom for more than 183 days, excluding days of arrival and departure in any tax year (April 6 to April 5).

8.31 If the individual is able to remain outside the United Kingdom for more than half the year but still spends a considerable amount of time in the United Kingdom, there is a further test that the Inland Revenue will apply in determining whether the individual is resident for tax purposes. If the individual averages, over a four-year period, more than 90 days physically in the United Kingdom in each tax year, then the Revenue will deem the individual to be resident from the beginning of the 5th tax year. If, however, it becomes apparent before the end of the 4th year that the 90-day test will be exceeded, then the Revenue will deem residence from an earlier date. Indeed, if it is clear that it was the individual's intention always to exceed the 90-day test as from the beginning, the Revenue will deem the individual to be UK resident for tax purposes from the moment of arrival in the United Kingdom.

Domicile. The other factor that affects an individual's liability to UK tax is the concept of *domicile.* Under UK law an individual has one (and only one) domicile. This concept is not to be confused with the idea of accommodation, since it is more closely linked to the concept of a 'permanent home'.

8.32 A person is born with a domicile of origin, which will generally be his father's domicile at the date of his birth. This can be changed when the individual is still a minor by the father changing his domicile. Upon reaching the age of majority, an individual can acquire a domicile of choice by making a positive decision to abandon his domicile of origin and to settle in a new country.

Income Tax

8.33 Where it is established that an individual is a UK-resident non-domiciliary, income tax is chargeable on all income arising in the United Kingdom and on any income arising outside the United Kingdom that is remitted to the United Kingdom.

8.34 The concept of remittance covers not only the physical importation of money but also deemed remittance, whereby the individual has the use of, or enjoyment of, money in the United Kingdom that has arisen outside.

8.35 As a UK resident, an individual is entitled to certain allowances and is taxed on the total of his income on a sliding scale. All UK individuals are entitled to a personal allowance, and in addition there are other allowances, such as a married couples' allowance, as well as extra allowances for age and disability for which various conditions must be satisfied.

Capital Gains Tax

8.36 Gains on the disposal of assets are taxable in the hands of individuals who are resident or ordinarily resident in the United Kingdom.

8.37 However, if the individual is not domiciled in the United Kingdom, in the case of a sale of an asset situated outside the United Kingdom, only proceeds that are actually or constructively remitted to the United Kingdom will be subject to capital gains tax. Capital gains are deemed to be remitted where they are in some form or other enjoyed or used in the United Kingdom.

8.38   A non-domiciled UK resident individual is therefore taxable on the difference between the sales proceeds and the cost of purchase of any relevant assets.

Inheritance Tax

8.39   Liability to inheritance tax for a non-domiciled individual arises only on assets physically situated in the United Kingdom at the time of death. However, it should be noted that as well as the normal meaning of domicile discussed above, the Inheritance Tax Act also deems as a UK domiciliary, for inheritance tax purposes, any person who has been resident in the United Kingdom in 17 out of the past 20 years.

8.40   Inheritance tax applies to the transfer of any asset from one person to another, whether or not on the event of a death. Most lifetime gifts, however, are treated as exempt if the transferor survives for seven years.

Income Accounts and Capital Accounts

8.41   Any earned income that is paid for services conducted outside the United Kingdom can, by the use of separate employment contracts, be paid outside the United Kingdom and, as long as not remitted, will be free of UK tax.

8.42   It is possible to avoid the UK tax on non-UK-source income. The UK Revenue does, however, deem remittances to the United Kingdom to be income first, capital gains second, and capital last, unless proved otherwise.

8.43   In order to differentiate between these, an individual should set up, outside the United Kingdom, three separate accounts before arrival in the United Kingdom:

- The first will be all the available cash before arrival in the United Kingdom. This will be a 'clean' capital account, and as such moneys can be remitted to the United Kingdom from this account without any UK tax consequences. This account should, however, not receive any injections other than the proceeds of sale of assets that are exempt from capital gains tax in the United Kingdom (e.g. your principal private residence, motor vehicles, etc.).

- The second account should be the income account. This will receive all non-UK source income, both from non-UK employment and from non-UK investments. Moneys from this account should never be remitted to the United Kingdom, as they would be immediately liable to UK tax.

- The third account should be used for the proceeds of sale of any non-UK assets concluded while the individual is resident in the United Kingdom. As with the income account, any remittance from this third account will be immediately liable to UK tax.

8.44   By the setting up of these accounts it will therefore be possible for the foreigner to prove to the UK Revenue, by the production of bank statements, that any remittances to the United Kingdom are from tax-free capital.

8.45   If it is necessary to bring any assets into the United Kingdom at the time of establishing residence here, it would be advisable to consider 'bed and breakfasting' (selling an asset and immediately repurchasing it) any assets that would be subject to UK capital gains tax. This would therefore raise the base cost of the assets, so lowering any ultimate gain and reducing any tax liability on eventual sale. This, of course, should be done before actually establishing residence in the United Kingdom. It follows that the consideration of future needs is advisable.

8.46   The foreigner should retain his membership in his church, business, and social club in the foreign country and continue to emphasise in all documents (such as his will) that he considers his place of permanent residence and domicile to be in the foreign country.

8.47   When the foreigner completes his future UK tax returns, he should indicate that he is still domiciled in the foreign country.

RESIDENCE AND DOMICILE PLANNING

8.48   It is no understatement that residence is the one single factor that can change dramatically the tax bill of an individual or a company, possibly running the full range from zero tax to the top marginal rate.

8.49   The reason for this is that residence is the principal connecting factor in most tax systems. Residence normally decides, for most double taxation purposes, which will be the primary taxing country enjoying the right to tax general or specific taxable events. Since tax systems vary considerably, the ultimate effective tax burden may be a function of which tax system has the first bite of the cherry and which comes in second position, or in no position at all. The residence tests in tax treaties mostly tend to produce an all or nothing result.

8.50   Take the following simple example of an exceedingly effective tax plan that owes its effectiveness to the fact that the countries are treaty countries, both of them high tax countries with different tax systems.

Example

A family emigrates from a country — say South Africa — that would, under its domestic tax system, still regard them as a resident for tax purposes, if they were to immigrate to a country where there is no relevant tax treaty — say Monaco or the Bahamas. Setting up trusts would have no effect on their tax liability, since, under the domestic tax system in question, they would still be liable to tax on the income and gains of the trust, and the beneficiaries of this trust would, in due course, be liable to gifts or inheritance tax.

Now add a new factor: the same family immigrates instead to a country — say France — where they are liable to tax in the ordinary way. However, in the country of immigration, they and their heirs or beneficiaries would not be liable to tax on the income, capital gains or assets of a trust that had been set up *prior* to their immigration.

8.51   In the above example, the fact of being resident in France, for tax treaty purposes, and hence not resident in South Africa for tax treaty purposes, can provide the magic wand of tax planning, since it may produce an instant conversion of onshore into offshore. However, in such matters, proof is of the greatest importance.

8.52   Residence is normally a critical factor in determining the content of the taxable base. However, setting up a residence offshore will seldom on its own terminate residency status in another taxing country.

8.53 Offshore Planning Strategies for Individuals

8.53 It is important to bear in mind that an individual may be resident for tax purposes in more than one country. In most cases, he will be treated in each country as if it were his only place of residence. In certain countries, however, an individual may acquire a secondary residence, thus incurring what will usually be a lesser tax burden in such country.

8.54 For example, an alien having a secondary residence in France is subject to income tax on a base computed at three times the estimated rental value of his home or on his income from French sources, whichever is the higher (*Code général des Impôts*, art. 164–C).

8.55 Domicile and citizenship may also be material considerations. For the United Kingdom, see paras 8.28–8.47 above.

8.56 In the United States, on the other hand, citizenship is a material factor in determining tax liability, while in most other countries citizenship is merely of marginal relevance for tax purposes.

Example

The taxpayer, who had renounced his citizenship of the United States and established a bona fide residence in the Bahamas, was held to be a non-resident alien and was not taxable as a US citizen. He was, however, in receipt of income, earned while he was still a citizen, from sources within the United States, and it was held that this income was to be included under s 872(a) of the Internal Revenue Code.

His wife, who had not renounced her citizenship, was chargeable with reporting one-half of the income as community property.

8.57 In certain legal systems that follow UK law in this regard, a corporation is treated as being resident in the country in which its central management and control is exercised, and not necessarily in the country of its place of registration or incorporation.

8.58 Since connecting factors, such as residence, domicile, citizenship, source of income, or situs of property, are not necessarily mutually exclusive, double taxation of the same taxable event may ensue.

8.59 Furthermore, anti-avoidance provisions may have the effect of maintaining or creating a connecting factor with a taxing jurisdiction or of preventing the reduction of the potential tax burden through the alteration of one or more connecting factors.

Example

The Danish Department of Finance was called upon to give a ruling as to whether Danish emigrants who established residence in Monaco would continue to be subject to Danish income tax.

According to Danish tax law, liability to tax on the basis of residence normally terminates if proof is submitted to the effect that the taxpayer is subject to income tax in a foreign country according to the rules for residents of that country.

The issue that arose for consideration by the department was whether this rule was applicable to a taxpayer who is subject to tax in Monaco. There is no individual income taxation in Monaco; the only taxes levied on individuals there are indirect taxes and duties, principally consumption and turnover taxes.

The department ruled that these taxes do not have any resemblance to Danish income taxation, and Danish emigrants to Monaco would hence still be subject to resident tax liability in Denmark.

8.60   Similar anti-avoidance measures in the US Internal Revenue Code (s 877 and 2107) lay down that a non-resident individual who has given up his US citizenship will continue to be taxable as a US taxpayer if he lost his citizenship within ten years preceding the taxable year.

ARTICLE 4.2 OF THE OECD MODEL TAX CONVENTION

8.61   Article 4.2 of the OECD Model Convention deals with the question of residence as follows:

'Where by reason of the provisions of paragraph 1 of this article an individual is a resident of both Contracting States, then his status shall be determined in accordance with the following rules:

(a)   He shall be deemed to be a resident of the Contracting State in which he has a permanent home available to him; if he has a permanent home available to him in both Contracting States, he shall be deemed to be a resident of the Contracting State with which his personal and economic relations are closest (hereinafter referred to as "his centre of vital interests").

(b)   If the Contracting State in which he has his centre of vital interests cannot be determined, or if he has not a permanent home available to him in either Contracting State, he shall be deemed to be a resident of the Contracting State in which he has an habitual abode.

(c)   If he has an habitual abode in both Contracting States or in neither of them, he shall be deemed to be a resident of the Contracting State of which he is a national.

(d)   If he is a national of both Contracting States or of neither of them, the taxation authorities of the Contracting States shall determine the question by mutual agreement.'

OECD Commentary on Article 4.2

8.62   The OECD Commentary on paragraph 2 of Article 4 relates to the case where, under the provisions of paragraph 1, an individual is a resident of both Contracting States.

8.63   To solve this conflict special rules must be established which give the attachment to one State in preference over the attachment to the other State. As far as possible, the preference criterion must be of such a nature that there can be no question but that the person concerned will satisfy it in one State only, and at the same time it must reflect such an attachment that it is felt to be natural that the right to tax devolves upon that particular State.

8.64   The Article gives preference to the Contracting State in which the individual has a permanent home available to him. This criterion will frequently be sufficient to solve the conflict, e.g. where the individual has a permanent home in one Contracting State and has only made a stay of some length in the other Contracting State.

8.65 Offshore Planning Strategies for Individuals

8.65 Sub-paragraph (a) means, therefore, that in the application of the Convention (that is, where there is a conflict between the laws of the two States) it is considered that the residence is that place where the individual owns or possesses a home; this home must be permanent, that is to say, the individual must have arranged and retained it for his permanent use as opposed to staying at a particular place under such conditions that it is evident that the stay is intended to be of short duration.

8.66 As regards the concept of home, it should be observed that any form of home may be taken into account (house or apartment belonging to or rented by the individual, rented furnished room). But the permanence of the home is essential; this means that the individual has arranged to have the dwelling available to him at all times continuously, and not occasionally for the purpose of a stay which, owing to the reasons for it, is necessarily of short duration (travel for pleasure, business travel, educational travel, attending a course at a school, etc).

8.67 If the individual has a permanent home in both Contracting States, paragraph 2 gives preference to the State with which the personal and economic relations of the individual are closer, this being understood as the centre of vital interests.

8.68 If the individual has a permanent home in both Contracting States, it is necessary to look at the facts in order to ascertain with which of the two States his personal and economic relations are closer. Thus, regard will be had to his family and social relations, his occupations, his political, cultural or other activities, his place of business, the place from which he administers his property, etc. The circumstances must be examined as a whole, but it is nevertheless obvious that considerations based on the personal acts of the individual must receive special attention. If a person who has a home in one State sets up a second in the other State while retaining the first, the fact that he retains the first in the environment where he has always lived, where he has worked, and where he has his family and possessions, can, together with other elements, go to demonstrate that he has retained his centre of vital interests in the first State.

How the Residence Tiebreakers Work

8.69 In cases where taxpayers are considered to have permanent homes in both countries, the relevant tiebreakers are thus:

- the State with which their personal and economic relations are closer (i.e. the centre of vital interests), i.e.:

  — family and social relations,

  — occupations,

  — political, cultural and other activities,

  — place of business,

  — place from which their property is administered,

  — personal acts in general,

  — and failing clarity on the above, the State of which they are citizens.

ESTATE PLANNING CASE STUDY

Background

8.70   Estate and gift tax planning should take place when the parties are in good health and outside of any emergency situation, and it should be updated from time to time as circumstances change and relationships evolve.

8.71   In Anglo-Saxon legal systems, estate taxation is primarily governed by the law of domicile, which normally grants to one jurisdiction the principal right to tax. Domicile for estate purposes is quite distinct from residence with respect to taxation of income. In principle, rules are laid down in case law and in treaty provisions that enable domicile to be determined unambiguously even in cases of multiple residence.

8.72   This determination turns on what may be very detailed issues of fact (down to the minutiae of one's arrangement of one's social intercourse) yet may have major consequences for the heirs of an estate. A key issue in planning is to try to meet the major criteria rather than relying on the unpredictable interpretation of details. As the case study indicates, a key factor will generally be the status of one's domestic arrangements in both the jurisdiction in which one wishes to maintain a domicile and the one in which one wishes merely to reside temporarily.

8.73   The decedent was an Australian woman married to a US citizen.

8.74   The decedent and her husband jointly owned homes in Australia (New South Wales); her husband owned a home in the United States; and they spent varying proportions of the year in each of the two homes. The decedent's estate also included stock in foreign corporations.

8.75   The determination of the decedent's domicile/residence will have an effect on estate tax and probate in US and Australian law.

Domicile

8.76   It is a general principle of private international law that the state of domicile has the widest jurisdiction in the imposition of inheritance and estate taxes. It is in theory the state of domicile that can impose taxes on the transfer of the decedent's intangibles. The taxing power of the domiciliary state covers substantially all property of a decedent except real or tangible personal property located outside of its jurisdiction.

US Law of Domicile

8.77   The American Law Institute Restatement of the Law defines domicile as follows:

> 'Domicile is the place with which a person has settled connection for certain legal purposes; either because his home is there, or because that place is assigned to him by law.'

US cases tend to define domicile as the 'place where one has his true fixed, permanent home and principal establishment and to which, whenever he is absent, he has the intention of returning'.

8.78   In determining the decedent's place of domicile for US estate tax purposes, a series of additional criteria has been laid down by case law:

8.79 Offshore Planning Strategies for Individuals

- every person has a domicile at all times, and, at least for the same purposes, no person has more than one domicile at a time;

- home is the place where a person dwells and that is the centre of his domestic, social, and civil life;

- the domicile of origin is the domicile that a person has at birth;

- a domicile of choice may be acquired by a person who is legally capable of changing his domicile;

- in addition to legal capacity, acquisition of a domicile of choice requires both physical presence and an attitude of mind;

- to acquire a domicile of choice in a place, a person must be physically present there;

- to acquire a domicile of choice in a place, a person must intend to make that place his home for the time at least;

- a domicile once established continues until it is superseded by a new domicile.

8.79 The real problems that arise are in respect of the provisions concerning the domicile of a person having two dwelling places and the position of a married woman. Generally speaking, when a person with capacity to acquire a domicile of choice has more than one dwelling place, his domicile is in the earlier dwelling place unless the second dwelling place is his principal home. A wife who lives with her husband has the same domicile as him unless the special circumstances of the wife make such a result unreasonable.

8.80 The actual home of a decedent, and, if he has several homes, his principal home — the one with which he has been associated most intimately — is thus his domicile.

8.81 A change of domicile may be made for any reason whatever, provided that there is an intention to abandon one domicile and acquire another and that the acts of the person affected confirm the intention. But mere intention to effect a shift of domicile is not sufficient, and the motive prompting the change (whether tax avoidance or not) is immaterial. Facts alone are determinative as to the reality of a purported domiciliary shift. However, the burden of showing a change from a former domicile is upon the party asserting the change.

8.82 Because of the presumption against change of domicile, despite material facts pointing to such a change, the question of a possible double domicile may arise.

8.83 Courts in two different states may each find that the decedent's domicile was located there. The decedent could not have had two domiciles, but there may be conflicting findings as to where the domicile was when the property owner died. In such case, there seems no escape from the imposition of two domiciliary taxes upon the succession to the estate, aside from the practical difficulties of collection.

8.84 It would seem entirely possible that courts of different jurisdictions may have occasion to adjudicate differently as to domicile with the practical result that a person may have several domiciles when it comes to payment of inheritance taxes, and his heirs may be compelled to pay the full amount of tax in the several states on his whole intangible personal estate, providing there be found sufficient property in the states decreeing domicile differently to satisfy the tax on the whole estate.

Australian Law of Domicile

8.85 A person will be a resident of Australia for the purposes of the Income Tax Assessment Act 1936, as amended, if that person is either a resident in the ordinary sense of the word or is a person who satisfies certain tests set out in the definition, i.e.:

- a person whose domicile is in Australia, unless the commissioner is satisfied that his permanent place of abode is outside Australia; or

- a person who has actually been in Australia continuously or intermittently during more than one half of the year of income, unless the commissioner is satisfied that his usual place of abode is outside Australia and that he does not intend to take up residence in Australia.

8.86 Residence in the ordinary sense is a question of fact. A person resides where he lives. However, as an exception to this general rule, the first test above creates a presumption of residence with regard to anyone within Australian domicile. The presumption is rebuttable by reference to certain facts.

8.87 Australia accepts the English common law tests of domicile, which, stated shortly, are as follows. The law ascribes to all persons a domicile and only one domicile. At birth all persons acquire a domicile of origin, which, in the case of a legitimate child, is the domicile of his father. This domicile continues until a new domicile is established, either, in the case of the infant, by a change in the domicile of the appropriate parent or, in the case of an adult, by the acquisition of a domicile of choice. To acquire a domicile of choice, the law requires not only that residence has in fact been set up in a new country or state but also that the person whose domicile is in question intends remaining in this new place of residence permanently. The onus of proving a change of domicile is upon the person alleging it.

8.88 The decedent could be regarded as having lost her Australian residence if the tax authorities were satisfied that she had a permanent place of abode outside Australia. Here the word *permanent* means 'indefinite', so a person who had a home in the United Kingdom and who was working on an indefinite basis in Australia or the United States might cease to be a resident of Australia notwithstanding that ultimately that person intended to return home at the end of a tour of duty or for the purposes of retirement.

8.89 Loss of Australian domicile would furthermore require the severance of links with Australia and the absence of any intention to return there, neither of which is necessarily implied by the possession of a permanent place of abode outside Australia.

Applicable Taxes

8.90 In the United States, there are both federal and state estate and inheritance taxes. In Australia and the State of New South Wales, there are none.

8.91 It is therefore very important to determine whether the decedent was domiciled in Australia or in the United States.

The Domicile/Residence of the Decedent from an Australian Perspective

8.92 Residence is defined by the tests quoted above. These tests are independent of each other. Thus, a person need satisfy only one test to be a resident of Australia.

8.93 Offshore Planning Strategies for Individuals

8.93 Although the question of residence is a conclusion of fact, the courts, when considering this question, take into account various factors. In determining whether a person resides in a particular country for a year of income, it is necessary to consider the following:

- whether the individual is physically present in the country at some time during the year of income;

- the nationality of the person;

- the history of his residence and movements;

- his mode of life;

- the frequency, regularity, and duration of his visits to the country;

- the purpose of any visits;

- the reason for any absences from the country during the year;

- family and/or business ties with the country; and

- whether a place of abode is maintained by the person in the relevant country or is available for his use while he is there.

8.94 The expression 'place of abode' means, for these purposes, the house in which a person lived or the country, city, or town in which he was for the time being to be found. Further, it was considered that 'permanent' was used in the sense of something that was to be contrasted with that which was temporary or transitory but that it did not mean everlasting.

8.95 It appears that the decedent did not have her permanent place of abode outside Australia since her stays outside Australia were of a temporary nature and no intention to remain outside the country was formed.

The Domicile/Residence of the Decedent from a US Perspective

8.96 The imposition of US federal estate tax upon the estate of the decedent will depend upon two factors:

- whether the decedent was a citizen or resident of the United States at the time of her death; or

- whether the decedent held any assets with a US situs at the time of her death.

8.97 The decedent remained an Australian citizen throughout her life. Thus, the first issue is whether the decedent was a 'resident' of the United States at the time of her death.

Residency Determined by 'Domicile'

8.98 Although the US Internal Revenue Code contains a statutory definition of the term *resident*, by its terms that definition does not apply for estate tax purposes. Instead, for US federal estate tax purposes, a decedent is a resident only if she was 'domiciled' in the United States at the time of her death.

8.99 The decedent spent a significant amount of time in the United States. This satisfies the physical presence test. Thus, the question of domicile turns on whether the decedent had an intention to remain there permanently. Reported cases indicate that the courts will look to a variety of objective factors to test the ties of the decedent to Australia:

- the frequency with which the decedent returned to Australia and the length of her stays there;

- whether she owned and maintained a home in Australia;

- whether her home in the United States was maintained primarily for pleasure;

- the location of her family and friends;

- whether she maintained club, church, or social memberships in Australia;

- whether there were any written declarations of intention in wills, applications for visas, or other such documents; and

- various other items that may be applicable solely in the decedent's situation.

8.100   On the basis of the facts, it appears that the majority of the foregoing factors would support the decedent's intention to retain her Australian domicile. For example, the decedent returned to Australia at least once a year and remained there for at least three months out of every year, and usually for more than six months. Furthermore, she owned and maintained a home in Australia but only rented her home in the United States. Her home in Australia was in Sydney, but her home in the United States was in Aspen, Colorado. Some cases have discounted the importance of a residence if it is maintained at or near a resort area for pleasure purposes.

8.101   The fact that the decedent possessed a permanent US visa (a 'green card') will certainly provide some evidence that she intended to become a US resident. In addition, her marriage to a US citizen and resident will also provide some evidence that she intended to become a US resident. It is important to note, however, that no cases were identified in which either of these factors was determinative. The fact that the decedent filed a US federal income tax return should carry no weight whatsoever in determining her residency status for estate tax purposes.

8.102   Accordingly, based on the facts assumed herein, it appears that the objective indicia of intent support the decedent's intention to remain domiciled in Australia.

Status of Assets

8.103   Since the decedent remained both a citizen and a resident of Australia at her death, only those assets with a situs in the United States can be included in her estate for US federal estate tax purposes. For US federal estate tax purposes, stock of a foreign corporation is deemed to have a foreign situs, regardless of the location of the stock certificate, the stock transfer offices, or the sources of income.

US–Australia Estate Tax Treaty

8.104   The estate tax treaty between Australia and the United States does not address either of the issues analysed above. The treaty leaves the question of domicile to be determined by the local law of Australia and the United States. In addition, the treaty has no situs rules as to corporate stock; thus, the situs determination is again left to local law. As a result, the treaty does not alter the conclusions that the decedent should be treated as an Australian resident.

Conclusion

8.105   On the facts of the above case study, and in view of the applicable US and Australian law, the decedent had an Australian domicile at the time of her death.

8.106   Therefore, there was no estate tax liability in the United States and no requirement to make any report for the purposes of estate tax.

8.107   In the absence of any applicable Australian federal or state taxes, no Australian tax liability arises in respect of the estate.

CITIZENSHIP AND PASSPORTS

Acquiring a New Citizenship

8.108   Many offshore persons need more than just residence. Citizenship can be the critical problem — and usually a more difficult one— to resolve. The United States, for example, taxes on the basis of citizenship, and shedding US citizenship may be a painful procedure.

8.109   The other side of the coin is the acquisition of citizenship. Frequently the problem is solved by producing an Irish grandparent as the passport to Irish citizenship. An Italian ancestor can do the same for Italy, and a Jewish ancestor for Israel. But for many the wrong citizenship can be a greater hardship than just tax liability; and the search for a new citizenship is generally quite arduous.

8.110   France is a relatively hospitable country, particularly for people who have three or more children or who have a degree from a French university. Austria may accept you if you give a huge and well-placed donation and show a special love for all that is Austrian (which means rather more than Mozart and Strauss). For most countries, however, you need 3–5 years residence to qualify for citizenship.

8.111   Flaky passports from Latin America are mostly little more than travel documents of doubtful validity. Perhaps some 40 years ago, your parents were travelling through an isolated village in Bolivia when your mother unexpectedly gave birth to you. It was a bumpy llama ride that triggered her labour. Fortunately, some old villagers still remember the incident well and will sign a document certifying that you were born there. The rest is easy: citizenship, passport, driver's license, exemption from military service. How about a change of name for the same trouble? Or anything else you fancy? You can even come out of the procedure 12 years younger. See 'Strategic Checklists' at the end of this chapter.

Types of Passports

8.112   In addition to the simple passports based on citizenship, there are also a number of other classes that may meet the needs of an individual seeking to move offshore.

Marriage of Convenience Passports

8.113   A number of countries, including many European countries, grant immediate citizenship to persons who marry citizens. It may even be enough to have a 'serious relationship'. Female spouses often receive preferential treatment. Males usually have to have a period of residence as well as a marriage of convenience before getting their passports.

Non-citizenship Passports

8.114 Although passports are usually only issued to citizens, sometimes passport-like documents are issued that are little more than travel permits. Sometimes, too, passports are issued that look identical to normal passports notwithstanding that the bearer is a non-citizen.

Provisional Passports

8.115 Some Latin American countries grant citizenship to property owners. During the waiting period for such citizenship a *cedula*, or national identity card, may be granted and even a provisional passport if the property owner needs to travel. These documents may appear to be identical to regular passports.

Honorary Diplomatic Passports

8.116 Honorary consul diplomatic passports are sometimes awarded to friends of the country or to international business people who are considered useful. These diplomatic passports are usually treated seriously throughout the world.

Service Passports

8.117 Service passports are of limited application but may be granted to certain classes of government employees.

Refugee Passports

8.118 Stateless or persecuted persons may be granted refugee passports to enable them to travel beyond the country of asylum.

REMUNERATION OF OFFSHORE EMPLOYEES

Objectives

8.119 It is necessary to find a way to remunerate employees for the contributions they make to a multinational group's international activities. A second important need is for international mobility, with employees rendering services wherever the changing needs of the Group take them. Linked to the above needs is the need to provide flexibility regarding the provision of retirement benefits for employees.

8.120 In structuring the proposed arrangements, it is important to focus on the provision of internationally competitive rewards with specific attention being paid to:

● salaries and similar cash entitlements,

● bonuses,

● share participation, and

● retirement benefits

by means of tax-efficient simple, dual or multiple contractual arrangements.

8.121 Attention should also be directed at the establishment of an employment structure that is consistent with other benefits and which provides for:

● contractual relationships with standard conditions;

- a reward and benefit framework;
- primary conditions of employment;
- flexibility in employment benefits;
- competitiveness.

Tax Considerations

8.122 Payments that are effected offshore for services performed offshore will normally escape tax. However, it is always necessary to take into account the domestic and treaty rules governing each specific situation. In particular, persons resident (or in some cases domiciled, in the strict Anglo-American sense of the word) in countries that tax worldwide income will be liable in respect of offshore income.

8.123 In each of the countries concerned there are specific tax rules determining the incidence of tax liability of residents working abroad.

8.124 In addition, a tax treaty between the country of residence of an employee and the country where the services are performed may contain specific rules governing the apportionship of earnings.

Non-tax Considerations

8.125 Non-tax issues will, however, in most cases have a greater impact on the overall position of the employees. All of the rules and general considerations governing the remuneration of employees, their conditions of employment, and their benefit packages, have to be taken into account, every bit as much as tax factors, in the design of an international employment structure.

Exchange Control

8.126 Wherever employees are resident in a country that imposes exchange control restrictions, they are normally limited in their freedom to keep their funds abroad. In such cases, it is usual for the employer to be faced with a request that an offshore trust of some kind be set up by the employer in such a way that a portion of the remuneration may be received abroad without this constituting a breach of the exchange control regulations concerned.

Employment Structure

Contractual Relationship Between the Employer Company/ies and Employees

8.127 Employees could be employed solely by one of the companies in the Group, with all provisions relating to their employment embodied in one sole contract. Alternatively, employees could be retained or employed under dual or multiple contracts as follows:

- in respect of home duties, by the home company; and
- in respect of foreign duties, by the offshore headquarters company.

8.128 The rationale for using the headquarters company in respect of international duties would be to allow them to build up a tax-free retirement fund in hard currency in respect of international duties and to ensure that they will not be taxed at home in respect of income derived from international duties.

Administration

8.129   It is important that the activities of the headquarters company should not be regarded by the local tax authorities as actually being part of local activities. In order to ensure this, the following practical aspects should, *inter alia*, be attended to:

● central management and control;

● retainer and employment contracts should be initiated at the headquarters of the headquarters company and signed by the headquarters company;

● accounting and administration should physically be done by and at the headquarters of the headquarters company;

● cost recoveries and invoicing should be handled by the headquarters company.

Contractual Relationship Between the Headquarters Company and Local Companies

8.130   The headquarters company could enter into formal agreements with the local companies in terms of which the headquarters company will provide certain services (including secondment services) to the local company at an agreed fee. These agreements should be correctly drafted to ensure that this is clearly a service provided by the head-quarters company and not a contractual relationship between the employee and the local company.

8.131   Each time an employee is sent to work for a new local company for the first time, he or she should receive an appropriate letter of direction from the headquarters company.

Conditions of Employment

General

8.132   It may not be possible to harmonise all of the conditions of employment applicable at the headquarters company level, with the prevailing conditions of employment in the many local companies.

8.133   The conditions of employment that should be focused on are:

● remuneration (salary package);

● bonuses;

● benefits;

● tax equalisation; and

● terms of employment, which should be addressed fully before the conclusion of the employment contract.

Remuneration (Salary Package)

8.134   Employees of multinational companies who have dual contracts generally receive packages that are apportioned in accordance with actual services rendered in the various jurisdictions.

8.135   The apportionment of remuneration between the respective employment companies under dual contracts should be justifiable in terms of actual time spent in the home country and in other jurisdictions.

8.136 However, marginal flexibility exists in terms of apportionment of remuneration, for example, a ratio of 1.5:1 in favour of offshore remuneration, on the basis of annual calculations, can usually be justified by the need to travel, the nature of offshore duties, and so on. This ratio is generally acceptable to the tax authorities in most countries. Higher weightings could be regarded as a diversion of local remuneration to other jurisdictions by the local tax authorities, thus triggering their intervention. Regular reviews of the weightings used versus actual time spent on duties, should be undertaken.

8.137 The international portion of the remuneration may be adjusted to offshore market conditions to accommodate the cost of living differentials and to secure services. In appropriate circumstances, special allowances may be paid to compensate for lifestyle adjustments (e.g. hardship allowances).

8.138 In the case of some countries, it may be worthwhile noting the concept of a flexible salary package, in terms of which employees may (within certain limits) structure tax efficient packages on a cafeteria basis by means of a salary sacrifice. This kind of arrangement may be more difficult to implement in some countries because of adverse tax legislation. Package structuring will be implemented only in appropriate circumstances (where it is practical and manageable). Insofar as the headquarters company will apply a policy of tax equalisation, employees will largely be discouraged from package structuring.

8.139 By applying a policy of tax equalisation, the employer bears the cost of additional taxes or reaps the reduction in taxes that applies in the various jurisdictions where the services are rendered. The employee's net salary (after-tax salary) therefore remains unchanged.

Bonuses

8.140 Annual and other bonuses for international services should be attached exclusively to the work of the employees and their successes in connection with such work, outside of the home country. In this regard, it is important to note that if there is any fudging of the lines, all or a part of the bonuses in question could be attached by the local Revenue to a local source.

Benefits

8.141 *Retirement benefits.* To ensure that contractual arrangements are legitimate, retirement benefits (including the funding thereof) should mirror the distribution of earnings — which in turn should be aligned with the actual and physical rendering of services in the various jurisdictions.

A defined-contribution provident fund could also be set up offshore and benefits could be aligned with the most favourable of the local funds.

8.142 *Exchange control.* In the case of exchange control, regulations affecting certain persons who render services on a non-continuous basis to an offshore company, consideration might perhaps be given to the provision of retirement benefits via a discretionary trust. The discretionary trust will be funded by the headquarters company, and employees will sacrifice income equal to their own contributions. The trust will invest the funds and pay the proceeds to the beneficiaries on retirement or resignation. It is recommended that the beneficiaries should have no legal entitlement to the benefits. A protector should be appointed to ensure through a letter of wishes that beneficiaries will ultimately receive benefits (i.e. their portion of the investments of the trust).

8.143 *Tax treatment.* The deductibility of contributions for tax purposes will be determined in accordance with relevant local tax laws in the jurisdiction where services are rendered, since contributions will be funded from such earnings. The growth in the fund will be exempt from tax, and the benefits will normally also be free of tax. Withholding taxes on dividends received by the trust will not be recoverable. Planning may furthermore ensure that benefits can be taken in lump-sum form free from tax anywhere.

8.144 *Share incentive schemes.* Different types of share incentive schemes are possible, depending on whether shares are granted outright or distributed as options and whether the incentive scheme has immediate or deferred effect.

8.145 The issue of shares to employees in terms of a bonus is straightforward, as the bonus is taxable as normal remuneration — on payment.

8.146 The issue of shares in terms of a deferred sale scheme may have more complex tax implications in some countries where the difference between the issue price and market value of the shares on the date of exercise of the option is taxable. Usually this difference becomes tax-free if certain conditions are met, typically that a specified period lapses between exercising the option and selling the shares.

8.147 If the issue of shares is related to services rendered locally, the local tax legislation would normally apply. If the issue of shares is related to services rendered offshore, local tax legislation will not necessarily apply.

8.148 *Insurance.* Life cover premiums qualify for tax deduction, the proceeds form part of taxable income in the hands of the employee, but the employer qualifies for a tax deduction on payment of the proceeds to the estate of the deceased employee. The employer is therefore tax neutral, the premiums are tax deductible, and the proceeds are taxable in the hands of the employee.

8.149 Accident cover premiums qualify for a tax deduction, and employees are taxed on the proceeds.

8.150 Care must be taken to examine all issues, for example, whether premiums may qualify for deductions, the position of the estates of deceased employees, whether the employer would be tax neutral, and whether the proceeds would be taxable in the hands of the employee.

8.151 The deductibility of the cost of the premiums would generally depend on the tax legislation of the jurisdiction in which the services are rendered.

8.152 Cash could be offered in lieu of life cover, as the tax treatment normally does not differ from cash payments unless a discount on the premiums can be achieved through economies of scale. Employees could then be permitted to decide whether they wish to self-insure.

8.153 *Medical coverage.* The funding of medical schemes is, in most countries, tax deductible in the hands of the employer, and employees are not taxed on the funding or the benefits.

8.154 It may not be practical to provide medical benefits at the headquarters company level, as the employees will be rendering services in other jurisdictions; so it may be preferable to simply extend the local scheme internationally.

Ancillary Issues

8.155   The following ancillary issues may also need to be addressed:

- confidentiality;
- non-solicitation clauses;
- agreements on conflicts of interest;
- legal jurisdiction matters, etc.

STRATEGIC CHECKLISTS

PROOF OF RESIDENCE AND DOMICILE

The following non-exhaustive checklist, for each pertinent country, may, depending on the specific facts, contain useful guidance for the purpose of determining the question of residence of you or your client. Change the wording as appropriate if you are addressing the residence position of a third person or a decedent.

- Where is your permanent place of residence?

- Do you have a secondary place of residence? If so, where?

- Is it clear which is your permanent place of residence?

- Do you have a home, other than your principal place of residence, that you return to with any degree of frequency? If so, how frequently and for what duration?

- In which countries were you physically present at some time during the tax year, and for how many days respectively in each? Historically, what is the frequency, regularity, and duration of your past visits to each such country?

- What is your mode of life from a residency point of view?

- What is the purpose of any visits that you made to other countries during the tax year?

- What is the reason for any absences from the country in question during the tax year?

- What are your family and/or business ties with each country in question?

- If married, where does your spouse live?

- If you have minor children, where do they go to school?

- Is a place of abode is maintained by you in another country or countries, or available for your use while you are there?

- Where is your principal place of employment?

- How much time do you spend working there?

- How much time do you spend living there in total, including working time?

- How much time do you spend working at other places of employment in other countries?

- How much time do you spend outside of the country of your principal place of employment in total?

- Where are your principal business ties, other than your employment itself, located?

- Where are your personal ties, other than spouse and children, located?

- Of which clubs, church/es, or associations are you a member, and in which countries?

- Where were you born?

- What was your nationality at the time of your birth?

- What is your nationality now?

- What was your father's nationality at the time of your birth?

- Where was your father domiciled at the time of your birth?

- Have you made any written statement or statements relating to your place of residence in wills, applications for visa, or other such documents, relating to either your place of residence or of domicile?

RESIDENCE TIEBREAKERS IN TAX TREATIES

In cases where taxpayers are considered to have permanent homes in both treaty countries, the relevant tiebreakers are:

- the country with which their personal and economic relations are closer (i.e. the centre of vital interests), i.e.:

  — family and social relations;

  — occupations;

— political, cultural and other activities;

— place of business;

— place from which their property is administered;

— personal acts in general;

● and failing clarity on the above, the country of which they are citizens.

ACQUIRING A NEW CITIZENSHIP

A second passport, providing proof of citizenship and (usually although not invariably) access to the benefits associated with citizenship, may require one or more of the following:

● Conditions to be met:

— place of birth;

— parent's or grandparent's nationality;

— remoter ancestry;

— religion;

— military service;

— spouse, concubine, or similar relationship;

— meritorious service (very);

— special arrangements (very).

● Evidence to be produced:

— valid current passport;

— birth certificate;

— police good-conduct certificate;

— medical certificates;

— financial statements;

— evidence of languages;

— character references;

— religious certificates;

— a compliant spouse;

— patronage;

— money.

CITIZENSHIP REQUIREMENTS FOR SPECIFIC COUNTRIES

Australia, Canada, New Zealand	Three years, but this period may be shortened for special categories of immigrants.
Austria	Can be almost instant in the case of persons with the right patronage and attitudes, and certain classes of refugees.
Belize	A non-refundable economic contribution to the country of US$50,000 can earn you both citizenship and a passport.
Bolivia	Special formulas exist.
Brazil	The right contacts can get you a passport in as little as three weeks.
Dominican Republic	Can be very quick if you buy a home and some bonds as well.
France	Military service or three or more children or a university degree; plus a measure of permanence in France.
Germany	Some classes of refugees receive immediate citizenship and passports. Descent from a proven German citizen (especially from a passport-holder) can also work.
Honduras	A matter of price.
Israel	The Law of Return makes an instant passport available to anyone of Jewish descent.
Italy	Citizenship is easy in the case of 'ethnic Italians' or public benefactors.
Paraguay	Special formulas exist.
Portugal	Ownership of a property in Portugal for seven years may be deemed to meet the residence requirements for naturalisation purposes.
St. Kitts and Nevis	The purchase of approved real estate to the value of a minimum of US$50,000; or making an investment in

	an approved enterprise may earn you both citizenship and a passport.
Spain	Two years residence only if you are from a former Spanish colony, i.e., most of Latin America except Brazil.
Switzerland	Start with 12 consecutive years of residence and money (remember *'pas d'argent, pas de Suisse'*).

REMUNERATION PACKAGES OF OFFSHORE EMPLOYEES

- Contractual relationships.

- Primary conditions of employment.

- Salaries.

- Similar cash entitlements.

- Bonuses.

- Share participation.

- Retirement benefits.

- A reward and benefit framework.

- Flexibility in employment benefits.

- Competitiveness.

- Tax equalisation.

- Terms of employment.

- Confidentiality.

- Non-solicitation clauses.

- Agreements on conflicts of interest.

- Legal jurisdiction matters, etc.

DEPARTING EXPATRIATES ATTEND LIST

An expatriate leaving home usually has a long checklist:

- buying or renting property in a new country;

- overseas removal;

- pre-retirement savings and investment;

- the pension position;

- social security benefits;

- private medical treatment and health care;

- exchange control;

- tax in both countries.

9 New Developments Affecting Offshore Trusts and Asset Protection

---

STRATEGIC ISSUES, OPPORTUNITIES AND CAVEATS

THE TRUST STRUCTURE

- The trustees stand, broadly speaking, in the shoes both of the creator of the trust, who may be living or dead, and of the beneficiaries.

- The trustees' powers of dealing with the property entrusted to them are to be gathered from the true construction of the trust instrument, if any, as supplemented or restricted by the principles of equity and by statutory provisions.

- In most countries, the court exercises ultimate control over all trusts.

- As a general rule, it is the Anglo-Americans that have the monopoly of the offshore trust business.

- *Caveat:* Though entities such as the Liechtenstein *Anstalt* and *Stiftung* may be useful, they sometimes suffer non-recognition in other legal systems.

TAX TREATMENT OF TRUSTEES

- In most countries, the income of the trust bears tax in the hands of the trustees.

- In the normal course, it is the trust's assets that will be used to pay the taxes, and not the trustee's personal assets.

TAX TREATMENT OF BENEFICIARIES

- The following generally form part of the total income of the beneficiary (though there are significant differences in the various tax systems):

  — income in which the beneficiary has a vested interest, whether this is paid to him or accumulated;

  — sums in the nature of income applied for the benefit of the beneficiary under the terms of the trust;

  — sums in the nature of income paid to or applied for the benefit of the beneficiary in exercise of a discretion.

- *Caveat:* To determine whether a sum forms part of a beneficiary's total income, it may be necessary to ascertain, not whether the sum arises from capital or income of the trust, but whether it is received by the beneficiary in the quality of income.

TAX TREATMENT OF SETTLORS

- The income from certain types of settlement may in certain countries be deemed for tax purposes to be income of the settlor.

- Sometimes there are provisions that require the settlor to pass on to the trustees or beneficiaries the benefit of any reliefs he may receive in respect of the trust income concerned, and empower the settlor to recover from the trustees or beneficiaries the amount of any additional tax liability he incurs in respect of such trust income.

- *Caveat:* The settlor is frequently in the firing line of anti-avoidance provisions.

CAVEATS REGARDING THE LEGAL LIABILITY OF OFFSHORE TRUSTEES AND TRUST COMPANIES

- The trustees should exercise the same standard of care as the prudent person of business in the exercise of one's own affairs.

- In the use of investment powers, the standard of care is that of a prudent businessperson. A higher standard of care is expected from a professional than a lay trustee.

- A trust company should not place itself in a position where its duty and interest may conflict.

- A trustee may not profit from the trust.

- If trustees sell trust property to themselves, or sell their own property to the trust, the transaction is voidable (the 'self-dealing' rule).

- If trustees purchase the beneficial interest of a beneficiary, the sale is voidable unless the trustees have taken no advantage from their position, made full disclosure, and the sale is fair and honest (the 'fair-dealing' rule).

- Trustees should not place themselves in a position where a duty to one set of beneficiaries conflicts with their duty to another set of beneficiaries.

- Where trustees control a company, they must ensure that they receive sufficient information about the company's board and decisions taken, so as to allow the trustees to protect the value of their shares.

SUPERIORITY OF OFFSHORE ASSET PROTECTION TRUSTS (ATPS) OVER DOMESTIC TRUSTS

- There is enhanced ability to retain benefit and control.

- Offshore trusts are not automatic targets.

- Offshore trusts create practical barriers.

- Offshore trusts are ultimately more protective.

- The choice of location of the trust assets is not the same issue as the choice of location of the trust itself.

- A properly drafted foreign situs APT allows the trustees to invest trust assets in any part of the world.

- The ultimate safety valve is the ability of the APT, as an international instrument, to invest and reinvest assets in any part of the world.

- *Caveat:* Watch for fraudulent conveyance considerations. If there is an identifiable creditor problem — whether pending, threatened, or expected — the scope of planning opportunities is severely narrowed

ASSET PROTECTION AND THE STATUTE OF ELIZABETH

- Under the 1571 Statute of Elizabeth it is sometimes possible to set aside transfers into trust even if the settlor transferred the property many years before the debt arose and, at the time of making the transfer, had no indication that the particular debt would arise in the future.

- *Caveat:* This provision of English law has also been introduced into the law of a number of legal systems based on English law, and this includes many of the states in the United States nd many of the tax havens of the world.

CASES OF VALIDITY OF TRUSTS COMING UNDER CHALLENGE

- Offshore trusts are a minefield of potential exposure to legal liability, in particular regarding:

  - controls over trustees by the settlor;

  - transfers in the case of an existing debt;

  - settlors serving as trustees;

  - matrimonial disputes.

- The settlor's role should not extend beyond establishing and funding the trust, appointing the trustees, determining the beneficiaries and laying down under what circumstances they are to benefit.

- Settlors should be made aware of the fact that, once the property has been transferred to the trust fund, they should have no direct control over the trust or access to the trust assets.

- *Caveat* A settlor driven trust may be void where the settlor seems to 'give' without really giving.

- *Caveat* Where a protector is used so as to enable the settlor to continue to exercise control over the trust or to access the trust assets, this too may put the validity of the trust in issue.

ALTERNATIVE OFFSHORE VEHICLES TO THE OFFSHORE TRUST

- Limited liability companies.

- Companies limited by guarantee.

- Bearer share companies.

- Contractual arrangements, such as an option or an agency.

- Contractual relationships relating to possession, such as bailment.

- Various pour-over devices whereby assets and rights can be moved from one vehicle to another.

LEGAL NATURE OF THE TRUST

9.1 The word 'trust' refers to the duty or aggregate accumulation of obligations that rest upon a person described as a trustee. The responsibilities are in relation to property held by him or under his control. The trustee is obliged to administer the trust property in the manner lawfully prescribed by the trust instrument (trust deed or settlement), or in the absence of specific provision, in accordance with equitable principles or statute law. The administration will thus be in such a manner that the consequential benefits and advantages accrue, not to the trustee, but to the beneficiaries.

9.2 The Anglo-Saxon trust is merely a bundle of rights and obligations in equity and is thus not strictly speaking a legal entity. Though the law of trusts varies from system to system, those patterned on the English law of trusts resemble one another closely, differences usually being of statutory origin. In the case of civil law systems where the trust is to be found it is invariably a creature of statute.

9.3 According to *The Oxford Companion to Law*, a trust is an arrangement for the holding and administration of property under which property or legal rights are vested by the owner of the property or rights (truster) in a person or persons (trustees) which they are then to hold or to exercise for or on behalf of another (*cestui que trust* or beneficiary), or others, or for the accomplishment of a particular purpose or purposes. The essence of the concept is the separation of legal and beneficial ownership, the property being legally vested in one or more trustees but in equity held for and belonging to others. The concept of trust is the most important contribution of English equity to jurisprudence. It is not derived from Roman law, from such institutions as *fidei commissa*, and its origin is doubtful. Significance in its development attaches to the idea of conscience, which was treated as important by the early chancellors, who were ecclesiastics. Statutes have only to a small extent affected English trust law, though the few statutes are important.

9.4 The trustees stand in a fiduciary relation and must hold the property or exercise the rights in a fiduciary capacity. In many relationships, e.g. partnership, a person stands towards another or others in a fiduciary relationship and may be deemed a trustee for some purposes.

9.5 A trust may be created expressly, by statute, by *inter vivos* declaration, or by will, or arise by operation of law, which includes constructive trusts and resulting trusts. It may be a private trust, for the benefit of individuals, or a public trust for charitable or public purposes. It may extend to any property or interest in property, which a person can transfer, or assign, or dispose of. It may be in favour of any person, or for charitable or other lawful purposes. The objects of the trust must be declared with sufficient certainty to permit the court to enforce it.

9.6 Where a trust is created expressly there must be an adequate declaration of trust and certainty of intention, as to subject matter, and as to objects or persons to be benefited.

9.7 A constructive trust is, in a sense, a remedy that arises by operation of law where the legal holder of property would, for instance, be unjustly enriched if he kept the property, and where the interest should actually be transferred to or held for the benefit of some other person. Frequently, a constructive trust attaches to property, which a person holding property in trust has acquired by means of his ownership of or dealings with that trust. A resulting trust arises where an intention to create a trust is indicated, but the trust is not fully declared or fails in whole or in part, or where property is put in the possession of a person ostensibly for his own use but truly to effect a purpose which fails, or where property is put in someone's possession without intimation that he is to hold it in trust, and where retention of the beneficial interest by the purchaser is presumed intended and is held to be equitable.

9.8 The courts have over the centuries greatly elaborated principles laying down the rights, powers, and duties of trustees. In particular, high standards have always been demanded of trustees in respect of care for the trust estate, careful investment, strict accounting, fair apportionment between income and capital, duty to pay the right beneficiaries, and absence of personal profit or self-interest and trustees have frequently been held liable to repay to the trust losses caused by lack of care or other breach of trust. Trust property can be recovered from a third party who has obtained it unless he obtained a legal title, for valuable consideration, and without notice that his acquisition was in breach of trust.

9.9 Equity has always shown great favour to charitable trusts, which comprise trusts for the relief of poverty, for the advancement of education, for the advancement of religion, and for other purposes beneficial to the community, and the court will not allow a charitable trust to fail because the purpose is uncertain but will give effect to the trustor's intention by settling a scheme for administration of the trust to give effect as nearly as possible to the trustor's intentions.

9.10 A trustee must accept or disclaim office, and persons may be authorised to appoint new trustees, or the court may do so. A trustee may retire but remains liable for things done while he was a trustee, or may be removed by the court. A trustee must not make use of trust property for his private advantage and must account for profit made out of his trust. As a general rule, in the absence of a provision relating to remuneration, a trustee is not entitled to any remuneration. Also, in many cases, the trustee would not be empowered to acquire trust property, and dealings with beneficiaries may be voidable.

9.11 The trustees' duties are to take possession of and preserve the trust property, be diligent and prudent in administering it, act personally, be impartial as between beneficiaries, keep accounts and give information to the beneficiaries as required, and invest the trust funds in the manner permitted by statute. If in doubt, trustees are entitled to obtain the opinion of the court as to the right course of action, and they may have specific questions determined by the court.

9.12 The court now has wide powers to approve arrangements varying or revoking the trusts or enlarging the powers of the trustees.

9.13 Breach of trust is any act in contravention or excess of the duties imposed on the trustees by the trust, including neglects, omissions, and dishonesty, and trustees are liable in so far as loss has resulted to the trust estate. They may be relieved from liability by provision in the trust deed, or by the court under statutory power. Beneficiaries can obtain no relief against trustees if they concurred or acquiesced in the breach of trust.

9.14 There is no generally accepted definition of the word 'settlement' but it may be defined as any disposition of property, of whatever nature, by any instrument or number of instruments, whereby trusts are constituted for the purpose of regulating the enjoyment of the settled property successively among the persons or classes of persons nominated by the settlor. However, for certain tax purposes the word 'settlement' is given a much wider meaning.

9.15 The trust concept has analogies with, but is distinct from, the *fidei commissa* of civil law systems, which is really a different concept altogether. For this reason, certain countries, such as Panama, Liechtenstein, and Monaco, have introduced trusts by statute. However, these creatures of statute lack the body of equitable principles that characterise the Anglo-American trust.

TAX TREATMENT OF TRUSTS

9.16 In many countries, the income of the trust bears tax in the hands of the trustees, either by deduction at source or by direct assessment.

9.17 Trustees stand, broadly speaking, in the shoes both of the creator of the trust, who may be living or dead, and of the beneficiaries. Their powers of dealing with the property entrusted to them are to be gathered from the true construction of the trust instrument, if any, as supplemented or restricted by the principles of equity and by statutory provisions. In most countries, the court exercises ultimate control over all trusts. In the normal course, a trustee is not personally liable for tax. It is the trust's assets that will be used to pay the taxes, not the trustee's personal assets.

9.18 The following generally form part of the total income of the beneficiary (though there are significant differences in the various tax systems):

- income in which the beneficiary has a vested interest, whether this is paid to him or accumulated;

- sums in the nature of income applied for the benefit of the beneficiary under the terms of the trust;

- sums in the nature of income paid to or applied for the benefit of the beneficiary in exercise of a discretion.

9.19 New Developments Affecting Offshore Trusts

9.19 Income in which the beneficiary has a contingent interest, and which is accumulated, does not generally form part of the beneficiary's income as it arises.

9.20 The income from certain types of settlement may in certain countries be deemed for tax purposes to be income of the settlor; sometimes there are provisions that require the settlor to pass on to the trustees or beneficiaries the benefit of any reliefs he may receive in respect of the trust income concerned, and empower the settlor to recover from the trustees or beneficiaries the amount of any additional tax liability he incurs in respect of such trust income.

9.21 To determine whether a sum forms part of a beneficiary's total income, it may be necessary to ascertain, not whether the sum arises from capital or income of the trust, but whether it is received by the beneficiary in the quality of income.

THE OFFSHORE TRUST

9.22 The Medieval trust became a tax avoidance technique which worked so effectively that by the end of the last century the trust was well and truly in position to fulfil its prime vocation of income tax and estate tax avoidance.

9.23 Inevitably, the trust became a target of UK and US anti-avoidance measures. But since the first moves to restrict the free operation of tax avoidance were domestic, the wealthy simply moved their trusts offshore. Anti-avoidance measures gradually came to be directed also at the offshore trust.

9.24 A prime example of a far-reaching anti-avoidance measure is the UK imposition of tax liability on a UK resident who has power to enjoy income of any person (a term which includes companies and trusts) outside the United Kingdom. Although there must be a 'transfer of assets' to bring the provision into play, this can be a transfer between two non-residents and it is practically impossible to conceive of a situation where an offshore entity could be set up without there being a transfer of assets within the meaning of the section.

9.25 For the most part, it is the Anglo-Americans that have the monopoly of the offshore trust business. But there is one contender that has done extraordinarily well with its own inventively and marketing skills — Liechtenstein. There are two original Liechtenstein creations: the *Anstalt* or establishment, and the *Stiftung* or foundation.

9.26 The most common and best known of the Liechtenstein entities is the *Anstalt* or establishment. The *Anstalt* is the duck-billed platypus of offshore creatures. A curious mixture of a company and a trust, it is formed in much the same way as a regular company, but has beneficiaries as well. The most unusual feature is that the supreme authority of the *Anstalt* vests in the current holder of the founder's rights. For this reason, the certificate evidencing the founder's rights is often transferred or assigned from one person to another in blank without any name filled in — thus making the certificate the approximate equivalent of a bearer share document for all the shares of a corporation. The current holder of the founder's rights has the power to amend the articles of incorporation and to appoint or remove directors. He can also appoint beneficiaries and determine their rights. If beneficiaries are not designated, the founder's rights constitute an asset in the estate of the holder upon his death.

9.27 Because of these oddities the *Anstalt* does not find a ready niche in the legal systems of other countries. Some courts refuse to accept that an *Anstalt* is a separate legal entity at all. Sometimes they treat the *Anstalt* as a company and sometimes as a trust, their choice seeming to turn on little more than the way they can raise more tax. To make things worse, most European tax administrators assume that a taxpayer who has dealings with an *Anstalt* is hiding assets and income.

9.28   The *Stiftung* or foundation has many of the features of a trust. It has been described as a charitable foundation with non-charitable beneficiaries, a sort of equivalent of a family Red Cross. If an eligible family member asks the *Stiftung's* board for money he is likely to get it; an outsider will not. There are no founder's rights. The board administers the assets and may even have the power to designate beneficiaries and determine their rights.

9.29   Again, it is far from obvious whether a foreign court would classify a *Stiftung* as a trust or as an association; and in some systems it might even be taxed as if it were a company.

9.30   All of these factors conspire to make the Liechtenstein *Anstalt* and *Stiftung* somewhat less than the ideal entities for most purposes.

OFFSHORE TRUST CASES AFFECTING THE WEALTHY

When and Why the Courts may set Aside Trusts

9.31   There are a number of cases in which US courts showed reluctance to set aside offshore trusts. We look at a number of recent cases where foreign structures were successfully attacked. The implications of these cases are of major significance to settlors, trustees, beneficiaries, and creditors of settlors and beneficiaries. The assumptions of the past relating to the legal effect of letters of wishes and trustees' file notes will have to come under review. So will the assumptions made regarding the effectiveness of certain divesting techniques.

Controls over Trustees by the Settlor

9.32   If a settlor of a trust controls the trustee or trust assets, the trust may be a sham or the alter ego of the settlor. Persons transferring assets to a trust, knowing that a claim has been filed or is about to be filed against such assets, should expect that the courts might well set aside the benefits otherwise available.

9.33   The trustee, as legal owner, has fiduciary duties to beneficiaries in a trust relationship. Controlling the trustee may cause a court to classify the settlor as a principal, with the trustee as his agent, or treat the trust as the alter ego of the settlor. *Rahman v Chase Bank Trust Co Ltd* [1987/88] JLR 81 set aside a foreign trust as a sham stating 'to give and to retain is not possible'. The court found that Rahman controlled the trust and made all decisions relating to management of trust assets. In *George v Zmuda* 731 F 2d 1417 (9th Cir, 1984), foreign business trusts were found to be 'paper entities structured solely to avoid taxes'.

9.34   The Bahamian appellate in *Grupo Torras SA* approved the 1994 High Court Mareva injunction freezing trust assets since the settlor had 'substantial or effective control' (*Private Trust Corp v Grupo Torras SA* [1997/98] 1 OFLR 443). The Bahamian courts found the trust made the settlor's money 'available to himself as an object of the trust'. The Bahamian courts said the trust gave absolute discretion to the trustees; however, the trustees acted at the settlor's whim, stating:

'If it be established that the Bluebird Trust was a vehicle over which Sheikh Fahad [settlor] exercised substantial or effective control, the court would pierce the corporate structure of PTC [the trustee] and regard Sheikh Fahad as beneficial owner of the . . . trust.'

9.35 The Bahamas court, discussing the standard 'flee' clause, stated:

'It is unnecessary to pass on the validity or enforceability of such a provision . . . [I]ts very presence . . . sets off alarm bells . . . of a potential judgment creditor.'

9.36 However, the judge stated that 'nothing but a pre-emptive Mareva injunction could shut the stable door before the horse bolts'. These statements regarding the flee clause by the Bahamian judge cause concern to international practitioners. However, on 16 April 1999, the Court of Appeals reversed a 1994 Mareva injunction granted by the High Court in England, holding that there is no jurisdiction to grant a Mareva injunction when no substantive cause of action was filed against the defendant. The Court of Appeals stated that when the High Court issued the Mareva injunction in 1994, there was no substantive claim filed against the appellants (defendants) anywhere, and no Mareva injunction has been granted in such circumstances. See *Meespierson (Bahamas) Ltd v Grupo Torras SA* Civil Appeal No 41 of 1998. Nevertheless, on 25 June 1999, the High Court found that Sheikh Fahad and others had committed fraud and assessed damages against them ('The Grupo Torras Case', Vol. IV, No. 5 Offshore Red 103).

Transfers in the Case of an Existing Debt

9.37 In another case, a debtor transferred most of his assets to an offshore trust, knowing that his personal guarantee of his corporation's debt was being called. The Bankruptcy Court denied bankruptcy discharge to the debtor (*Marine Midland Bank v Portnoy* 1996 US App LEXIS 28974 (Bankr SDNY Oct 7, 1996)).

9.38 In the matter of *Stephan J Lawrence* (United States Bankruptcy Court Southern District of Florida, case No 97–14687, BKC-AJC), the debtor transferred assets to a Mauritius trust a few days before judgment was rendered against him. The judge stated that the matter may be transferred to the US Attorney-General or the FBI on possible perjury, the attorneys who advised the bankrupt may be sued, and the debtor may go to jail.

9.39 The court reinstated a Mareva injunction against US settlors in *Orange Grove Owners Association. v Orange Grove Partners* (Plaint No 208/94) (6 November 1995, unreported), High Ct Rarotonga, Civil Div. In interpreting the Cook Islands International Trust Acts of 1984, the court said, 'It should not be lightly assumed that Parliament intended to defeat the claims of creditors by allowing international trusts to be used to perpetrate a fraud against a creditor.' Creditors bought condominiums from settlors in November 1988 and 1989. Problems were discovered in 1991, with action brought in California State Court in April 1992. Judgment was entered on 13 April 1994, for the creditors. The settlors transferred assets to a Cook Islands trust from late 1993 until early 1994.

9.40 Settlors requested the Cook Islands Court to recognise the California judgment and satisfy the judgment from trust assets. The settlors alleged that the action was not filed within two years of the date of the accrual of the cause of action. The settlors defined that date as the date on which the act or omission occurred. The court defined the jury's verdict as the applicable date.

9.41 Cook Islands legislation subsequently clarified the date of a cause of action: 'the date of the cause of accruing shall be the date of that act or omission which shall be relied upon' (§13B(8)(a), Cook Islands International Trusts Act of 1984, as amended).

Settlors Serving as Trustees

9.42 In *Federal Trade Commission v Anderson and Anderson* (CV-S-98-669-LDG (RLH) (*D Nev* 1998)), the FTC claimed the Andersons committed fraud. The judge ordered the Andersons to repatriate offshore trust assets to the United States. The Andersons continued to serve as trustees of the trust and sent a request for the funds to be returned pursuant to the court order. The trust contained a typical 'anti-duress' provision, and the request for the return of the assets was denied. The Andersons were automatically removed as trustees and the judge ordered the Andersons to be jailed.

9.43 The US government was granted a default judgment to foreclose on federal tax liens against taxpayer's assets that were held in offshore trusts (*Deryll Wayne Pack v United States* 77 AFTR 2d para 96–476; see also, *United States v Reinhard P Mueller* 77 AFTR 2d para 96–457).

9.44 A leading case of trustee mismanagement is *Bartlett v Barclays Bank Trust Co Ltd* [1980] 1 All ER 139. The bank, a major shareholder, remained passive regarding the directors' proposals. The younger-generation beneficiary managers made two speculative investments resulting in financial disaster. The English Court of Appeals stated that, 'It was a trustee's duty to conduct trust business with the care that a reasonably prudent businessman would extend to his own affairs.'

9.45 In *West v Lazard Bros Co (Jersey) Ltd* [1993] JLR 165, the court refused to uphold a standard form exoneration clause.

Matrimonial Disputes

9.46 In another case, a physician transferred assets to a Cook Islands trust to protect against malpractice claims. Some time later, the physician's wife commenced divorce proceedings in New York. At the same time, she commenced litigation in the High Court of the Cook Islands, resulting in a Mareva injunction restricting the doctor and trustee from disposing of the trust assets pending the determination of the wife's claim. The New York Court acknowledged no jurisdiction over trust assets, saying the physical location of marital property was not relevant. It awarded the wife one-half the value of the trust assets on the date of the transfer to the offshore trust, not to be duplicative, however, of any award from the Cook Islands court *Riechers v Riechers* (No 21833/94 (1 July 1998, unreported), NY Sup Ct.

Duty of Care of Trustees

9.47 In *Bartlett et al v Barclays Bank Trust Co Ltd* ([1980] 1 All ER 139), the trustee was a trust company controlled by Barclays. The principal trust asset was a private company in which the trustee had a controlling interest. Years after the inception of the trust and the death of the settlor, the bank and trust corporation had no representation on the company's board. Without consulting the trustees, the company embarked on two very speculative investments. One produced a huge loss, the other made a very small profit. The company's board had never provided the bank with any information, nor did the bank insist on receiving it. As such, the trustees were not even aware of the investment.

9.48 The judge in the case stated the following:

'So far, I have applied the test of the ordinary prudent man of business. Although I am not aware that the point has previously been considered, except briefly in *Re*

Waterman's Will Trusts, I am of the opinion that a higher duty of care is plainly due from someone like a trust corporation which carried on a specialised business of trust management. A trust corporation holds itself out in its advertising literature as being above ordinary mortals. With a specialist staff of trained trust officers and managers, with ready access to financial information and professional advice, dealing with and solving trust problems day after day, the trust corporation holds itself out, and rightly, as capable of providing an expertise which it would be unrealistic to expect and unjust to demand from the ordinary prudent man or woman who accepts, probably unpaid and sometimes reluctantly from a sense of family duty, the burdens of trusteeship. Just as, under the law of contract, a professional person possessed of a particular skill is liable for breach of contract if he neglects to use the skill and experience which he professes, so I think that a professional corporate trustee is liable for breach of trust if loss is caused to the trust fund because it neglects to exercise the special care and skill which it professes to have.'

9.49   The court held as follows:

- the trustee's duty was to conduct business with the care of a reasonably prudent businessman conducting his own affairs;

- as a professional corporate trustee (such as the bank) a higher duty of care was owed than would have been the case if it were a lay trustee (i.e. the bank was thus liable for loss caused to a trust by neglect to exercise the special care and skill it professed to have);

- the bank had a duty as a trustee to receive adequate information on the company's activities to make use of such information so as to protect the interests of the beneficiaries (the only information the bank had asked for was that dispensed at the annual general meetings).

9.50   In the Jersey case of *West v Lazard Bros & Co (Jersey) Ltd* [1993] JLR 165, the trustees acted with extreme ineptitude and negligence. The trustees transferred the interest which the settlor (Frederick West) had in his home (about 34%) to a company for £1 without his involvement. The result was that West lost most of his money.

9.51   The trustees sought to rely upon an exemption clause in the trust deed which provided, in essence, that the trustees would not be liable for any act, unless this was as a result of fraud. As such, the trustees sought to exclude liability as a result of negligence. However, West had never even seen the trust deed (which was a standard deed utilised by the trustees).

9.52   The court found the comprehensive exclusion clause as being repugnant to the fundamental concept of a trust and also contrary to Article 26(9) of the Jersey Trust law which held: 'Nothing in the terms of a trust shall relieve, release or exonerate a trustee from liability for breach of trust arising from his own fraud, wilful misconduct or gross negligence.' The court found the trustees liable on the basis of gross negligence.

9.53   In another Jersey case, *Midland Bank Trustee v Federated Pension Services Ltd* [1995] JLR 352, a decision was taken by the inexperienced trustees without consulting with solicitors beforehand. The professional trustees committed an alleged breach of trust in that the transfer of trust property to new trustees was delayed. In the ensuing period, the trust assets were placed on deposit with a bank, which resulted in the loss of the benefit of a rise in the stock market during the same period. In this case, like *West v Lazard Bros*, an exclusion clause in the trust deed sought to exclude liability.

9.54   However, unlike the *West* case, the court did not find that the trustees' negligence amounted to wilful default or gross negligence, but simple default. As such, the trustees were protected by the exclusion clause in the relevant trust deed. The court held that clauses that seek to exonerate trustees from liability are to be interpreted narrowly and strictly.

LEGAL LIABILITY OF OFFSHORE TRUSTEES AND TRUST COMPANIES

Cardinal rules

9.55   A trust company should not place itself in a position where its duty and interest may conflict.

9.56   A trustee not profit from the trust. If a trustee sells trust property to himself or herself, or sells his or her own property to the trust, the transaction is voidable (the 'self-dealing' rule). If a trustee purchases the beneficial interest of a beneficiary, the sale is voidable unless the trustee has taken no advantage from his or her position, made full disclosure, and the sale is fair and honest (the 'fair-dealing' rule).

9.57   A trustee should not place himself or herself in a position where a duty to one set of beneficiaries conflicts with his or her duty to another set of beneficiaries.

9.58   Where trustees control a company, they must ensure that they receive sufficient information about the company's board and decisions taken, so as to allow the trustees to protect the value of their shares.

9.59   The trustees should exercise the same standard of care as the prudent person of business in the exercise of one's own affairs. In the use of investment powers, the standard of care is that of a prudent person of business making investments for those for whom he or she feels morally bound to provide. A higher standard of care is expected from a professional than a lay trustee.

Offshore Trust Pitfalls

9.60   Offshore trusts are a minefield of potential exposure to legal liability. At the very least, the settlor, the trustee, and the protector should beware of the following pitfalls.

9.61   A trust may be void where the settlor seems to 'give' without really giving. The settlor's role should not extend beyond establishing and funding the trust, appointing the trustees, determining the beneficiaries and laying down under what circumstances they are to benefit. Settlors should be made aware of the fact that, once the property has been transferred to the trust fund, they should have no direct control over the trust or access to the trust assets.

9.62   Where a protector is used so as to enable the settlor to continue to exercise control over the trust or to access the trust assets, this too may put the validity of the trust in issue. The protector is an additional party in the trust equation and acts as guardian over the trust and the trustee. The protector would be able, for example, to relocate the trust to a safer or more convenient jurisdiction in case of danger (this was the origin of the *Cuba clause*). The powers of the protector are embodied in the trust deed, and the problem arises where the settlor side-steps these provisions and uses the protector to limit the powers of the trustees in a manner incompatible with the provisions of the trust deed — say as a tool whereby the settlor could exercise the power of hiring and firing the trustees.

9.63 Lack of clarity as to the respective roles of the parties to the trust relationship can be fraught with danger. The trustees need to appreciate that the settlor is not their client or customer, and that they should refrain, in discussions or correspondence, from such references. The concept of the settlor as client or customer is in conflict with the fundamental definition of a trust as laid down in Article 2 of the Hague Convention, which makes it clear that the trustees stand in a fiduciary relationship to the beneficiaries.

9.64 Another danger lies in the tendency of trustees and others engaged in trust formation to resort to a standard trust deed, rather than to design the trust in the light of the specific circumstances of the prospective settlor, his family, and his business. Again, the need to update the trust arrangements should not be left out of account.

9.65 Trust arrangements ought always to plan for income tax, estate tax, and wealth tax burdens that may fall on the settlor, the trustee, or the beneficiary, at home or abroad.

ASSET PROTECTION TRUSTS

9.66 The term *asset protection trust* (APT) is a term of art referring to the trusts that are specifically designed to address the limits to the uses of standard trusts. It is of course arguable that the term is a misnomer since nearly every trust may be considered to have asset protection as one of its objectives.

9.67 Asset protection, as its name indicates, is aimed at protecting companies and individuals from creditors, real and phoney, from spouses and children, from partners and employees.

9.68 Aside from protecting assets, a number of other estate and financial planning objectives can be achieved through the use of a foreign situs APT. Generally, the APT is considered to be the most effective asset protection planning tool available.

Superiority of Offshore Asset Protection Trusts Over Domestic Trusts

9.69 As an asset protecting planning device, foreign situs trusts are generally considered to be superior to domestic trusts for the following reasons:

● *Enhanced Ability to Retain Benefit and Control.* Domestic trust law generally restricts the extent of benefit and control that a settlor can retain following establishment of the trust. A maxim of domestic law is that one does not place property out of a creditor's reach if the property has not been placed out of the transferor's reach. Accordingly, a domestic trust settled when the settlor's seas are calm may nevertheless remain vulnerable to the reach of creditors during the settlor's lifetime to the extent benefit or control is retained by the settlor.

● *Offshore Trusts not Automatic Targets.* Because a domestic trust remains subject to local jurisdiction, it can be expected to be a target in litigation against the settlor if the trust corpus is substantial. Due to geographical, jurisdictional, and other factors (such as whether the judgments and orders of a domestic court will be recognised by a foreign court ('comity'), an APT is not nearly as likely to be the same automatic defendant as a domestic trust.

● *Offshore Trusts Create Practical Barriers.* The mere fact that an APT is a foreign entity will have a definite impact on a creditor's decision either regarding instituting suit in the first instance or concerning how far the creditor is willing to go to pursue assets. Factors such as:

— the psychological barrier of dealing with foreigners and foreign legal systems;

— the costs of pursuing litigation overseas (particularly if a new, non-contingency-based suit must be brought against the defendant in the foreign court);

— the added uncertainty of prevailing under foreign law; and the increased time required to litigate abroad;

— substantially enhance the protection the trust assets will enjoy should a problem develop in the future.

● *Offshore Trusts Ultimately more Protective.* The trust law of certain offshore jurisdictions may be more specific and protective than is the trust law of the domestic jurisdiction.

9.70 It should be noted that certain states (e.g., South Dakota, Alaska, and Delaware) have adopted ATP legislation, which offers many of the features to be found in the IOFCs themselves.

Selecting the Appropriate Offshore Jurisdiction

9.71 There are a number of considerations that should be analysed in choosing the offshore jurisdiction whose laws will govern an APT.

9.72 A number of offshore financial centres, such as the Bahamas, Belize, the Cayman Islands, the Cook Islands, Cyprus, Gibraltar, and the Turks & Caicos Islands, satisfy these conditions to varying degrees. Though recently enacted legislation clarifies to some extent the myriad of issues relating to when and under what circumstances a creditor of a settlor can reach assets of the settlor's trust, a great deal of uncertainty in this area exists under domestic as well as English common law.

9.73 The laws of the Bahamas, the Cayman Islands, Cyprus, the Cook Islands, and certain other jurisdictions provide a fixed period of time following a transfer within which a creditor must commence a suit against the trust or its settlor or both.

9.74 Other important provisions to look for in APT legislation are dealt with in the asset protection trust law of Gibraltar, Turks & Caicos, and the Cook Islands. Moreover, a number of other offshore financial centres, such as the Bahamas, the British Virgin Islands, Bermuda, Guernsey, Jersey, and the Isle of Man, are enhancing their asset protection trust legislation.

9.75 The United Kingdom is able to bring pressure to bear on its Overseas Territories (notably Bermuda and the Cayman Islands) to open their financial records to official investigators; this has led Belize to introduce new mutual funds and other financial services legislation.

Aggressive *versus* Non-Aggressive Trust Legislation

9.76 Belize has the most aggressive trust law. Belize provides for immediate protection for trust assets and Belizean courts will not invalidate a trust or enforce a foreign judgment based on the claims of creditors in an insolvency proceeding (thereby not recognising the fraudulent transfer). Anyone desiring to levy against trust assets must prove, in a Belizean court, that the trust was established by duress, fraud, mistake, undue influence, misrepresentation or that the settlor was incapable under Belize law of creating a trust.

9.77 The most conservative trust jurisdiction with so-called asset protection laws is the Cayman Islands. The Cayman Islands has a six-year statute of limitations that gives claimants the right during a six-year period after the establishment and funding of the Cayman Islands trust to prove in the appropriate Cayman court that the settlor made a fraudulent transfer. If successful in such proof, the claimant has a right to levy against the trust assets.

9.78 Jurisdictions that have similar trust laws, with a two-year statute of limitations and other variances, include St. Vincent and the Grenadines, Nevis, the Bahamas, Mauritius, and others. The trust laws of these jurisdictions provide that a creditor's action to void an allegedly fraudulent conveyance to a trust must be commenced within two years after the trust was established or the assets sought were conveyed to it. The Cook Islands, St. Vincent and the Grenadines and Nevis further provide that where the trust is established or the assets transferred to same the trust before the expiration of two years from the date that the creditor's cause of action accrued, the creditor must commence an action before the expiration of one year from the creation of or transfer of assets to the trust. The Nevis International Exempt Trust Ordinance, 1994, states that 'The term "cause of action" means the earliest cause of action capable of assertion by a creditor against the settlor of a trust or, as the case may be, against the settlor of property upon a trust by which that creditor has established (or may establish) an enforceable claim against the settlor.' The Nevis International Exempt Trust Ordinance also provides that 'The entry of judgment in any proceeding shall not constitute a separate cause of action.' Jurisdictions such as the Cook Islands and Nevis require the creditor to prove beyond a reasonable doubt that the property was settled into the trust with the principal intent to defraud that particular 0creditor.

9.79 The Isle of Man trust law does not provide for asset protection benefits; however, the Isle of Man High Court held that the transfer of assets to an Isle of Man trust cannot be set aside by creditors whose debts were not known or ascertainable at the time of the transfer.

Location of Trust Assets

9.80 The choice of location of the trust assets is not the same issue as the choice of location of the trust itself. A properly drafted foreign situs APT allows the trustees to invest trust assets in any part of the world.

9.81 Through the concurrent use of other planning techniques, such as a foreign limited partnership ('FLP'), the settlor can be given direct control and management over the protected assets without being a trustee and without compromising the protection afforded.

Deterrent Effect of APTs

9.82 Although a domestic court should recognise the settlor's choice of law and bona fide purposes for the APT planning, a safety valve is necessary to protect against the possibility that a court will disregard the settlor's decision as to choice of law and will apply domestic law in an effort to reach the trust assets.

9.83 The ultimate safety valve is the ability of the APT, as an international instrument, to invest and reinvest assets in any part of the world. The option exists for the trustees to best exercise their fiduciary duty to protect trust assets by diversifying investment of the assets outside any jurisdiction in which a problem may be foreseen, thereby forcing the battle over the assets into one or more foreign courts.

Foreign Tax Considerations

9.84   A correctly drafted APT provides neither tax benefits (other than tax benefits that one can achieve through a living or testamentary trust) nor tax detriments. Because an APT is not a tax-motivated structure, it should not saddle the settlor with any additional domestic or foreign tax burden.

9.85   An APT that is structured correctly and governed by an appropriate foreign jurisdiction is not subject to any income, gift, estate, transfer, excise, or like tax in the selected jurisdiction. The foreign jurisdictions that have enacted APT legislation generally treat APTs as 'exempt trusts' as long as none of the beneficiaries is resident in the jurisdictions.

Fraudulent Conveyance Considerations

9.86   If there is an identifiable creditor problem — whether pending, threatened, or expected — the scope of planning opportunities is narrowed. For this reason, asset protection planning is best implemented when the legal seas are calm. Attempting to protect assets when the legal seas turn choppy may be like trying to buy fire insurance during a fire.

9.87   The issue arises as to whether one is free to plan for potential problems with creditors when one has no pending or threatened litigation and has not otherwise been involved in a situation that could reasonably be expected to develop into a problem with a creditor in the future.

9.88   The common law system favours the free alienability of property. If there is no creditor entitled to protection under applicable fraudulent conveyance law, one is generally free to do with property as one deems fit. One is free to consume, destroy, sell, or make gifts of assets. Assets may be sold or given to an entity or a trust, whether domestic or foreign. The issue as to whether a transfer is fraudulent or not, does not in general turn on the identity of the transferee.

9.89   Although most fraudulent conveyance law seeks to protect present as well as subsequent creditors, the definition of 'subsequent' creditor is not so broad as to include all the nameless, faceless persons whom the transferor has yet to meet or give cause to complain (i.e., future potential creditors). The class of subsequent creditors is a relatively narrow one and includes those persons against whom the transferor harboured an actual intent to injure or defraud as of the date of the transfer, or persons who are injured as a result of the transferor conducting his affairs with reckless disregard for the rights of others following a transfer of property.

9.90   However, it has been held that while subsequent creditors are entitled to protection under fraudulent conveyance law, future potential creditors are not. The 'no harm, no foul' approach is expressed as follows: 'If there were no creditors, the conveyance could not be fraudulent to them.'

Avoiding Risks

9.91   A properly structured APT should contain all necessary checks and balances in a carefully drafted trust deed. Moreover, as an international vehicle, the APT can hold assets in any part of the world; the assets need not be physically held in the jurisdiction the laws of which govern the APT's administration, interpretation, or validity. For so long as, and to the extent that, assets are held in an FLP, the general partner (not the trustees) has direct control over, and management of, the protected assets.

9.92 Another material issue is whether a party may some day be in the awkward position of either having to repatriate assets or else be held in contempt of court.

9.93 A well-drafted APT would, under such a circumstance, make it impossible for the assets held by the trust to be repatriated. Impossibility of performance is usually a complete defence to a civil contempt charge. An exception exists if the party claiming impossibility of performance is responsible for the creation of the impossibility. For this exception to apply, however, there must be a nexus in time between the order in question and the creation of the impossibility. This nexus would be lacking if the APT were established and funded at a proper time.

9.94 Another material issue is whether a domestic court can be expected to recognise the foreign-based planning when assets remain physically at home.

9.95 In the context of an APT, the danger would be that a court would disregard the choice of law made by the settlor and determine that trust assets are indeed available to satisfy a creditor's claim.

9.96 For this reason, it frequently makes sense for the foreign trustee, in exercising its fiduciary duty to protect trust assets, to diversify those assets out of the jurisdiction in which the settlor's problem may be developing. Through this protective step, the battle over the assets can be forced into the foreign court, which would apply its protective legislation.

9.97 An effective offshore tax plan is one that anticipates the worst case foreseeable at the time it is designed and implemented.

ASSET PROTECTION AND THE STATUTE OF ELIZABETH

The Problem

9.98 Since the creation of a trust involves the settlor transferring legal ownership of property to trustees who hold that property upon terms outlined by the trust deed, on the face of it, from the moment the trust is properly constituted the property comprised within the trust is no longer the property of the settlor and ceases to be available to discharge a liability owed by the settlor to a creditor or otherwise. The trust, and particularly the offshore trust, would seem to be the obvious asset protection mechanism. In a sense, this premise is legally correct. But the mechanism may nonetheless not work, owing to an important provision in a 1571 English law, known as the Statute of Elizabeth, which has also been introduced into the law of a number of legal systems based on English law, and this includes many of the states in the United States and most of the tax havens of the world.

9.99 Under such legislation it is sometimes possible to set aside transfers into trust even if the settlor transferred the property many years before the debt arose and, at the time of making the transfer, had no indication that the particular debt would arise in the future.

9.100 For example, in UK law the provisions under which a disposition into trust may be challenged are contained in the Insolvency Act 1986, dealing with transfers made at an undervalue and preferences.

9.101 Under US Federal Law the equivalent provisions are contained within s 548 of the Bankruptcy Reform Act of 1978, as amended, and in state law within the Uniform Fraudulent Conveyance Act of 1918, which currently applies in 18 states including New York, and the Uniform Fraudulent Transfer Act which currently applies in 17 states including California.

9.102 Most other developed countries have laws which have a similar effect to those noted above and in many common law jurisdictions it is difficult to determine whether, and to what extent, the Statute of Elizabeth applies.

9.103 With the above in mind, laws governing asset protection trusts have been developed by certain jurisdictions to provide an extra degree of protection to that afforded by a normal trust and to remove the doubts over whether a trust arrangement does completely protect the trust assets. This has been achieved by enacting legislation which specifically overrides the Statute of Elizabeth type legislation and states that, subject to certain conditions being fulfilled, no application for the return of trust property will be entertained irrespective of judgments obtained outside the offshore jurisdiction.

9.104 In a wave of recent developments, one offshore base after another is changing its laws to accommodate asset protection trusts. Three jurisdictions (among others) which are commonly used to shelter asset protection trusts from the application of the Statute of Elizabeth are Gibraltar, the Turks & Caicos Islands, and the Cook Islands.

9.105 It should be noted that the Statute of Elizabeth is not and never was part of the Isle of Man law.

Gibraltar Asset Protection Trusts

9.106 Trust law in Gibraltar is based on English Common law, and Gibraltar recognises and gives full effect to the concept of trusts.

9.107 The legislation creating the concept of the asset protection trust is the *Bankruptcy (Amendment) Ordinance* 1990 and the *Bankruptcy (Register of Dispositions) Regulations* 1990.

9.108 The *Bankruptcy (Amendment) Ordinance* 1990 amends the *Bankruptcy Ordinance* to the effect that a disposition of assets by a settlor into a trust will not be voidable at the instance of a creditor provided the following conditions are met:

● the settlor is an individual;

● the settlor is not insolvent at the date of the disposition;

● the settlor does not become insolvent in consequence of the disposition;

● the settlement is registered in accordance with the Regulations.

9.109 The disposition must be registered in order to gain the protection allowed for under the law. The requirements of registration are specified in s 5 of the *Bankruptcy (Register of Dispositions) Regulations* 1990. A disposition may be simply registered by providing the Registrar with the following minimal information:

● the name and address of the trustee;

● the name of the disposition;

● the date of making the disposition and the duration thereof, i.e. the perpetuity of the trust;

● the country of ordinary residence of the settlor.

9.110 The application is accompanied by undertakings from the trustee making the application for registration to the effect that:

● the settlor has satisfactorily completed forms of inquiry establishing the financial position of the settlor and inquiring as to any claims which are being made against the settlor or which will or might be made in the future;

● the trustee has taken all reasonable steps to substantiate the information within the forms of inquiry mentioned above;

● the trustee has obtained an affidavit of solvency from the settlor.

9.111   A fee of £300 is payable upon registration of the trust and a renewal fee of £100 annually thereafter.

9.112   The details contained on the Register are available only to the Financial & Development Secretariat and are specifically not available for public inspection. The law contains secrecy provisions which make it a criminal offence for any person to reveal these details.

9.113   Gibraltar has attempted to insure that asset protection trusts are not used by those seeking to avoid a current or contingent liability which is within their knowledge at the time of making the disposition and have imposed very high standards on those administering and setting up trusts.

Turks & Caicos Islands Asset Protection Trusts

9.114   Section 61 of the Turks & Caicos Islands *Trust Ordinance* 1990 specifically refers to asset protection trusts and estates:

'1.   If by virtue of a disposition made by or on behalf of a settlor his property becomes trust property which is the subject of a Turks & Caicos trust, and:

    (a)   the settlor is an individual;

    (b)   the settlor is not insolvent when the disposition is made; and

    (c)   the settlor does not become insolvent by reason of the disposition, that disposition shall not be voidable at the instance of any creditor of the settlor.

2.   In any proceedings in which the provisions of this section are to be applied the burden of proof of the fact that a settlor is or has been insolvent shall be upon the person asserting that fact.'

9.115   It is not necessary to register the trust in order to gain the protection of the Ordinance and the effect of the law is that applications through the Courts of the Turks & Caicos made by a creditor of the settlor for the return of the trust property would be bound to fail as long as the provisions of the Ordinance have been adhered to.

9.116   Any trust which is set up and administered within the Turks & Caicos automatically gains the added protection of the asset protection legislation without further formality or registration.

9.117   The legislation abolishes all rules regarding perpetuity and accumulation periods. A Turks & Caicos trust may therefore last indefinitely and there is no requirement to distribute income.

9.118   Protectors are given statutory recognition as being persons whose consent the trustees must obtain before exercising a power or discretion. The legislation specifically provides that the Protector shall not be deemed to be a trustee.

9.119   A trustee is not required to disclose information to any person except for accounting information which need only be revealed to the beneficiaries.

9.120   The legislation provides that the interest of a beneficiary may be reduced or terminated in the event of that beneficiary becoming insolvent or any of his property becoming liable to sequestration by a creditor.

9.121   The legislation stipulates that a trust may be revocable either wholly or in part. There is a modern trend of creating revocable trusts and there has been some doubt in other jurisdictions as to whether such trusts are initially valid, so this provision lends great clarity to the law in this area.

9.122   Provision is made that the terms of the trust may allow for changing the law from that of the Turks & Caicos to the law of another jurisdiction provided that the trust deed stipulates that the change cannot invalidate any other terms of the trust and that the change is consistent with the intention of the settlor.

Cook Islands International Trusts

9.123   The 1995 amendments to the International Trusts Act 1984 are designed to reinforce the element of certainty in the Cook Islands trust law. The following are the most significant elements.

9.124   An amendment removes the requirement for an international trust to be limited to a period no longer than 100 years, and applies automatically to all new international trusts. Provision is made for existing international trusts to adopt the new law. The validity of existing trusts and their flexibility are preserved because a settlement may provide for bequests to vest on the occurrence of an event or within a time limit. A 'safety-net' provision counters the danger that a trust without a perpetuity period might be void for uncertainty.

9.125   The exercise of a power contained in a trust instrument to change the governing law of the trust is conclusive of that change. Provision is made for continuity of trust relationships and trust validity of transfers of property to or from the trustee to continue, in spite of a change in the governing law. A trust may be governed by different laws in respect of different aspects of its management and administration, and the trust instrument may also provide for a change in the governing law of a trust in the event of a specified event or state of affairs, permitting the urgent removal of a trust from one jurisdiction to another.

9.126   The trustee may delegate any or all of the trustee's powers, functions or discretion's, including management of trust property (but excluding powers of disposal concerning distributions to beneficiaries). In so doing, the trustee is required to exercise the standard of care of a 'reasonable and prudent man of business'.

9.127   A trust instrument may provide a trustee with a general power to undertake any kind of investment in any property, equivalent to that of a natural person.

9.128   Any person or group may be appointed a custodian trustee, and any action concerning the trust property must be brought or defended in the name of the custodian trustee. Upon termination of a custodian trustee's appointment, any restriction upon the powers of a managing trustee lapse and the managing trustee assumes all trustee functions, unless the trust instrument provides otherwise.

9.129   A trust instrument may effectively be executed in counterpart in different places and times within or without the Cook Islands. The period allowed for registration of an international trust is 45 days from the date of establishment of the trust, which period may be extended at the Registrar's discretion.

9.130   It is possible for a trust to adopt a name for the purpose of identification and for the trust instrument to authorise the trustees to have trust property registered in that name rather than in the name of the trustees. Legal title remains in the trustees. The trustees may delegate the function of holding title to trust property as between themselves.

9.131   There is segregation of trust property from that of a trustee's own property in the event of the trustee's insolvency. A trustee must exercise the care, diligence and skill that a prudent person would exercise in managing the affairs of others.

9.132   The trust instrument may provide for one or more persons to be a 'nominated person' to represent all or any beneficiaries who are minors or yet to be ascertained.

9.133   A trustee's contractual liability to third parties may be effectively limited to an amount no greater than the value of the trustee's right to be indemnified out of the assets of the trust.

9.134   There is a provision expressly permitting majority decision-making by the trustees.

9.135   A 'protector' means a person who has the power to appoint or remove a trustee, or who controls whether by vote or otherwise, the trustee's exercise of powers.

9.136   There is specific recognition of both purpose trusts (in favour of an object) and trading trusts (where third party rights may be prescribed and thus controlled).

9.137   More recently, however, the Cook Islands is encountering more and more difficulty in keeping its goalposts straight. Courts in different high tax jurisdictions have been putting in issue, the validity of Cook Islands structures.

9.138   The Ninth Circuit Court of Appeals upheld the ruling of the District Court for the District of Nevada in finding a couple in contempt for refusing to repatriate moneys from a Cook Islands asset protection trust. (*Federal Trade Commission (FTC) v Affordable Media* (No 98–16378)). The decision by the US court shows a serious resolve on the part of onshore jurisdictions to frustrate aggressive asset protection schemes entered into by taxpayers within their control.

9.139   Responding to this and similar judgments by the courts of other countries, the Cook Islands promulgated the 1999 International Trusts Amendment Act containing a number of very important modifications to the law. These changes were designed to make the Cook Islands asset protection trust a more effective shield against creditors and contingency fee lawyers. The main new provisions are:

●   The burden of proof is placed on the creditor to establish that an amount awarded in a foreign court is limited to compensation for actual loss and does not include 'punitive', 'vindictive', 'retributory' and 'exemplary' damages.

●   The creditor may not use a foreign judgment as a basis to attack trust fund property, unless the creditor first proves (a) that he has exhausted all claims against the settlor's other property; and (b) that all rights of appeal concerning that judgment have been exhausted. Note: this provision does not apply retroactively if at the time of settlement, establishment, or disposition, an award had already been made against the settlor by a court in a foreign judgment.

- A protector does not incur the liability of a trustee or fiduciary. The role of protector is interpreted as meaning someone who has power to appoint and remove trustees and veto the use of the trustees' powers.

- A trustee is permitted to release information to attorneys or to any person or class of persons whose help the trustee regards as essential for trust management and administration.

- Any trust that changes its proper law to that of the Cook Islands will be treated as if it were governed by Cook Islands' law from the date of the settlement.

ALTERNATIVES TO THE OFFSHORE TRUST

The Need for Alternative Offshore Vehicles to the Offshore Trust

9.140   The demand for offshore and onshore structures to provide legal mechanisms for the defence of family property is colossal. In the past decades, the preferred vehicle has been the so-called asset protection trust. The massive increase in the use of offshore trusts over the past 30 years, often in jurisdictions with either no, or inadequate, trust law, has led to a corresponding explosion in litigation. In the last two or three years there has been a succession of decisions which have raised large question marks over the future use of offshore trusts as assumptions that have been made for years have been overturned.

9.141   As we have seen above, serious difficulties are now being encountered in the use of offshore trusts.

9.142   In the first instance, the trust has, at its heart, a number of essential fundamentals that clients frequently refuse to accept as part of the trust relationship. For example, there is a fundamental requirement that the trustee should take full legal ownership and control of the assets. Many a client seeking an asset protection vehicle is horrified to find that he loses control of his hard-earned assets to some foreigner in a remote jurisdiction who could, in strict law, take decisions entirely independently of him.

9.143   Then, devices such as letters of wishes (letters of intent), trustees' file notes, and special functions of the protector, are coming increasingly under attack as being nothing more than an extension of settlor control. Reporting requirements for settlors of offshore has made life very much more difficult for overseas trustees. For example, non-resident trustees of trusts with US beneficiaries must appoint an agent who is authorised to disclose information on the trust to the IRS, when requested.

9.144   The duties and responsibilities of trustees have always been onerous. In the last few years, a number of important court decisions have considerably increased their exposure. Combining this with the fact that, by definition, the asset protection trust is operating in an area where litigants are trigger happy, overseas trustees are now very concerned at the potential risks, and finding it almost impossible to obtain insurance cover. Where the settlor (or grantor) retains control over the 'trust' (whether directly or through a protector) the product is not a trust as the law of equity understands it. It is in legal terms an agency arrangement, or perhaps a bailment, and entirely different legal rules apply.

9.145   Trusts are '*in personam*'. A trust is a creature of equity, that branch of traditional English law which is concerned with remedies in personal disputes. This means that any court that administers equity can apply equitable remedies, irrespective of the proper law of the trust. Despite legislation in one or two jurisdictions which have attempted to prevent trusts being the subject of attack by creditors, the fact is that a trust is a creature of equity, and it is a fundamental principle of equity that an equitable remedy cannot be invoked to deny an equitable remedy to another person. This has led to a crisis in trust law, with some court decisions coming down strongly against the validity of the 'trusts' in question.

9.146   The transfer of assets so as to deny a creditor, whether present or future, the ability to access trust assets has been considered fraudulent since the 16th century (the so-called Statute of Elizabeth), and the principle is embodied in all modern Anglo-Saxon jurisdictions (including tax havens). Although the issue may be one of bankruptcy law, the implicit fraud is sufficient for a court of equity to decline to enforce the provisions of a trust set up 'without clean hands'. Indeed such trusts may be considered void, and not merely voidable. In order to remedy this, a few jurisdictions have legislated to define the circumstances in which a transfer will be considered fraudulent and otherwise. Some of this legislation is satisfactory in that it merely clarifies an existing principle. However, one or two jurisdictions have introduced legislation which many lawyers, and increasingly the courts, consider has unacceptably swung the balance the other way, thereby creating major difficulties at the equitable heart of trust law.

9.147   As a consequence of the above, establishing an asset protection trust that minimises these risks and difficulties, while remaining effective, has become more and more difficult and more and more expensive.

9.148   There has thus arisen a need for new forms of vehicles that will be safer and more efficient in their application, and cheaper to administer.

9.149   One useful and practical such vehicle is the limited liability company (LLC), which can be used either independently or in conjunction with a trust, which may be either onshore or offshore. However, in ways it may be preferable to set up an asset protection LLC on its own without a trust. The advantage is simplicity and lack of expense. The disadvantages (unless combined with trusts) are a limited tax planning capability and reliance on one line of defence only.

9.150   The offshore partnership has also been used as a family property protection vehicle for some time, but it too has drawbacks. For a start it has unlimited liability and no legal personality. Even a limited partnership is unable to provide legal personality.

9.151   In addition, a number of alternative structures have been brought into use for offshore operations, for example:

●   companies by guarantee;

●   bearer share companies;

●   contractual arrangements, such as an option or an agency;

●   contractual relationships relating to possession, such as bailment;

●   various pour-over devices whereby assets and rights can be moved from one vehicle to another.

The International Business Company (IBC)

9.152   Over the years both company law and company taxation has become more and more complex. In nearly every country, there has been growing an awareness that company law does not differentiate adequately between the multinational corporate entity which employs thousands, and the simple company used, for example, to hold a property, and which employs nobody. As a result, there has been increasing pressure to 'deregulate' small private companies. In Europe, this pressure has resulted in substantial relaxation of disclosure requirements for small companies.

9.153   The pressure led, in the Caribbean, to the introduction of the phenomenally successful International Business Company or IBC. It has effectively created a brand new type of company, with minimal administrative and reporting requirements, but equally, with considerable restrictions on both its design capability and its uses. It is not possible, for example, to structure such a company as a foundation or other form of quasi-trust. A creditor of a shareholder can, following a judgment, take possession of the shares, and thus control of the company.

The Limited Liability Company (LLC)

9.154   The Limited Liability Company (LLC), as originally conceived in Wyoming, has now spread throughout the US and beyond.

9.155   Frequently, the modern offshore LLC is merely a variant of the IBC. The most significant large-scale potential of an offshore LLC is for use instead of an IBC or other corporate form for simple situations. However, in the Isle of Man, it is an entirely separate form of business organisation.

9.156   The Isle of Man adopted the Wyoming legislation as its model and legislated the Limited Liability Companies Act 1996 specifically, with the intent of ensuring that an Isle of Man LLC would always meet the criteria in the former regulations of the US Internal Revenue Code under which it could be classified as a partnership. With the introduction of the Check-the-Box Regulations in 1997, the Isle of Man LLC could, for US tax purposes, be a constructive trust, depending on the drafting of the Articles of Organisation. Under the US tax rules, if it is not a trust it will be, by default, a corporation, but could elect to be treated as a partnership.

9.157   For Isle of Man Income Tax purposes, an Isle of Man LLC will always be taxed as a partnership, and, if owned by non-resident members and having no Isle of Man source income, can be exempt from all Isle of Man direct taxation.

9.158   The Isle of Man LLC is able to provide what many clients need in an offshore structure: corporate personality, limited liability, minimal administrative requirements with no directors, a manager with such powers only as the members choose to give him, asset protection, safety in that there are no shares, bearer or otherwise, to be lost or alienated, no loss of control, minimal disclosure.

9.159   The Isle of Man LLC is formed by two or more persons registering with the Registrar of LLCs, the Articles of Organisation of the LLC, and, simultaneously, entering into an Operating Agreement.

9.160   At the same time as the Articles are signed, the parties enter into the Operating Agreement. These provide for the internal governance of the LLC and the rights of the members amongst themselves.

9.161   The constitutional documentation of an Isle of Man LLC consists of (a) the Articles of Organisation, and (b) the Operating Agreement.

9.162   The Articles of Organisation deal with a few major points, such as the name of the LLC, the identity of the members, the capital introduced by each member, the principles governing the admission of new members, and the ability of surviving members to continue the business in the event of a member dropping out as a result of death, resignation, or otherwise. After the Articles of Organisation have been registered, the Registrar of LLCs will issue a Certificate of Registration, and the LLC is in business. The document embodying the Articles of Organisation is a public document.

9.163   The Operating Agreement, on the other hand, is a private document entered into by the members and dealing with the internal governance of the LLC. Although a few matters must be dealt with as required by the Limited Liability Companies Act 1996, the Operating Agreement is largely drafted to suit the members. Though the LLC is an entity that originally owed its existence and its significance to the US federal taxation system, it is also of considerable significance to non-US persons, and new uses for the LLC keep emerging.

The Single Premium 'Whole of Life' Policy

9.164   The single premium 'whole of life' policy is an exceptionally efficient type of offshore planning vehicle. The key planning device lies in the following principal feature: the Policy may be on a single life, joint life or multiple lives last death basis. This is possibly the most attractive planning technique available.

9.165   In addition, this type of policy normally provides for all or most of the following features:

- the flexibility of a personal investment portfolio, offering tax efficiency, combined with the benefits of a life policy;

- a minimum required initial investment that is not excessive (frequently in the area of $50,000, with a minimum additional investment of $5,000);

- investment freedom offering access to: products in managed, sector and specialist funds; fixed interest securities, stocks and shares quoted on any recognised stock exchange; eurobonds and currency deposits; deposit and building society funds, etc.;

- a share exchange facility enables the transfer of existing holdings into the Policy;

- an authorisation for regular withdrawals to be taken monthly, quarterly, half-yearly, yearly or as needed (caveat tax implications);

- full or partial encashment (though an early withdrawal charge may apply);

- the possibility of linking the Policy to an offshore bank account;

- automatic life assurance cover providing often 101% of the encashment value, free of charge;

- additional life cover, providing increased protection for dependants;

- a facility whereby additional cover (sometimes of up to 120% of the encashment value) can be arranged (though usually subject to medical evidence);

- investment of up to 100% of contributions invested, depending on charging structure selected;

- the option to appoint a personal investment advisor with delegated switching authority;

● availability to international investors, aged between 18 and 89 at commencement.

9.166   The Policy thus allows investment in a wide range of different investments, enabling a personalised portfolio to cater for specific needs, i.e. offshore funds or authorised unit trusts, managed, sector and specialised funds, stocks and shares, fixed interest securities, eurobonds and various currency deposits. The facility to transfer existing shareholdings etc straight into the Policy is useful, and in this way an existing trust could simply be backed into the policy.

9.167   In the case of certain jurisdictions policyholders are protected worldwide by authorised life assurance companies schemes. For example, the Isle of Man Life Assurance (Compensation of Policyholders) Regulation 1991 protects investors with compensation of up to 90% of the value of their policies being paid in the event that their insurer became unable to meet its liabilities, and without there being an upper monetary limit.

The Executive Investment Bond

9.168   The Executive Investment Bond combines the flexibility of a personal investment portfolio, with the tax-efficiency of the whole of life policy.

9.169   All assets could be lodged within the Bond. Units in collective investment schemes or the stocks, shares and securities, are legally owned by the financial institution. They are held on the financial institution's behalf by a custodian trustee. The Bond then operates through an 'investor's account', which is notionally divided into units. These are allocated to the account at a price based on the value of the underlying assets.

9.170   The advantages of the bond are, above all:

● convenience of holding diverse assets in one portfolio;

● reduced stockbroking fees;

● significant initial discounts from fund management groups;

● opportunities for greater tax-efficiency;

● ability to transfer in existing quoted shareholdings;

● almost total investment freedom;

● flexibility to change the investment portfolio at any time;

● easy access to capital;

● a regular income facility;

● the option to provide additional life cover.

9.171   Companies normally provide an in-depth valuation statement quarterly. This valuation keeps the policyholders informed of the Bond's progress, providing full information on asset movement, income accrual, cash withdrawals and charges.

9.172   The investment can be automatically split into a number of separate policies. Each policy can then be partially or completely encashed without cancelling the entire Bond.

9.173   The policyholders can also take regular withdrawals to provide an income, perhaps on a monthly or annual basis, though an early withdrawal charge may apply to withdrawal, income payment or full or partial surrender.

9.174　The Bond thus offers the option of taking withdrawals at regular intervals, providing a steady source of income.

Scope of Alternative Offshore Structures

9.175　All high-tax jurisdictions have some form of anti-avoidance legislation directed against the use of offshore structures. Such anti-avoidance legislation, has, in many countries, made offshore tax planning increasingly difficult, and persons with offshore trusts and underlying companies are now commonly being advised to forget about offshore tax planning and bring the assets onshore.

9.176　However, it is important to note that this legislation generally focuses on what the taxpayer *owns* (e.g. the shares in a company, or an interest in a trust or foundation) but does not always pay the same attention to the benefit of a contract, which the taxpayer enjoys. It is here that there is scope for a measure of international tax planning.

9.177　A common example of the benefit through contract planning rather than through ownership planning is, of course, the contract of life assurance. This comes in many forms, one of the best being a profits endowment policy, with a single premium: i.e. I pay £x to an insurance company; the insurance company invests the money and rolls up the dividends; at the end of the term — say 10 or 20 years — I get the cash equivalent of the rolled up fund, less the insurance company's charges; but if I die before then, my estate gets a certain sum.

9.178　In countries where a taxpayer can simply take out an endowment policy with a company in an offshore centre, no tax consequences may follow until the policy matures or is surrendered, i.e. the insurance company devotes the life cover part of the premium to paying for the life cover, and it may reinsure the whole or part of that risk elsewhere, in such a way that the life cover money is invested, and the income and gains from the portfolio are accumulated.

Example

The taxpayer is a US corporation; the client is a non-resident alien owning some European manufacturing companies and a major stake in a US corporation.

He wishes to make his profit in the manufacturing companies and charge a high price to the US corporation, which buys and distributes the product. This would inevitably attract transfer pricing difficulties.

His solution to the problem might be in the following manner: he could put the manufacturing companies under an offshore holding company and put the holding company under an offshore trust for the benefit of the employees of the manufacturing companies. The holding company then employs him at a salary which effectively absorbs the manufacturing profit. The transfer pricing problem would thus be eliminated, through substituting contract for ownership.

Example

The next example is similar, but here the client is about to take up residence in the United States.

In this case, the offshore employee trust creates a company in an IOFC and it is that company which enters into the employment agreement. The important feature of the employment agreement is that the compensation arising under it is deferred, the amount being put aside into a separate account under an employment trust.

Once again, the essence of the transaction is that what the client enjoys is a contract and not ownership.

Fiscally Transparent Entities

9.179   It should not be assumed that the taxpayer has total freedom to classify an entity in the most beneficial manner from the tax point of view.

Example

The French Supreme Court has decided an important case involving recognition under the French–Dutch treaty of transparent partnerships for French withholding tax rate purposes. Royalties paid by a French payor to a Dutch CV transparent entity were treated as received by its partners, that were Dutch BVs. This holding enables the parties to enjoy the benefits of reduced French withholding as well as the reduced tax rates in the Netherlands. See 2000 WTD 72-4.

Example

The IRS Regulations (30 June 2000) with respect to the availability of treaty benefits in the case of payments to fiscally transparent entities, provide helpful examples of their application. The intention of the regulations is to implement the provisions of s 894 to prevent treaty benefits (largely withholding tax reductions) from being available in circumstances where the characterisation of an entity as transparent or non-transparent is different as between the treaty country partners. The Regulations apply to hybrid entities (treated as transparent for US purposes but non-transparent for the foreign country purposes) as well as so-called domestic reverse hybrid entities (non-transparent for US purposes but transparent for the foreign country purposes). In essence, the regulations require that an item of income be derived (received for the pertinent tax purposes) by a recipient entity or an interest holder in such entity, with such items taken into account on an item-by-item basis.

STRATEGIC CHECKLISTS

SELECTION FACTORS FOR THE OFFSHORE ASSET PROTECTION JURISDICTION

- Whether the jurisdiction's trust law is favourable, well defined, and protective.

- The political, economic, and social stability of the jurisdiction.

- The jurisdiction's reputation in the world business community.

- The tax laws of the jurisdiction.

- Whether language barriers exist.

- Whether the jurisdiction has modern telecommunications facilities.

- Whether the jurisdiction offers adequate legal, accounting, and financial services.

- The standard of proof that a creditor must meet in attempting to show fraudulent intent on the part of the transferor.

- The extent to which a transferor may retain benefit in, and control over, an APT without exposing the APT to the transferor's creditors.

- The relevance of the settlor's solvency following transfers to the APT.

- The recognition to be given to judgments and orders of foreign courts that may affect an APT, its trustees, and its assets.

- What conditions must be satisfied in order to freeze trust assets.

IOFCS HOLDING THEMSELVES OUT AS ASSET PROTECTION JURISDICTIONS

- The Bahamas

- Belize

- The Cayman Islands

- The Cook Islands

- Cyprus

- Gibraltar

- The Turks & Caicos Islands

ALTERNATIVE STRUCTURES

- Limited liability companies.

- Companies limited by guarantee.

- Bearer share companies.

- Contractual arrangements, such as an option or an agency.

- Contractual relationships relating to possession, such as bailment.

- Various pour-over devices whereby assets and rights can be moved from one vehicle to another.

FEATURES TO LOOK FOR IN SINGLE PREMIUM POLICIES

- The flexibility of a personal investment portfolio, offering tax efficiency, combined with the benefits of a life policy.

- A minimum required initial investment that is not excessive (frequently in the area of $50,000, with a minimum additional investment of $5,000).

- Investment freedom offering access to: products in managed, sector and specialist funds; fixed interest securities, stocks and shares quoted on any recognised stock exchange; eurobonds and currency deposits; deposit and building society funds, etc.

- A share exchange facility enables the transfer of existing holdings into the Policy.

- An authorisation for regular withdrawals to be taken monthly, quarterly, half-yearly, yearly or as needed (*caveat* tax implications).

- Full or partial encashment (though an early withdrawal charge may apply).

- The possibility of linking the Policy to an offshore bank account.

- Automatic life assurance cover providing often 101% of the encashment value, free of charge.

- Additional life cover, providing increased protection for dependants.

- A facility whereby additional cover (sometimes of up to 120% of the encashment value) can be arranged (though usually subject to medical evidence).

- Investment of up to 100% of contributions invested, depending on charging structure selected.

- The option to appoint a personal investment advisor with delegated switching authority.

- Availability to international investors.

FEATURES TO LOOK FOR IN EXECUTIVE INVESTMENT BONDS.

- Convenience of holding diverse assets in one portfolio.

- Reduced stockbroking fees.

- Significant initial discounts from fund management groups.

- Opportunities for greater tax-efficiency.

- Ability to transfer in existing quoted shareholdings.

- Almost total investment freedom.

- Flexibility to change the investment portfolio at any time.

- Easy access to capital.

- A regular income facility.

- The option to provide additional life cover.

STRATEGIC ISSUES, OPPORTUNITIES AND CAVEATS

THE INTERNET AS A RESEARCH TOOL

- It has become increasingly necessary for tax planners to have access to a large and up-to-date library covering laws, regulations, and practices of many jurisdictions. The Internet can in part fulfil this function. Thus the Internet has become one of the most powerful tools at the disposal of any tax planner.

- Information on the Internet can be cheaply and relatively effortlessly updated as new information becomes available.

- *Caveat:* Current and correct information is always a necessity and the lack thereof can result in incorrect planning. Owing to the unreliability of much of the information on the Internet, this planning tool has great weaknesses as well as strengths.

GOOD, BAD AND UNCERTAIN WEBSITES

- There are many sites, particularly in the financial services sector, with up-to-the-moment information.

- However, finding a site, which updates even relatively often and regularly, is not necessarily as common as one might think.

- Within the category of 'bad' sites that do not have the required up-to-date information, there is a (not much) smaller subcategory of even worse sites that are poorly designed to the extent that it takes longer than normal to determine that the site does not contain the desired information.

- *Caveat:* The immense time and effort required in order to decide which sites are good and which are not may prompt the researcher to give up on the Internet route and choose a more traditional method of research.

GOVERNMENT AND REVENUE PAGES

- Revenues have an interest in providing a comprehensive Internet service since it is far cheaper to provide an automated response to taxpayers' questions than to have a large staff complement specifically dedicated to answering the questions of the general public.

- *Caveat:* Many Revenue websites are not updated as frequently as one would be entitled to expect.

10.1 The Internet in the Offshore Tax Planning Process

TAX TREATIES ONLINE

- Tax treaties are of critical importance in international tax planning.

- According to the OECD, there are currently over 1,500 tax treaties in force today, with more being signed and ratified on a steady basis.

- *Caveat:* No single site containing tax treaties is comprehensive, and conventional research tools must be employed in order to obtain copies of many tax treaties.

THE INTERNET AS A RESEARCH TOOL

10.1 The Internet is the greatest advance in the communication of information since the telephone and the fax machine. Never before has so much information been so readily available to so many people. In every conceivable manner and by every conceivable method, the Internet has had a profound effect in all areas within its considerable and ever growing domain. While the reliability of the available information is often questionable, there is no doubt that with proper use the Internet is one of the most powerful tools at the disposal of any researcher.

10.2 Like any other research tool, the Internet has its strengths and its weaknesses.

10.3 The nature of international taxation and international tax planning is such that current and correct information is always a necessity and the lack thereof can result in incorrect planning. The past decade has seen more change in economic and tax policies than the previous three decades before it. With this volatility and the expansion of international trade and private foreign investment, it has become increasingly necessary for tax advisors to have a large and up-to-date library covering laws, regulations, and practices of many jurisdictions. Besides being an expensive and time-consuming exercise, maintaining or even getting the necessary resources in the first place is likely to be difficult and often impossible. Finding the correct information is made even more difficult when there is a discrepancy between the printed regulations and their implementation in practice. In less economically developed countries, the regulations are sometimes not available for public perusal. Until the advent of the Internet, this effectively meant that one was dependent on second-hand information or spending fortunes on lengthy consultations with foreign experts. Without the financial and technical constraints experienced in the case of hard copy publications, the Internet has made vast amounts of information accessible to the public that is often both accurate and timely.

10.4 Information on the Internet can be cheaply and relatively effortlessly updated as new information becomes available. Whether this updating is actually done is another matter altogether — perpetual updating is a rarity, and finding a site that updates even relatively often and regularly is not necessarily as common as one might think. This is mainly because of the amount of effort and expense still required to maintain the currency of a website in spite of the relative ease with which the maintenance can be performed. Also to be taken into account is the benefit to the website administrator of maintaining a current website. Logic dictates that if the benefits derived from a correct and current site are not greater than the effort and expense required to maintain the correctness and currency then it will not be in the interests of the site-administrator to expend time and money in this regard.

10.5 However, in spite of this, there are many sites, particularly in the financial services sector, with up-to-the-moment information. The primary reasons for this are twofold: (a) there exists a large and financially significant market for current information in this field, and (b) as a consequence, there are still many site-administrators with a vested interest in making information available.

10.6 One of the main reasons for the failure of searches for specific information on the Internet is the fact that even though there are many sites that are accurate and reliable, there are many more that are not. Often the immense time and effort (and anguish) spent deciding which sites are good and which are not will prompt the researcher to give up on the Internet route and choose a more traditional method of research.

10.7 Within the category of 'bad' sites that do not have the required up-to-date information, there is a (not much) smaller subcategory of even worse sites that are poorly designed to the extent that it takes longer than normal to determine that the site does not contain the desired information. These sites can be a tremendous impediment and delay in the finding of a good site, particularly when one can get several thousand (and sometimes hundreds of thousands) 'hits' on any given search.

10.8 The remainder of this chapter will deal with methods of finding these site-administrators quickly, checking the reliability and currency of the information found on a site, and how to stay abreast of current developments in this dynamic field.

THE TYPES OF INFORMATION

Domestic Tax Law and Practice

10.9 Every international tax plan contains at least two and frequently many more domestic tax systems.

International Tax Law and Practice

10.10 The advisor also has to consider each jurisdiction's treatment of international tax issues.

Tax Treaties

10.11 Working in multiple jurisdictions introduces an aspect of tax planning not found in local tax planning. Tax treaties are extremely important if one is to avoid or at least to mitigate the effects of double taxation.

Case Law

10.12 Even though one may have the latest texts of a jurisdiction's laws and regulations, it may also be very useful to have access to the jurisdiction's case law, particularly in the case of Anglo-Saxon jurisdictions.

Tax and Other Incentives

10.13 Besides the laws and regulations that are documented, there may be tax and other incentives available to companies involved in certain activities and under certain conditions that may have considerable impact on the choice of jurisdiction. Finding out about these incentives on the Internet is generally rather difficult.

10.14 The Internet in the Offshore Tax Planning Process

Pending Changes

10.14 It is very important to be aware of potential future changes to the law and regulations, and their likely impact on the overall tax and business position.

Non-Tax Factors

10.15 Tax is not the only factor of concern when designing a tax plan. One always has to judge whether the benefits of implementing a tax plan outweigh the costs to the business in terms of implementation costs and possible restrictions in activity. Clearly it would not be advisable to implement a tax plan if the benefits are less than the costs. Amongst other non-tax factors, one also has to take into account such matters as exchange control (where applicable), exchange rate volatility, legal and administrative systems, political and economic stability, professional commercial and banking facilities, language, and generally accepted accounting procedure.

Foreign Consultants

10.16 Finally, although the Internet does provide some measure of independence from consultation with foreign experts, it is important to realise that the Internet does not eliminate the need for consultation.

GOVERNMENT AND REVENUE PAGES

10.17 A redoubtable problem that one encounters when searching for information on the Internet is the mass of out-of-date, factually incorrect, and misleading sites. In a large proportion of cases, these sites are indistinguishable from the useful sites, and often display impressive animation and graphics, thereby giving one the overall impression that the site is up-to-the-minute and administered by the world's leading authorities, when in fact the contrary is often the case.

10.18 Even when one manages to find a site that one can rely on with a good measure of confidence, the particular details that are the subject of the search may be incomplete or totally absent.

10.19 It is therefore very valuable and much appreciated that the vast majority of revenue services in developed countries have moved to administering their own websites. Such websites normally contain basic information for resident taxpayers, relevant tax forms, news items, and in some cases more specialised information. These sites may also contain regulations for cross-border transactions, anti-avoidance issues, and treatment of non-resident individuals, companies and trusts, and a whole host of other useful information. Sometimes too the wording of the relevant acts and laws may be available for online perusal or for downloading. And, should one not be able to find some particular information, provision is often made to be able to contact the revenue directly by e-mail.

10.20 The turnaround time and the quality of the response vary from revenue site to revenue site. Queries will normally be answered in one to three working days, seldom taking longer than two weeks. Rarely, is no response received. The reliability of the responses is normally good, for the reason that the revenue has an interest in making sure that the public 'gets it right'.

10.21 A large expenditure item on any revenue service's budget is an enquiry department of one sort or another. Regardless of the size of a given jurisdiction's taxpaying population, an average revenue service can expect to field literally millions of questions and enquiries annually. This is a problem faced by many companies and other organisations, in varying degrees of scale and intensity.

10.22   The revenues of the world have an interest in providing a comprehensive Internet service since it is far cheaper to provide an automated response to taxpayers' questions than to have a large staff complement specifically dedicated to answering the questions of the general public. Having a well-designed and accessible website does not eliminate the need for a customer care staff, but it does dramatically reduce the total number of staff members needed for this task. Even though extra staff members are required to create and maintain the website, the number of extra staff members needed for this new task is generally far lower than the number of staff replaced by the new system.

Example

Singapore Revenue Website *(http://www.iras.gov.sg/)*

The Singapore Revenue site is an extremely simplified revenue web page, containing little more than the usual array of standard forms and press releases. Only the most basic information is made available, with sections on income tax, property tax, Singapore's 38 existing tax treaties, and a far from comprehensive collection of other miscellaneous tax related documentation and legislative summaries. The site does not even make provision for direct contact with the relevant departments.

IRS Website *(http://www.irs.gov/)*

The IRS site has, since its inception, been one of the world's leading revenue sites. Though containing useful links to topics of interest to local US taxpayers, the IRS site is rather impractical for tax professionals. An excellent and innovative feature is thus the presence within the site of a 'Tax Professional Corner' *(http://www.irs.gov/bus_info/tax_pro/index.html)*. This section contains many useful links to sites specifically aimed at the tax practitioner, including, for example, sections containing tax law, official IRS forms, advanced tax rulings, instructions and publications; information on continuing professional education; and tax products and software. There are also references to international tax issues, but these are well buried in the mass of information, and hard to access. Nevertheless, the IRS site does make provision for direct e-mail contact.

UK Inland Revenue Website *(http://www.inlandrevenue.gov.uk/home.htm)*

Superior features of this site are its logical organisation and ease of use, even while keeping as vast body of information as does the IRS site.

The UK Revenue Site contains all the basics, with excellent sections for tax practitioners (with a bimonthly tax practitioner bulletin), enterprises, individuals and others, and containing also subsections with technical notes and reports. Of great value are the sections for non-residents and the legislation section containing statutory instruments, draft legislation, and tax treaties.

To add to this, a detailed list of direct contact information (different details for different categories of queries) helps make the Inland Revenue site perhaps the best example of a revenue site on the Web.

TAX TREATIES ONLINE

10.23　Tax treaties are the building blocks of any international financial plan. According to the OECD, there are currently over 1,500 tax treaties in force today, with more being signed and ratified on a steady basis. Tax treaties are of critical importance in international tax planning, since paying tax in one jurisdiction can be onerous enough in many cases, and having to pay tax in multiple jurisdictions can conceivably lead to a tax burden on greater than 100% of profits.

10.24　Double tax agreements work by setting out the connecting factors to the parties to the agreement in such a way that at most one of the parties would be entitled to tax income for any single given transaction or operation. Although most if not all tax treaties today are based on the OECD Model Tax Treaty Convention on Income and Capital, a large proportion of double taxation agreements do have a number of material differences, and it is important to have access to the text of a double taxation agreement if one intends to use it in a tax plan.

10.25　In some cases, it may be possible to engage in treaty shopping and to make use of tax treaties of jurisdictions not directly related to a particular operation.

10.26　The following are examples of sites containing some useful tax treaty databases.

Example

Windstar Technologies　*(http://www.windstar-tech.com/new/htmltreaties/indextreat.html)*

Windstar Technologies' website is an easy-to-use directory of 57 of the United States' in force tax treaties. The full text for all of the treaties in the directory is available. Windstar Technologies also sells tax-treaty related software that helps you determine if you are able to make use of a particular treaty, what the criteria are that one must satisfy to be able to use a particular treaty, and what the withholding rates would be under a particular treaty. This software is available for purchase on the Windstar site.

Danziger's Website *(http://www.danzigerfdi.com)*

This site has a very simple layout that allows one to get a good idea of the entire site at a glance. Although not comprehensive by any means (no site is at the moment), Danziger's FDI has the full text of over 400 tax treaties between many of the world's major jurisdictions, with new treaties being added all the time. In addition to the treaty information, the site has sections dealing with investment locations, export processing zones, free trade zones, and investment organisations. This site is well worth a visit if you need to find the text for a particular tax treaty, though one weakness in the site is the lack of links.

11   Harmful Tax Competition Measures

STRATEGIC ISSUES AND CAVEATS

OECD'S POSITION ON HARMFUL TAX COMPETITION

- The existence of low or no income taxes is not in itself enough to constitute harmful tax competition.

- Countries remain free to decide their own tax rates, with checks and balances coming from competitive forces of the global marketplace.

- *Caveat:* When low or no taxes are combined with other legislative or administrative features, such as 'ring-fencing', a lack of transparency, or the absence of exchange of information, then harmful tax competition may arise.

GEOGRAPHICALLY MOBILE SERVICE ACTIVITIES

The following situations may have undesirable effects when seen from the perspective of the other country:

- the first country is a tax haven and, as such, generally imposes no or only nominal tax on that income;

- the first country collects significant revenues from tax imposed on income at the individual or corporate level but its tax system has preferential features that allow the relevant income to be subject to low or no taxation;

- the first country collects significant revenues from tax imposed on income at the individual or corporate level, but the effective tax rate that is generally applicable at that level is lower than the tax rate levied in the other country.

FINANCIAL AND RELATED SERVICE ACTIVITIES

- The main focus of the OECD's work is on financial and other service activities because these are the activities that are the most geographically mobile and therefore the most sensitive to tax differentials.

- Tax havens located outside the OECD area and harmful preferential tax regimes in OECD countries are particularly involved in these activities.

- OECD Member countries have concluded that they need to act collectively as well as individually to curb harmful tax competition and to counter the spread of harmful preferential tax regimes directed at financial and service activities.

11.1 Harmful Tax Competition Measures

- The Committee on Fiscal Affairs has already engaged in a dialogue with countries in the Asia-Pacific region, Latin America, Africa and in the former Soviet Bloc.

- Since it is difficult for individual countries to combat effectively the spread of harmful preferential tax regimes, a co-ordinated approach and international co-operation are being intensified to avoid competitive bidding by countries for geographically mobile activities.

THE OECD RECOMMENDATIONS AND GUIDELINES

- Multilaterally: (a) the tax haven list, and (b) the guidelines.

- At the national level: (a) adoption of controlled foreign company (CFC) or equivalent legislation, and (b) transfer pricing guidelines.

- Bilaterally: (a) intensified exchanges of information on tax havens and preferential tax regimes, and (b) possible termination of tax treaties with tax havens.

- *Caveat*: A provision is being considered for the OECD's Model Tax Convention that would deny entities operating under harmful tax regimes access to certain or all of the Convention's benefits.

PROPOSALS OF THE FORUM ON HARMFUL TAX PRACTICES

- Proposed restriction of deductions for payments to tax haven entities.

- Proposed imposition of withholding taxes on certain payments to residents of countries that engage in harmful tax competition.

- Proposed revision of residence rules.

- Proposed reversal of onus of proof in transfer pricing rules and guidelines

- Proposed introduction of new thin capitalisation rules.

- Proposed use of a wide range of non-tax measures in order to address harmful tax competition.

- Proposed monitoring to ensure that financial innovation is not used to assist harmful tax competition.

THE EFFECTS OF GLOBALISATION AND LIBERALISATION ON HARMFUL TAX PRACTICES

11.1 The past decades have seen a rapid spread of preferential tax regimes in high tax countries as well as in the tax havens themselves. Liberalisation and globalisation have led a number of governments to introduce special tax structures; today virtually every high tax country has adopted some type of preferential tax regime. Over recent years, the number of tax havens has more than doubled, while the value of investments into low tax jurisdictions has expanded exponentially.

11.2   Because these tax policies may result in the siphoning off of parts of countries' tax bases, this proliferation of what are considered harmful preferential tax regimes and tax havens has become a growing concern for governments.

11.3   Globalisation is a major economic process that breaks down economic barriers between nations and leads enterprises to develop global strategies. It was the liberalisation of national economies that opened the way for globalisation, just as the emergence of new technologies made that globalisation happen.

11.4   Liberalisation is at the core of the OECD's work and is aimed at facilitating cross-border flows of trade and investment. The OECD has made considerable efforts to eliminate double taxation, which is an obstacle to cross-border activities. Furthermore, the OECD is now undertaking similar efforts to curb harmful tax practices that are considered to have detrimental effects on world economic growth.

11.5   The perception of the OECD is that, if this situation is not redressed, governments may increasingly be forced to engage in competitive tax bidding in order to attract or retain mobile activities, thus leading to a 'race to the bottom', in which location and financing decisions become primarily tax driven.

11.6   Developments within the G7, the European Union (EU), the OECD, and beyond are leading to a common approach against what is considered harmful tax practices. Similarly, countries in the Asian-Pacific region, Latin America, Africa, and in the former Soviet bloc are addressing these issues. In some ways, these countries are more exposed to tax havens and competitive bidding for financial and service activities since many of them lack the administrative capacity to implement sophisticated counteracting measures.

THE HARMFUL TAX COMPETITION REPORT OF THE OECD

The Report and the Recommendation to Member Governments

11.7   In May 1996 the ministers called upon the OECD to 'develop measures to counter the distorting effects of harmful tax competition on investment and financing decisions and the consequences for national tax bases, and report back in 1998'. The G7 heads of state endorsed this request at their 1996 summit, urging the OECD to 'vigorously pursue its work in this field, aimed at establishing a multilateral approach under which countries could operate individually and collectively to limit the extent of these practices'.

11.8   The OECD's Committee on Fiscal Affairs launched its project on harmful tax competition, and its report was presented to the ministers. The report addresses harmful tax practices in the form of tax havens and harmful preferential tax regimes in OECD countries and their dependencies and in non-Member countries. It focuses above all on geographically mobile activities, such as financial and other service activities.

11.9   In approving the report on 9 April 1998, the OECD Council adopted a recommendation to the governments of Member countries and instructed the committee to pursue its work in this area and to develop a dialogue with non-Member countries. Luxembourg and Switzerland abstained in Council on the approval of the report and the adoption of the recommendation.

11.10 Harmful Tax Competition Measures

The OECD's Position

11.10 The OECD´s position on preferential taxes is stated clearly. The existence of low or no income taxes is not in itself enough to constitute harmful tax competition. Rather, when low or no taxes are combined with other legislative or administrative features, such as 'ring-fencing', a lack of transparency, or the absence of exchange of information, then harmful tax competition may arise. The OECD report provides a framework for identifying harmful regimes and suggests counter-measures for them. Accordingly, harmonising tax rates across countries or installing minimum tax levels is not the aim. Countries will remain free to decide their own tax rates, with checks and balances coming from competitive forces of the global marketplace. This will encourage countries to adopt 'best practice' policies on taxation.

11.11 The report makes a distinction among three situations in which the tax levied on income from geographically mobile financial and other service activities in one country is lower than the tax that would be levied on the same income in another country:

- the first country is a tax haven and, as such, generally imposes no or only nominal tax on that income;

- the first country collects significant revenues from tax imposed on income at the individual or corporate level but its tax system has preferential features that allow the relevant income to be subject to low or no taxation; or

- the first country collects significant revenues from tax imposed on income at the individual or corporate level, but the effective tax rate that is generally applicable at that level is lower than the tax rate levied in the other country.

11.12 Each of these situations may have undesirable effects when seen from the perspective of the other country. However, the report is careful not to suggest that there is some general minimum effective tax rate on income below which a country would be considered to be engaging in harmful tax practices.

Focus on Financial Services

11.13 The main focus of the OECD's work is on financial and other service activities because these are the activities that are the most geographically mobile and therefore the most sensitive to tax differentials. Tax havens located outside the OECD area and harmful preferential tax regimes in OECD countries are particularly involved in these activities.

The OECD's Concept of 'Tax Haven'

11.14 The OECD report focuses on the following factors to determine whether a jurisdiction is a tax haven:

- the jurisdiction imposes no or only nominal taxes and offers itself, or is perceived to offer itself, as a place to be used by non-residents to escape tax in their country of residence;

- practices of the jurisdiction prevent the effective exchange of relevant information with other governments on taxpayers benefiting from the low or no tax jurisdiction;

- a lack of transparency exists;

- there is an absence of a requirement that the activity be substantial, since this would suggest that a jurisdiction may be attempting to attract investment or transactions that are purely tax driven; and

- there is no or only nominal taxation within the jurisdiction.

11.15   If combined with a situation in which the jurisdiction offers itself as a place where non-residents can escape tax in their country of residence, any of the above factors may be sufficient to identify a tax haven.

11.16   The OECD's concept of 'tax haven' thus refers to tax jurisdictions that offer themselves as a place that non-residents can use to escape tax obligations in their countries of residence. A number of factors identify these jurisdictions, in particular the virtual absence of taxes (combined with minimum business presence requirements) and a lack of legislative and administrative transparency. Bank secrecy and other features that prevent effective exchange of information are also discernible. Using these definitions, a list of jurisdictions identified as tax havens has been published in order to help form the basis for unilateral or collective countermeasures.

The OECD's Concept of 'Harmful' Preferential Tax Regimes

11.17   Four key factors are used by the OECD to assist in identifying harmful preferential tax regimes:

- the regime imposes a low or zero effective tax rate on the relevant income;

- the regime is 'ring-fenced';

- the operation of the regime is non-transparent; and

- the jurisdiction operating the regime does not effectively exchange information with other countries.

11.18   A low or zero effective tax rate is the necessary starting point for an examination of a preferential tax regime.

11.19   The concept of 'harmful' preferential tax regimes thus refers to low tax regimes — provided for either in the general tax legislation or as administrative measures — that are primarily tailored to tap into the tax bases of other countries. Characteristics of such regimes are their low effective taxes combined with 'ring-fencing', whereby they are partly or fully insulated from the domestic economy. Furthermore, there is often a lack of legislative and administrative transparency, as well as difficulties in accessing information. The potentially harmful regimes in the OECD area tend to target banking, financing, insurance, location of headquarters, and distribution and similar services, although of themselves these are legitimate commercial activities.

Collective Action

11.20   Recognising the positive aspects of the new global environment in which tax systems operate, member countries have concluded that they need to act collectively as well as individually to curb harmful tax competition and to counter the spread of harmful preferential tax regimes directed at financial and service activities. Since it is difficult for individual countries to combat effectively the spread of harmful preferential tax regimes, a co-ordinated approach and international co-operation are being intensified to avoid competitive bidding by countries for geographically mobile activities. Consequently, a strong case is made for reinforcing existing measures and for intensifying international cooperation when formulating a response to the problem of harmful tax practices.

11.21   The Committee on Fiscal Affairs has already engaged in a dialogue with countries in the Asian-Pacific region, Latin America, Africa and in the former Soviet Bloc. Ministers have asked the OECD to explore further how contacts with non-Member countries can be intensified.

11.22 Harmful Tax Competition Measures

THE RECOMMENDATIONS AND THE GUIDELINES

11.22 In order to deal with harmful preferential tax regimes, OECD countries agreed to non-binding Guidelines for Dealing with Harmful Preferential Tax Regimes. They have undertaken to eliminate within five years of the adoption of the OECD's report on harmful tax competition (or, if a particular 'grandfather clause' applies, no later than 31 December 2005) the features of those preferential tax regimes identified as harmful under the guidelines.

11.23 In addition to the tax haven list and the guidelines, both of which are of a multilateral character, recommendations are made on how the OECD countries might strengthen their domestic and bilateral measures against harmful tax practices. At the national level, OECD countries are encouraged to adopt controlled foreign corporation (CFC) or equivalent legislation. This generally enables the home country of the parent to exercise taxing rights over lowly taxed foreign subsidiaries that the parent controls. The OECD countries are also encouraged to adhere to certain defined standards in providing tax rulings and to apply strictly the 1995 OECD Transfer Pricing Guidelines, which provide for internationally agreed-upon standards for establishing prices on intra-group transactions.

11.24 Bilaterally, OECD countries are encouraged to intensify their exchange of information on tax havens and preferential tax regimes. A provision is being considered for the OECD's Model Tax Convention that would deny entities operating under harmful tax regimes access to certain or all of the Convention's benefits. Furthermore, the OECD report asks countries to consider terminating any treaties they might have with tax havens.

11.25 After defining the factors to be used in identifying harmful tax practices, the report goes on to make 19 wide-ranging recommendations to counteract such practices. The recommendations set out in the report and the accompanying guidelines address the problem of harmful tax practices from different angles. Taken together, the recommendations with the guidelines represent a comprehensive approach by Member countries for dealing with the problems of harmful tax competition created by tax havens and harmful preferential tax regimes. Some of the recommendations encourage countries to refrain from adopting harmful tax competition or to eliminate measures constituting harmful tax competition. Others are aimed at offsetting the benefits for taxpayers of certain forms of harmful tax practices. Still others address the issue indirectly by focusing on tax evasion and avoidance, because many forms of harmful tax competition are aimed at taxpayers willing to engage in tax evasion and tax avoidance.

11.26 The effectiveness of many of the recommendations concerning domestic legislation and tax treaties depends in part upon whether they can be implemented in a co-ordinated way. Consequently, one of the main recommendations is for the establishment of a forum on harmful tax practices in order to monitor the application of the guidelines and to undertake an ongoing evaluation of existing and proposed regimes. The forum would assess the effectiveness of countermeasures and to propose ways to improve their effectiveness. It would also be responsible for monitoring the implementation of the other recommendations.

11.27 The guidelines are:

- Refrain from adopting new measures, or extending the scope of or strengthening existing measures (in the form of legislative provisions or administrative practices related to taxation) that constitute harmful tax practices.

- Review existing measures for the purpose of identifying those measures, in the form of legislative provisions or administrative practices related to taxation, that constitute harmful tax practices. These measures should be reported to the Forum on Harmful Tax Practices and should be included in a list within two years from the date on which these guidelines are approved by the OECD Council.

- Remove, before the end of five years (starting from the date on which the guidelines are approved by the OECD Council), the harmful features of preferential tax regimes. However, in respect of taxpayers who are benefiting from such regimes on 31 December 2000, the benefits that they derive will be removed at the latest on 31 December 2005. This will ensure that such particular tax benefits have been entirely removed after that date. The list of harmful tax practices will be reviewed annually to delete those regimes that no longer constitute harmful preferential tax regimes.

- Make certain requests. Each Member country may request that a measure be examined by the Member countries, through the Forum on Harmful Tax Practices, when it believes that an existing measure not already included in the list (or a proposed or new measure of itself or of another country) constitutes a measure that might qualify as a harmful tax practice. The purpose of this examination is to include the measure in the list. The measure may be in the form of a legislative provision or administrative practice related to taxation. The Forum may issue a non-binding opinion on that question.

- Co-ordinate, through the Forum, national and treaty responses to harmful tax practices adopted by other countries.

- Use the Forum to encourage actively non-Member countries to associate themselves with these guidelines.

FORUM ON HARMFUL TAX PRACTICES

11.28   The OECD established the Forum on Harmful Tax Practices in order to provide a framework for implementation of the 19 recommendations contained in the report. The Forum's role is to oversee the implementation and development of the recommendations and engage in a dialogue with non-Member countries that share the concerns of OECD members. In addition to these recommendations, the report identifies a series of areas where further study could result in new recommendations. The Forum will be used to examine these areas.

11.29   The OECD report contains proposals for the examination of issues of harmful tax competition to be explored, apart from the issue of geographically mobile financial and other service activities. It is proposed that, in the context of the Forum, member countries and interested non-member countries will continue to examine these issues with the aim of developing new recommendations.

- *Restriction of deductions for payments to tax haven entities.* A number of countries have rules imposing restrictions on the deduction of payments made to tax haven countries or rules imposing a reversal of the onus of proof in case of such payments.

- *Imposition of withholding taxes on certain payments to residents of countries that engage in harmful tax competition.* Many countries currently have legislation that imposes withholding taxes on various types of payments to non-residents but eliminates or substantially reduces the rate of withholding tax on payments made to residents of treaty countries.

It is considered by the OECD that the imposition of withholding taxes at a substantial rate on certain payments to countries that engage in harmful tax competition, if associated with measures aimed at preventing the use of conduit arrangements, would act as a deterrent for countries to engage in harmful tax competition and for taxpayers to use entities located in those countries.

- *Residence rules.* Revising the definition of corporate residence might be considered a possible measure to counteract the use of foreign corporations to avoid domestic tax. Accordingly, one option is to extend the domestic tax definitions of corporate residence so that a foreign corporation controlled by residents would be considered to be resident. Control for this purpose could be limited to the control of the affairs of a corporation as exercised by its board of directors or management. Alternatively, control could be determined by reference to the ownership of its shares. Several countries already treat corporations as residents if the corporation's management and control are located in the country. However, this concept of control is easily manipulated by taxpayers, in contrast to the share ownership concept of control.

  On the treaty side, the definition of 'resident of a Contracting State' could be restricted to expressly exclude certain entities subject to no or little tax. One possibility is to narrow the scope of the definition of resident in the OECD Model Tax Convention to exclude other taxpayers who are liable to tax in a country but do not in fact pay tax on all of their income like ordinary residents. Moreover, a specific rule might be adopted to deny certain treaty benefits to corporations resident in countries that exempt foreign branch income. For example, the benefit of reduced withholding taxes might be denied to such a corporation with respect to amounts attributable to a foreign branch located in a tax haven. Furthermore, the definition of resident could be revised to exclude legal entities that take advantage of specified regimes that constitute harmful tax competition.

- *Application of transfer pricing rules and guidelines.* The application of transfer pricing rules may constitute a useful counteracting measure to the situation in which significant income may be attributed to a foreign entity that performs few, if any, real activities. (Transfer pricing rules typically start from an analysis of the true functions performed by each part of a group of associated enterprises.) It is suggested that rules affecting a reversal of onus of proof in certain cases might help to address the specific circumstances of tax havens and regimes that constitute harmful tax practices.

- *Thin capitalisation.* A large number of OECD countries apply general or specific legislative rules to address cases of base erosion that are attributable to the thin capitalisation of resident companies by non-residents. Such rules can act as a block against the tax-free repatriation of domestic profits to entities that may be located in tax havens or in countries that provide, directly or indirectly, favourable taxation of interest income from foreign subsidiaries. Some domestic rules, however, such as the setting of safe harbour debt/equity ratios, can, conversely, be used to facilitate harmful tax competition.

  The Committee intends to explore whether it should recommend to Member countries lacking such rules that they consider their introduction, especially with respect to safe harbours. The committee also intends to review existing domestic rules.

- *Financial innovation.* Financial markets are constantly evolving, and innovative financial products are continually being created. Such instruments have the potential to be used to assist harmful tax competition, as well as being used for legitimate business purposes. For example, derivative products, in addition to hedging interest rate risk, can be used to create synthetic loans. Such 'loans' give the taxpayer the same economic effect as if a loan had been made, but with the potential to avoid withholding tax and thin capitalisation rules. The Committee intends to keep monitoring this area to insure that financial innovation is not used to assist harmful tax competition.

- *Non-tax measures.* The Committee also intends to explore the possibility of addressing harmful tax competition using a wide range of non-tax measures.

RECENT DEVELOPMENTS

11.30 Recently, the project has evolved into a more co-operative effort, with a particular emphasis on the elimination of tax practices and regimes that facilitate non-compliance with tax law. Jurisdictions outside the OECD area have been consulted. Business involvement by means of the Business and Industry Advisory Committee (BIAC) to the OECD has encouraged the move towards a more co-operative approach toward tax compliance.

Tax Havens

11.31 In June 2000 Bermuda, Cayman Islands, Cyprus, Malta, Mauritius, and San Marino made a commitment to eliminate their harmful tax practices by the end of 2005. Of the other 35 jurisdictions identified as meeting the tax haven criteria, 32 have already contacted the OECD seeking further co-operative dialogue. Some of these jurisdictions have already made commitments (the Isle of Man, the Netherlands Antilles, and the Seychelles) and others are expected to do so shortly.

11.32 To assist this process, the OECD has agreed that a jurisdiction may either make a bilateral commitment or base its commitment on the recently issued Collective Memorandum of Understanding (see http://www.oecd.org/media/release/nw00-123a.htm). In either case a commitment can be made by means of a press release reflecting government action rather than a formal letter being sent from a Minister to the Secretary-General of the OECD. In order to achieve greater transparency, all commitments will be made public.

11.33 Early in January 2001, a meeting, hosted by the Government of Barbados in association with the Commonwealth and the OECD, was convened to improve the dialogue between the OECD countries and jurisdictions primarily of the Caribbean region. The intention was to identify the common principles and shared concerns to guide this work. On 1 February 2001, a third meeting took place in Paris primarily for European jurisdictions and on February 15–16 a similar regional meeting took place in Tokyo for the Asian Pacific countries. These regional meetings have achieved a better understanding of the project and have encouraged jurisdictions to intensify their bilateral dialogue with the OECD Member countries working towards the objective of having a minimum number of jurisdictions on the List of Uncooperative Tax Havens.

Works within the OECD Member Countries

11.34 The work on eliminating harmful tax practices within OECD Member countries is expected to meet the deadline of April 2003, as set out in the OECD Ministerial Council decision. The OECD Forum on Harmful Tax Practices is continuing its review of the 47 OECD tax regimes identified as being potentially harmful.

OECD and Commonwealth Co-operation

11.35 ECD and Commonwealth countries have agreed on a way forward in efforts to achieve global co-operation on harmful tax practices through a dialogue based on shared support for the principles of transparency, non-discrimination and effective exchange of information on tax matters.

11.36 The agreement was achieved at a two-day meeting co-organised by the OECD and the Commonwealth in Barbados, and attended by representatives of more than 40 jurisdictions including OECD and Commonwealth countries and jurisdictions in the Caribbean

11.37 Harmful Tax Competition Measures

and neighbouring region. A number of international and regional organisations were also represented, including the IMF, the World Bank, Caricom, the Caribbean Development Bank, the Inter-American Development Bank, the Centre for Inter-American Tax Administrators and the Pacific Islands Forum.

11.37 Discussion at the 8–9 January 2001 High-Level Consultations in Barbados showed that there is much common ground between participants on the substantive issues, although there remain some divergences on process. Wide consent has been attributed to the broad principles, i.e. transparency, non-discrimination and effective exchange of information.

11.38 Agreement build upon this to create a small tightly knit joint Working Group of representatives from the Commonwealth, Caricom, Pacific Island Forum and OECD countries and territories was set up with a two-fold task:

- To take the three principles noted above and to find a mutually acceptable political process by which these principles could be turned into commitments. This process, if successful, would replace the OECD's process in the context of its Memorandum of Understanding.

- To examine how to continue the dialogue begun in Barbados. The Group will examine how the recently created Global Forum on taxation can evolve into a truly inclusive Global Forum, which would promote global co-operation on tax matters. It will also identify further relevant tax issues for consideration by such a Forum.

Work with non-OECD Countries

11.39 The OECD's Committee on Fiscal Affairs (CFA) is actively following up a meeting held in Paris last June, which brought together 29 OECD countries and an identical number of economies outside the OECD. The aim of this meeting was to see how far non-Member jurisdictions shared the concerns of the OECD Member States, and to explore how they could be more closely involved with this work. A number of additional bilateral and multilateral contacts are planned to encourage others to work with OECD countries to counter the spread of harmful tax practices.

The Involvement of the Business Community

11.40 The BIAC Taxation Committee has created a liaison group to work with the Forum on Harmful Tax Practices to ensure that the views of the business community are heard.

OECD MEMBER COUNTRY PREFERENTIAL REGIMES

11.41 The OECD Forum on Harmful Tax Practices has identified below preferential tax regimes as potentially harmful:

Insurance

Australia	Offshore Banking Units
Belgium	Co-ordination Centres
Finland	Åland Captive Insurance Regime
Italy	Trieste Financial Services and Insurance Centre
Ireland	International Financial Services Centre
Portugal	Madeira International Business Centre
Luxembourg	Provisions for Fluctuations in Re-Insurance Companies
Sweden	Foreign Non-life Insurance Companies

Financing and Leasing

Belgium	Co-ordination Centres
Hungary	Venture Capital Companies
Hungary	Preferential Regime for Companies Operating Abroad
Iceland	International Trading Companies
Ireland	International Financial Services Centre
Ireland	Shannon Airport Zone
Italy	Trieste Financial Services and Insurance Centre
Luxembourg	Finance Branch
Netherlands	Risk Reserves for International Group Financing
Netherlands	Intra-group Finance Activities
Netherlands	Finance Branch
Spain	Basque Country and Navarra Co-ordination Centres
Switzerland	Administrative Companies

Fund Managers

Greece	Mutual Funds/Portfolio Investment Companies (Taxation of Fund Managers)
Ireland	International Financial Services Centre (Taxation of Fund Managers)
Luxembourg	Management companies (Taxation of management companies that manage only one mutual fund (1929 holdings))
Portugal	Madeira International Business Centre (Taxation of Fund Managers)

Banking

Australia	Offshore Banking Units
Canada	International Banking Centres
Ireland	International Financial Services Centre
Italy	Trieste Financial Services and Insurance Centre
Korea	Offshore Activities of Foreign Exchange Banks
Portugal	External Branches in the Madeira International Business Centre
Turkey	Istanbul Offshore Banking Regime

Headquarters regimes

Belgium	Co-ordination Centres
France	Headquarters Centres
Germany	Monitoring and Co-ordinating Offices
Greece	Offices of Foreign Companies
Netherlands	Cost-plus Ruling
Portugal	Madeira International Business Centre
Spain	Basque Country and Navarra Co-ordination Centres
Switzerland	Administrative Companies
Switzerland	Service Companies

Distribution Centre Regimes

Belgium	Distribution Centres
France	Logistics Centres
Netherlands	Cost-plus/Resale Minus Ruling
Turkey	Turkish Free Zones

Service Centre Regimes

Belgium	Service Centres
Netherlands	Cost-plus Ruling

11.42   Harmful Tax Competition Measures

Shipping

Canada	International Shipping
Germany	International Shipping
Greece	Shipping Offices
Greece	Shipping Regime (Law 27/75)
Italy	International Shipping
Netherlands	International Shipping
Norway	International Shipping
Portugal	International Shipping Register of Madeira

Miscellaneous Activities

Belgium	Ruling on Informal Capital
Belgium	Ruling on Foreign Sales Corporation Activities
Canada	Non-resident Owned Investment Corporations
Netherlands	Ruling on Informal Capital
Netherlands	Ruling on Foreign Sales Corporation Activities
United States	Foreign Sales Corporations

TAX HAVENS

11.42   The jurisdictions listed below were found to meet the tax haven criteria of the 1998 OECD Report. These evaluations were endorsed by the Council on 16 June 2000:

Andorra
Anguilla (Overseas Territory of the United Kingdom)
Antigua and Barbuda
Aruba (a Member of the Kingdom of the Netherlands)
Commonwealth of the Bahamas
Bahrain
Barbados
Belize
British Virgin Islands (Overseas Territory of the United Kingdom)
Cook Islands (New Zealand)
The Commonwealth of Dominica
Gibraltar (Overseas Territory of the United Kingdom)
Grenada
Guernsey/Sark/Alderney (Dependency of the British Crown)
Isle of Man (Dependency of the British Crown)
Jersey (Dependency of the British Crown)
Liberia
The Principality of Liechtenstein
The Republic of the Maldives
The Republic of the Marshall Islands
The Principality of Monaco
Montserrat (Overseas Territory of the United Kingdom)
The Republic of Nauru
Netherlands Antilles (a Member of the Kingdom of the Netherlands)
Niue (a fully self-governing country in free association with New Zealand)
Panama
Samoa
The Republic of the Seychelles
St. Lucia
The Federation of St. Christopher & Nevis
St. Vincent and the Grenadines

Tonga
Turks & Caicos (Overseas Territory of the United Kingdom)
US Virgin Islands (External Territory of the United States)
The Republic of Vanuatu

EUROPEAN UNION

11.43 Work on harmful tax competition has also been carried out in the European Union (EU). The EU Council agreed on 1 December 1997 to a package of measures that will tackle harmful tax competition in order to help to (a) reduce distortions in the single market, (b) prevent excessive losses of tax revenue, and (c) develop tax structures in a more employment-friendly way. The package includes a Code of Conduct on business taxation, taxation of savings income, and the issue of withholding taxes on cross-border interest and royalty payments between companies. The Code of Conduct identifies potentially harmful regimes in the field of business taxation and gives factors for the assessment of harmful regimes. It includes a commitment not to introduce new harmful tax regimes and to roll back existing regimes.

11.44 Under the Code, a standstill on unfair tax competition came into operation on 1 January 1998; the Commission is now conducting a review of tax practices in each Member State. Member States have at least five years to dismantle unfair tax regimes — the EU Commission had proposed a two-year phase-out period — but some exceptions, such as an unspecified rollback period for Ireland's 10% corporation tax rate for manufacturers, have been negotiated.

11.45 The Code is flanked by a package of measures, including a commitment to deal with taxes on savings (including withholding taxes on bank interest payments and share dividends) as well as a commitment to draft a directive on interest and royalty payments between companies.

11.46 Particular attention is being paid to peripheral parts of the EU such as the Canary Islands and Madeira. Member States are also called upon to promote the Code in their own dependencies, such as the United Kingdom for the Channel Islands and Gibraltar, and the Netherlands for the Netherlands Antilles.

11.47 Several favourable corporate tax regimes for foreign and domestic companies, such as those in the Netherlands, Belgium, and, more recently, Denmark also fall under scrutiny. Under the Code, all unfair tax regimes are to be withdrawn by 1 January 2003.

11.48 The Irish government has signalled that it will oppose EU interference in domestic tax policy by announcing plans to enshrine future corporation tax cuts in its legislation. It is concerned that other Member States opposed to tax competition will seek to dismantle the bilateral tax deal struck with the European Commission.

11.49 The EU Competition Commission has drawn up draft guidelines to end discriminatory tax treatment that governments might exploit to protect domestic companies or attract foreign companies. The new rulebook states that all forms of exceptional tax treatment — special deductions or accelerated depreciation of assets, credits, exemptions or deferment of tax debt — can be prohibited under the Treaty of Rome's rules against the granting of illegal State aid. General measures that apply throughout the economy and do not give preference to certain sectors or regions will still be allowed, but regional aid schemes will have to be submitted to the Commission for prior approval on the basis of the new guidelines. If a scheme is found to be unlawful, the Directorate-General for Competition will instruct the government concerned to claw back the value of the illegal tax break plus interest.

11.50 Harmful Tax Competition Measures

11.50 While the EU Code and the OECD Guidelines are broadly compatible, particularly regarding the criteria used to identify harmful preferential tax regimes, and mutually reinforcing, the scope and operation of the two differ. The OECD Guidelines are clearly limited to financial and other service activities, whereas the Code looks at business activities in general, although with an emphasis on mobile activities. The review procedure reflects the different institutional frameworks within which each organisation operates, and the OECD Guidelines are explicitly aimed at a much broader geographic grouping. The OECD work goes beyond harmful preferential tax regimes to encompass tax havens; it also focuses on exchange of information. In addition, as noted above, the EU Code is part of a package of measures, whereas the OECD Guidelines are accompanied by the 19 detailed recommendations relating to the specific issues of harmful tax competition.

CASE STUDY: JERSEY

Edwards Report

11.51 The official British government report on the trusts and banking industry in Jersey, Guernsey, and the Isle of Man by former Treasury official Andrew Edwards paid tribute to the manner in which their fiduciary business is conducted and regulated. This has vindicated the claims of the three jurisdictions that they belong in the top drawer of the world's offshore financial centres.

11.52 Following the British government's *Edwards Report* on regulation in the Channel Islands and the Isle of Man, UK officials are conducting a similar review of other British dependent offshore centres, including Anguilla, Bermuda, the British Virgin Islands, the Cayman Islands, Gibraltar, Montserrat, the Turks & Caicos Islands, Gibraltar, Bermuda, and the British Virgin Islands have been updating their regulatory systems over the past 18 months. Gibraltar introduced rigorous new laws to bring it in line with EU directives as far back as 1995. Its financial regulations now are equal in standard to the UK Bermuda and the British Virgin Islands also have introduced legislation in line with the standards of the world's leading offshore jurisdictions. However, Anguilla, the Cayman Islands, Montserrat, and the Turks & Caicos Islands do not yet meet required standards.

11.53 At the present time, Jersey is moving strongly to the forefront of both onshore and offshore jurisdictions in the licensing and regulating of trust and company service providers. In this respect, Jersey is becoming a leader in financial regulation, and is currently ahead of the United Kingdom. In fact, the 1998 *Edwards Report* to the UK Home Secretary confirmed that the arrangements in place in Jersey were to a large measure in conformity with the internationally accepted standards of financial regulation. The Report stated that Jersey, as well as Guernsey and the Isle of Man were in the top division of offshore finance centres. However, the Report recommended a number of changes in order to raise standards by extending the depth of regulation. The *Edwards Report* included over 150 individual proposals, conclusions and expressions of opinion.

Task Force

11.54 Since then Jersey set up a Task Force, with two key objectives: (a) to ensure that the Island maintains its high regulatory standards, and (b) to ensure that the Island's reputation and economic interests are fully protected.

11.55 The Task Force has endorsed most of the Edwards's conclusions and recommendations. A large number of these proposals had already been implemented or have been accepted in principle and are now in the process of being implemented.

Disclosure of Beneficial Ownership of Corporations

11.56 Jersey has long had a policy of requiring confidential disclosure of beneficial ownership for all new incorporations. The *Edwards Report*, however, went very much further in seeking the confidential disclosure of the beneficial ownership of foreign incorporated entities that are administered in Jersey. The Task Force has rather adopted the policy of not enforcing routine disclosure in such cases but rather to require that persons administering foreign incorporated entities should maintain records and make the information available to the Jersey authorities when so requested in the context of a criminal or regulatory investigation.

Investment Business

11.57 The Investment Business Law 1999 extends the high standard of regulation that applies to banks, insurance companies, and fund managers, now also to investment managers, dealers, and advisors. This will enable the Commission of the Financial Services Board to apply to the Courts for the handing over of unlawful profits and restitution in the case of investor losses. The Commission is empowered to refuse or revoke a license or make a public statement about any person who has breached a provision of the Investment Business Code. Of particular significance is the acceptance by the Task Force to change a provision in the law that currently prohibits the Commission from responding to overseas regulators' requests for assistance in respect of customers of Jersey regulated businesses even in cases where the customers are subject to regulatory action by the requesting authority.

Licensing and Regulation of Trust and Company Administrators

11.58 Jersey is moving strongly to the forefront of both onshore and offshore jurisdictions in the licensing and regulating of trust and company service providers. In this respect, Jersey is becoming a leader in financial regulation, and is currently ahead of the United Kingdom.

All Crimes Legislation

11.59 The Proceeds of Crime Law 1999 brought Jersey legislation substantially into line with the United Kingdom. The Jersey anti-money laundering law now more than holds its own with the legislation in force in most of the member countries of the OECD and the European Union, and makes Jersey the offshore financial centre that is co-operating the most effectively in the international fight against organised financial crime.

STRATEGIC CHECKLISTS

THE OECD'S CONCEPT OF 'TAX HAVEN'

- The jurisdiction imposes no or only nominal taxes and offers itself, or is perceived to offer itself, as a place to be used by non-residents to escape tax in their country of residence.

- Practices of the jurisdiction prevent the effective exchange of relevant information with other governments on taxpayers benefiting from the low or no tax jurisdiction.

- A lack of transparency exists.

- There is an absence of a requirement that the activity be substantial, since this would suggest that a jurisdiction may be attempting to attract investment or transactions that are purely tax driven.

- There is no or only nominal taxation within the jurisdiction.

- The jurisdiction offers itself as a place where non-residents can escape tax in their country of residence.

THE OECD'S CONCEPT OF 'HARMFUL' PREFERENTIAL TAX REGIMES

- The regime imposes a low or zero effective tax rate on the relevant income.

- The regime is 'ring-fenced'.

- The operation of the regime is non-transparent.

- The jurisdiction operating the regime does not effectively exchange information with other countries.

PENDING DEVELOPMENTS WORLDWIDE

- Stricter 'all crimes' legislation.

- Stricter money laundering provisions.

- Removal of the time limit on prosecutions.

- Police and criminal evidence law.

- International co-operation.

- Extra staffing of law enforcement services.

- Fraud and financial investigation procedures.

- Licensing and regulation of trust and company service providers.

- Changes in companies regulation.

- Changes in trust legislation.

- Disclosure of beneficial ownership of corporations.

- Toughening of audit and disclosure requirements.

- Registration of foreign incorporated entities.

- Business rescue measures.

- Customer protection schemes.

- Financial services ombudsman.

- Insurance regulation.

- Investment business regulation.

- Possible new tax treaties and exchange of information agreements.

- Restriction of deductions for payments to tax haven entities.

- Imposition of withholding taxes on certain payments to residents of countries that engage in harmful tax competition.

- Revision of residence rules.

- Stricter application of transfer pricing rules and guidelines.

- Tightening of thin capitalisation rules.

- Attack on certain financial innovation.

- New uses of non-tax measures to restrain harmful tax practices.

STRATEGIC ISSUES AND CAVEATS

SCOPE OF NEW MEASURES

- 'All Crimes' and 'Money Laundering' are becoming part of the ordinary legal systems worldwide, and extend even to IOFCs.

- *Caveat* Penalties are very considerable and extend in certain countries also to life imprisonment.

KEY AREAS OF ACTIVITY OF THE FINANCIAL ACTION TASK FORCE (FATF)

- Establishing standards.

- Reviewing money laundering methods and countermeasures.

- Monitoring the implementation of anti-money laundering measures by member governments.

- Promoting the widest possible international action against money laundering.

- Adoption of countermeasures by non-member countries.

MAIN ISSUES OF INTERNATIONAL CONCERN

- Vulnerabilities resulting from Internet banking.

- The increasing reach of alternative remittance systems.

- The role of company formation agents and their services.

- International trade-related activities as a cover for money laundering.

- The practice in some jurisdictions of an 'indirect obligation' to report suspicious transactions related to some criminal offences, whereby making a report provides a defence against a charge of money laundering, rather than a direct obligation to make a report.

- The practice in some jurisdictions of allowing intermediaries to introduce businesses to banks and financial institutions where the obligation to verify customer identity was an obligation for the introducer instead of the bank.

- Difficulties in establishing the beneficial ownership of some legal entities, including companies issuing bearer shares and trusts.

- The existence and development of the IBCs which can be formed by intermediaries and be subject to fewer verification and disclosure requirements than applied to the company sector as a whole.

- The lack of a stringent scheme to apply the new rules of customer identification for accounts open prior to their entry into force.

FINANCIAL SERVICES OVER THE INTERNET

- A growing number of existing mainstream financial institutions, as well as a few pure Internet banks, already provide a range of transactional services.

- The potential money laundering risks arise from the extreme difficulty for banks offering such capabilities to positively establish the identity of a particular transactor or even determine the location from which the transaction is made.

- The capability of accessing an account from beyond national borders raises the question of how to determine regulatory or investigative jurisdiction when online activity might indicate money laundering.

- The FATF considers it important to examine the implications that such technology might have on current customer identification practices.

ISSUES RAISED BY WIRE TRANSFERS OF FUNDS

- The FATF has for a long time worked with the Society for Worldwide Interbank Financial Telecommunication (SWIFT) on measures which would help to prevent wire transfers being misused by money launderers. SWIFT has 7,000 member institutions, which process 5 million messages totalling US$ 5–6 trillion each day.

- Western Union has an anti-money laundering and suspicious activity report systems (SARs), and works with the United States Treasury Department to develop regulations concerning SARs.

PRINCIPAL SOURCES OF MONEY LAUNDERING PROCEEDS

- Narcotics trafficking.

- Proceeds from various types of fraud activity.

- Use of accounts with false names.

- Structuring transactions.

- Currency smuggling.

ALTERNATIVE REMITTANCE SYSTEMS AS THE BACKBONE OF MONEY LAUNDERING SCHEMES

- Black Market Peso Exchange.

- Hawala/Hundi.

- Certain Chinese/East Asian remittance systems.

TRADE ACTIVITY

- The FATF has observed a growing trend for trade activity to be used both as a cover for money laundering and as an actual money laundering mechanism.

- Although frequently appearing in the context of alternative remittance systems, trade-related money laundering is not exclusively associated with such systems.

- Customs officials responsible for import/export controls have access to useful information on cross-border movement of goods; however, this information is not always exploited fully from the perspective of potential money laundering activity.

INCREASED PRESENCE OF CERTAIN PROFESSIONS IN MONEY LAUNDERING OPERATIONS

- Bankers.

- Trust officers.

- Attorneys and solicitors.

- Notaries.

- Accountants.

- Company formation agents.

COMPANY FORMATION AGENTS

- The role played by company formation agents in money laundering is becoming increasingly clear.

- Taking advantage of the agent's expertise in varying company registration procedures, together with the banking or corporate secrecy of certain jurisdictions, the money launderer may create a barrier of legitimate seeming corporate structures that further separates the money launderer from his illegal proceeds.

- For the most part, company formation agents are not specifically held to anti-money laundering rules, and extending such rules to cover this sector may represent a solution on a national level.

> • The possibility is being considered to promote a minimum standard in company formation procedures — e.g. limiting the number of directorships held by an individual, and striking companies off the register upon failure to comply with necessary procedures.

FINANCIAL ACTION TASK FORCE ON MONEY LAUNDERING (FATF)

12.1 Money laundering knows no frontiers. Money laundering is ubiquitous. Money laundering is an evolving activity. It follows that, in order to be effective, any action to combat money laundering must rely on effective cooperation between experts from a wide range of disciplines: legal and judicial, financial and regulatory, and law enforcement.

12.2 The main issues of concern include:

• the vulnerabilities of Internet banking;

• the increasing reach of alternative remittance systems;

• the role of company formation agents and their services; and

• international trade-related activities as a cover for money laundering.

12.3 The Financial Action Task Force (FATF) was established by the G7 Summit in Paris in 1989 in order to examine measures to combat money laundering. The FATF is not a permanent international organisation. Its mandate has to be renewed periodically, usually for five-year stretches.

12.4 In 1990, the FATF issued Forty Recommendations for action against money laundering. These recommendations were revised in 1996 to reflect changes in money laundering trends. Membership of the FATF comprises 27 governments and 2 regional organisations (European Commission and Gulf Co-operation Council); major financial centres of North America, Europe and Asia are all represented. Current Members include Argentina; Australia; Austria; Belgium; Brazil; Canada; Denmark; Finland; France; Germany; Greece; Hong Kong; China; Iceland; Ireland; Italy; Japan; Luxembourg; Mexico; the Netherlands; New Zealand; Norway; Portugal; Singapore; Spain; Sweden; Switzerland; Turkey; the United Kingdom; and the United States.

12.5 The delegations of the task force's members are drawn from a wide range of disciplines, including experts from the ministries of finance, justice, interior and external affairs, financial regulatory authorities, and law enforcement agencies.

12.6 In 1998, FATF Ministers and the European Commissioner for Financial Services endorsed the report prepared by the FATF that defines a five-year plan — 1999–2004 — to spread the anti-money laundering message to all continents and regions of the globe. To this end, ministers urged FATF to foster the establishment of a worldwide anti-money laundering network. The network would be based on adequate expansion of the FATF membership, the development of FATF-style regional bodies (such as the Caribbean FATF and the Asia/Pacific Group on Money Laundering), and close co-operation with all relevant international organisations, in particular the United Nations Office for Drug Control and Crime Prevention (UNODCCP) and the International Financial Institutions.

12.7 'All Crimes' and 'Money Laundering' Measures

12.7 The FATF survey of money laundering typologies clearly noted the emergence of new areas of money laundering, such as electronic money, new payment technologies, remittance businesses, non-financial professions, the insurance sector, and stock exchange dealers.

12.8 As the primary objective of its current mandate, the FATF is committed to promoting anti-money laundering initiatives in all continents and regions of the globe and to building a worldwide anti-money laundering network. This strategy consists of three main components: enlarging the FATF membership, developing credible and effective FATF-style regional bodies, and increasing co-operation with the relevant international organisations.

12.9 The FATF continued its collaboration with these relevant international organisations/bodies rather than launch new initiatives, and participated in several anti-money laundering events organised by other bodies. To increase the effectiveness of international anti-money laundering efforts, the FATF and the other organisations and bodies endeavour to co-ordinate their activities through an annual co-ordination meeting and meetings of five regional ad hoc groups (Africa, Asia/Pacific, Caribbean, Central and Eastern Europe and South America). These meetings take place in the margins of the FATF Plenaries.

12.10 The success of the FATF's work so far demonstrates that there is no alternative international organisation, body, or group, that has the necessary expertise of a multidisciplinary nature with the experience and ability to assume the responsibilities of the FATF in a flexible and efficient way.

KEY AREAS OF ACTIVITY

12.11 The FATF has concentrated above all on the following key areas of activity:

- establishing standards;

- reviewing money laundering methods and countermeasures;

- monitoring the implementation of anti-money laundering measures by member governments; and

- promoting the widest possible international action against money laundering and the adoption of countermeasures by non-member countries.

Anti-money laundering efforts focus above all on three main areas:

- to spread the anti-money laundering message to all continents and regions of the globe;

- to improve members' implementation of the Forty Recommendations;

- to strengthen the review of money laundering methods and counter measures.

12.12 Considerable progress has been made by FATF members in implementing anti-money laundering measures. By mid-1999, every member had undergone two evaluations of its anti-money laundering system. The first round of evaluations dealt with the question of whether all members had adequately implemented the Forty Recommendations, while the second round dealt with the effectiveness of the anti-money laundering system for each member.

12.13 Over the past decade, the FATF has played a key role in building an international consensus on the measures that need to be taken to combat money laundering. It has also helped to persuade many countries to implement these measures. In the process, it has helped to create a 'network' of money laundering experts in each of the FATF members, improving co-operation and the flow of information, both at the domestic level and internationally. However, although the FATF's Forty Recommendations have gained some international prominence, a large number of countries around the world have not implemented anti-money laundering systems.

OBJECTIVES OF THE FATF

12.14   The medium- to long-term objectives of the FATF are (1) to develop credible and effective FATF-style regional bodies and (2) to expand its membership to include strategically important new members. At the beginning of 2005, the FATF should ideally have achieved its objective of promoting the establishment of a worldwide anti-money laundering network. It is proposed that an assessment of the FATF's achievements and strategy between 1999 and 2004 and its future should be carried out in 2003–2004.

Objective 1: Establish a worldwide anti-money laundering network in all continents and regions of the globe

12.15   This worldwide anti-money laundering network is to be based on:

- an adequate expansion of the FATF membership to strategically important countries that already have certain key anti-money laundering measures in place, that is, criminalisation of money laundering, mandatory customer identification, and suspicious/unusual transactions reporting by financial institutions;

- the development of FATF-style regional bodies, especially in areas where FATF is not sufficiently represented and strengthening of the work of bodies that already exist (CFATF, Asia/Pacific Group on Money Laundering, Council of Europe, OAS/CICAD, and OGBS); and

- close co-operation with relevant international organisations, in particular the United Nations bodies and the International Financial Institutions.

Objective 2: Improve the implementation of the Forty Recommendations in FATF members

12.16   This objective involves the following elements:

- an enhanced self-assessment process, and

- a third round of simplified mutual evaluations for all FATF members starting in 2001, focusing exclusively on compliance with the revised parts of the recommendations, areas of significant deficiencies identified in the second round, and the general effectiveness of the countermeasures.

Objective 3: Strengthen the review of money laundering trends and countermeasures

12.17   Because money laundering is an evolving activity, it is considered crucial for FATF members to acquire the best possible experience with and knowledge of money laundering trends and techniques. It is similarly considered to be of great importance to assess the effectiveness of the FATF recommendations and to extend the geographical scope of the future typologies exercises, with the possible need for new countermeasures.

12.18   On 17 May 1998, the G8 Heads of State and Government 'welcomed the FATF decision to continue and enlarge its work to combat money laundering in partnership with

12.19 'All Crimes' and 'Money Laundering' Measures

regional groupings' and 'placed special emphasis on the issues of money laundering and financial crime, including issues raised by offshore financial centres'.

MONITORING THE IMPLEMENTATION OF ANTI-MONEY LAUNDERING MEASURES

12.19   A considerable part of the FATF's work focuses on monitoring the implementation by its members of the Forty Recommendations. FATF members are clearly committed to the discipline of multilateral surveillance and peer review. All members have their implementation of the recommendations monitored through a two-pronged approach:

● an annual self-assessment exercise; and,

● the more detailed mutual evaluation process under which each member is subject to an on-site examination.

The Self-Assessment Exercise

Legal Issues

12.20   Almost all members are in compliance with a large majority of the recommendations. All members have enacted laws to make drug money laundering a criminal offence, and all but three members have enacted a law that prohibits the laundering of the proceeds of a range of crimes in addition to drug trafficking.

Financial Issues

12.21   Almost all members comply fully with customer identification and record-keeping requirements for banks, but there are some persistent gaps in coverage with respect to certain categories of non-bank financial institutions. The serious concerns regarding the anonymous passbooks for residents in Austria have not been resolved, however, and are being pursued through the FATF non-compliance procedures.

12.22   In relation to the requirement for financial institutions to report suspicious transactions and related measures, the position is generally regarded as quite satisfactory in relation to banks and almost as good for non-bank financial institutions. However, there is still room for improvement regarding (1) non-bank financial institutions, (2) the need to pay attention to large, unusual transactions, and (3) the obligation to develop internal controls. Almost all bank members have now established anti-money laundering guidelines and taken steps to guard their banks against control or acquisition by criminals. Though there have been improvements, a number of countries still need to take similar measures for all categories of non-bank financial institutions.

12.23   The FATF has stated that there is also a pressing need in the United States to finalise and implement the proposed regulations to significantly enhance anti-money laundering controls over many categories of non-bank financial institutions. These are particularly *bureaux de change*, money remitters, cheque cashiers, issuers and sellers of money orders and travellers cheques, casinos, and securities brokers and dealers. The United States has also been urged to place additional money laundering controls on insurance companies.

The Mutual Evaluation Process

12.24   The second and major element for monitoring the implementation of the FATF recommendations is the mutual evaluation process. Each member is examined in turn by the FATF on the basis of a report drawn up by a team of three or four selected experts drawn from the legal, financial, and law enforcement fields of other members. The purpose of this exercise is to provide a comprehensive and objective assessment of the extent to which the country in question has moved forward in implementing effective measures to counter money laundering and to highlight areas in which further progress may still be required.

FATF EXPANSION

12.25   The FATF has decided to expand its membership to a limited number of strategically important countries which could play a major role in their regions in the process of combating money laundering.

12.26   The minimum and *sine qua non* criteria for admission are as follows:

- to be fully committed at the political level: (i) to implement the 1996 Recommendations within a reasonable timeframe (three years), and (ii) to undergo annual self-assessment exercises and two rounds of mutual evaluations;

- to be a full and active member of the relevant FATF-style regional body (where one exists), or be prepared to work with the FATF or even to take the lead to establish such a body (where none exists);

- to be a strategically important country;

- to have already made the laundering of the proceeds of drug trafficking and other serious crimes a criminal offence; and

- to have already made it mandatory for financial institutions to identify their customers and to report unusual or suspicious transactions.

ISSUES OF PARTICULAR CONCERN FOR ANTI-MONEY LAUNDERING PURPOSES

Principal sources of money laundering proceeds

12.27   Narcotics trafficking continues to represent the single largest source of criminal proceeds throughout the world.

12.28   Nevertheless, the proceeds from various types of fraud activity make up an increasing portion of illegal funds originating from some jurisdictions. The increased presence of certain professions — especially attorneys, solicitors, notaries, and accountants, often in connection with company formation agents, in money laundering operations is noticeable.

12.29   In addition to some of the more complex money laundering techniques, a number of less sophisticated methods continue to be observed, including use of accounts with false names, structuring transactions and currency smuggling.

Issues of interpretation

12.30   A number of issues have arisen in several jurisdictions (noted above), which raised questions of interpretation. These are, in particular:

- The practice in some jurisdictions of an 'indirect obligation' to report suspicious transactions related to some criminal offences, whereby making a report provides a defence against a charge of money laundering, rather than a direct obligation to make a report.

- The practice in some jurisdictions of allowing intermediaries to introduce businesses to banks and financial institutions where the obligation to verify customer identity was an obligation for the introducer instead of the bank.

- Difficulties in establishing the beneficial ownership of some legal entities, including companies issuing bearer shares and trusts.

- The existence and development of the IBCs which can be formed by intermediaries and be subject to fewer verification and disclosure requirements than applied to the company sector as a whole.

- The lack of a stringent scheme to apply the new rules of customer identification for accounts open prior to their entry into force.

Financial services over the Internet

12.31 With the increasing offering of financial services over the Internet, it is the potential for conducting financial transactions on-line that presents one of the most significant vulnerabilities to money laundering at present. A growing number of existing mainstream financial institutions, as well as a few pure Internet banks, already provide a range of transactional services. The potential money laundering risks arise from the extreme difficulty for banks offering such capabilities to positively establish the identity of a particular transactor or even determine the location from which the transaction is made. The capability of accessing an account from beyond national borders raises the question of how to determine regulatory or investigative jurisdiction when on-line activity might indicate money laundering. However, no money laundering cases have been detected yet which involve this mechanism. The FATF considered this issue important enough to require further attention, if only to examine the implications the technology might have on current customer identification practices.

Alternative remittance systems

12.32 Alternative remittance systems are often shown to be the backbone of some money laundering schemes throughout the world. The FATF considered three major systems — Black Market Peso Exchange, Hawala/Hundi, and the Chinese/East Asian systems — which, although different in regional, economic, or cultural origins, share a number of common characteristics. These systems give the money launderer the key ability to move funds rapidly over great distances leaving little or no audit trail. They represent a significant challenge to the investigator who must often surmount cultural, ethnic or linguistic barriers in order to detect and penetrate such systems. Remedies to the problem of alternate remittance systems could include expanding and more thoroughly implementing.

Company formation agents

12.33 The role played by company formation agents in money laundering is becoming increasingly clear. Taking advantage of the agent's expertise in varying company registration procedures, together with the banking or corporate secrecy of certain jurisdictions, the launderer may create a barrier of legitimate seeming corporate structures that further separates him from his illegal proceeds. For the most part, company formation agents are not specifically held to anti-money laundering rules, and extending such rules to cover this sector may represent a solution on a national level. This response to the problem does not address the issue of services provided from locations outside of the jurisdiction. One other possibility might be to promote a minimum standard in company formation procedures — perhaps limiting the number of directorships held by an individual, or striking companies off the register upon failure to comply with necessary procedures. Implementing such standards will only work, however, if they are adhered to by all jurisdictions.

Trade activity

12.34 The FATF has observed a growing trend for trade activity to be used both as a cover for money laundering and as an actual money laundering mechanism. Although frequently appearing in the context of alternative remittance systems, trade related money laundering is not exclusively associated with such systems. Several examples were cited this year in which laundering operations through import or export of merchandise were not tied to alternative remittance. Customs officials responsible for import/export controls have access to useful information on cross-border movement of goods; however, this information is not always exploited fully from the perspective of potential money laundering activity.

Issues raised by wire transfers of funds

12.35 The FATF has for a long time worked with the Society for Worldwide Interbank Financial Telecommunication (SWIFT) on measures which would help to prevent wire transfers being misused by money launderers. SWIFT has 7,000 member institutions, which process five million messages totalling US$ 5–6 trillion each day.

12.36 Western Union, participating for the first time in an FATF Forum, described their anti-money laundering and suspicious activity report systems (SARs). Western Union has developed compliance programs — which include interviews with customers requesting large value transactions — and voluntary co-operation with law enforcement agencies which are aimed at preventing and detecting money laundering operations. Western Union works with the United States Treasury Department to develop regulations concerning SARs.

FATF COLLABORATION WITH INTERNATIONAL ORGANISATIONS AND NON-MEMBERS

12.37 The FATF collaborates with the relevant international organisations and bodies rather than launching new initiatives. In particular, the FATF participates in anti-money laundering events organised by other bodies so that it can observe the developments taking place in non-members, particularly the adoption of money laundering countermeasures. The United Nations Global Program on Money Laundering will contribute significantly to the implementation of these measures through the provision of training and technical assistance.

12.38 To increase the effectiveness of international anti-money laundering efforts, the FATF and other organisations and bodies endeavour to co-ordinate their activities. Regional and international bodies concerned with combating money laundering have regular co-ordination meetings. As part of this mission, the FATF co-operates closely with international and regional organisations concerned with combating money laundering, including the following:

● Asia/Pacific Group on Money Laundering (APG);

● Caribbean Financial Action Task Force (CFATF);

● Council of Europe;

● Commonwealth Secretariat;

- European Bank for Reconstruction and Development;

- International Monetary Fund (IMF);

- Inter-American Development Bank (IDB);

- Inter-American Drug Abuse Control Commission (CICAD);

- Interpol;

- International Organisation of Securities Commissions (IOSCO);

- Offshore Group of Banking Supervisors (OGBS);

- United Nations Office for Drug Control and Crime Prevention (UNODCCP); and

- World Bank and the World Customs Organisation (WCO).

12.39 The FATF's strategy for relations with non-members is directed toward supporting the various activities of other regional and international bodies involved in the fight against money laundering. A select committee of the Council of Europe and the Offshore Group of Banking Supervisors has commenced mutual evaluations of the anti-money laundering measures taken by their members.

12.40 The FATF has adopted a policy for assessing the implementation of anti-money laundering measures in non-member governments. The rationale for this policy is that the implementation of a mutual evaluation procedure will encourage countries and territories not only to get on with implementing anti-money laundering laws but also to improve the countermeasures already in place. The task force has already validated and supported the mutual evaluation processes of other bodies that have agreed to carry out mutual evaluations of their members. In this respect, the FATF determined that the CFATF, the Council of Europe, and the OGBS's mutual evaluation procedures conformed with its own principles. The FATF has sought formal political endorsement of the procedures and the Forty Recommendations from those governments of the members of the OGBS that are not represented in either the CFATF or the FATF.

12.41 The FATF has furthered its co-operation with these bodies. First, it stands ready to provide assistance in the training of mutual evaluators of non-FATF bodies. Secondly, FATF member countries will supply observer examiners, if requested by one of the three bodies mentioned above.

DEVELOPMENT OF FATF-STYLE REGIONAL BODIES

Caribbean Financial Action Task Force

12.42 The Caribbean Financial Action Task Force (CFATF), which is the oldest FATF-style regional body, has a membership of 25 States from the Caribbean basin. The current CFATF members (Aruba and the Netherlands Antilles are part of the Kingdom of the Netherlands, which is a member of FATF) are: Anguilla, Antigua and Barbuda, Aruba, the Bahamas, Barbados, Belize, Bermuda, the British Virgin Islands, the Cayman Islands, Costa Rica, Dominica, Dominican Republic, Grenada, Jamaica, Montserrat, the Netherlands Antilles, Nicaragua, Panama, St. Kitts and Nevis, St. Lucia, St. Vincent and the Grenadines, Suriname, Turks & Caicos Islands, Trinidad & Tobago, and Venezuela.

12.43 The Caribbean Financial Action Task Force (CFATF) endorsed the original Forty FATF Recommendations in the Kingston Declaration of November 1992. (In the Kingston Declaration, the governments of the CFATF members also made a commitment to implement the 19 additional CFATF Recommendations. The CFATF has been conducting a typologies exercise to evaluate and determine whether any interpretative notes and/or amendments to the FATF revised Recommendations and the CFATF Nineteen recommendations are appropriate.) The main objective of the CFATF is to achieve the effective implementation of, and compliance with the Nineteen CFATF and the Forty FATF Recommendations.

12.44   The CFATF has instituted measures to ensure the effective implementation of, and compliance with, the recommendations. The CFATF Secretariat monitors members' implementation of the Kingston Ministerial Declaration through the following activities:

● self-assessment of the implementation of the recommendations;

● ongoing programme of mutual evaluation of members;

● co-ordination of, and participation in, training and technical assistance programmes;

● bi-annual plenary meetings for technical representatives; and

● annual Ministerial meetings.

12.45   To further its mandate to identify and act as a clearing-house for facilitating training and technical assistance needs of members, the Secretariat works closely with regional Mini-Dublin Groups, the diplomatic representatives of countries with interest in the region. Prominent here are Canada, France, the Netherlands, the United Kingdom and the United States. There is also close liaison with CARICOM, the Caribbean Customs Law Enforcement Council (CCLEC), the Centre Interministériel de Formation Anti Drogue (CIFAD) in Martinique, the Association of Caribbean Chiefs of Police (ACCP), the Commonwealth Secretariat, and the International United Nations Drug Control Program (UNDCP).

12.46   Supported by, and in collaboration with, UNDCP, the CFATF Secretariat has developed a regional strategy for technical assistance and training to aid effective investigation and prosecution of money laundering and related asset forfeiture cases. The development of this regional strategy parallels and closely co-ordinates with similar initiatives by the European Commission and with efforts arising from the Summit of the Americas Ministerial in Buenos Aires.

12.47   Interestingly, the Cayman Islands Criminal Conduct Law has been judged to be the most comprehensive anti-money laundering piece of legislation in the Caribbean. It goes so far as to make it a criminal offence to assist in the retention, acquisition, possession, concealment, or transfer of proceeds of all serious crimes, and requires financial institutions and professional advisors to report all suspicious or unusual transactions.

Asia/Pacific Group on Money Laundering

12.48   A Working Party meeting of the Asia/Pacific Group on Money Laundering (APG) was held in Beijing in July 1997. Countries in the region have started to exchange information and examine the strengths and weaknesses of their systems through the mechanism of jurisdiction reports. Measures are also proposed for improving technical assistance and training, enhancing mutual legal assistance, and improving co-operation with the financial sector. The Working Party also recognised that, although regional differences need to be taken into account, the FATF Forty Recommendations provide guiding principles for action in establishing an effective anti-money-laundering system. The FATF stands ready to assist the APG in its consideration of how international standards such as the Forty Recommendations can best be implemented in the region.

12.49   The Asia/Pacific Group on Money Laundering (APG) currently consists of 19 members from South Asia, Southeast and East Asia and the South Pacific. The current

12.50   'All Crimes' and 'Money Laundering' Measures

members of the APG are: Australia; Bangladesh; Chinese Taipei; Fiji; Hong Kong; China; India; Japan; Malaysia; New Zealand; Pakistan; Indonesia; Republic of Korea; the Philippines; Samoa; Singapore; Sri Lanka; Thailand; United States, and Vanuatu.

12.50   The revised Terms of Reference for the APG, adopted in Tokyo on 10–12 March 1998, recognised that the FATF's Forty Recommendations are accepted international standards. The Tokyo meeting represented the full establishment of the APG as a cohesive regional group following on from the earlier awareness-raising efforts.

Council of Europe (PC-R-EV)

12.51   The Select Committee of Experts on the Evaluation of Anti-Money Laundering Measures (PC-R-EV) was established in September 1997 by the Committee of Ministers of the Council of Europe, to conduct self and mutual assessment exercises of the anti-money laundering measures in place in the 22 Council of Europe countries which are not members of the FATF. The membership of the Committee is comprised of certain of the Council of Europe member States which are not members of the FATF: Albania, Andorra, Bulgaria, Croatia, Cyprus, Czech Republic, Estonia, Georgia, Hungary, Latvia, Liechtenstein, Lithuania, Moldova, Malta, Poland, Romania, Russian Federation, San Marino, Slovakia, Slovenia, Macedonia, and Ukraine.

12.52   The PC-R-EV is a sub-committee of the European Committee on Crime Problems of the Council of Europe (CDPC). The PC-R-EV has pursued a significant mutual evaluation program. The PC-R-EV has in the last year put in place a mechanism for oral progress reports to be given to the plenary by all countries one year after their report was adopted. The Council of Europe also contributes fully and effectively to the development of the worldwide anti-money laundering network.

Commonwealth

12.53   In October 1997, the Commonwealth Heads of Government (CHOGM) welcomed the endorsement by Finance Ministers of the updated Forty Recommendations of the FATF.

12.54   The Commonwealth members that are not members of FATF (the Commonwealth members that are members of the FATF are: Australia, Canada, New Zealand, Singapore, and the United Kingdom) are: Antigua and Barbuda, the Bahamas, Bangladesh, Barbados, Belize, Botswana, Brunei Darussalam, Cameroon, Cyprus, Dominica, Gambia, Ghana, Grenada, Guyana, India, Jamaica, Kenya, Kiribati, Lesotho, Malawi, Malaysia, Maldives, Malta, Mauritius, Mozambique, Namibia, Nauru, Nigeria, Pakistan, Papua New Guinea, St. Kitts and Nevis, St. Lucia, St. Vincent and the Grenadines, Samoa, Seychelles, Sierra Leone, Solomon Islands, South Africa, Sri Lanka, Swaziland, Tonga, Trinidad and Tobago, Tuvalu, Uganda, the United Republic of Tanzania, Vanuatu, Zambia, and Zimbabwe.

12.55   Commonwealth Heads of Government have repeatedly called for concerted action to combat money laundering. A joint meeting of finance and law officials has been set up to develop a co-ordinated approach aimed at:

● improving domestic co-ordination through national interdisciplinary co-ordinating structure;

● dealing with the special problems concerning money laundering in countries with large parallel economies;

- strengthening regional initiatives for more effective implementation of anti-money laundering measures; and

- self-evaluating the progress made in implementing anti-money laundering measures in the financial sector.

The Eastern and Southern African Anti-Money Laundering Group (ESAAMLG)

12.56 The ESAAMLG, a FATF-style body for 14 countries in the region, was launched in August 1999. A Memorandum of Understanding based on the experience of the FATF and other FATF-style regional bodies was agreed. All members are Commonwealth countries, committed to the Forty FATF Recommendations. The current members of the ESAAMLG are Botswana, Kenya, Lesotho, Malawi, Mauritius, Mozambique, Namibia, Seychelles, South Africa, Swaziland, Tanzania, Uganda, Zambia, and Zimbabwe.

Other Regional Groups

12.57 At the December 1999 Summit of the Heads of State and Government of the Economic Community of West African States (ECOWAS) in Lomé (Togo), it was decided to establish an inter-governmental group against money laundering.

12.58 In February 2000, it was announced that Finance Ministers from 34 Western Hemisphere countries, meeting under the auspices of the Hemispheric Financial Affairs Committee in Cancun, Mexico, had called upon all member countries to support and participate in financial action task forces, either the CFATF or the new South American Financial Action Task Force, whose creation Argentina and Brazil have pledged to lead. In addition, MERCOSUR has clearly expressed its support for the creation of this new group at its April 2000 meeting in Buenos Aires.

OTHER INTERNATIONAL ANTI-MONEY LAUNDERING INITIATIVES

United Nations

12.59 The Global Program against Money Laundering (GPML), a research and technical co-operation program, implemented by the United Nations Office for Drug Control and Crime Prevention (ODCCP), is now in operation. Its aim is to increase the effectiveness of international action against money laundering through comprehensive technical co-operation services offered to governments. The program is carried out in co-operation with other international and regional organisations. In the context of the GPML, the UNODCCP organised several important international anti-money laundering events in 1997–1998, including two awareness-raising seminars for West Africa in Ivory Coast on 1–3 December 1997, and for South Asian countries, plus Myanmar and Thailand, in New Delhi on 2–4 March 1998.

12.60 In December 1997, participants in the United Nations Workshop on Money Laundering recommended that states adopt or take into account the Recommendations of the Financial Action Task Force on Money Laundering.

12.61 In March 1998, a United Nations Conference on Money Laundering recommended that 'in drafting their legislation, States should have regard to the standards set out in the forty recommendations of the Financial Action Task Force on Money Laundering'.

12.62 'All Crimes' and 'Money Laundering' Measures

12.62 The United Nations General Assembly met on 8–10 June 1998, in New York, for a special session devoted to the fight against the illicit production, sale, demand, traffic, and distribution of narcotic drugs and psychotropic substances and related activities, including money laundering. In a declaration of 10 June 1998, the United Nations General Assembly in Special Session on the world drug problem recalled that the 1996 Resolution 5 of the United Nations Commission on Narcotic Drugs noted that 'the forty recommendations of the Financial Action Task Force . . . remain the standard by which anti-money laundering measures adopted by concerned States should be judged. . .'.

12.63 The General Assembly adopted a Political Declaration in which the Member States of the United Nations:

• undertake to make special efforts against the laundering of money linked to drug trafficking, and

• recommend that states that have not yet done so adopt by the year 2003 national anti-money laundering legislation and programmes in accordance with relevant provisions of the Vienna Convention and a package of measures for countering money laundering, adopted at the same session.

12.64 In early 1999, the United Nations started the negotiation of a Convention against Transnational Organised Crime. Among the important provisions of the draft convention are measures against money laundering. In particular, the draft convention currently contains an article requiring nations to criminalise money laundering (Article 4).

12.65 The FATF endorses this requirement for appropriate serious offences. The draft convention also contains an article, which would require States to develop comprehensive anti-money laundering domestic regulatory and supervisory regimes (Article 4 bis). The FATF attaches specific importance to a version of draft Article 4 bis which would require each State Party within its means, to develop the domestic regulatory and supervisory regime under the terms of the article on the basis of the Forty Recommendations of the FATF and other relevant initiatives such as the Caribbean Financial Action Task Force, the Commonwealth, the Council of Europe, the Eastern and Southern African Anti-Money Laundering Group, the European Union, and the Organisation of American States.

12.66 The Global Programme against Money Laundering (GPML) is a research and technical co-operation initiative implemented by the UN Office for Drug Control and Crime Prevention (ODCCP).

12.67 Its aim is to increase the effectiveness of international action against money laundering through comprehensive technical co-operation services offered to governments. The Programme is carried out in co-operation with other international and regional organisations.

Offshore Group of Banking Supervisors

12.68 The conditions for membership of the Offshore Group of Banking Supervisors (OGBS) include a requirement that a clear political commitment be made to implement the FATF's Forty Recommendations. The current membership of the OGBS includes Aruba, Bahamas, Bahrain, Barbados, Bermuda, Cayman Islands, Cyprus, Gibraltar, Guernsey, Hong Kong, China, Isle of Man, Jersey, Labuan, Macao China, Malta, Mauritius, Netherlands Antilles, Panama, Singapore, and Vanuatu. In addition, the following members of the OGBS, which are not members of the FATF or the CFATF, are formally committed to the Forty Recommendations through individual Ministerial letters sent to the FATF President during 1997–1998: Bahrain, Cyprus, Gibraltar, Guernsey, Isle of Man, Jersey, Malta, Mauritius, and Vanuatu.

Organisation of American States/Inter-American Commission for Drug Abuse Control (OAS/CICAD)

12.69   The CICAD Group of Experts to Control Money Laundering has continued to monitor implementation of the Buenos Aires Plan of Action. (In December 1995, the ministers responsible for addressing money laundering in the States of the Western Hemisphere met in Buenos Aires, where they endorsed a Statement of Principles to combat money laundering and agreed to recommend to their Governments a Plan of Action reflecting this Statement of Principles for adoption and implementation. The Plan of Action specifically provided that the Governments intended to institute ongoing assessments of the implementation of the Plan of Action within the framework of the OAS. This and other activities identified in this Plan were remitted to the CICAD for action.) As for its Model Regulations, CICAD approved changes, subsequently adopted by the 29th OAS General Assembly, to expand the predicate offences giving rise to money laundering offences as well as to include offshore banks as entities required to comply with banking regulations.

Inter-American Development Bank

12.70   The Inter-American Development Bank (IDB), in conjunction with the Banking Superintendent of Colombia and the Andean Development Corporation, sponsored a seminar on the subject of asset laundering during the 1998 annual meeting of the Board of Governors in Cartagena de Indias, Colombia. The session addressed the multi-faceted aspects of asset laundering activities, as well as international approaches to combat money laundering on the basis of presentations made by the United Nations, the OAS/CICAD, the IDB, the IMF, the Federation of Latin American Bankers Association, and the FATF. The seminar ended with certain common goals, focusing on a multilateral approach to combating asset laundering in Latin America and the Caribbean, as well as current and future activities in the region.

12.71   The IDB was encouraged to:

- use its own funds and seek additional funding for programmes, including the training of supervisors, regulators, and financial institutions, particularly on the detection and prevention of new laundering techniques on a regional and/or national basis;

- serve as a clearing-house for such proposed programmes, sources of funding, and potential executing entities;

- strengthen the dialogue between private banking sectors and government regulators; and

- use its good offices to encourage implementation of effective laws and regulatory frameworks to address the issue of asset laundering.

Gulf Co-operation Council

12.72   The Gulf Co-operation Council (GCC) is in the unique position of being a member of FATF but with non-FATF member countries as its constituents. Noticeable progress has been made to improve the implementation of effective anti-money laundering systems within the GCC States.

The Financial Services Industry

12.73   One of the FATF's goals is to encourage co-operation with the private sector in the development of policies and programmes to combat money laundering. To further this aim, a Forum was convened with representatives from the financial services industry and accounting professions. The purpose of this event was to discuss with the private sector, areas of common interest and the best way to develop measures to prevent and detect money laundering through the financial community.

12.74   The Forum was attended by representatives from FATF members, national banking, financial and accounting associations, companies such as SWIFT sc, and Western Union, delegates from international financial services industry and accounting organisations, European Banking Federation, International Banking Security Association, European Insurance Committee, European Savings Banks Grouping, International Federation of Accountants, European Federation of Accountants and the Federation of European Stock Exchanges.

12.75   Four general topics were addressed in the Forum: current money laundering trends, feedback to institutions reporting suspicious transactions; the role of the accounting profession in identifying and discouraging money laundering and the issues raised by the wire transfers of funds.

12.76   The International Federation of Accountants (IFAC) emphasised the importance for financial institutions of an internal control framework.

NON-CO-OPERATIVE COUNTRIES OR TERRITORIES

Scope of the Problem

12.77   Recent years have seen a considerable increase in the number of jurisdictions, which offer financial services without appropriate regulation or control, coupled with very strict banking secrecy. Over the last ten years, many countries have developed measures to combat money laundering. However, any weak link in international arrangements jeopardises the entire international financial system.

FAFT Progress in dealing with Non-Co-operative Countries And Territories

12.78   FATF has accomplished considerable progress in its work on non-co-operative countries and territories. Since the end of 1998, the FATF has embarked on substantive work on the problems raised by countries and territories which do not co-operate in the combat of money laundering. The work which FATF has undertaken on non-co-operative jurisdictions is fully in line with measures elaborated by the international community to consolidate the international financial system and render it more transparent. The aim of the work is to enhance the level of protection for the world financial system and to prevent the circumvention of the anti-laundering measures introduced over the last ten years.

12.79   To ensure transparency and sound operation in the international financial system, and the effective prevention of financial delinquency, FATF has established an Ad Hoc Group to discuss in more depth the action to be taken with regard to these countries and territories. The scope of the work extends to all major financial centres, offshore or onshore, whether they are FATF members or not. The FATF recommends that financial institutions should give special attention to business relations and transactions with persons, including companies and financial institutions, from the non-co-operative countries and territories.

12.80   At its February 2000 Plenary meeting, the FATF set up four regional review groups (Americas; Asia/Pacific; Europe; and Africa and the Middle East) to analyse the anti-money laundering regimes of a number of jurisdictions.

Problem countries

12.81   Serious systemic problems have been identified in the following jurisdictions: Bahamas, Cayman Islands, Cook Islands, Dominica, the Grenadines, Israel, Lebanon, Liechtenstein, Marshall Islands, Nauru, Niue, Panama, Philippines, Russia, St. Kitts and Nevis, and St. Vincent.

12.82   The FATF has urged all countries and territories which are part of the global financial system to change any rules or practices, which impede the fight against money laundering.

The Austrian Case

12.83   On 3 February 2000, in accordance with its policy for members who do not comply with the Forty Recommendations, the FATF decided to suspend Austria as one of its members in June 2000 unless action was taken on the issue of anonymous passbooks. Following this unprecedented move, the Government of Austria took the appropriate steps to meet the conditions required by the FATF and thus avert suspension of membership.

List of Criteria for Defining Non-Co-operative Countries or Territories

Loopholes in financial regulations

● No or inadequate regulations and supervision of financial institutions.

● Inadequate rules for the licensing and creation of financial institutions, including assessing the backgrounds of their managers and beneficial owners.

● Inadequate customer identification requirements for financial institutions.

● Excessive secrecy provisions regarding financial institutions.

● Lack of efficient suspicious transactions reporting system.

Obstacles raised by other regulatory requirements

● Inadequate commercial law requirements for registration of business and legal entities.

● Lack of identification of the beneficial owner(s) of legal and business entities

Obstacles to international co-operation

● Obstacles to international co-operation by administrative authorities.

● Obstacles to international co-operation by judicial authorities.

● Lack of efficient suspicious transaction reporting system.

The importance of criminalising money laundering

12.84   Criminalisation of money laundering is the cornerstone of anti-money laundering policy. It is also the indispensable basis for participation in international judicial co-operation in this area. Hence, failure to criminalise laundering of the proceeds from serious crimes (Recommendation 4) is a serious obstacle to international co-operation in the international fight against money laundering.

STRATEGIC CHECKLISTS

PARTICULAR AREAS OF INTERNATIONAL CONCERN

- The single European currency and large denomination banknotes.

- The role of the foreign legal entities.

- New payment technologies.

- The inability to identify and authenticate parties that use the new technologies.

- The lack of transparency of transactions.

- The lack or inadequacy of audit trails, record keeping, or suspicious transaction reporting by the technology provider.

- The use of higher levels of encryption (thus blocking out law enforcement access).

- Transactions that fall outside current legislative or regulatory definitions.

- Smartcards.

- Online banking.

- E-cash.

- The gold market.

- Hawala/Hundi alternative remittance system .

- Derivatives and securities markets.

FATF MONEY LAUNDERING TYPOLOGIES

- Accounting firms.

- Structuring schemes.

- Gold smuggling.

- Insurance policies and real estate.

- Front companies.

- Money transfers.

- Offshore financial centres, solicitors, and other financial services providers.

- Insurance.

- Bureaux de change.

- The derivatives market.

FATF CO-OPERATION WITH OTHER INTERNATIONAL ORGANISATIONS

- Asia/Pacific Group on Money Laundering (APG).

- Caribbean Financial Action Task Force (CFATF).

- Council of Europe.

- Commonwealth Secretariat.

- European Bank for Reconstruction and Development.

- International Monetary Fund (IMF).

- Inter-American Development Bank (IDB).

- Inter-American Drug Abuse Control Commission (CICAD).

- Interpol.

- International Organisation of Securities Commissions (IOSCO).

- Offshore Group of Banking Supervisors (OGBS).

- United Nations Office for Drug Control and Crime Prevention (UNODCCP).

- World Bank and the World Customs Organisation (WCO).

Appendix 1   Strategic Checklists for Offshore Companies

BAHAMAS

Checklist for IBCs

- Once incorporated, IBCs are very cost effective, and they are guaranteed tax exemption for 20 years. However, because of a lack of public registers, ownership is difficult to prove. IBCs are not recommended for high-profile trading operations.

- IBCs are governed by the International Business Companies Acts of 1989 and 2000, and the common law.

- Certain words are prohibited from being used in the company name, for instance, *Assurance*, *Bank*, or *Building Society*. Names must end with an appropriate suffix such as *Incorporated*, *Société Anonyme*, or *Limited*.

- Incorporation takes one to two days. No minimum capital is required. There is no requirement regarding information being furnished to the authorities prior to incorporation or prior to tax status being granted.

- Shelf companies are available.

- Capital duty is payable on a sliding scale. From BAH0 to BAH5,000, duty is payable at BAH100. From BAH5,001 to BAH50,000, duty is payable at BAH300, and from BAH50,001, it is payable at BAH1,000.

- A minimum of one shareholder is required. Bearer shares are no longer allowed.

- A minimum of one director is required. Corporate directors are permitted, and there is no restriction on the residence of directors.

- A company secretary is not mandatory. A corporate secretary is permitted, and there is no restriction on the secretary's residence.

- An IBC must have a registered office and a registered agent.

- The memorandum and articles of association, the registered office, and the registered agent are on the public file. Copies of the register of members and register of directors must be kept at the registered office, with an impression of the company seal.

- The company must have a seal and registers of members and directors.

- There are no requirements regarding the keeping and filing of accounts. Annual returns are not required.

- There are no requirements regarding the holding of meetings.

- An annual fee of BAH100 is payable to the government if the authorised capital does not exceed BAH5,000.

- Exchange controls do not apply to IBCs. There are no double tax treaties.

- Migration of IBCs to and from the Bahamas is facilitated, also allowing for the immediate transfer in or out of assets.

BARBADOS

Checklist for IBCs

- The company name must end in *Incorporated, Corporation,* or *Limited.* Consent is required for the use of words such as *Bank* or *Insurance.* The registrar of companies often refuses to approve names with words such as *International* or *Global.*

- It takes two to three days to incorporate a company. Shelf companies are not available. The minimum capital requirement is US$1,000. Capital duty of US$390 is payable.

- Prior to granting of an IBC license, the details of shareholders must be submitted to the Ministry of Finance.

- At least one shareholder is necessary. Bearer sharers are not allowed, but shares of no par value are. It should be noted that Barbados law does not provide for shares of par value.

- At least one director is required. Corporate directors are allowed, and there is no restriction on directors' residence.

- A company secretary is mandatory. There is no restriction on the residence of the secretary.

- A registered office is required, although a registered agent is not. Statutory records and registers are lodged with the registered office.

- Audited accounts are required only when the total assets exceed US$500,000. They do not have to be filed. An annual return is not necessary.

- Directors are obliged to meet once a year, and shareholders are to meet within 18 months of incorporation, and thereafter, within 15 months of the previous meeting.

- An annual fee of US$100 is payable to the government.

- Exchange controls do not apply to IBCs.

BERMUDA

Checklist for Ordinary and Exempt Companies

- Bermuda ordinary and exempt companies are governed by the Companies Act 1981. Companies must include *Limited* or *Ltd* in their names, and the use of words such as *Bank* is restricted.

- Incorporation can take up to five working days. Shelf companies are not available, although old companies may be. The identity of the beneficial owner must be disclosed to the authorities prior to incorporation.

- The minimum capital required is US$12,000, and capital duty of 0.25% is charged on the authorised capital. No duty is charged on exempt companies.

- A minimum of one shareholder is required. Bearer shares and shares of no par value are not permissible.

- A minimum of two directors is required. Corporate directors are not allowed, and Bermudian directors are no longer necessary. There are no restrictions on where meetings may be held.

Appendix 1

- A local registered office is necessary, although a registered agent is only needed if resident directors are appointed. The share register, share certificate book, minutes of shareholders' and directors' meetings, and accounts must be kept at the registered office, although the accounts are not open to inspection.

- Corporate books and a seal are necessary, and they are usually kept at the registered office.

- A company secretary is mandatory. A corporate secretary is allowed, and there is no restriction on the secretary's residence.

- The share register, register of directors and officers, certificate of incorporation, and memorandum and articles of association are available on the public file.

- An annual return is not necessary for exempt companies.

- Provision is made for migration or redomiciliation.

BRITISH VIRGIN ISLANDS

Checklist for IBCs

- Prior approval of the name is required when registering a company. Some words are sensitive, e.g., *Royal* and *Imperial*. The name must end in *Limited*, *Corporation*, *Incorporated*, *Société Anonyme*, or *Sociedad Anonima*, or abbreviations thereof.

- It can take one day to incorporate a company. Shelf companies are available. The usual minimum capital required is US$50,000.

- The minimum number of shareholders required is one. Bearer shares or shares of no par value are possible.

- The minimum number of directors required is one. Corporate directors are allowed, and there is no restriction on the residence of directors.

- A company secretary is not mandatory. A corporate secretary is allowed, and there is no restriction on the place of residence of directors.

- There must be a registered office and a registered agent.

- No information is required by the authorities prior to incorporation or prior to tax status being granted. The memorandum and articles and the registered office and agent are available on the public file. Copies of the register of members and directors (if maintained) and an impression of the seal must be kept at the registered office. Both corporate books and a seal are required and may be kept anywhere.

- Accounts are not required and do not have to be filed anywhere. An annual return is not required.

- There are no restrictions on when meetings should be held.

- Migration and redomiciliation are not provided for.

- The annual licence fee payable to the government is US$300 if the capital does not exceed US$50,000, and US$1,000 if it does. There is no filing fee.

CAYMAN ISLANDS

Checklist for Non-Resident and Exempt Companies

- A non-resident company's name must end with *Limited* or *Ltd*. There is no restriction on the ending of exempt companies' names. The use of words such as *Bank* and *Insurance* is restricted.

- It takes three to five days to incorporate a company. Shelf companies, although unusual, are available. Prior to incorporation, an undertaking must be made not to engage in local business.

- The usual minimum capital required for exempt companies and for non-resident companies is US$50,000. Capital duty on incorporation of an exempt company is a minimum of US$500, and for a non-resident company, a minimum of US$427.

- At least one shareholder is required. With regard to exempt companies, bearer shares and shares of no par value are allowed, but no such shares are possible for non-resident companies.

- There must be at least one director. Corporate directors are allowed, and there is no restriction on the place of residence of the directors.

- A company secretary is not necessary. Corporate secretaries are permissible, and there is no restriction on the secretary's residence.

- There must be a registered local office, but there is no requirement for a registered agent.

- No documents are required to be kept at the registered office in respect of exempt companies, but the registers of members, directors, mortgages, and charges must be kept in respect of non-resident companies.

- The address of the registered office and a copy of the memorandum and articles of association are available on the public file.

- Corporate books and a seal are required in both cases.

- An audit is not necessary, but books reflecting the true financial state of the company must be kept, although there are no filing requirements.

- A limited form of annual return is required for exempt companies, and a full form is required for non-resident companies.

- There are no restrictions on the meetings of non-resident companies. With regard to exempt companies, one directors' meeting per year must be held in the islands, but there is no restriction on annual general meetings.

COOK ISLANDS

Checklist for International Companies

- The registrar's approval of the company name is required, and words such as *Bank*, *Trust*, and *Insurance* are restricted to use by special licence holders.

- It takes one day to incorporate an international company. A limited number of shelf companies are available. No information is required by the authorities prior to incorporation.

Appendix 1

- The usual minimum capital required is US$1 million. Fees charged are not based on the company's capital.

- No capital duty is charged.

- A minimum of one shareholder is required. Bearer shares and shares of no par value are possible.

- A minimum of one director is required. Corporate directors are allowed, and there is no restriction on the directors' residence.

- A company secretary is mandatory. Corporate secretaries are allowed, and at least one joint secretary must be a Cook Islands resident.

- A registered office is required, but a registered agent is not. The registered office must keep registers of directors, members, secretary, and charges, as well as the company books and seal.

- The company name and registered office are available on the public file.

- Accounts must be maintained, but they need not be filed. An audit is not required. An annual return is required.

- There is no restriction on the holding of meetings.

- Provision is made for the migration and redomiciliation of companies.

CYPRUS

Checklist for Offshore Companies

- Prior reservation of the company name is required, and many words are considered sensitive. The name must end with *Limited*. Prior to offshore status being granted, bank references and copies of passports must be given to the Cyprus Central Bank.

- It takes two to three days to incorporate an offshore company. Shelf companies are available. The usual minimum capital is C£1,000, and in the case of offshore companies, this must be issued.

- The minimum number of shareholders is two. Bearer shares and shares of no par value are not allowed.

- A minimum of one director is required. Corporate directors are not allowed, and there is no restriction on the directors' residence.

- A company secretary is mandatory. A corporate secretary is allowed, and there is no restriction on the secretary's residence.

- Offshore companies need a local registered office, but there is no need for a registered agent. The registered office must keep the company register.

- The memorandum and articles of association, directors, secretary, shareholders, share capital, registered office, mortgages and charges, and sometimes accounts are available on the public file.

- Corporate books and a seal are necessary and are kept at the registered office.

- Accounts are required and must be filed, but they are not available to the public. An annual return is also required.

- There is no restriction on the holding of meetings.

- There is no provision for migration or redomiciliation.

GIBRALTAR

Checklist for Companies

- Prior approval of the company name is not required, but it must end with *Limited*. Many words are sensitive, such as *Royal, Holdings, Group, Gibraltar, International, Bank,* and *Insurance*.

- It takes five to seven days to incorporate a company, although same-day incorporation can be obtained for an additional fee of G£30. Shelf companies are available, but application for exemption may only be made after acquisition of the company.

- Exempt companies must have at least G£100 of paid-up share capital or its currency equivalent. Capital duty of 0.5% is payable.

- At least one shareholder is required, but it is more usual to have two shareholders. Bearer shares are possible but impractical, and shares of no par value are not allowed.

- A minimum of one director is required. Corporate directors are allowed, and directors may be residents of Gibraltar.

- A secretary is mandatory only for exempt companies. Corporate secretaries are allowed, and they must be residents of Gibraltar.

- A registered office in Gibraltar is required, but a registered agent is not. References with regard to the beneficial owner must be supplied to the agents and may be required by the authorities before exemption is granted. The registers of members, directors, mortgages, and charges must be kept at the registered office.

- The directors, shareholders, registered office, memorandum and articles of association, annual return, mortgages, and charges are available on the public file.

- Corporate books and a seal are required and are usually retained at the registered office.

- Accounts must be filed. An annual return is required.

- There is no restriction on the holding of meetings.

- Tax of G£225 (or G£200 for a non-resident exempt company) is payable annually. A filing fee of G£26 is also charged for the annual returns.

GUERNSEY

Checklist for Companies

- Prior approval is required for a company name. Words such as *Insurance* and *Assurance* require additional approval. The company name must end with *Limited*.

- Incorporation takes 7 to 13 days. Shelf companies are not available. Beneficial ownership, as well as the intended trading activities of the company, must be disclosed to the authorities prior to incorporation or exempt status being granted.

- The usual minimum capital is G£10,000. A capital duty of 0.5% is payable, with a minimum of G£50.

- The minimum number of shareholders is two. Bearer shares and shares of no par value are not allowed.

- A minimum of one director is required. Corporate directors are allowed, and there is no restriction on the directors' residence.

Appendix 1

- A company secretary is mandatory. Corporate secretaries are allowed, and there is no restriction on the secretary's residence.

- A registered office is required, but a registered agent is not. The registers of directors and members, the secretary's details, and the minute books must be kept at the registered office.

- The share capital, registered office, shareholders, and directors are available on the public file.

- Corporate books and a seal are required and are usually kept at the registered office.

- Active resident companies must keep accounts and file them with the revenue authority. Exempt companies must also keep accounts but do not need to file them. Annual returns are required.

- There is no restriction on the holding of meetings.

- Exempt companies pay G£500 annually. A filing fee of G£100 is payable by those companies required to file accounts.

HONG KONG

Checklist for Companies

- All company names must end with the word *Limited*. Words such as *Royal* and *Imperial* are not permitted.

- It takes two to three weeks to incorporate a company, and shelf companies are available. No information is required by the authorities prior to incorporation.

- The usual minimum authorised share capital is HK$10,000. Capital duty of 0.6% is payable.

- At least two shareholders are required. Bearer shares and shares of no par value are not permitted.

- At least two directors are necessary. Corporate directors are allowed, and there is no restriction on their residence.

- A company secretary is mandatory. Corporate secretaries are allowed, and the secretary must be in Hong Kong.

- A company must have a registered office in Hong Kong, but there is no need for a registered agent. The registered office must keep the registers of members, secretaries, directors, mortgages, and charges and the minute book.

- The memorandum and articles of association and information as to directors, the secretary, shareholders, the registered office, annual returns, and mortgages and charges are available on the public file.

- An annual return is required.

- There is no restriction on the holding of meetings.

- Companies that do not earn income in Hong Kong are exempt from tax. An annual return filing fee of HK$75 is payable, as is a business registration fee.

- No provision is made for the migration or redomiciliation of companies.

ISLE OF MAN

Checklist for Companies

● Company law is based on English common law, as codified in the Companies Acts 1931 to 1993.

● Prior approval of the company name is necessary, and many words are sensitive, for instance, *International, Bank, Royal, Trust, Holdings,* and *Group.* The name must end with *Limited* or *Public Limited Company.*

● It takes two to four days to incorporate a company in the Isle of Man. Shelf companies are available, but application for non-resident or exempt or international status must be made after acquisition. No information is required by the authorities prior to incorporation or prior to tax status being granted, except with regard to banking, insurance, and some other finance-related operations.

● It is customary to have at least two shareholders. Bearer shares are possible, but shares of no par value are not.

● All companies, whether resident, non-resident, international, or exempt, must have at least two directors. Corporate directors are not allowed. With resident companies, the directors are normally resident. With non-resident companies, the directors must be non-resident. With international and exempt companies, at least one director must be resident.

● All companies, whether resident, non-resident, international, or exempt, must have a secretary. With resident and non-resident companies, corporate secretaries are allowed, and there is no restriction on the secretary's residence. With international and exempt companies, corporate secretaries are not allowed, and the secretary must be resident and professionally qualified.

● Registered offices are required in all cases, but registered agents are not. The registers of directors, secretaries, members, mortgages, and charges must be kept at the registered office.

● The registered office, directors, shareholders, secretary, memorandum and articles of association, annual return, mortgages, and charges are available on the public file.

● A corporate seal is not necessary. The corporate books and seal are usually kept at the registered office.

● International and resident companies must file accounts with the revenue authority, but these are not on public record. Non-resident and exempt companies must also maintain accounts, but they do not need to have them audited or file them with the revenue authority.

● An annual return is required in all cases. The annual return filing fee is £42.

● Non-resident companies may not hold meetings on the Isle of Man. There is no restriction on the location of meetings for all other companies.

JERSEY

Checklist for Companies

● Resident companies are taxed at a rate of 20% of profits. Exempt companies pay a flat rate of J£500 per annum.

Appendix 1

- The Companies Law 1991 governs companies in Jersey.

- Company names must be approved in advance. Certain words are considered sensitive, such as *Royal* and *International*. All names must finish with the word *Limited* or its abbreviated form.

- It takes about three days to incorporate a company, although same-day service is available at an additional cost of J£40. Shelf companies are not available. Beneficial ownership must be disclosed to the authorities prior to incorporation or to tax status being granted, and references may also be required.

- The usual minimum capital is J£2. A capital duty of 0.5% is charged, with a minimum of J£50.

- At least two shareholders are required. Bearer shares and shares of no par value are not possible.

- A minimum of one director is required. Corporate directors are not allowed, and there is no restriction on the directors' residence.

- A company secretary is mandatory. A corporate secretary is allowed, and there is no restriction on the secretary's residence.

- A registered office is required in Jersey, but a registered agent is not.

- The registered office, shareholders, annual return, and memorandum and articles of association are available on the public file.

- Corporate books and a seal are required and are usually kept at the registered office.

- Resident companies must keep accounts that must be filed with the revenue authorities. Exempt companies also have to keep accounts, but they do not have to be filed.

- An annual return is required. The annual return filing fee is J£120.

- There is no restriction on the holding of meetings.

LABUAN

Checklist for Companies

- Company names must be reserved to check for availability. Some words are sensitive and require the minister of finance's approval, for example, *Finance*, *Bank*, *Trust*, *Royal*, *Insurance*, and *Security*.

- Incorporation takes three to five days. Shelf companies are not available. Offshore companies in general need not furnish the authorities with information as to beneficial ownership prior to incorporation, although banks and insurance companies must.

- The usual minimum capital is between US$18,000 and US$20,000. There is no capital duty.

- At least one shareholder is required. Bearer shares and shares of no par value are not allowed.

- At least one director is required. Corporate directors are allowed, and there is no restriction on the directors' residence.

- A secretary is mandatory. Corporate secretaries are allowed, and offshore companies must have a resident secretary.

- Offshore companies must have a registered office but need not have a registered agent. The registers of directors, secretaries, members, transfers, mortgages, debentures, debenture holders, and interest holders must be kept at the registered office. Corporate books and a seal are also usually kept at the registered office.

- No information is available on the public file.

- Trading companies must keep accounts. These do not have to be filed if the company elects to pay RM20,000 tax per annum.

- An annual return is required. An annual return filing fee of RM100 is payable.

- There are no restrictions on the holding of meetings, unless proof of residency is required, in which case meetings must be held in Labuan.

- Trading companies must pay either 3% of net audited profits or RM20,000 per annum in tax.

LIBERIA

Checklist for Corporations

- Any name that is not in use may be used. The name must end with a word such as *Limited* or *Incorporated*. The name may be in any language.

- Same-day incorporation is possible through the International Trust Company of Liberia. Documents are available within two to three days. Shelf companies are available. The authorities do not require any information prior to incorporation.

- There is no usual minimum capital. No capital duty is payable.

- At least one shareholder is required. Bearer shares and shares of no par value are possible.

- If the number of shareholders is less than three, there may be the same number of directors. If the number of shareholders is three or more, there must be at least three directors. Corporate directors are allowed, and there is no restriction on the directors' residence.

- A secretary is mandatory. Corporate secretaries are not allowed, and there is no restriction on the residence of the secretary.

- Corporations do not need a registered office in Liberia, but they must have a registered agent (the International Trust Company of Liberia).

- The registered agent's address and articles of association are available on the public file.

- Accounts do not have to be kept or filed. An annual return is also not required.

- Corporate books and a seal are necessary but may be kept anywhere.

- There is no restriction on the holding of meetings.

- An annual fee of US$150 is payable to the government.

LIECHTENSTEIN

Checklist for Companies

- The corporate name may contain any words and be in any language, but the name of the corporate body (such as *Akteingesellschaft*, *Limited*, or *Anstalt*) must be registered in full.

285

Appendix 1

- Incorporation takes five to ten days. Shelf companies are available.

- The establishment, foundation, and trust enterprise must have a minimum capital of CHF30,000. The limited company must have a minimum capital of CHF50,000.

- A capital duty of 3% is payable, although there are some exceptions for foundations and trust enterprises.

- A minimum of one member or founder is required. Bearer shares and shares of no par value are allowed, although it is more usual to have bearer shares.

- A holding or domiciliary company must have one resident director who is professionally qualified. The same applies to a trust enterprise. There are no residency requirements for members of a foundation council or the founder of an establishment. Corporate directors are allowed.

- There are no legislative provisions regarding secretaries.

- Companies with exempt status must have a local trustee or lawyer, who will charge a representation fee. Registered and non-exempt companies do not have to have local agents.

- No information is required by the authorities prior to exempt status being granted. For resident and non-exempt companies, a business licence may be required where the company is engaged in banking, insurance, or other commercial activities.

- The corporate name, domicile, type, date of registration, board members, signatory rights of board members, purpose, representation, and share capital are available on the public file.

- Resident and non-exempt companies must keep certification at their registered offices that all prerequisites concerning nationality and professional qualifications have been met. In general, the memorandum and articles of association, registration correspondence, and confirmation that the minimum formation capital has been deposited with a bank must also be kept.

- Corporate books and a seal are not required.

- All companies that are engaged in commercial activity, whether within or outside Liechtenstein, must maintain and file accounts. Exempt companies that are not engaged in commercial activity (for instance, foundations, trust settlements, holding companies, and companies engaged in personal asset management) do not have to file accounts.

- Resident companies must file an annual return. Exempt companies do not have to comply with this provision.

- There is no restriction on the holding of meetings.

- Resident and non-exempt companies pay tax of between 7.5% and 20% on profits and 0.2% tax on capital, including reserves. Exempt companies pay a flat rate of 1% on their capital and surplus, with a minimum of CHF1,000 per annum.

MADEIRA

Checklist for Companies

- Prior approval of the company name is required. Foreign names are permitted, but the name must include the main activity of the company.

- Incorporation takes four to six weeks. Shelf companies are available. No information is required by the authorities prior to incorporation.

- The minimum capital required for stock corporations is Esc 5 million, and for limited liability companies, Esc 400,000. There is no capital duty.

- Limited liability companies must have at least one shareholder, and stock corporations must have five or more. Stock corporations may issue bearer shares after the initial share capital is paid up in full, but shares with no par value are not permitted.

- At least one director is required for either form of company, and there is no restriction as to the directors' place of residence. Stock corporations may have corporate directors, but limited liability companies may not. Madeira companies do not have secretaries.

- A registered office is necessary. All legal documents, minute books, and official accounting books and records must be kept at the registered office.

- The registered office, directors, shareholders, mortgages, object clause, share capital, and form of binding are available on the public file.

- Annual accounts and a tax return must be filed with the tax authorities. These are not a matter of public record for limited liability companies, but they are for stock corporations.

- Meetings must be held at the registered office.

- An annual filing fee of US$1,000 is payable to the government.

MALTA

Checklist for Companies

- The company name must end with *Limited* or *Ltd*.

- Incorporation takes seven to ten days. Shelf companies are not available.

- The minimum capital required is Lm 500 or its foreign currency equivalent. No capital duty is payable.

- At least two shareholders are necessary. Bearer shares and shares of no par value are not allowed.

- A minimum of one director is required. Corporate directors are permitted, and there is no restriction on the directors' residence.

- A company secretary is mandatory. Use must be made of a Maltese nominee company.

- A registered office is necessary, as is a registered agent that must be a Maltese nominee company. The share register must be kept at the registered office.

- The memorandum and articles of association are available on the public file, but beneficial ownership is not disclosed.

- A corporate seal is not necessary.

- Corporate accounts must be kept but need not be filed.

- An annual return must be made with a declaration that the company still satisfies the relevant regulations.

- There is no restriction on the holding of meetings.

- Trading companies pay an annual fee of Lm 1,000 and are taxed at a rate of 5%. Non-trading companies pay an annual fee of Lm 500 and are exempt from tax. Shipping companies pay an annual fee of Lm 100 and are also exempt from tax.

Appendix 1

MAURITIUS

Checklist for International Companies

- International companies are not resident for tax purposes.

- Prior approval of the company name is required, and words such as *Assurance*, *Chartered*, and *Bank* are sensitive.

- Incorporation takes two days, and shelf companies are available. A register of members must be submitted within 30 days of incorporation.

- There is no usual minimum capital and no capital duty.

- At least one shareholder is required. Bearer shares have been abolished.

- At least one director is required. Corporate directors are allowed, and there is no restriction on the directors' place of residence.

- A company secretary is not mandatory. Corporate secretaries are allowed, and there is no restriction on the secretary's residence.

- A registered office and agent are necessary. All documents must be kept at the registered office.

- No information is available on the public file.

- Corporate books and a seal may be kept at the registered office.

- Accounts are not necessary and do not have to be filed.

- An annual return is not required.

- There is no restriction on the holding of meetings.

- An annual fee of US$100 is payable to the government.

- An international company does not have access to double taxation treaties.

Checklist for Offshore Companies

- Offshore companies are resident for tax purposes.

- Prior approval of the company name is required, and words such as *National*, *Chartered*, and *Government* are sensitive.

- Incorporation takes approximately two weeks, and shelf companies are not available. Disclosure of beneficial ownership is required by the authorities prior to incorporation.

- There is no usual minimum capital and no capital duty.

- At least two shareholders are required, although one corporate shareholder is permitted after incorporation. Bearer shares and shares of no par value are not allowed.

- At least two directors are required. Corporate directors are not allowed, and at least two directors must be resident to benefit from double taxation agreements.

- A company secretary is mandatory. Corporate secretaries are allowed, and the secretary must be resident in Mauritius.

- A registered office and agent are necessary. The registers of shares, directors, secretary, and members must be kept at the registered office.

- No information is available on the public file.

- Corporate books and a seal may be kept at the registered office, although the official seal may be dispensed with.

- Accounts are necessary and must be filed with the Mauritius Offshore Business Activities Authority within six months of the closure of a financial year. The Authority may order inspection and audit of an offshore company's books.

- An annual return is not required.

- Directors' meetings must be in Mauritius if the company is to be tax resident there. There is no restriction on the holding of shareholders' meetings.

- An annual fee of US$1,500 is payable to the government.

- An offshore company has access to numerous double taxation treaties.

MONACO

Checklist for SAMs (*Sociétés Anonymes Monégasques*)

- On incorporation, a SAM must publish its authorisation and statutes in the Official Journal and register with the government.

- If the SAM does not commence trading within two years of government authorisation, the authorisation will be revoked.

- There is no minimum share capital, but in practice authorisations will not be granted to SAMs with less than FF 1 million.

- At least two shareholders are required. Registered shares and bearer shares are permitted.

- At least two directors are required, one of whom must be a resident of Monaco.

- A company secretary is not necessary.

- A local office is required prior to authorisation being granted.

- Accounts must be kept and must be audited.

- No fees are charged.

- Migration and redomiciliation are not permitted.

NAURU

Checklist for Trading and Holding Corporations

- Nauru law recognises trading and holding corporations with limited liability.

- The name must end with *Corporation*, *Corp.*, *Incorporated*, or *Inc.*

- Incorporation takes 24 hours.

- A holding corporation requires at least one shareholder and one director. A trading corporation must have at least two shareholders and two directors. A registered director is required on adoption of standard articles of association.

- A holding corporation may adopt standard articles of association as provided in Table B of the Corporation Act 1972, sch 2. A trading corporation may adopt

Appendix 1

standard articles of association as provided in Table A of the Corporation Act 1972, sch 2.

- A resident secretary is a statutory requirement.

- A corporate seal is required and is usually kept at the registered office in Nauru.

- There is no minimum capital requirement, although the Nauru Agency Corporation expects a holding corporation to have at least A$100 and a trading corporation to have at least A$1,000.

- Bearer shares may be issued by a holding corporation but not by a trading corporation.

- The accounts of a holding corporation need not be audited by a registered corporation auditor. There are statutory provisions relating to the audit of trading corporations' accounts, but these have not yet come into force.

- Annual returns must be filed for licence renewal purposes.

- The central management and control of either corporation may be anywhere in the world.

- There is no restriction on the holding of meetings for either corporation.

NETHERLANDS ANTILLES

Checklist for Companies

- The corporate name must be cleared with the Ministry of Justice. Words such as *Royal* and *Bank* are prohibited. The name must end with *NV*.

- Incorporation takes five to ten days. Shelf companies are available. No information is required by the authorities prior to incorporation.

- The usual minimum capital is US$30,000, which must be issued and paid up to US$6,000. There is no capital duty.

- At least one shareholder is required. Bearer shares are possible, but shares of no par value are not.

- At least one director is necessary. Corporate directors are allowed, and there is no restriction on the directors' location, but a local representative is required.

- The concept of the company secretary is not known to Netherlands Antilles law.

- Companies must have a registered office in the Netherlands Antilles but need not have a registered agent. The registered office must keep the share register, minutes and resolutions, share transfer documents, and administrative and book-keeping records.

- The articles of association, address, capital, purpose clause, and personal details of the supervisory directors, managing directors, and attorneys are available on the public file.

- The concept of the corporate seal is not known under Netherlands Antilles law.

- Accounts must be kept but need not be filed.

- An annual return must be filed.

- There are no restrictions on the holding of board meetings, but shareholders' meetings must be held within the Netherlands Antilles.

- An annual contribution is payable to the Chamber of Commerce.

VANUATU

Checklist for International Companies

- The company name may be in any language or script, with any common ending. There is rapid feedback as to availability.

- Incorporation takes one day. A one-hour special service is available at an extra cost of US$100. Shelf companies are available. No information is required prior to incorporation.

- There is no authorised minimum capital, although US$100 is standard. There is also no capital duty. Capital can be in any currency.

- At least one shareholder is required. Bearer shares and shares of no par value are possible.

- At least one director is required. Corporate directors are allowed, and there is no restriction on the directors' place of residence.

- There is no requirement for a company secretary. Corporate secretaries are allowed, and there is no restriction on the secretary's location.

- Companies must have a registered office and a registered agent. Documents do not have to be kept at the registered office.

- The constitution, registered office, and registered agent are available on the public file.

- A company seal is optional.

- Accounts do not have to be kept or filed.

- An annual return is also not required.

- There is no restriction on the holding of meetings.

- An annual fee of US$300 is payable.

Appendix 2   Strategic Checklists for Offshore Trusts

BARBADOS

- There is no statutory schedule of standard trust powers.
- The maximum perpetuity period for non-charitable trusts is 100 years.
- At least one resident trustee is required.
- Trusts need not be registered.
- Trust documents may be in any language, but an English translation is required.
- There is no stamp duty or registration fee.
- Barbados trust law is based on English equity.
- Appeal lies to the Privy Council.
- The Hague Convention has not been implemented.
- Specific provision is made for the exclusion of foreign inheritance laws.
- Specific provision is also made for the non-recognition of foreign judgments.
- There is a specific 'asset protection' provision protecting a disposition to a trust from challenge by creditors.
- Instant immunity is granted from creditors' claims.
- Provision is made for non-charitable purpose trusts.

BERMUDA

- There is a statutory schedule of standard trust powers for the Bermuda trust.
- The maximum perpetuity period for non-charitable trusts is 100 years.
- At least one resident trustee is required.
- There is no requirement for the registration of trusts.
- Trust documents are normally in English.
- No stamp duty is charged.
- The law of trusts is based on English equity.
- Appeal lies to the Privy Council.
- The Hague Convention has been implemented in Bermuda.
- Specific provision is made for the exclusion of foreign inheritance laws.
- There is a specific provision dealing with the non-recognition of foreign judgments.
- There is a specific 'asset protection' provision (beyond that offered by general insolvency law) protecting a disposition to a trust from challenge by creditors.
- A special limitation period of six years is imposed on creditors' claims.
- Provision is made for (registrable) non-charitable trusts.

BRITISH VIRGIN ISLANDS

- The maximum perpetuity period for non-charitable trusts is 100 years.
- A resident trustee is not required.
- There is no requirement for the registration of trusts.
- Trust documents are normally in English.
- Stamp duty of US$50 is charged.
- The law of trusts is based on English equity.
- The Hague Convention has been implemented in the BVI.
- Specific provision is made for the exclusion of foreign inheritance laws.
- There is no specific provision dealing with the non-recognition of foreign judgments.
- There is no specific 'asset protection' provision (beyond that offered by general insolvency law) protecting a disposition to a trust from challenge by creditors.
- There is no special statute of limitations period for creditors' claims.
- Provision is made for non-charitable purpose trusts.

CAYMAN ISLANDS

- There is no statutory schedule of standard trust powers for trusts or exempted trusts.
- The maximum perpetuity period for non-charitable trusts is 150 years.
- A resident trustee is not required.
- Exempted trusts have to be registered.
- Trust documents are usually in English.
- A registration fee of US$48 is charged.
- The law of trusts is based on English equity.
- Appeal lies to the Privy Council.
- The Hague Convention has been implemented in the Cayman Islands.
- Specific provision is made for the exclusion of foreign inheritance laws.
- Specific provisions deal with the non-recognition of foreign judgments.
- There is a specific 'asset protection' provision (beyond that offered by general insolvency law) protecting a disposition to a trust from challenge by creditors.
- There is a special limitation period of six years for creditors' claims.
- Provision is made for non-charitable purpose trusts.

COOK ISLANDS

- There is no statutory schedule of standard trust powers.
- The maximum perpetuity period for non-charitable trusts is over 100 years.
- A resident trustee is usually required.

Appendix 2

- Registration is required in that a certificate must be filed with the registrar of international trusts.
- Trust documents are in English.
- A registration fee of US$200 is charged.
- The law of trusts is based on English equity.
- Special leave is required to appeal to the Privy Council.
- The Hague Convention has not been implemented in the Cook Islands.
- Specific provision is made for the exclusion of foreign inheritance laws.
- Specific provisions deal with the non-recognition of foreign judgments.
- There is a specific 'asset protection' provision (beyond that offered by general insolvency law) protecting a disposition to a trust from challenge by creditors.
- There is a statutory limitation period of two years for creditors' claims.
- Provision is made for non-charitable trusts.

CYPRUS

- There is no statutory schedule of standard trust powers.
- The maximum perpetuity period for non-charitable trusts is 100 years.
- At least one resident trustee is required.
- Trusts need not be registered.
- Trust documents are in English.
- A stamp duty of US$550 is payable.
- Cyprus trust law has a mixed common and civil law background.
- There is no right of appeal to the Privy Council.
- The Hague Convention has not been implemented.
- Specific provision is made for the exclusion of foreign inheritance laws.
- Specific provision is also made for the non-recognition of foreign judgments.
- There is a specific 'asset protection' provision protecting a disposition to a trust from challenge by creditors.
- A limitation period of two years is imposed on creditors' claims.
- Provision is made for non-charitable purpose trusts.

GIBRALTAR

- There is no statutory schedule of standard trust powers.
- The maximum perpetuity period for non-charitable trusts is 100 years.
- At least one resident trustee is required.
- Trusts need not be registered.
- Trust documents are in English.

- There is no stamp duty or registration fee.
- Gibraltarian trust law is based on English equity.
- Appeal lies to the Privy Council.
- The Hague Convention has been implemented.
- No specific provision is made for the exclusion of foreign inheritance laws.
- No specific provision is made for the non-recognition of foreign judgments.
- There is a specific 'asset protection' provision protecting a disposition to a trust from challenge by creditors.
- There is no limitation period on creditors' claims.
- No provision is made for non-charitable purpose trusts.

GUERNSEY

- There is no statutory schedule of standard trust powers in Guernsey.
- The maximum perpetuity period for non-charitable trusts is 100 years.
- A resident trustee is not required.
- Registration of a trust is not necessary.
- Trust documents are in English.
- There is no stamp duty or registration fee.
- The law of trusts in Guernsey has a mixed English equity and civil law background.
- Appeal lies to the Privy Council.
- The Hague Convention has been implemented.
- Specific provision is made for the exclusion of foreign inheritance laws.
- Specific provisions deal with the non-recognition of foreign judgments.
- There is no specific 'asset protection' provision (beyond that offered by general insolvency laws) protecting a disposition to a trust from challenge by creditors.
- There is no special limitation period for creditors' claims.
- No provision is made for non-charitable purpose trusts.

HONG KONG

- There is no statutory schedule of standard trust powers.
- The maximum perpetuity period of non-charitable trusts is 80 years.
- A resident trustee is not required.
- There is no requirement for the registration of trusts.
- Trust documents are in English and Chinese.
- There is no registration fee or stamp duty.
- The law of trusts is based on English equity.
- Appeal does not lie to the Privy Council.

Appendix 2

- The Hague Convention has been implemented.
- No specific provision is made for the exclusion of foreign inheritance laws.
- There is no specific provision dealing with the non-recognition of foreign judgments.
- There is no specific 'asset protection' provision (beyond that offered by general insolvency law) protecting a disposition to a trust from challenge by creditors.
- There is no special statute of limitations period for creditors' claims.
- No provision is made for non-charitable purpose trusts.

ISLE OF MAN

- There is no statutory schedule of standard trust powers.
- The maximum perpetuity period for non-charitable trusts is 80 years.
- A resident trustee is not required.
- Trusts do not have to be registered.
- Trust documents are in English.
- No registration fee or stamp duty is payable.
- The law of trusts is based on English equity.
- Appeal lies to the Privy Council.
- The Hague Convention has been implemented.
- No specific provision is made for the exclusion of foreign inheritance laws.
- No specific provisions deal with the non-recognition of foreign judgments.
- There is no specific 'asset protection' provision (beyond that offered by general insolvency law) protecting a disposition to a trust from challenge by creditors.
- There is no special limitation period for creditors' claims.
- No provision is made for non-charitable purpose trusts.

JERSEY

- There is a statutory schedule of standard trust powers.
- The maximum perpetuity period for non-charitable trusts is 100 years.
- A resident trustee is not required.
- Registration of a trust is not necessary.
- Trust documents are normally in English.
- There is no stamp duty or registration fee.
- The law of trusts in Jersey is based on English equity.
- Appeal lies to the Privy Council.
- The Hague Convention has been implemented.
- Specific provision is made for the exclusion of foreign inheritance laws.
- Specific provisions deal with the non-recognition of foreign judgments.

- There is no specific 'asset protection' provision (beyond that offered by general insolvency laws) protecting a disposition to a trust from challenge by creditors.
- There is no special limitation period for creditors' claims.
- Provision is made for non-charitable trusts.

LABUAN

- There is a statutory schedule of standard trust powers.
- The maximum perpetuity period for non-charitable trusts is life plus 21 years.
- A resident trustee is not required.
- Trusts do not have to be registered.
- Labuan trust documents may be in any language.
- There is no stamp duty or registration fee.
- The law of trusts is based on English equity.
- There is no right of appeal to the Privy Council.
- The Hague Convention has not been implemented.
- Specific provision has not been made for the exclusion of foreign inheritance laws.
- No specific provision deals with the non-recognition of foreign judgments.
- There is no specific 'asset protection' provision (beyond that offered by general insolvency law) protecting a disposition to a trust from challenge by creditors.
- There is no special limitation period for creditors' claims.
- Provision is not made for non-charitable purpose trusts.

LIECHTENSTEIN

- There is no statutory schedule of standard trust powers.
- The perpetuity period of non-charitable trusts is unlimited.
- At least one resident trustee is required.
- It is compulsory to register trusts.
- Trust documents may be in German or any other language.
- A registration fee of US$200 is payable.
- The law of trusts has a civil law background.
- The Hague Convention has not been implemented.
- No specific provision is made for the exclusion of foreign inheritance laws.
- There is no specific provision dealing with the non-recognition of foreign judgments.
- There is no specific 'asset protection' provision (beyond that offered by general insolvency law) protecting a disposition to a trust from challenge by creditors. However, a Liechtenstein *Stiftung* generally provides excellent asset protection.
- A special statute of limitations period of one year exists for creditors' claims.
- Provision is made for non-charitable purpose trusts.

Appendix 2

MAURITIUS

- There is a statutory schedule of standard trust powers.
- The maximum perpetuity period for non-charitable trusts is 50 years.
- One resident trustee is required.
- Minimal registration provisions pertain.
- Trust documents may be in any language.
- Mauritian trust law has a civil law background.
- No registration fee or stamp duty is payable.
- Appeal lies to the Privy Council.
- The Hague Convention has not been implemented.
- Specific provision is made for the exclusion of foreign inheritance laws.
- Specific provisions deal with the non-recognition of foreign judgments.
- There is a specific 'asset protection' provision (beyond that offered by general insolvency law) protecting a disposition to a trust from challenge by creditors.
- A special statute of limitations period of two years exists for creditors' claims.
- Provision is made for non-charitable purpose trusts.

MONACO

- There is no statutory schedule of standard trust powers.
- The perpetuity period of a non-charitable trust is unlimited.
- All trustees must be approved by the government.
- Registration of the trust is compulsory.
- Law 214 trust documents must be in French. Other trust documents may be in any language.
- No registration fee or stamp duty is payable.
- There is no appeal to the Privy Council.
- The Hague Convention has not been implemented.
- No specific provision has been made for the exclusion of foreign inheritance laws.
- There is no specific provision dealing with the non-recognition of foreign judgments.
- There is no specific 'asset protection' provision (beyond that offered by general insolvency law) protecting a disposition to a trust from challenge by creditors.
- No provision is made for non-charitable purpose trusts.

NAURU

- The rule against perpetuities does not apply.
- Trusts may be created with perpetual duration.
- Non-charitable purpose trusts are permitted.
- There is no registration requirement.
- There are no nationality or residence requirements for settlors, beneficiaries, or trustees.

VANUATU

- There is no statutory schedule of standard trust powers in Vanuatu.
- The maximum perpetuity period for a non-charitable trust is 80 years.
- A resident trustee is not required.
- There is no requirement for the registration of trusts.
- Trust documents may be in French or English.
- Stamp duty of US$130 is charged.
- The law of trusts is based on English equity.
- The Hague Convention has not been implemented.
- Specific provision has not been made for the exclusion of foreign inheritance laws.
- There is no specific provision dealing with the non-recognition of foreign judgments.
- There is no specific 'asset protection' provision (beyond that offered by general insolvency law) protecting a disposition to a trust from challenge by creditors.
- There is no special statute of limitations period for creditors' claims.
- No provision is made for non-charitable purpose trusts.

Index

300

Index

Index

Index

Index

Index

Index